HOPE AND CHRISTIAN ETHICS

The theological virtue of hope has long been neglected in Christian ethics. But as social, civic, and global anxieties mount, the need to overcome despair has become urgent. This book proposes the theological virtue of hope as a promising source of rejuvenation. Theological hope sustains us from the sloth, presumption, and despair that threaten amid injustice, tragedy, and dying; it provides an ultimate meaning and transcendent purpose to our lives; and it rejoices and refreshes us 'on the way' (*in via*) with the prospect of eternal beatitude. Rather than degrading this life and world, hope ordains earthly goods to our eschatological end, forming us to pursue social justice with a resilience and vitality that transcend the cynicism and disillusionment so widespread at present. Drawing on Thomas Aquinas and virtue ethics, this book shows how the virtue of hope contributes to human happiness in this life and not just the next.

Dr David Elliot is Assistant Professor of Moral Theology and Ethics at The Catholic University of America. He received his PhD in Moral Theology from the University of Notre Dame, followed by a three-year postdoctoral fellowship as Research Associate in Theological Ethics at Cambridge University, where he was concurrently a Research Associate in ethics at the Von Hügel Institute, St Edmund's College, Cambridge. His work on hope, *Passing Through the Sirens: The Trials of the Christian Wayfarer in the World* (2012) was recently awarded the Essay and Book Prize from the Character Project of the Templeton Foundation for contribution to the study of character.

Christian ethics has increasingly assumed a central place within academic theology. At the same time, the growing power and ambiguity of modern science and the rising dissatisfaction within the social sciences about claims to value neutrality have prompted renewed interest in ethics within the secular academic world. There is, therefore, a need for studies in Christian ethics which, as well as being concerned with the relevance of Christian ethics to the present-day secular debate, are well informed about parallel discussions in recent philosophy, science, or social science. New Studies in Christian Ethics aims to provide books that do this at the highest intellectual level and demonstrate that Christian ethics can make a distinctive contribution to this debate – either in moral substance or in terms of underlying moral justifications

(continued after the index)

HOPE AND CHRISTIAN ETHICS

DAVID ELLIOT

The Catholic University of America

CAMBRIDGE
UNIVERSITY PRESS

CAMBRIDGE
UNIVERSITY PRESS

One Liberty Plaza, 20th Floor, New York, NY 10006, USA

Cambridge University Press is part of the University of Cambridge.

It furthers the University's mission by disseminating knowledge in the pursuit of education, learning, and research at the highest international levels of excellence.

www.cambridge.org
Information on this title: www.cambridge.org/9781107156173
DOI: 10.1017/9781316659458

First published 2017

Printed in The United States of America by Sheridan Books, Inc.

A catalogue record for this publication is available from the British Library.

Library of Congress Cataloging-in-Publication Data
Names: Elliot, David, author.
Title: Hope and Christian ethics / David Elliot.
Description: New York, NY, USA: University of Cambridge, [2017] |
Includes bibliographical references and index.
Identifiers: LCCN 2017008240 | ISBN 9781107156173 (hardback)
Subjects: LCSH: Hope – Religious aspects – Christianity – History of doctrines. |
Hope – Religious aspects – Christianity. | Thomas, Aquinas,
Saint, 1225?–1274. | Christian ethics.
Classification: LCC BV4638 .E43 2017 | DDC 234/.25–dc23
LC record available at https://lccn.loc.gov/2017008240

ISBN 978-1-107-15617-3 Hardback

Cambridge University Press has no responsibility for the persistence or accuracy of URLS for external or third-party internet websites referred to in this publication and does not guarantee that any content on such websites is, or will remain, accurate or appropriate.

For England:
'For your servants love her very stones, are moved with pity even
for her dust.'

Psalm 102:14

This is how the present life of man on earth, King, appears to me
in comparison with that time which is unknown to us. You are
sitting feasting with your counsellors and thanes in winter time;
the fire is burning on the hearth in the middle of the hall and all
inside is warm, while outside the wintry storms of rain and snow
are raging; and a sparrow flies swiftly through the hall. It enters
in at one door and quickly flies out through the other. While it is
inside, it is safe from the winter storms; but after a few moments
of comfort, it vanishes from sight into the wintry world from
which it came. Even so, man appears on earth for a little while;
but of what went before this life or of what follows, we know
nothing. Therefore, if this new teaching has brought any more
certain knowledge, it seems only right that we should follow it.

The Venerable Bede, The Ecclesiastical
History of the English People, Bk II, Ch 13

Contents

General Editor's Preface

David Elliot's *Hope and Christian Ethics* is a very welcome addition to *New Studies in Christian Ethics*. Like all of the other contributors to the series he has observed carefully the two central aims of *New Studies in Christian Ethics*, namely:

(1) To promote monographs in Christian ethics which engage centrally with the present secular moral debate at the highest possible intellectual level.
(2) To encourage contributors to demonstrate that Christian ethics can make a distinctive contribution to this debate – either in moral substance, or in terms of underlying moral justifications.

And, like most other contributors to *New Studies in Christian Ethics*, David Elliot writes from a perspective within virtue ethics. In *Moral Passion and Christian Ethics* (2017) I argued that passion is too often neglected by other ethicists and even by virtue ethicists. He, in turn, argues that hope has been similarly neglected. In seeking to correct this, he takes full account of secular (sometimes naïve) criticisms of Christian hope, as well as tentative notions of hope shaped by philosophy and psychology. Yet he maintains that a proper Christian understanding of hope, taking account of both virtue ethics and eudaimonism, does have something important to add. Even if relatively neglected, he suggests, there are recent forms of ethics that do at least leave room for hope. So some purely secular accounts of hope 'show a structural openness to the conclusion that theological hope, if it were available, would resolve gaps they acknowledge in the kind of *eudaimonia* they think available'. An adequate understanding of hope as a theological virtue, he believes, should affirm such naturalistic versions of virtue and happiness while also directing us to eternal beatitude – just as Aquinas did before him. Beyond this observation he argues that, if theological hope were still a live option, it would greatly benefit human agency by enriching our happiness, especially if it could ground hope, not in some crude escape from this world, but instead in social justice enabled by grace *and* in eschatological anticipation. He takes the long struggle of abolitionists such as William Wilberforce as an example of how hope, grace, and social justice can properly work together even within the public domain.

These are not strident claims. Like most other contributors to *New Studies in Christian Ethics*, David Elliot avoids stridency and, in line with the two aims of the series, is concerned both to learn from the present secular debate *and* to shape it. I am delighted to welcome this fresh and thoughtful contribution from a significant emerging theologian.

ROBIN GILL

Acknowledgements

Gratitude is one of the few debts it is a joy to pay, and my own debts for completing this work are many. Though heavily reworked, this book began as a doctoral dissertation at the University of Notre Dame, and was completed through a research associate position at the University of Cambridge. At Notre Dame I benefitted from a Theology Department as generous as it was learned. Among many friends and colleagues, I would like to thank Paul Scherz, Adam Clark, Brian Hamilton, Angela Carpenter, and Luis Vera, who read portions of the manuscript and gave valuable feedback. I am particularly grateful to David Lantigua, whose friendship has been a source both of personal and theological enrichment. Gerald McKenny, David Clairmont, and Joseph Wawrykow read the entire work, and proved to be learned and inspiring teachers as well as candid critics. Jerry's early criticisms got me to seriously rework the first chapter, and his hospitality helped set the convivial tone we prized in the department. Joseph, besides teaching me everything I hope I know about grace, inspired me to study hope in the first place. In addition, Jerry's scepticism about Aquinas, and Joseph's unswerving allegiance to him, helped me to face squarely the need to work out a coherent methodology of my own. Since I would never have studied theological ethics without the inspiring influence of David Novak at the University of Toronto, I would like to thank him now for all the good he did me then. I am most especially grateful to Jean Porter, who was my dissertation adviser at Notre Dame and the teacher who influenced me most. Her stature as a scholar is only equalled by her wisdom and solicitude as adviser, director, and tireless advocate. Like a great many others who have worked with Jean, one's debt of gratitude prompts a vain search for the ultimate superlative which finally resigns itself to muted admiration.

I owe a great debt of gratitude to the School of Arts and Humanities and the Faculty of Divinity at the University of Cambridge. In an era of humanities cost-cutting and theological austerity, a three-year research postdoc for an early-career theologian at such an institution is an enormous gift. Besides its bracing academic context and a superb set of colleagues, I am grateful for the School and Faculty's generous financial support for my position, which supplied the time and resources to complete this book. My thanks also go to Philip McCosker for practical help during my first year, and to the Flutter family for their extraordinary hospitality. In our home village of Melbourn, Cambridgeshire, I am grateful to Susan Cane and Mary Bailey for their regular welcome, and for opening the doors of All Saints Church to us each morning.

I am particularly indebted to Sarah Coakley, whose skill and devotion as a mentor at Cambridge have been truly exceptional. In addition to her advice, conversations, and hospitality, I am thankful to Sarah for reading and providing comments on the early book draft, and for championing its publication. My thanks also go to Susan Parsons and William Mattison for their encouragement, support, and suggestions. I am immensely grateful to Robin Gill, the editor of this series, whose encouragement for this book project was remarkable from the outset. His turnaround speed shows a courtesy that must be rare among editors, and his guidance and support have been unfailingly wise. I am also grateful to my anonymous reviewers for Cambridge University Press for helpful comments and suggestions.

This book includes some adapted and reworked material from earlier publications. The first chapter draws very lightly on my articles 'Defining the Relationship Between Health and Well-Being in Bioethics', in *The New Bioethics* 22.1 (Spring 2016): 4–17; and 'The Turn to Classification in Virtue Ethics: A Review Essay', in *Studies in Christian Ethics* 29.4 (November 2016): 477–488. In the fifth chapter, the section 'Possibilities for a Hopeful Death' draws on my 'The Theological Virtue of Hope and the Art of Dying', in *Studies in Christian Ethics* 29.3 (August 2016): 301–307. Chapter 6 adapts material from 'The Christian as *Homo Viator*: A Resource in Thomas Aquinas for Overcoming "Worldly Sin and Sorrow,"' in the *Journal of the Society of Christian Ethics* 34.2 (Fall/Winter 2015): 101–121. I am grateful to the editors of these journals for their kind permission to rework some of this material.

Thanks of a quite different nature are owing to my family for their love, pains, encouragement, and support. To my mother and father, who gave me life, faith, and upbringing, and enabled my academic path. To my grandmother, Mary Lannigan, whose extraordinary love and support saw me through an undergraduate degree. To my parents-in-law, Don and Susan Ellis, for their love, hospitality, support, and the gift of their daughter. To our children, who make off-hours something like a Dickensian romp, opening our eyes to wonder and joy. Lastly, to my best friend and beloved wife, Sarah, 'who is a wandering home for me'. I am incalculably in her debt for our children, our home, and our love. Her vision of things is a vision of beauty I aspire towards and delight to see ever more fully unfolded.

In a familiar tale of the Venerable Bede, Pope Gregory the Great looks upon the pagan Anglo-Saxons at the slave market and 'fetching a deep sigh from the bottom of his heart' utters his famous missionary pun: would that the Angles were co-heirs with the angels! Concerning the subsequent mission to the English, urged by Gregory and led by St. Augustine, Bede writes: 'Some believed and were baptized, admiring the sweetness of their heavenly doctrine' (*dulcedinem doctrinae eorum caelestis*). In Bede's telling, Christian hope played an essential role in the fruition of English spirituality. Naturally I seek to address readers everywhere. But in the spirit of *pietas*, and with the hope that in its own small way it might recall the 'reason for the hope that is in us' (1 Peter 3:15), this book is dedicated to England.

Introduction

The rise of virtue ethics in the past decades has led to many treatments of the cardinal and theological virtues. Justice, prudence, courage, charity, and the rest have inspired a great many books, articles, dissertations, and conferences. But one ship has not been lifted by this rising tide: the theological virtue of hope. Its preoccupation with what we loosely term 'heaven' is often derided as an opiate for earthly misery, a foothold for gloomy asceticism, a distraction from social justice, and a brake on human progress. Hope's perceived otherworldliness and obscurantism have made it a stock target of cultured despisers from Celsus and Hume to Marx and Russell. 'The country of the Christian is not of this world', Rousseau wrote disparagingly. 'This short life counts for so little in their eyes' that for Christians 'the essential thing is to get to heaven' and out of 'this valley of sorrows'.[1] Such criticisms of hope vary in quality from gratuitous abuse to bits of instructive hyperbole which unmask destructive forms of hope. But combined with eschatological squeamishness among many Christian ethicists themselves, the result is that reflection on hope as a theological virtue has for some time been 'closed for repairs'.[2]

Ironically, alongside this neglect has been a growing sense that we very much need more hope, not less. We live in the wake of a worldwide financial crisis, ecological bad news is plentiful, democratic vitality and social justice have lost serious ground to political cynicism and plutocratic interests, human life and dignity are flouted with impunity, family breakdown has sharply risen, and geopolitical instability and terrorism abound. With so many anxieties in economics, politics, and society, the Western cultural mood has soured and fears of permanent decline have set in. The social toxins of pessimism, apathy, and cynicism have predictably spread, and the threats of demoralisation and despair have become very real. Even if we resist simplistic diagnoses and shun declinist narratives, we have good reason to worry about the present hope deficit. Kant took the question 'for what may I hope?' to be a primary human one. To persist in shelving it as morally trifling would be unreflective, inert, and reckless. The need for renewed hopefulness is plain, and this has led to a casting about for sources of revitalisation. It has also, very tentatively, led to the thought that one of these resources may lie with theology, which first identified hope as a virtue, and for centuries made it central to Western thought and practice.

This book will take up that thought, and propose that one source for renewed hopes – in my view, the most profound and resilient source – is the theological virtue of hope. As this may suggest, my approach to hope is broadly one of 'virtue ethics'. That label is largely one of convenience, and it has annoyed many of its own practitioners, but it does capture a shared commitment to examine agency, character, and ethical life as a whole rather than as a set of isolated actions, duties, and consequences.[3] This focus brings to the fore certain questions which were generally neglected within Kantian and Utilitarian ethics, but which were pivotal to Greek, Roman, medieval, and some recent thought. Most basically: 'What does it mean to live the good life, and what kind of character should we cultivate to do so?'

My overall goal will be to show that the virtue of hope makes an important and recognisable contribution to the good life, primarily in terms of personal happiness, but secondarily in terms of social goods. Theological hope sustains us from the demoralisation and despair that threaten amid injustice, suffering, decline, and death; it provides an ultimate meaning and transcendent purpose to our lives; and it rejoices and refreshes us 'on the way' (*in via*) with the prospect of ultimate reconciliation and lasting beatitude. It also forms us to pursue social goods with a resilience and vitality that help to overcome the cynicism and disillusionment so common at present. To make plausible the claim that hope benefits us in these ways, I give a textured account of the hopeful life, describing how it rises above despair and presumption, and what it gains by doing so.

One early goal of virtue ethics was to move beyond the 'generalised self' of quandary ethics and ahistorical theories to the 'concrete self' located in narrative and given a history. But full treatments of individual virtues, from fortitude to charity, have rarely succeeded in showing what it concretely looks like to live that virtue in the various dimensions of human existence. The danger is that academic ethics then does little justice to the ethical life of 'situated selves'.[4] Part of my goal, therefore, is to describe what a hopeful life actually looks like in some detail while resisting overdetermination of the forms it may take. To this end I draw on and engage a variety of thinkers, disciplines, and genres; from the liturgy to literature, in the belief that the hopeful life has often been richly described in such nonstandard sources of ethical reflection.

My general point of departure is the work of St. Thomas Aquinas, whose brilliant work on hope I find the best precedent from which to branch out. No case begins in mid-air, and mine assumes many Thomistic claims as a methodological given. But though it will be deeply indebted to Aquinas, this book will not be primarily exegetical, and I will not employ Aquinas as an oracle. Obviously, if one treats his work as dogma and clutches the *Summa* as a talisman, it is easy in one sense to refute all critics by simply rehearsing the appropriate *respondeo*. But the immediate and ironic result of this would be to unduly marginalise Aquinas himself. Such arguments from authority predictably backfire as those outside the groupthink circle realise with a groan that what they hoped to engage as a live option they can at best admire as a period piece. At the same time, one must dialectically work from a tradition or context that takes many things as a given in order to get at the further questions one is addressing. Otherwise we could hardly get beyond throat-clearing exercises in methodology.[5] I will therefore adopt a middle path between a foundationalist project and what Thomas Nagel calls a 'view from nowhere'.[6] Operating from broadly Thomistic premises, my assumption will be that those premises sustain a viable discursive tradition that is intellectually respectable enough to be the starting place for serious work on hope. To bear out this claim would require a wholesale change of topic and a different work entirely. But at the same time, I will address contemporary objections to Thomistic hope where relevant, reply in my own terms rather than ply arguments from authority, and make extensive proposals about hope that go beyond (though I hope not *against*) what Aquinas says.

In addition to lay audiences concerned with rehabilitating hope, I have three scholarly audiences particularly in mind. The first are scholars of Christian ethics. The last time eschatological hope was a leading topic in theology was with the valuable but limited 'Theology of Hope' of Jürgen Moltmann. But even this discussion occurred mostly within systematic theology and never quite set the agenda in ethics. Yet this neglect of hope is not a modern idiosyncrasy. Within ethics hope generally has been kept in soft focus as the junior partner of faith and charity, consistently valued but conceptually underdeveloped. Given that there are only three theological virtues, the conspicuous neglect of one of them in theological ethics is, to say the least, awkward; and quite obviously should be corrected. But I expect that the long neglect of hope, the urgent need for it, and the rise in virtue theory have brought about favourable conditions for work on hope to be of immediate interest within Christian ethics.

My second intended audience are those who specialise in social justice, Christian or otherwise. I particularly want to address those who worry that hope deflects from social justice concerns by changing the subject: in this case, to heaven. In one liturgical formula, hope anticipates 'those heavenly habitations, where the souls of them that sleep in the Lord Jesus enjoy perpetual rest and felicity'.[7] I fully accept, and repeatedly insist on, the centrality of eschatology to theological hope. Discreetly hushing this up strikes me as disingenuous, and is of no use whatsoever.

It is incoherent to seek to borrow the moral capital of Christian hope while pretending that the eschatology which supplies it *just isn't there*. But equally, I argue that virtuous hope does not detract from this life and world, but acknowledges their integrity and honours their goodness, taking up and ordaining the earthly projects of prudence, justice, fortitude, charity, and other virtues to the eschaton itself. As mediated through charity and applied to justice, hope seeks happiness not just for oneself, but for the whole community, and so is not a 'selfish' virtue that grinds down solidarity. Indeed, the vice of presumption opposed to hope consists partly in refusing works of social justice and mercy in the 'presumption' that the common good is optional to those seeking eternal life. To show what this socially engaged hope looks like, I turn to the beatitudes of Christ's Sermon on the Mount.

I suggest that the beatitudes depict the paradigmatic form of the hopeful life: one in which we pursue the future kingdom while entangled in people's brokenness on earth. Understood this way, the hopeful life builds social commitments into its eschatological purposes.

My third intended audience is made up of moral philosophers, primarily neo-Aristotelians and others working on the virtues, and secondarily Kantians and Utilitarians. Philosophers such as Aristotle, Philippa Foot, and Rosalind Hursthouse argue that the virtues benefit their possessors by conducing to happiness, flourishing, or *eudaimonia*. Yet they add that our embodied finitude leaves happiness vulnerable to misfortune. The *eudaimonia* of even the virtuous will likely be marred, and may ultimately be wrecked, by some combination of poverty, disease, hunger, violence, pain, loss of livelihood, injustice, broken relationships, illness, decline, and tragedies of all kinds. Since these frustrate not just general desires, but many crucial priorities, the result is that we cannot be as happy in this life as we *reasonably* wish to be. Utilitarians acknowledge this depressing fact and worry that the demands of morality compete with what we need to be happy. Kant adds that the moral order, to be coherent, requires that happiness eventually be proportioned to moral worth. That such proportioning does not happen in this life is by his lights a direct threat to the intelligibility of the moral order itself.

The ills which limit happiness in these ways constitute a depressing gap between the kind of happiness we want and the kind we can reliably get. The response of philosophical ethics to this 'eudaimonia gap', as I call it, tends towards melancholy resignation. By contrast, I argue that the virtue of hope is a far more promising way of negotiating the gap. Hope believes that we can ultimately attain a far better happiness than what the eudaimonia gap allows, it sustains us from the discouragement and despair that threaten amid life's trials, and it buoys us up with the anticipation of a lasting beatitude that no disaster can reverse. In so doing, hope recognisably conduces to happiness in this life and not just the next. It also makes an important difference to how we regard the problems which continue to limit our happiness, and to whether we become demoralised by them.

This book's first chapter seeks to show why and in what sense the human condition needs theological hope. Unlike Augustine, Aquinas thought we *could* be happy in this world through a virtuous life that is characteristically enjoyable. He was quick to add that happiness in this life is imperfect, and yet it does remain genuine. I believe this view is correct and to be hailed with relief. It heads off from the outset any model of hope that is based on a denigration of this life and world. Yet obviously even the virtuous and happy suffer in this life from inevitable and major limitations which torment them, from tragedy to injustice, and it is here that hope is of evident and immediate value.

Granted a 'eudaimonia gap', hope's proposal of a perfect happiness that transcends the gap in its finality is in an interesting position. The gap does not entail, or necessarily even suggest, the existence of an object which could fill it (as Matthew Arnold wrote: 'Nor does the being hungry prove that we have bread'). But it does indicate that if a plausible candidate for closing the gap could be found, this would be 'good news' rather than just 'curious news' to us. The result, I suggest, is an intriguing test case for how the claim 'grace perfects rather than abolishes nature' can be shown rather than just told.

My proposals do not generate an 'apologetics' of hope. But as the philosopher Raymond Geuss has noted, apologetics is now premature. 'Parish-pump atheists still exist', he writes, 'but I suspect that the real danger for religious believers nowadays is not counter-belief or theoretical objections, but indifference'. This 'increase in sheer brute indifference – Why should we care *one way or the other* – rather than active unbelief or unwillingness to listen' is, he suggests, the 'greatest threat' to Christianity.[8] The first chapter tries to give reasons for why we should care one way or the other about Christian hope – why it is of evident and vital interest to us all – and it draws widely on the philosophers for sometimes reluctant, sometimes emphatic, support of a certain kind. My hope is that these interdisciplinary payoffs will put new life into the often halting relationship between philosophers and theologians. Readers who feel less need for philosophical spadework to bolster the claims of theological hope may wish to work through this chapter briskly.

Chapter 2 sets forth Aquinas' theology of hope in some detail. The account now becomes markedly theological, so that what was earlier described as the gap is largely ascribed to sin and its immediate and remote effects. I first seek to answer why Aquinas deserves a fresh hearing given that many think of Moltmann as *the* theologian of hope. It is certainly true that we are all greatly in Moltmann's debt. Along with Wolfhart Pannenberg, he helped to rescue eschatology from the image of embarrassing conversation-stopper which the demythologisers had given it. In addition, his biblically rich account refuses hope's equivalent of cheap grace at all points by its stress on social *praxis*, and by founding hope on Christ's Resurrection rather than on some baptised optimism. Yet Moltmann's account is implicated in a lot of Hegelian and Marxist baggage that has dated rather badly. Moreover, his panentheism with its developing and disempowered God cannot ensure that the eschaton ends happily rather than tragically. The ironic result is that Moltmann deflates hope in crucial ways, making the search for alternatives important.

'So faith, hope, and charity abide, these three' (1 Cor 13:13). The greatest of these may be charity, but hope's place in this great synecdoche of Christian virtue is well earned. Following the bleak despair of Good Friday, the Resurrection of Jesus Christ surprised his disciples with dazzling intensity. It was 'hot ice and wondrous strange snow', in Shakespeare's phrase, and it impressed upon early Christians the ultimate vindication of hope. The Easter mystery inspired the belief that nothing – not even death – could prevent the coming of God's kingdom. Unsurprisingly, the early Church espoused a confident, jubilant, and triumphal hope. By contrast, later patristic and medieval theology tempered this enthusiasm with sober warnings against presumption and counsels to ascetic patience.

Thomas Aquinas inherited a tradition of Latin theology whose greatest authority was Augustine and whose medieval benchmark was Peter

Lombard. In his *Sentences*, Lombard defined hope vaguely as a form of expectation, but left its practical – and therefore its moral – role unclear.[9] Aquinas took a serious interest in hope from early in his career, and sought to clarify its nature and role with some thoroughness. He defines hope's object as a 'future good possible but arduous to attain'.[10] Specifically Christian hope for Aquinas is a virtue rather than a feeling or species of optimism. In particular, it is a virtue of the will, which accounts for its resilience. But unlike the natural and 'acquired' virtues formed through habituation and effort, hope is a supernatural and 'infused' virtue gratuitously poured out by grace.[11] Like faith and charity, hope is also a 'theological' virtue in that its immediate object is God. But whereas faith knows God as first truth and charity loves God as the universal good, hope loves God as our personal good – namely, as our perfection and beatitude.

Aquinas says that theological hope empowers us in two ways, making its object twofold. The first is 'eternal life, which consists in the enjoyment of God'.[12] This is the 'final cause' or end for which hope longs. The second is 'the divine assistance ... on whose help [hope] relies'.[13] This is the 'efficient cause' or means on which hope leans. By hope we seek and long for God as the source of our beatitude, and we rely on grace to motivate us through the joys and challenges of our earthly pilgrimage.

Hope's goal is thus eternal happiness attained through the beatific vision of God, which is precisely a 'future good possible but arduous to attain'. In medieval terminology, the convert ceases to be *homo erro*: the 'human wanderer' lost in the mazes of serious sin. He or she is regenerated as *homo viator*: the 'human wayfarer' on the journey or pilgrimage to eternal beatitude.[14] This registers both a cheerful and a cautionary note. Instead of going nowhere, we are 'on the way' (*in via*). But by the same token, we *have not yet arrived*. As with Dante after he leaves the dark wood, there is a challenging journey for the Christian to make. He or she has not yet become *homo comprehensor*: the 'possessor' of perfect beatitude in the heavenly homeland (*in patria*). The major task of hope is to help one through the journey over the many challenges that stand between us and that final destination.

Many argue that theological hope offers false consolation. They claim to detect in it the 'siren-songs of old metaphysical bird-catchers', in Nietzsche's phrase, singing 'you are more, you are higher, you are of a different origin!'[15] Pagan and secular critiques of hope are well known, and I examine some of these. But hope has also drawn friendly fire from Christians who think it a hindrance or even a threat to the tasks of charity. Hope's senior prosecutor in this sense is the Christian agapist Timothy

Jackson. In his bracing and influential *Love Disconsoled*, Jackson argues that hope taints charity with mercantile motives by subverting charity into a sort of spiritual cash with which to buy heaven. Against this common criticism I argue that hope informed by charity desires consummate happiness through union with the divine friend. Since communion with a friend is the proper reward of friendship, hope does not seek an external or mercenary reward. More generally, I argue that the image of antagonism between hope and charity should be overcome, and illustrate how hope benefits the tasks of charity itself.

The remaining chapters form the theological core of the book. Chapter 3 addresses the positive flip-side of the eudaimonia gap. Many thinkers have believed that human beings are haunted by an elusive but ineradicable desire for complete fulfilment, or at least for some ideal of individual or social good beyond what we seem to be able to get in this life. The 'restless heart' theme of St. Augustine is one famous iteration, but there are countless others, some less wistful. The general desire is expressed in many forms, from religion, philosophy, music, and art, to shopping, sports, travel, and politics. I refer to it semi-technically as the *desiderium*: the ongoing desire for an ideal of happiness or completion that we never fully attain and never truly exhaust. This does not imply resentment with the world since we may rightly be grateful and appreciative for the good we can get even while lamenting lost possibilities and present injustices. But while we may be truly if partially happy in this life, not all of us get that far, and nobody permanently and securely does. Hope encourages us by promising that the *desiderium* for a fuller good or more ideal happiness is not vain, narcissistic, or absurd, but a created need which finds entire fruition in eternal life. Trusting in God's grace and confidently looking forward to perfect beatitude and lasting peace, Christians have reason to 'rejoice in hope' (Rom 12:12). That sensibility has been badly neglected. Yet such rejoicing, I argue, is not a devotional wallflower. It cultivates the habit of hope, and its absence leaves a vacuum into which sloth or *acedia* easily settles.

Hope's rejoicing has a Christological basis. We are in transition between what the New Testament calls the 'ages' or *aiones*, but that transition is *from* the old and *to* the new *aion* where the kingdom will be fully manifest and the gap fully closed. If the new *aion* is still inbreaking, and the Resurrection is its first fruits, then the Resurrection is ahead of the times, so to speak. It is incomparably newer than the old *aion* whose bad news still litters the headlines. The Empty Tomb therefore remains not just good, but (what we too easily forget) 'news': precisely the sort of thing over which to rejoice in awe. So while retaining an important place for lament, mere pessimism and disenchantment are not options for the hopeful. Expressed through practices of thanksgiving and praise, rejoicing should deeply colour the tenor of the hopeful life: for Christ is risen and has gone 'to prepare a place' for us (John 14:3).

Chapter 4 addresses hope's opposed vice of presumption, which comes in two forms. The first occurs when one refuses to seek God's grace or forgiveness out of either self-reliance or self-righteousness. The second occurs when one refuses to repent or perform good works in the belief that salvation is easy or guaranteed, and therefore requires no moral or spiritual toil. As an analogue of the first, I examine Jeffrey Stout's Emersonian construal of piety in his widely influential book *Democracy and Tradition*. Stout regards piety as something like the form of the virtues for democratic citizens. It gratefully acknowledges 'the sources of one's existence and progress through life', such as one's country, parents, and community.[16] He sincerely invites Christians to accept piety as shared moral ground with secularists like him. But Stout redacts piety so that it will necessarily exclude any role for grace, forgiveness, or redemption. He regards these broadly Augustinian items as 'blights on the human spirit' that wreck democratic self-reliance and self-respect. Stout's ethic is in many respects a secular analogue of Pelagian presumption which habituates agents to stiffly reject any dependency on grace or a Saviour. Since this cannot co-exist for very long with self-aware Christian practice, I argue that Stout's proposal that Christians accept his redacted piety turns out to be a coy subversion of Christianity itself. Since Stout is one of the most influential religious thinkers in the English-speaking world today, his overall agenda for influencing Christians – which to a large degree turns on redefining piety for them – has important ramifications.

With regard to complacent or morally lazy presumption, I examine 'moralistic therapeutic deism': a self-satisfied and impenitent spirituality which presumes upon salvation, and has been described by Christian Smith and others as the majority religion of today's youth. To resist such presumption, I follow Aquinas in saying that hope benefits from its 'gift of fear'. While most would like to return that gift unopened, I suggest that spiritual fear, understood with serious nuances, has a unique and valuable moral role that rewards examination. One important consequence of falsifying presumption is to justify the place of repentance. But intelligent criticisms have been levelled against repentance itself: for instance, that it results in unacknowledged moral injury. Nietzsche is our most subtle critic here. He construes repentance as the implicit effort partly to erase yourself by breaking with your past. This makes it both self-violent and self-deceiving. I counter that grace makes it possible to repent of your past and at the same time accept it as constitutive of who you are, making reconciliation and enhanced plenitude available to us in a way that denial of guilt and self-righteousness would not. The rest of the chapter addresses the stereotype of hope as aloof and socially quietist, arguing that apathy towards social justice is a hallmark not of hope, but of its opposed vice of presumption. Through the mediation of charity, love of neighbour as oneself is extended to hope for neighbour as oneself, giving hope a *social* interest.

Chapter 5 addresses hope particularly in terms of our vulnerability to *acedia*, demoralisation, and the vice of despair. One conspicuous reason the hopeful rely on grace is for strength in trials. Hope changes our perspective on suffering, discouragement, injustice, tragedy, and death. By making clear that our present situation is not permanent and by relying on grace to sustain us, hope precludes undue dejection and despair. As Isaiah says: 'They that hope in the Lord shall renew their strength; they shall take wings as eagles; they shall run and not be weary; they shall walk and not faint' (Is 40:31). This takes concrete shape in what we might loosely call the prayer of leaning. Here one recalls that God is trustworthy in light of the mercies shown throughout salvation history, from the Red Sea to the Empty Tomb, making credible the belief that one's own journey can be completed with divine help. This recollection may impinge upon the will with a sense of encouragement, trust, and resilience (as in 'I can do all things in him who strengthens me', Phil 4:13), and lead us to recommit to persevere on the journey.

But lest things look simplistic, I distance my account of hope from the genre of naïve consolation. While sensible consolations may arrive like water in the desert, hope does not guarantee emotional solace. Even the hope of psalmists and saints has been challenged by 'the dark night'. Having nothing to fall back on when the slough of despond arrives, naïve hope can win only Pyrrhic victories in the moral life and is defenceless against despair. This is why it is necessary to emphasise that hope is a virtue of the will: one that keeps one going not just until, but also amid, the loss of characteristic enjoyment and even moderate cheerfulness. The corollary is that losing feelings of hope does not entail losing the virtue of hope. However horrible it may seem, those who *feel* no hope can still *go on* hoping. And having an alternative to despair is itself a kind of consolation.

In connection with its arduousness I examine John Bowlin's view of hope as a Stoic virtue immune to fortune. This model, I argue, would reduce hope to a mere parade-ground exercise and deflate concern for neighbour by regarding the tragedies and injustices they face as easily overcome by a super-powered hope. While hope is apt to sustain us when fortune goes awry, trials may tempt us to give up. Whether by sudden existential shocks or the slow attrition of the years, a *taedium vitae* may set in and induce sloth or despair. In contrast to a Stoic view which sees hope operating with serene invincibility, I therefore emphasise hope's faithful, trusting, but also dogged reliance on grace to get one through life's challenges.

One unique challenge of life is the inevitability of death. Dying and death are notoriously ignored, hidden, and denied in our youth, entertainment, and consumer culture. The spiritual geography charted by traditional eschatology has blurred for most, making death an impenetrable enigma whose approach may herald bewilderment, resignation, or despair. I seek to reassert and refurbish the place of hope in a contemporary *ars moriendi* or 'art of dying'. Specifically, I propose a renewed *ascesis* of hope whose shared eschatological vision and practices help keep us from despair and prepare us for a 'good death'.

As such challenges imply, the hopeful life is complex and bittersweet. I suggest that insight into the complications for hope and happiness may be gleaned from the beatitudes in the Sermon on the Mount. Like hope, each of the beatitudes seeks a 'future good possible but arduous to attain': eternal happiness sought through the arduous path of spiritual poverty, mourning, hungering after justice, and so forth. I propose that theological hope is the 'form' or rationale of the beatitudes as a whole. Since the beatitudes are socially committed, this supports my broader claim that hope does not tacitly wink at apathy and self-absorption.

The last two chapters examine the civic, social, and cultural dimensions of hope. Early Christians aimed to be 'in the world but not of the world'. Christ himself told his disciples to expect from it a certain resistance: 'If the world (*kosmos*) hates you, know that it has hated me first' (John 15:18). Christian hope has traditionally viewed 'the world' in some sense as a tension, a problem, or even an adversary. The fear that some Manichean thought lurks behind this makes ignoring the phenomenon tempting but facile. In Chapter 6 I try to shed light on hope's terrestrial hang-ups by retrieving the concept of 'worldly sin' or 'worldliness': a category which despite its contemporary neglect was a major figure in the older tradition. Worldliness is the excessive attachment to external and this-worldly goods such as wealth, status, pomp, fame, reputation, honours, power, and influence. It is undue concern for splendour and 'success in the world's eyes'. By its very nature it calls the journey of hope to a halt through the idolatry of created goods and a peculiar kind of gentle despair which disdains the eschatological good as vague, boring, remote, and perhaps threatening.

As a remedy for this worldliness I draw on hope's specific beatitude, poverty of spirit, which involves detachment from hubris, domination, and greed in a state of acknowledged creaturely dependence on God. Given that worldliness itself is vicious and dehumanising, hope's opposition to it frees the wayfarer to be 'for the world' with respect to social justice and the cultivation of the good society. The implication is that hope is *contra mundum* in a highly qualified sense that allows us to be *pro mundo* in another and much more important sense.

Hope ultimately seeks a future and eternal good through membership in a transcendent *polis*, believing that 'here we have no lasting city, but seek one which is to come' (Heb 13:14). It may thus seem to regard the world as a dissolving phantasmagoria, and many Christians have spoken this way, lending support to critics who argue that Christianity harbours an inner logic of otherworldliness and obscurantism. In the final chapter I concede that hope at its most dualistic, Platonic, and Stoic is guilty as charged, and make no effort to repair those ruins. But Aquinas takes embodiment seriously, which means taking local and social existence seriously. Hope considered in this way has reason to regard Christian wayfarers as 'dual citizens', bound in piety to love and honour their earthly as well as the heavenly homeland. This encourages a genuine attachment to one's people and shared way of life, from relishing local holidays to quoting the national poets. Rather than sanctioning jingoism or uncritical patriotism, such love makes space for fraternal correction of one's social context as an act of charity. Dante's complex relationship to his native Florence is my model here. Social criticism uttered from this moral space will stem from piety's solicitude and love's anxiety, not the clinically detached and aloof moral disgust of those who feign flight from and abdicate responsibility for their social context – a move which inevitably frays social bonds and foments cynicism. Hope's unconditional priority is God, but, taking my cue from Aquinas, I suggest that hope may invest itself in the social body as a 'proximate end' that may be referred to God as our 'ultimate end'. So even if 'here we have no lasting city', it is false to believe that our social identifications in this life are morally and spiritually trifling. Indeed, if they were, it would make little sense to believe that 'the glory and the honour of the nations' will be brought *into* the heavenly city (Rev 21:26).

Chapter 7 also examines how hope may benefit society. The goal of theological hope is eternal beatitude with God, but the virtue also ordains created goods and temporal causes to that ultimate end. These goods and causes are the special business of virtues such as justice, prudence, courage, and charity. But when hope takes account of their projects, as I argue it should, hope coordinates the work of more 'this-worldly' virtues to its own eschatological end. Hence many Christians conspicuous for theological hope were also conspicuous for social hopes – for example, the great medieval saints who tirelessly advocated and worked for the poor, the British evangelicals and Quakers whose efforts helped abolish the slave trade, and the work of Martin Luther King Jr. in the civil rights movement. Such reformers sought first the kingdom of heaven, and yet they plainly contributed to the earthly city in extraordinary fashion, continuing to respond to social setbacks with patience, forgiveness, resilience, and tenacity long after the conventional optimists of their context had called it a day. Trusting in divine strength and 'hoping against hope' (Rom 4:18), their efforts were not founded on the prediction that everything *would* become better, but only on the belief that important things *could* become better. The result is something better than mere optimism or embittered despair: a vision which gives to this-worldly projects a transcendent horizon and stake while sustaining the hopeful with the confidence that divine help will not be lacking and that grace is operative in their contexts.

Scripture intriguingly states that the nations themselves will be 'healed' (Rev 22:2) in the eschaton, becoming most truly and perfectly themselves, fulfilled rather than abolished. Drawing on Aquinas, I suggest that the social achievements of the hopeful may at their best be not just a movement towards, but a foretaste or premonition, of the perfect social happiness proper to the beatified communion of saints. While the hopeful should not expect an earthly kingdom or secular utopia, the belief that our social identities may be long-term objects of redemption gives added reason for the hopeful to be socially invested and work for reform. The lives of the saints suggest this may be done with a refreshing lack of cynicism that corresponds to the spiritual 'youthfulness' (*iuventas*) traditionally ascribed to hope, and compared to which despair is a kind of spiritual senility. Hope can powerfully help us to sustain vitality and curb demoralisation when the results of our personal and social endeavours prove flawed. In a period when severe civic and social anxieties continue rapidly to mount, this can only be good news. Throughout the work I stress that God, the Father, Son, and Holy Spirit, is hope's primary concern and basic object. As seems fitting, I therefore end by discussing how we might best conceive of the beatific vision so as to make better sense of both our ultimate and our everyday aspirations.

CHAPTER I

The Eudaimonia Gap

Affliction is inseparable from our present state: it adheres to all the inhabitants of this world, in different proportions indeed, but with an allotment which seems very little regulated by our own conduct. It has been the boast of some swelling moralists, that every man's fortune was in his own power ... and that happiness is the unfailing consequence of virtue. But, surely, the quiver of Omnipotence is stored with arrows, against which the shield of human virtue, however adamantine it has been boasted, is held up in vain: we do not always suffer by our crimes; we are not always protected by our innocence.

                Samuel Johnson, Essay no. 120, *The Adventurer*

In this alone we suffer:
Cut off from hope, we live on in desire.

       Dante, *Inferno*, canto IV (the 'Limbo of the virtuous pagans')

Hope seeks beatitude, making happiness central to any account of hope. Happiness, in turn, is a dominant category in many schools of ethics. The philosopher Julia Annas noted that 'The question 'In what does my happiness consist?' is the most important one in ancient ethics'.[1] The same could be said for patristic, early, and high medieval ethics. Augustine takes it as noncontroversial that 'all men agree in desiring the ultimate end, which is happiness'.[2] Origen, the Cappadocian fathers, Chrysostom, Boethius, Anselm, Lombard, Bonaventure, Albert the Great, and other representative sources of late antiquity and the Middle Ages certainly agreed about it.[3] The ultimate end of human action was identified with happiness: the *eudaimonia* of Greek philosophy, the *makarios* of the Beatitudes, and the *felicitas* and *beatitudo* of Latin philosophy and theology. As will be discussed, the concept of happiness was morally layered in such traditions. It is a genuinely ethical category and not just a psychological search for mere contentment beneath philosophical scaffolding.

Aquinas on Happiness

Thomas Aquinas plainly belongs to this eudaimonist tradition. 'Happiness is the complete good', he writes, 'which satisfies desire altogether; otherwise it would not be the ultimate end, if something yet remained to be desired'.[4] The literature explicating Aquinas on happiness is centuries old, has recently been renovated, and is so well trodden that no lengthy excursion need detain us. For my purposes all that is necessary is to state a few working assumptions and direct those eager for fine print to the relevant literature.

Aquinas proposes that the ultimate end of human striving is happiness (*beatitudo*). As Servais Pinckaers usefully notes, happiness has an 'objective' and a 'subjective' side for Aquinas.[5] The former refers to the 'object' in which happiness consists, and the latter to the attainment and possession of happiness on the part of the agent as a 'subject'. For Aquinas the object of happiness in the fullest sense is God. He argues at length that goodness as such, rather than any particular good, is the object of the will (an important corollary of which is that his eudaimonism is not egoistic).[6] No particular good, however lovely it may be, can completely and permanently satisfy us such that we will never need or want anything else ever again. Aquinas says that only the full and everlasting attainment of God in the beatific vision could do that. The will is further distanced from its object by the unavoidable presence in this life of innumerable evils which impede and destabilise whatever good we do have. Only through attaining goodness as such – in which there is no admixture of evil – could the will fully and securely rest in its proper object. But this 'is to be found, not in any creature, but in God alone', who is goodness itself.[7]

The 'subjective' side of happiness concerns the attainment, possession, and enjoyment of happiness on the part of the agent. Happiness is not simply a state of the habits or of the passions. The implication – which shows that our contemporaries face Aquinas across a wide conceptual gulf – is that mere contentment does not even account for the subjective side of happiness, let alone its objective side. Instead of a psychological state such as general contentment or satisfaction, Aquinas says that the subjective side of happiness is essentially an activity (*operatio*): 'For happiness is man's supreme perfection. Now each thing is perfect in so far as it is actual; since potentiality without act is imperfect. Consequently happiness must consist in man's ultimate act'.[8]

For Aquinas, happiness is the flourishing or perfection of a rational being. But perfection does not occur by sitting idly by. It comes through the actualisation or development of the human potential for excellence: by making the case what could and should be the case. This is achieved through performing the activities that develop our human capacities. What kind of activities are these? Aquinas agrees with Aristotle that they are *virtuous* activities. Subjectively speaking, happiness is primarily 'activity (*operatio*) in accordance with virtue', or as we might say, 'living virtuously'.⁹

Virtues are 'habits' (*habitus*) understood as stable dispositions of the intellect, will, and passions which perfect agency by inclining us to act well. Each virtue perfects one or more human capacities (*potentiae*). Put in terms more familiar to us, a virtue *develops* a human capacity to engage in pursuits and attain goods that conduce to human flourishing. Our capacities are many, of course: they range over the intellectual, volitional, or affective dimensions of our humanity. We are not born with these capacities developed. As with language acquisition or fine motor skills, formation is required. The virtues have a crucial role here in that they dispose our capacities to function harmoniously, so that we get beyond a fissiparous, haphazard, and self-divided way of life, and more stably pursue our comprehensive good.¹⁰

Despite the top-heavy role of virtue, this is not a recipe for moral purism. The idea is that practising virtue will be characteristically enjoyable to the virtuous. This enjoyment is not reducible to narrowly moral pleasures, such as the joys of a good conscience. For one thing, developing one's humanity through pursuing worthwhile aims that register real achievements does make life more enjoyable. Beyond that, the virtues themselves are not austerely moral. They denote an organised set of attitudes and trained habits which shape our very taste and enjoyments. To get at this, Aquinas, like Aristotle, distinguishes between the merely continent or self-controlled, and the truly virtuous.¹¹ Unlike the continent, the virtuous characteristically enjoy acting virtuously. But this is a result of art and not just of nature. By consistently acting at or 'practising' a virtue we may, over time, cultivate the disposition or *habitus* of that virtue. Charity, temperance, honesty, generosity, prudence, and so forth, are the product of a way of life that ideally should begin in early childhood, encouraged through stories, education, religion, the imitation of role models, discipline, praise, rewards, practices, routines, and habituation. These encourage the modes of perception and stock responses proper to the virtuous.

As Aristotle notes, to be virtuous it is not enough to do what the just or temperate person does; we must do it *as* the just or temperate person does it: from a settled character and with the appropriate intention, manner, judgment, timing, sensibility, and so forth.[12] Those who have the *habitus* that disposes to virtuous activity typically engage in the appropriate acts with a certain ease, promptness, and pleasure. Far from doing one's duty with gritted teeth and fevered brow, virtue is almost a *style*.[13]

Aquinas describes enjoyment as 'unimpeded activity, or what perfects an activity'.[14] He approves Aristotle's description: 'For a good man *qua* good delights in virtuous actions and is vexed at vicious ones, as a musical man enjoys beautiful tunes but is pained at bad ones'.[15] A fine illustration of this is to be found in *Persuasion*, where Jane Austen says that Anne 'had delicacy that must be pained' by Henrietta's bad conduct towards Charles Hayter.[16] As violinists enjoy the exercise of their skill and shudder at a false note, so the virtuous characteristically enjoy the exercise of virtue and are repulsed by vice. By contrast, the continent still find it difficult to do what virtue requires, like an apprentice violinist who sweats over a piece a professional would play with grace.[17] Hence while various moral struggles remain for the virtuous, the virtuous life is characteristically enjoyable, and being virtuous, its enjoyments are of the best kind. Recent work in empirical psychology lends support to this view.[18]

In terms of its 'subjective' side, happiness is primarily the perfection brought about by 'activity (*operatio*) according to virtue' which develops our human capacities, and in which we characteristically take enjoyment.[19] As this suggests, for Aquinas happiness does not just consist in *having* the virtues, but beyond that, in *practising* the virtues. The relevant *operatio* does not just refer to discrete actions, but to the activity of our life as a whole. This is achieved with consistency through adopting a certain way of life – specifically, a virtuous life of some fairly determinate form.

To show what the happy life might look like, Aquinas like Aristotle bundles the possibilities into three recognisable options: the hedonistic life, which he elbows aside as vicious, and the active and contemplative lives.[20] The active life devoted primarily to practical virtues such as justice and prudence in a life of labour and service is genuinely happy. Such actions perfect human capacities, their objects are great goods, and they dispose to right relationship with God. But happiest of all, he insists, is the contemplative life devoted primarily to wisdom and to divine things. In part this is because the contemplative life goes more directly to ends, whereas the active life is more saddled with means: 'The active life, which is busy with many things, has less of happiness than the contemplative life, which is busied with one thing, i.e. the contemplation of truth'.[21] Aquinas also acknowledges a 'mixed life' of both contemplative and active pursuits.

The highest of all activities corresponds to the highest form of happiness. It comes only with the beatific vision of God in the next life construed as a contemplative act of the intellect in which the will adheres to God with overflowing love and delight. In it all evils will be expelled and our 'mind will be united to God by one, continual, everlasting activity'.[22] Here the objective and subjective sides of happiness perfectly meet. But obviously we cannot attain such bliss now. Aquinas insists on our essential embodiment, and unlike the Stoics he thinks happiness enjoys no immunity from the world of fortune in which our bodies entangle us.[23] The activities of the contemplative and active lives (in which happiness consists) will often be interrupted, impeded, and even foiled by sickness, ignorance, weariness, lack of resources, lack of time, and misfortunes of all kinds. Aquinas therefore concludes that 'a certain participation of happiness can be had in this life', but that perfect happiness (*perfecta beatitudo*) 'cannot be had in this life'.[24] But as a Christian he believes that complete fruition can be had in the next life. Insofar as happiness is inevitably imperfect, it therefore points towards hope rather than resignation or despair.

The Eudaimonia Gap as Interdisciplinary Problem

In this world, we rightly want to overcome evils we cannot adequately overcome, and pursue goods and projects whose scope falls short of our best aspirations. This bad news for happiness I call the 'eudaimonia gap'. As stated in the introduction, this book will not try to argue for all of Aquinas' positions from the ground up. Instead, it will methodologically presuppose many of his claims to provide the discursive context needed to get at the questions I am really addressing. Aquinas' general account of happiness is one such presupposition, and I leave those interested in a full and renovated defence of that account in good hands.[25] But since I am making normative claims, I will treat those presuppositions as in principle defeasible, and will address relevant questions and objections in their own terms. The rest of this chapter will take up that task with respect to the eudaimonia gap. My aim will be to show that what I call the gap is not just an idiosyncratic postulate of Aquinas, but a major problem for the human condition which makes the prospect of hope important to believers and nonbelievers alike. To bear this out, I turn from Aquinas to a wider sampling of philosophers and interlocutors who corroborate my diagnosis of the gap, and often wistfully ponder whether hope may be our best answer to it.

I take it that the happy life of 'activity in accordance with virtue' is a rich, admirable, and worthwhile life. Yet that life is burdened with problems inherent to embodied finitude and our vulnerability to fortune. I will suggest that the resulting gap is something we rightly wish to be rid of and work to close, but that even our best efforts are doomed to 'reach beyond our grasp', and fall well short of our praiseworthy aims. I will further suggest that the gap is not just a niggling annoyance, but a grave problem which frustrates many of our most important individual projects and social causes. The eudaimonia gap describes a crisis, not just an irritant. If it is possible to resolve it at all, the prospect of doing so will be a *priority*.

To show that such claims are not issued by theological *fiat*, I turn now to the work of philosophers who wrestle with the gap and conclude that we cannot close it adequately by human means. My primary interlocutors here are Aristotelian and neo-Aristotelian. Specifically, I will examine Aristotle himself and two very prominent contemporary virtue ethicists, Philippa Foot and Rosalind Hursthouse. But to avoid appearances of philosophical parochialism, and to show just how widespread are the philosophical headaches caused by the eudaimonia gap, I will also examine Kantian and Utilitarian treatments of the problem.

The gap leads most of my interlocutors to affirm happiness even while reluctantly trimming down our expectations, giving way to resignation tinged by melancholy. But it leads others to ask if we might hope to attain a happiness which at present is better-than-possible, but which divine agency might make possible beyond this life. Partly in light of such accounts, I argue that the eudaimonia gap leaves space for the theological virtue of hope to greatly enrich us in pursuit of the happy life.

The Limits of Aristotelian Happiness

Aristotle believed that happiness does not consist in the goods of fortune, bodily goods, or even the possession of the virtues. Like Aquinas, he describes happiness as 'activity (*energeia*) in accordance with the virtues' and describes it as characteristically enjoyable.[26] It requires some of the goods of fortune: minimally as raw material for exercising certain virtues and maximally because certain goods are themselves needed for the happy life. The consequence is that *eudaimonia* must not suffer too much from what Aristotle calls impediments (*empodia*) to virtuous activity.[27] The scope of *eudaimonia* itself is not just a favoured year or decade, but a completed life.[28] *Eudaimonia* for Aristotle is 'a *lifetime's* virtuous activity'.[29] He does not think of happiness as a future reward, like a happy retirement. As

J. L. Ackrill notes, *eudaimonia* is best thought of as 'living well' in what amounts to 'the best possible life' for a person.[30]

Aristotle claims that goals, activities, and virtues are on a scale not just of good versus bad, but of good, better, and best. In the tenth book of the *Nicomachean Ethics* he seems to say that *eudaimonia* – or the best kind of it – will be in accord with the best kind of virtuous activity. This will correspond to the peculiar function (*ergon*) of humans as rational animals: a function especially noble (*kalon*) and even divine (*theion*). The peculiar *ergon* of humans is reason (*nous*). So for Aristotle, the most complete (*teleion*) form of *eudaimonia* will be devoted to this function.[31] What this amounts to depends on a further distinction between theoretical and practical reason. Practical reason and its virtue of practical wisdom (*phronesis*) deliberate about means ordered to ends other than themselves. By contrast, theoretical reason with its virtue of theoretical wisdom (*sophia*) is 'loved for its own sake; for nothing arises from it apart from the contemplating, while from practical activities we gain more or less apart from the action'.[32] In a much-debated passage of *Nicomachean Ethics* Book X, Aristotle appears to conclude that the summit of *eudaimonia* is a life devoted to theoretical reason (*theoretike energeia*): the contemplative life of intellectual research. As a genuine exercise of human virtue, the life of action and practical wisdom is also happy, but happy 'in a secondary degree'.[33]

At this point problems arise for the scope of *eudaimonia*. Unlike Plato, Aristotle thinks that the human is not a soul with a body, but a body-soul composite. Plato's Socrates defiantly told his persecutors that: 'No one can harm a good man either in life or death'.[34] As is well known, a certain mind-body dualism is behind this claim. Aristotle's hylomorphic model of embodiment allows no such insulation from luck since it leaves the body and therefore the self vulnerable to fortune. It follows that the virtuous activity the happy person undertakes is likewise vulnerable since bad luck and injustice really can harm us. Given that *eudaimonia* is virtuous activity, it follows that merely having the virtues cannot suffice for happiness.[35]

Not only is tragedy an impediment to *eudaimonia*. Our very nature as a body-soul 'composite' (*synthetou*) puts certain dead weights on the contemplative life.[36] The body's clamorous needs and the world that body thrusts us into frequently hinder contemplation. We need food, exercise, and instruments to do research and to keep fit for it. Moreover, as political animals, we face duties our communities impose upon us. Hence even the contemplative must practise the moral virtues 'in so far as he is a man and lives with a number of people'.[37] But Aristotle regards these as interruptions: 'they are, one may say, even impediments (*empodiai*), at all events to his contemplation'.[38] So even barring serious bad luck, our composite nature means that contemplative happiness hits a certain ceiling. The chronic neediness and frailty of the body, and the interruptions of ordinary life mean that contemplative activity will be intermittent and restricted in scope.[39]

There is much debate over just how privileged contemplation is in Aristotle's overall account of *eudaimonia*, and whether Book X of the *Nicomachean Ethics* may be in tension with the rest of the Aristotelian corpus on this point. The most satisfactory view appears to be that Aristotle depicts contemplation as one part (i.e., the best part) of *eudaimonia* (i.e., the best form of *eudaimonia*).[40] But resolving this dispute is not necessary here since Aristotle thinks the active or so-called secondary form of happiness is even more dependent on externals and vulnerable to luck than contemplative happiness.[41] So however the contemplative and active questions are resolved, the impediments foreseen for *eudaimonia* apply to both.

Routine hindrances to *eudaimonia* exist even in the absence of tragedy. As Aristotle notes, it is not just the person 'who meets with fortune's like Priam's' whose happy life has problems. Impediments to *eudaimonia* include more familiar and frequent woes than Priam's, or than 'death on the rack'. Martha Nussbaum has discussed these in some detail. They include unruly passions, weariness, sickness, diminishing enjoyments, political problems, and tensions or failures in one's friendships and in one's relationships generally.[42] Since these may afflict one's family, friends, and *polis*, one is vulnerable to their misfortunes, too; for Aristotle regards it as a 'very unfriendly doctrine' that misfortune to someone's fellows 'should not affect his happiness at all'.[43] Impediments to a friend's happiness may hinder my own *eudaimonia*, even without abolishing it.[44] All of these 'impediments' (*empodiai*) are more familiar and frequent aspects of the eudaimonia gap, and show that one does not just have to be plunged in tragedy to have one's *eudaimonia* regrettably cramped and pinched, even if it remains intact, admirable, and worthwhile on the whole. Aristotle does not dwell on the point, but the inevitability of aging, decline, and death both for oneself and one's fellows makes this picture even bleaker and ensures that *eudaimonia* exists on an arc that is certain eventually to plummet. Absent crippling debility, Aristotle would presumably not see happiness as wholly voided for those whose 'way of life/ Is fall'n into the sere, the yellow leaf'. But if *eudaimonia* is virtuous activity, then for the many who undergo significant mental and physical decline – especially near or at death – impediments to *eudaimonia* would problematically build up. This makes pagan and secular *eudaimonia* quite different from

Christian beatitude with its eschatological telos.[45] Aristotle's happy life is anticlimactic in the sense that the best bits come earlier, and the later bits tend to a slow, weary unravelling.

Despite talk of impediments to happiness and nods to what I have called the eudaimonia gap, Aristotle insists that we should not lower our aspirations. In the teeth of limitations posed by our composite nature, he flings out a kind of defiance: 'We must not follow those who advise us, being men, to think of human things, and being mortal, of mortal things, but we must, so far as we can, make ourselves immortal, and strain every nerve to live in accordance with the best thing in us'.[46] This 'best thing in us' for Aristotle is our theoretical reason (*nous*). In what can only be taken as exultant hyperbole, Aristotle even claims that our *nous* 'would seem actually to be each man, since it is the authoritative and better part of him'. By living the contemplative life we identify with theoretical reason, the part of us that is akin to the gods. But the life a purely rational being could live *we* cannot due to embodiment and fortune. 'Such a life would be too high for man; for it is not in so far as he is man that he will live so, but in so far as something divine is present within him'.[47] We can get much but not all of the happiness possible to a rational being due to our bodies and our vulnerability to luck.

Aristotle reserves perfect *eudaimonia* to his purely contemplative gods. Compared to their unhindered *eudaimonia* our measure of happiness is small. By identifying with our *nous* ('this would seem to actually be each man') we are, so to speak, playing at being Aristotelian gods. The pretence of 'immortalising' will ultimately be shattered by our composite nature with its vulnerability and mortality, but the identification-exercise has an elevating effect. It leads us to 'strain every nerve' to get nearer to heights of virtuous achievement that we will never quite reach. Yet without this straining we would achieve less. It is rather like a bit actor imitating a genius of the stage to boost his performance, or the ascetic goal to 'whip th' offending Adam out' while expecting all too human results. Looking up to God and the gods as the paradigms of perfect *eudaimonia*, Aristotle concludes: 'we are happy, but only as men'.[48] The qualifying tone is deflationary, as in 'we compete well, for lightweights'.

Nonetheless, Aristotle's account of happiness does not give way to whining angst. He lacked the existentialist temperament and stressed the great good of the *eudaimon* life such as it was. This befits the aspirations and labours he saw as proper to the 'magnanimous man' who rises to lofty occasions. Perfect *eudaimonia* may be 'too high for man'. But Aristotle responds with the goal of 'making ourselves immortal' and closing what

I call the eudaimonia gap 'so far as we can'.[49] The will to overcome the gap is there, even if the means are somewhat wanting.

The Limits of Neo-Aristotelian Happiness

The eudaimonia gap is also regretfully acknowledged by many leading scholars of virtue. The contemporary 'turn to virtue' began in the late 1950s–1970s and was pioneered by philosophers Elizabeth Anscombe, Philippa Foot, and Iris Murdoch at the Universities of Oxford and Cambridge. During those years its status was that of an eccentric but respected insurgency movement. Only in later work and figures did it achieve great fame and impact. Alasdair MacIntyre's 1981 *After Virtue* perhaps represents, like Barth's *Epistle to the Romans*, the symbolic 'bombshell going off in the playground' of academics. But many who rejected his diagnosis of modernity saw virtue as a missing piece in ethics whose absence helped explained various Utilitarian and Kantian dead-ends. During the mid-1980s, virtue became something of a gold rush, collecting many of the era's finest ethical minds.[50] As of the late 1990s, something called 'virtue ethics' was being described from graduate seminars to nursing ethics textbooks as a third major approach to ethics, alongside consequentialism and deontology.

The approaches to virtue have varied, sometimes starkly. Within philosophy, the most popular has been neo-Aristotelian, with a sizeable minority gathered around Plato, the Stoics, Hume, and others. As this suggests, the label 'virtue ethics' is largely one of convenience. My focus will be on the more common – and, in my view, more compelling – neo-Aristotelian approach. Rejecting the fantasy of dualism's escape-hatch from frailty, bad luck, and tragedy, this approach has wrestled with the eudaimonia gap under various names. I will examine the representative and influential work of Philippa Foot and Rosalind Hursthouse, probing the limits they ascribe to happiness, and why they even toy with religious hope as a way out of demoralisation and despair.

Philippa Foot

Philippa Foot's 2001 book *Natural Goodness* crowned decades of pioneering work in virtue ethics. It challenged orthodox pieties surrounding the 'naturalistic fallacy' by claiming that virtue conduces to happiness and empowers us to flourish as members of our own distinct species. It also fully acknowledged the limits of happiness, or what I am calling the eudaimonia gap. She does not focus on everyday limits to happiness, but on misfortunes that may destroy it. Since these depend on contingencies we cannot transcend, Foot's melancholy conclusion is that the unlucky may have to forgo happiness. Still more interesting for my account are her cryptic musings about the possibility that religious hope might deal with the gap more adequately than philosophical regret.

Foot claims that happiness is the kind of flourishing proper to the human species. As rabies hinders the flourishing of a dog, and blindness hinders the flourishing of an owl, so vice hinders the happiness of a human. Nature and ethics, fact and value, are much closer than popularly believed.[51] To live a happy life is to flourish according to the human life-form through going about things virtuously and pursuing the ends required by our species. If successful, such a life will be characteristically marked by '*the enjoyment of good things*, meaning enjoyment in attaining, and in pursuing, right ends'. This is different from saying that happiness just is subjective enjoyment or contentment. She mentions an asylum patient who was 'happy all day collecting bits of garbage in the yard', and rhetorically asks whether eighty years of foolish giggling or squeaking could be thought of as a good and fully human life, regardless of whether someone liked it. The sense that something important is missing from such lives retains the intuition that happiness is not just subjective enjoyment, but enjoyment with appropriate objects and a fitting way of life.[52] This is pursued through activities, and enjoyment is of activities. So this brings Foot close to Aristotle's definition of happiness as 'activity in accordance with virtue' that is characteristically enjoyable.[53]

This edifying account fully accords with Aristotle and his heirs. But it also raises troubling questions. For instance, what does Foot make of virtues such as justice, honesty, and courage which may cause us to become despised, harmed, persecuted, tortured, or killed? Certainly they may benefit the community, but can we say the courageous are benefited by what harms them, or flourish through what kills them? Such puzzles land Foot in an Aristotelian in-house debate over which of the following best describes the *eudaimon* overtaken by tragedy: 1) they lose *eudaimonia* and fall into misery;[54] 2) their *eudaimonia* is diminished but not abolished; or 3) they lose not *eudaimonia* but rather 'blessedness' (*makarios*) construed as a kind of '*eudaimonia* plus', i.e., *eudaimonia* plus some of the goods of fortune and characteristic enjoyment seen as a kind of 'lustre' or 'adornment' supervening on *eudaimonia* itself.[55] With Martha Nussbaum and against T. H. Irwin and Julia Annas, Foot argues for position 1). But that position raises the spectre of virtue conflicting with happiness. Granted that conflict, virtue ethics, and eudaimonism might part ways at the *experimentum crucis*, wrecking Foot's whole project. Position 1) also raises the question of whether virtue is an essential or merely contingent benefit to humans: whether virtue's benefiting properties are ultimately at the mercy of fortune.

Foot considers these problems and presents a set of exemplars to help navigate them. They are a group of young Germans imprisoned and killed for bravely resisting the Nazis, and whose thoughts are recorded in letters sent to their sweethearts and families. The letters were later published in a book called *Dying We Live*.[56] Foot calls them the Letter-Writers, and describes them as exceptionally virtuous and suited to happiness. Out of justice and sustained by fortitude, they refuse to go along with Nazi demands. Predictably, this leads to imprisonment and execution. So did their virtues make them sacrifice happiness, Foot asks? It seems so. They lost their families, loved ones, and futures. Then should they have sacrificed their virtues in pursuit of happiness, and given in to Nazi demands? Foot replies in the negative, and adds that they would not have felt that happiness *could* be found by abandoning the course of virtue.[57]

According to Foot, two essentials are required for happiness: a) a virtuous way of life or virtuous activity; and b) characteristic enjoyment. The problem is that costly virtues such as justice and courage may cause a) and b) to come apart. If so, then virtue might in a strange twist backfire on the very happiness it conduces to and for which tendency it was deemed an objective benefit in the first place. The relationship between virtue and happiness might then look competitive. This would raise the dark question: might one have to pick one over the other should push come to shove? Foot rejects that view. Since true happiness requires virtue, one cannot seek happiness through vicious courses. She notes that 'only goodness can achieve' *eudaimonia*, but 'by one of the evil chances of life it may be out of the reach of even the best of men'.[58] So the virtuous agent in tragedy does not seek virtue over happiness. Fortune makes it 'that a happy life had turned out not to be possible for him. We cannot ignore this interpretation … if we identify happiness with the human good'.[59] To put it in double-effect language: the good agent in tragedy intends virtue while foreseeing but not intending the probable loss of *eudaimonia*.

The consequence of Foot's view is that happiness is ultimately at the mercy of fortune. The unlucky experience not just a eudaimonia gap, but a eudaimonia collapse. At least, this is Foot's theoretical view. But her actual set of exemplars raises another possibility which she finds tantalising if personally off-limits: the prospect of Christian hope.

The Nazi-resisting Letter-Writers of Foot's test case are meant to illustrate the theoretical points about what happiness requires and how the virtuous may have to forgo it. Imprisoned and awaiting execution for their witness, they are Foot's equivalent of Aristotle's 'man on the rack' who cannot possibly be happy. Yet Foot notes an anomaly in her test case: her exemplars do not actually appear to be miserable, putting the hypothesis and evidence in tension. Making clear that she is a 'card-carrying atheist', Foot nevertheless feels she must point out that: 'Readers of these letters have been struck by the extraordinary sense of happiness they radiate, which has perhaps to do with the fact that practically all the writers were devout Christians (with belief in) God'.[60] The letters are in fact replete with Christian hope. Because of this hope the Letter-Writers believe that virtue does not require them to forgo happiness full stop. Knowing just how much they are losing now, they nevertheless believe their virtuous course will ultimately lead to complete and irrevocable happiness. Hence the apt title for their collected letters: *Dying We Live*. The 'extraordinary sense of happiness they radiate' makes clear that hope does not just make them trust in future happiness; it also confers a certain present happiness amid tragedy. The motto of Foot's exemplars could easily be the Scriptural phrase 'rejoicing in hope, patient in tribulation' (Rom 12:12).

Foot alludes to 'the extraordinary sense of happiness (the Letter-Writers) radiate'; a sense which she cannot explain, but which she simply says 'puzzled (me) for years'.[61] The source of her puzzlement seems fairly clear. On the one hand, Foot *qua* virtue theorist sees that hope really is happy-making for those who have it. On the other, Foot *qua* atheist is puzzled that a hope for which she sees no theoretical justification nevertheless does us good. The overall impression is of muted but significant support for the view that hope does what Foot thinks the virtues are supposed to do: *benefit* us. Her belief that happiness is at the mercy of luck is something she dislikes but regretfully accepts as the best that secularism can do. Yet she is at the same time intrigued by a better prospect founded on a hope she does not share, but whose results she finds compelling.

Rosalind Hursthouse

Rosalind Hursthouse's book *On Virtue Ethics* has been described by Simon Blackburn, Roger Crisp, and others as the defining and comprehensive exposition of virtue ethics. It shares with Foot's *Natural Goodness* the goal of tethering virtue and *eudaimonia* to naturalism. But its proposals for how to achieve this are far more detailed and programmatic.

Hursthouse claims that virtue ethics can be made objective using three theses: (1) the virtues benefit their possessor by enabling *eudaimonia*; (2) the virtues make their possessor a good human being; and (3) the two theses interrelate in that what is happy-making for agents is what makes them good *qua* human, as rational and social animals of a specific kind.[62] The virtues benefit by making the appetites, needs, parts, and operations of a human well endowed for attaining four main natural ends. These in turn are: (1) individual survival; (2) continuance of the species; (3) characteristic freedom from pain and characteristic enjoyment; and (4) the flourishing of the social group. The human being empowered by virtue who attains these four ends is *eudaimon*.[63]

Well aware of the problems posed by luck, Hursthouse concedes that her formula is a rule of thumb, not an infallible gimmick. All virtues are not always enjoyable. And virtue does not suffice for *eudaimonia* anyway. Honesty and charity foster personal and social goods, but in some cases may get you harmed or killed. But just as a 'health regimen' is our best chance for attaining health, so a virtuous life is the 'only reliable bet' for attaining happiness. A regimen of regular exercise, healthy eating, and quitting smoking conduces to health. But it does not *guarantee* it. You might keep a health regimen but still die young of a heart attack or in a car wreck. Hursthouse thinks that a 'virtue regimen' has a similar relationship to happiness:

> The claim is not that possession of the virtues guarantees that one will flourish. The claim is that they are the only reliable bet – even though, it is agreed, I might be unlucky and, precisely because of my virtue, wind up dying early or with my life marred or ruined.[64]

Though it is more elaborate, Hursthouse's view is much like Foot's when it comes to the relation of virtue and happiness, and the possibility that the virtuous may have to forgo happiness. But like Foot she acknowledges that religious hope complicates the picture in interesting ways.[65]

Hursthouse's ethical naturalism presupposes that the parts of human moral psychology work cooperatively towards the same end like well-conducted musicians playing together in an orchestra. But Bernard Williams has influentially argued against this, in part on evolutionary grounds: '(in) adding rationality to our social animality, nature has produced a sadly flawed and divided creature, an "ill-assorted *bricolage* of powers and instincts" '.[66] Hursthouse takes this challenge of inner division seriously and entertains possibilities of it. Child-rearing, for example, fosters the continuance of the species and the good of the social group. But what if the demands of child-rearing frustrate the agent's characteristic experience of enjoyment and freedom from pain? In that case, natural ends (2) and (4) only come at the expense of (3), making the agent look 'sadly flawed and divided'. Williams' famous case of the painter Gauguin makes a related point. In that case, the drive to develop one's talents and life projects conflicts with the good of one's family and community.

Whether to have children, whether to work or stay at home with the children, whether to put creativity and career over your family: such cases are not the stuff of tragedy, but track the inner conflict and rival demands which frustrate countless people. Williams pessimistically maintains that: 'Humans beings are to some degree a mess … beings for whom no form of life is likely to prove entirely satisfactory, either individually or socially'.[67] Happiness may therefore only be got through 'astonishing luck'. But something so unsure and unstable can hardly be made the basis of ethics. With the eudaimonia gap recast as a eudaimonia abyss, the project of consistently bridging the gap looks quixotic, and eudaimonism itself a failed project.

Hursthouse chastises this view as a form of 'tragic despair', and calls on her readers to oppose it. To this end she makes an intriguing appeal to practices of child-rearing. She notes that parents tend morally to educate their children partly through a stock of traditional stories and fairy tales which imply that the virtuous are generally better off and more happy than the vicious. We teach that while there are tragic exceptions, the brave, loving, and loyal hero or heroine, not the treacherous friend or wicked stepmother, should and generally does end happily. If we did not already believe in the beneficial power of virtue in human life – at least on the whole – such lessons would be absurd, even abusive. Yet we do not think we are lying to our children about life, or setting them up for disaster. Of course, there is no argument here. Hursthouse's point is that we behave as though we have *already* resolved this argument, and that we should attend to this. Performatively if not explicitly, we betray the fact that we have agreed with her and disagreed with Williams all along. Moreover, she takes her overall point as an appeal to necessity. The necessity is to pass on this kind of beneficent moral education to our children since the alternative is to form them to live by 'counsels of despair'.[68]

Against premature despair, Hursthouse argues that many are unhappy due not to tragedy, but to widespread vice. Yet she admits being unable to prove that the natural ends will never cannibalise each other or produce inner division. So while she believes her case for naturalistic virtue ethics is plausible, she hedges, concluding: 'The fact, if it is a fact, that human nature is, at best, harmonious, is a highly contingent one. It is a contingent fact, if it is a fact, that we can, individually, flourish or achieve *eudaimonia*'.[69]

By hanging everything on this string of 'ifs' and 'at bests' and 'extreme contingencies', Hursthouse exposes her case to the law of dwindling probabilities. This might strengthen Williams's hand, implying that *eudaimonia* is the result of 'astonishing luck' after all. But she rejects this view given her commitment to fight despair in ourselves and not to pass it down to our children. Her last appeal looks from the philosophical point of view almost like a *deus ex machina*. Concluding *On Virtue Ethics*, she says:

> Atheists may find it hard to recognize the point nowadays, but believing that human nature is harmonious is part of the virtue of hope … to believe in (God's) Providence was part of the virtue of hope; to doubt it is to fall prey to the vice of despair. And that seems to me to be right.[70]

Despite the salute to Providence, the hope in question is not really theological. Its goal is natural *eudaimonia*, not supernatural beatitude. The reference to God is hand-waving; and even if it were taken seriously, would only demand an inconspicuous deism. Yet the felt need for the move is revealing. Hursthouse wants to retrieve hope because she thinks the evidence for naturalistic eudaimonism fair but inconclusive. The belief that nature is (probably) harmonious will not get us far enough. We need a leap of hope, so to speak, to pass onto our children something more cheerful than the bleak thought that only by 'astonishing luck' could their lives be happy. She writes: 'hope, as a virtue, is not without its own validation. We could give it a sort of "necessary condition of our practice" justification'.[71] Hursthouse therefore makes hope something like a postulate of pure practical reason. Such hope will let us trust that nature is ultimately 'for us' in a way that mimics the Christian hope that Providence is 'for us'. This guarantees that we pass down to the next generation the belief that the life and world in which its members find themselves is characteristically comic rather than tragic.

Hedged teleological bets make Hursthouse clutch at hope as an ethical talisman. But we must not confuse this occasion for hope with its overall justification – any more than a given danger which occasions courage is the sole justification for courage as a virtue. Hursthouse may use hope as a shield for eudaimonism against Darwinian critique. But she does not think hope became a virtue only after and because Darwin published *The Origin of the Species*. Occasions of despair are many, and so Hursthouse's overall justification for hope is the need to resist any such despair. She closes her book with the single sentence: 'Keep Hope Alive'. So even if the destabilisation of teleology is overstated by Williams and given too much credit by Hursthouse, her retrieval of hope is of broader relevance.[72]

Hursthouse is plundering a religious virtue for usable gear.[73] Christians and others might gladly share some, but her proposal raises doubts. Hursthouse hopes in nature as though it were beneficently arranged by Providence. But why? Christians hope in Providence because they believe God is trustworthy. By contrast, Hursthouse hopes in human nature because she is not sure if it is trustworthy. She trusts in the nature she doubts because we as human beings have nowhere else to go. We cannot exit our humanity and so 'there is no practicable alternative' than hope for those who wish to resist 'counsels of despair'. This raises the possibility of asking whether there does exist an object which makes hope well placed. If there is such an object, then hope really does trust in something which merits trust. If there is not, then even if hope were somehow justified as a practical necessity, its ultimate ending would be tragic and absurd.

As Hursthouse furtively suggests, the perfect fit for such an object of hope is Divine Providence. Naturalistic hope trusts in nature as if it were providentially 'for us' while unsure of whether it is. Genuine trust in Providence removes this awkward play-acting by proposing an object proportionate to that hope: a genuine Providence which has made creation be actually and not just feignedly 'for us'. It is the difference between the trust of those who jump from a window believing a rescuer will catch them, and the trust of those who jump *as if* they will be caught while having no idea if anybody is there. Whether hope in Providence is itself justified depends on further beliefs, not least whether secularism is accurate. But if available, theistic premises would ground the hope Hursthouse wants far better than agnostic ones since they would affirm and not just feign a proportionate object.

Theology could also help with the serious problem that Hursthouse's account actually cannot resist despair at all. The object of her hope is not a future good we expect and long for, but the belief that human nature and virtue conduce to happiness. So what happens when *eudaimonia* is – as Hursthouse thinks it often will be – impossible for the virtuous due to tragedy? Since I cannot hope for what I know to be impossible, isn't despair reasonable at that point? Oddly enough, Hursthouse's hope would at this point come under no strain at all. The wrecked or marred *eudaimon* may still hope in teleology. Since *that* is the object of hope, misfortunes should never threaten despair. But surely it is pedantic and fickle to propose a model of hope which cannot account for how personal despair really is despair. And it would be a very strange hope which does not sustain me in trials and suffers no loss at the prospect of ruin. But in Hursthouse's model, I hope for no individuals: not for myself, my loved ones, my community, my country, or anyone particular at all. My hope is in human nature, making it a very thin kind of hope, rather like a vague 'faith in humanity'.

The practical work such hope does is very small. If I or my loved ones face the threat of ill health, lost livelihood, a ruined marriage, bankruptcy, destitution, ruin, or death, hope in teleology will be a poor sop. In no sense that matters to any particular people can it 'Keep Hope Alive', and so the ruined person is still 'prey to the vice of despair'. Only insofar as it is open to Providence might Hursthouse's hope be relevant in trying times.

Aristotelian and Neo-Aristotelian Discontents

Aristotle, Philippa Foot, and Rosalind Hursthouse all acknowledge the eudaimonia gap. Each believes we cannot attain *eudaimonia* as fully as we reasonably wish. For Aristotle, the gap is constituted by our composite, finite, and mortal nature which saddles happiness with various problems and makes us vulnerable to fortune. He sees a tension between the *eudaimonia* we can get and the greater form of it we are lofty enough to conceive of but too feeble to attain. The tension should not be overstated or either the possibility or the worth of happiness might appear in doubt. But the tension is there, and it is certainly compatible with Christian intuitions, not least the belief in salvation history, the Incarnation, and the Gospel as more than 'curious news'.

Foot and Hursthouse likewise acknowledge the limits of naturalistic eudaimonism, and stress even more than Aristotle that happiness is prone to misfortune. The best their naturalism can do amid very bad luck is to make us martyrs to virtue who mingle conscientiousness with melancholy resignation. But without committing themselves to theological premises, they frankly acknowledge the appeal of hope.

Hursthouse believes that philosophers should borrow from religious hope its transcendent assurance of trust in Providence and project that trust onto nature. I have claimed that actual trust in Providence would strengthen this hope. One would then believe that trust had been placed in a trustworthy object instead of just play-acting that it had while remaining agnostic on the question. Moreover, such trust would make hope far more resilient and relevant than Hursthouse's model as it stands. When tragedy arrives, we will need a much stronger tonic than an abstract trust in nature to 'Keep Hope Alive'.

Philippa Foot calls herself a 'card-carrying atheist'. But what does she point to when happiness faces not just a gap, but a collapse, and the claim that the virtues are happy-making is true only for the fortunate? She points to Christian exemplars for whom the virtue of hope is the most important sustainer of happiness amid misfortune. Foot's test case implies that while the losses incurred by tragedy are real, hope for durable happiness is not just for the well-off and lucky. Given the countless victims of horrific abuse, injustice, tragedy, famine, and natural disaster whose lives are tragically marred or ruined, the point is immensely important.

The Limits of Kantian and Utilitarian Happiness

Work drawing on Aquinas easily finds conversation partners in Aristotle and the neo-Aristotelians. The family resemblances between Thomism and Aristotelianism have been commented on for centuries. For this reason, it will strengthen my account to show that what I call the eudaimonia gap is not a private dogma of Thomists and Aristotelians which the rest of the philosophical world has never heard of. The eudaimonia gap, I am eager to demonstrate, has not been 'staged' in a philosophical show trial. A full account of parallels to the eudaimonia gap in the history of Western philosophy is of course beyond my scope. But I want to say enough to show that the problem has been widely felt in Western philosophical ethics to avoid suspicions of parochialism.

Something resembling the eudaimonia gap often haunts Kantians and Utilitarians. At different points in his career Kant himself registers dismay with Job's question of why the righteous languish and the wicked prosper. 'It is as if', Kant writes, we 'heard an inner voice that said: This is not how it should be'.[74] Such discontent led Kant to his 'postulates of pure practical reason'; particularly the postulates of God and immortality. His philosophy of religion is a notoriously tangled thicket of intellectual history. Moreover, there is no 'received interpretation' of how to harmonise everything Kant said about it over his career. But for my purposes, only a general sketch of his practical postulates will here be necessary.

Most relevant is his argument from the *Critique of Practical Reason*. There Kant states that the properly moral agent will not primarily seek happiness, but the moral duty that makes one worthy of happiness. Practical reason and the moral order require pursuit of the highest good, which broadly speaking is a state of affairs in which all agents achieve virtue, and where happiness is proportioned to their moral worth. 'In the highest good', Kant tells us, 'virtue and happiness are thought of as necessarily combined, so that the one cannot be assumed by practical reason without the other belonging to it'.[75] For Kant, the awareness of being moral makes one happier, but he denies what he thinks is the Stoic belief that happiness just is the self-awareness of being moral.[76] What he calls 'moral happiness' is just one part in happiness as a whole, and the 'whole' is a comprehensive and maximum satisfaction of need and desire in a being both rational and needy. As Kant says elsewhere, for such happiness 'a maximum, of well-being is needed in my present and in every future condition'.[77] But plainly such happiness is not fairly distributed according to moral desert in this life, and the consequence is a problem analogous to the eudaimonia gap.

Kant thinks it our duty to pursue the highest good. To do this, we must believe it is possible to get it. The problem is that the causal world does not effect the highest good. He therefore postulates both an afterlife and a 'supreme cause of nature' which ensures the highest good may be had in it. The requisite 'supreme cause' would require intelligence, will, beneficence, and omnipotence. In short, it is 'morally necessary to assume the existence of God'.[78] As Kant had already said in his first *Critique*, we should therefore postulate 'God and a future life' where 'every happiness awaits us as long as we do not ourselves limit our share of it through the unworthiness to be happy'.[79]

For someone who spent so much time knocking down traditional proofs for God's existence, these postulates seek to draw out Leviathan with a hook. Those who take them as small concessions or as a favour for his pious manservant Lampe are grossly mistaken. Kant's concern is not just with good people missing out on happiness; it is with solving an antinomy that poses a threat to the moral order itself. He thinks the duty to promote the highest good is 'an a priori necessary object of our will and inseparably bound up with the moral law'. So if God and the afterlife as conditions for the possibility of the highest good are not postulated, the moral law itself 'which commands us to promote it, must be fantastic and directed to empty imaginary end and must therefore in itself be false'.[80] The stakes could not be higher. As with Hursthouse's hope in nature as harmonious and in reality as comic, Kant's hope in a theistic afterlife is justified as a *practical* necessity. Hence he does not think the practical postulate justifies the theoretical conclusion 'God exists', but the practical conclusion 'we ought to believe that God exists'.[81]

Kant's argument is controversial, to say the least, and even most Kantians have long since dropped this fig leaf of traditional religion. But a minority of theistic Kantians, notably John Hare, have drawn on Kant in revisiting the questions of God, morality, happiness, and the afterlife. Something much like the eudaimonia gap appears in Hare's contribution to the recent volume, *God, the Good, and Utilitarianism*. The goal of the volume is to put Christian theologians into conversation with the Utilitarian ethicist Peter Singer. Hare's essay is a response to Singer's work, but he uses it as an opportunity to revisit the larger problems jointly faced by Kantians and Utilitarians when it comes to harmonising the pursuit of morality and happiness. As with Kant, the occasion for doing this is the fact that morality and happiness are separate, and that 'in this world they can come apart'.[82]

Kant's God will see to it that happiness is proportioned to moral worth in the afterlife. Since this ensures that the moral law is not falsified, it is a genuine *deus ex machina*. But Utilitarians do not quite face the same problem. They never held that a reified moral order would collapse if the cosmic scales were not righted. Nevertheless, Hare argues that Utilitarians cannot get off so easily but must face a terrible problem of their own that threw Sidgwick and Mill into crisis. The problem is that of whether and why the Utilitarian should prefer morality to happiness when the two conflict. Why not prefer self-interest to the universal interest? Or why not say there is just no reason to prioritise one over the other?

A theistic Kantian like John Hare is at least free from this worry. Like Kant, Hare appeals to a theistic order to postulate that moral worth will eventually be proportioned to happiness. But he is clear that in our deliberations the pursuit of duty has complete priority over the pursuit of happiness.[83] The incentive of happiness does not displace the maxim of duty; rather, post-mortem happiness is the reward of those who put duty over happiness. (Schopenhauer compares this to a tip slipped to a high-class waiter who pretends to be above such matters but definitely pockets the cash).[84] Should the exigencies of morality and happiness come into conflict, the conscientious Kantian will presumably 'do the right thing' and become a martyr to duty. But Hare argues that Utilitarians have no similarly considered reason for preferring the universal interest over their own self-interest. The story begins with Henry Sidgwick.

John Hare and Peter Singer, among others, believe Sidgwick to be the greatest of the Utilitarians.[85] Like all mainstream Utilitarians, Sidgwick claimed that one ought always to try to maximise one's balance of pleasure over pain and to do the same for every other sentient being, at whatever cost to oneself.[86] That maximisation is itself happiness, and one is happy to the extent the balance obtains. The egoistic hedonism which seeks individual happiness and the Utilitarianism proper which seeks the happiness of all are therefore both morally incumbent upon us.

The problem is that the interests of morality and happiness construed in this way may conflict or simply pull in different directions. So does one have trump power over the other, or is the result a dilemma that could result in agency paralysis? Unlike Kant and Hare, when Sidgwick, Singer, and Mill face this question they stammer uncertainties.

Sidgwick considered two possible solutions to this problem: one psychological and the other theological.[87] The first option expands the role of sympathy so as to create a psychological bridge between the agent's pleasures and pains, and the pleasures and pains of others. But this option does not hold up, as Sidgwick admits. Sympathy is strongest for those most identified with us, and it dwindles the further removed from one's circle of acquaintances one gets, making it veer closer to the egoistic rather than to the universal interest.

Singer follows Sidgwick here, noting that 'benevolent affections' add to fulfilment, but conceding that they 'very rarely lead us to act completely impartially'.[88] As to whether and why one should prefer morality to happiness given such facts, Singer likewise flounders: 'Ultimately there is no answer to this question.... We may decide to live ethically because that's what we want to do'. As the foundations of his ethical enterprise are called into question, Singer oddly takes refuge in literal arbitrariness. At the same time he suggests that if we are moral, 'We will feel better in ourselves' and find 'a kind of a harmony in our life. But I can't give a more definite answer than that'.[89] Singer can tell us what he thinks morality is, should we wish to be moral. But if and to the extent the demands of morality fail to make us 'feel better in ourselves', he gives no reason for why we *ought* to remain moral at this cost. He is ultimately stuck where Sidgwick was.

Hare does not pronounce Utilitarianism wholly discredited by this shaky handling of the problem. Instead, he draws our attention to Sidgwick's second, theological option for addressing it and invites Utilitarians to consider it again (particularly given the inadequacy of their first approach). According to this option, the happiness/morality tension could be resolved by positing a just and benevolent God who wills the maximum balance of pleasure over pain for all living beings, and who will effect this state of affairs in the afterlife. God becomes an orthodox Utilitarian, and this 'celestial Jeremy Bentham', as C. D. Broad has called him, will see to it in the next world that happiness is bestowed in proportion to moral efforts and punishment allotted in proportion to moral failings.[90] This would let us expect individual happiness in the next life in proportion as our moral pains hindered it in this life, addressing the tension at issue. With God cast as the afterlife balancer of moral worth/personal happiness disparities, we are back within shouting distance of Kant's postulates. One great difference is that Sidgwick neither accepts nor rejects his theological proposal, but stays neutral.[91]

John Hare believes that the theological postulates resolve the moral/ happiness tension for both the Kantian and the Utilitarian. Without a theistic model of Providence, he thinks we will lack various important moral resources, including 'the resources to hope that we are, so to speak, on the winning side even when things look hopeless'.[92] Although they get there by very different roads, Kantian and Utilitarian eschatology (insofar as they exist) end up in much the same place. That they sometimes get there at all is due to the worry that the moral and virtuous will not attain the happiness they deserve.

Both ethical schools are in fact struggling with something like the eudaimonia gap. The major difference between them and the Aristotelians I have examined has to do with differences between how the former's concept of morality and the latter's concept of virtue both relate to happiness. The Utilitarians I considered regard morality and happiness not just as distinct, but as separable and potentially in competition. By contrast, eudaimonist virtue ethics regards virtuous activity as the essential ingredient in a happy life. For the former, morality limits happiness in various ways. For the latter, virtue is a constituent in happiness rightly understood. The consequence is that morality as the Utilitarians I have examined read it vastly widens the eudaimonia gap. For them, religious hope would not just gesture at a fuller happiness we reasonably want and deserve. It would help justify the conviction that we should stay moral even when it hurts.

Kant and Hare think the moral law has a Janus-faced relationship with the eudaimonia gap. On the one hand, the moral law is a stern taskmaster which often demands sacrifice. On the other, conscientiousness makes space for moral satisfactions that make us happier. But in a different respect, the Kantian moral law exacerbates the eudaimonia gap – namely, by making it the definitive test case on which the integrity of the whole moral law is made to rest. For Kant, the gap makes the highest good impossible of pursuit or attainment, and he treats this as a cosmic crisis that only God and the afterlife could mend. But solving the gap is important for Kant mainly as a border skirmish in his all-consuming effort to keep the moral order inviolate. Depending on whether the gap is resolved, the moral law on his telling will either be vindicated or falsified as an 'empty imaginary end'. Having to bear this enormous burden, the eudaimonia gap on this account is far more oppressive than in my virtue ethics account. It not only signifies just a gap in happiness, but bears the full weight of the Kantian moral law's desperate effort to justify itself on pain of the moral order's wholesale collapse.

The implication is that the eudaimonia gap is not a problem staged by Aristotelians, Thomists, and eudaimonists. It is an issue acknowledged in different moral vocabularies and entangled with different considerations by mainstream Kantians and Utilitarians. Their problem effectively consists in the eudaimonia gap *plus* the added moral mess it creates for their theories. If anything, that added baggage makes the gap even more burdensome for them than for those who are philosophically closer to myself.[93]

Kant, Sidgwick, Mill, and others within these philosophical traditions regard a religious hope in Providence as the most promising solution to their versions of the gap whether or not they found themselves able to accept Christian hope on the whole.[94] This is not the place to detail the philosophical, let alone the theological problems I find in their attempted resolution of the gap, or in the spare account of hope most of them give. For my purposes, their appeals to a providential ordering are important not as going arguments for the afterlife, but as symptoms of a wider philosophical discontent with the gap which sees in religious hope the only fully adequate solution. The basic force of the eudaimonia gap is a problem not just within virtue ethics, but is a widely acknowledged philosophical anxiety.

The Normative Argument

In most of these philosophical discussions the silent guest is theology. With the exception of Aristotle, the philosophers examined help themselves to a concept of hope whose historical debt to Christianity is enormous. The hope taken as basic by these philosophers is in some cases Christian hope itself, and in others, it is what is left of theological hope after it has been wrenched from its doctrinal context, draped in the language of natural religion, and picked over as *bricolage* by major figures of modernity. In a grand reversal of St. Augustine's famous simile, in the latter case it is the Egyptians who despoil the Christians of their gold and fashion it into what they will.

The consequence is that this discussion occurs along an intriguing fault line between philosophy and theology. To propose that there is a eudaimonia gap is to claim that happiness is possible, but fraught with limits we reasonably wish to overcome, but which even the virtuous cannot adequately get past. Aristotle, Foot, and Hursthouse identify many bleak contours of the gap. But just as importantly, they do not exaggerate the extent of the gap, and they acknowledge the great value of the happy life still available to us. This balancing act strikes me as correct: honest enough to admit grave defects in the good life and in philosophy's coping mechanisms, but sober enough to shun the kind of hyperbole that loses sight of the good remaining. Acknowledging limits to happiness does not call its value into question any more than conceding a few faults in a beloved parent or spouse means denying their overall goodness or even greatness. The commitment to free ourselves of such impediments so far as we can is a good thing. Both the religious believer and nonbeliever can agree on this, though they may disagree on what the means are and how far the impediments can be got past. My claim at this point is that the commitment to overcome the impediments insofar as we can both for ourselves and others is important, good, and praiseworthy. To the virtuous it will be a priority and not just a vague wish. Many of the reasons why have been hinted at in my account of the eudaimonia gap as explicated in my interlocutors. But by way of summary I will describe the gap as I see it to advance my normative argument.

Earthly existence exposes us, our loved ones, our neighbours, and the whole human community to ills such as pain, misunderstanding, weariness, sickness, depression, injustice, frayed relationships, aging, decline, and tragedy. In its final extremity it exposes us to death, which on naturalistic terms is the final and irrevocable parting from those we love most, the permanent loss of all that we cared and worked for in this world. We are rightly consoled by the thought that larger goods we identify with, from one's children to one's country, will live on after we are dead and forgotten. But this in turn raises for nonbelievers the disquieting thought that all such goods and all possible secular goods – given the eventual demise of our sun, the heat death of the universe, and the extinction of all organic life – are fleeting judged by the cosmic clock, and on the losing side of cosmological history. The belief that nothing we do will make any difference in the end is disquieting, and sadly produces in some what Mill calls 'the disastrous feeling of not worth while'.[95]

The 'slings and arrows of outrageous fortune' deprive us over the course of our lifetime of priorities whose loss is grievous. At this point a cautionary note is in order. Happiness should not be confused with the possession of various goods. With Aquinas, I have described happiness as a life of *virtuous* activity that is characteristically enjoyable. But that way of life takes shape in and through the pursuit of the goods appropriate to a desirable human life.[96] Loss of important goods impedes virtuous activities and forfeits many virtuous enjoyments, so that happiness diminishes.

Besides important non-moral goods, such misfortunes threaten still more important moral goods. Serious concern for people, communities, and moral causes is proper to the virtuous. Lisa Cahill underscores this in her recent volume *Global Justice, Christology and Christian Ethics*, which describes and insists on the need to confront global structures of inequality, poverty, violence, and ecological destruction with all the tools of social justice and Christian hope.[97] Likewise, Gordon Graham challenges us to confront and account for deep, horrendous evils, from high school gun massacres to the wickedness of serial killers and of genocide before which secular accounts of moral evil often recoil.[98] Surely they are both right in pointing out these needs, and the indignation with which they confront what I call the gap is fitting. Outrages and injustices visited upon the human race are grievous. They could only fail to impede commitments of ours if we were indifferent to moral concerns and therefore vicious. Though one may affirm the essential goodness of creation, the virtuous person will surely not look upon poverty, war, starvation, oppression, corruption, torture, and genocide, and say, 'Nothing is deeply wrong in the world'. The virtuous and happy person is the just person, and the just person seeks happiness not just for himself or herself, but for the wider community. The fact that this larger good is so often and deeply injured is something we should be committed to overcome.

As impediments to the happy life, the presence of these evils is part of what it means to say that the happiness we rightly want we cannot fully get. We reasonably desire to avoid these evils, experience their presence as abhorrent, and fervently seek their removal. Since they constitute what impedes our happiness, the corollary is that by seeking individually and socially to overcome them, we are shown to will their contrary. But what is this 'willing the contrary' but an indirect admission that the impediments constitute a status quo opposed to many of our basic needs and virtuous projects? Correlatively, this suggests that the desire to attain a more complete and fuller form of happiness – i.e., a happiness *not* impeded in these ways – is good, reasonable, and praiseworthy. But precisely because we are finite, composite, mortal, and vulnerable to fortune, this aspiration falls deplorably short of its target. It is important to note that the result is not simply irritating. Given the misfortunes and evils that comprise it, the eudaimonia gap is a massively burdensome crisis which threatens us with demoralisation – that is, with a significant if not total weakening of moral and eudaimonic motivation.[99] If the crisis can be resolved in any sense, doing so will be a priority. But no adequate secular solution appears forthcoming, as my philosophical interlocutors lament. Hence the interest of theological hope in this conversation.

Theological hope promises that by divine agency we can eventually overcome the eudaimonia gap as much as we rightly want and attain full, secure, and lasting happiness. Such hope sustains us from the demoralisation and despair that threaten us in this life, it gives a transcendent meaning and dignity to our lives, it assures us that we were created by love and for love, and it encourages us with the anticipation of perfect beatitude. In that respect, hope negotiates the gap better in this life and looks forward to its total closure in the next. Just what this looks like in detail will be the subject of the chapters that follow.

Suppose I am correct that some forms of virtue ethics and eudaimonism see hope as desirable. I still have to show how this helps my overall case. It certainly does not demonstrate that ethics is crippled without hope, or by showing that in all respects ethics needs hope. Since I take hope to be a theological virtue, this would be tantamount to denying naturalistic virtue and happiness, both of which I affirm with Aquinas.[100] Nor do I claim that my account of hope and the eudaimonia gap demonstrates theism or some other religious view. Apologetics, as I stated in the introduction, is at this point of discussion premature. But drawing on some notable philosophers who show a certain openness, I claim that hope, if available, would resolve gaps they acknowledge in the kind of *eudaimonia* they think possible. More generally, I believe that if theological hope were a live option, it would greatly benefit human agency by enriching our happiness. A growing body of evidence in empirical psychology suggests much the same.[101]

To put it in legal language, I regard the philosophical resonances not as initial or primary evidence justifying hope, but as corroborating evidence which lends support to a proposition whose main evidence rests on other grounds. A witness' testimony to a hit-and-run would count as primary evidence. Suspicious dents found on the car of the accused would count as corroborating evidence. The dents support the testimony, but would not themselves suffice for a conviction. Similarly, I take my interlocutors to provide the latter (valuable but limited) kind of support for hope's desirability and benefit. Since my argument and genre is theological, the primary evidence for my claims comes from theological sources.

I believe the corroboration gives some respectable but not overwhelming support to my proposal that theological hope is a true virtue which enriches moral agency and human happiness. No theoretical or pragmatic argument for accepting the existence of hope's object is being smuggled in. All that has been claimed is that hope of a more than secular kind is of moral and eudaimonic advantage. What follows from that advantage in terms of deliberating about hope? I suggest several things. First, it removes certain obstacles to theological hoping; especially, it helps remove the worry that hope is a substitute for happiness rather than an ingredient in it. Second, it means nonbelievers have good reason at least to consider hope as a possibility since it is of considerable moral and eudaimonic advantage, and therefore of interest. This justifies what I will call an *accommodating* interpretation of hope from those who do not presently affirm it. An accommodating interpretation occurs when for good reasons one is amenable without being credulous towards the case for a certain position. Widely accepted examples are ready to hand: the cancer patient who is amenable to a doctor's prognosis that she could get better with treatment, the parents' willingness to believe a teacher's claim that their struggling child can improve, or our willingness in Britain during August 1940 to believe that victory was still possible. In such cases, acceptance of the position gives a much-needed boost of hope when moral and eudaimonic motivation are flagging.

To be disposed favourably to consider supporting reasons in such cases is reasonable provided the agent does not become dishonest or credulous by dispensing with the serious consideration of reasons.[102] Should the latter occur, the boundary between accommodating thinking and wishful thinking has been violated.

Accommodating interpreters will actively consider a position that would likely be ignored as unimportant if it did not seem in their interests. I noted earlier Raymond Geuss' point that apologetics is now premature, since 'the real danger for religious believers nowadays is not counter-belief or theoretical objections, but indifference'. The 'increase in sheer brute indifference – Why should we care *one way or the other* – rather than active unbelief or unwillingness to listen' is in his view the 'greatest threat' to Christianity'.[103]

In effect this chapter seeks to answer that question. The accommodating interpreter will be disposed to think well rather than ill of the accommodated position at the outset, giving it some benefit of the epistemic doubt while stopping well short of credulity by remaining open to evidence that could overturn a possible favourable assessment. An accommodating interpretation of theological hope by nonbelievers would require no more than this, and I believe it is justified given the argument of this chapter. Getting even this far would significantly improve relations between philosophy and theology – for example, by removing lingering traces of the Enlightenment struggle against superstition stereotype that frequently cramps relations between the two disciplines.

But on what grounds could hope be interpreted accommodatingly by the interested nonbeliever? One possibility is that secular philosophers who assume that theism has been shipwrecked since the days of Hume might engage more generously with philosophy of religion. As Jeffrey Stout notes, the discipline has made enormous advances since the 1980s, but most philosophers have held their noses, in part because old Enlightenment prejudices die hard, and in part because theism has seemed contrary to their interests.[104] Part of why I have engaged with secular philosophers in this chapter is to complicate that picture by suggesting that hope *is* in their interests, whether or not they find hope justified all things considered.

Another possibility is that philosophers will engage directly with theologians. Since hope is a theological virtue by origin and nature, there is much to be said for this approach. When Foot, Hursthouse, and others discuss hope, they are self-consciously nibbling around the edges of a theological virtue they keep in soft focus, perhaps to avoid taking on religious baggage before their philosophical peers. This renders their accounts of hope unhelpfully vague. By contrast, an accommodating but robust engagement of philosophers with theology would bring that virtue into bold relief, allowing for a sustained discussion of whether theological hope is simply 'curious news' or possibly good news for all concerned. 'What has Athens to do with Jerusalem?', Tertullian famously quipped, 'or the Academy with the Church?' Given the eudaimonia gap and the threat of demoralisation it poses, one plausible answer is the shared need to 'Keep Hope Alive'. The prospect of meaningful interdisciplinary work between theologians and philosophers is one both disciplines should welcome.[105]

The Positive Side of the Eudaimonia Gap

I have mostly put the eudaimonia gap in negative terms, stressing impediments to happiness. At the same time, the gap has a positive side which regards not limits to happiness, but the yearning for a greater share of it: perhaps even a total fulfilment. It is a second and more positive occasion for hope that is commonly experienced. To look at the gap from this perspective is to ponder what it would be like to have more of a good thing rather than to grouse about limits we would be rid of. Happiness can occasion reflexive desires. As the delights of courtship may leave one longing for a fuller and deeper union with the beloved, so partial happiness may prompt the wish for a more secure, more permanent, and fuller share of happiness than we ever arrive at. As one poet says, the very presence of happiness reminds us of the 'unmeasured price Man sets his life'. Though this may leave us 'feeling kindly unto all the earth', it may also make us 'more mindful that the sweet days day'.[106] In Augustinian and Thomistic terms, we are never *perfectly* happy. We never attain what Aquinas describes as 'the perfect good, which satisfies appetite altogether'.[107] Less will be said about this side of the gap here since it will be treated at length in the third chapter. But a brief prologue is fitting so that the gap does not look misleadingly one-sided.

For Aquinas, happiness is not mere contentment, but a virtuous way of life that develops our capacities for the good and is characteristically enjoyable.[108] But even virtuous agents with a fair degree of perfection and enjoyable life attain only a partial fulfilment which is transitory and limited at best: one which leaves them with more to do, more to pursue, and so forth. This opens up the possibility that they may begin to desire a fuller or even complete kind of happiness which seems beyond reach. This is partly why the prospect of a supernaturally enabled happiness has deeply attracted people in widely different contexts.

As previously discussed, the prospect of perfect contemplative happiness was a limit concept for Aristotle. But he is hardly alone in his poignant yearning for ideal happiness. Countless Greek, Roman, and Indian thinkers felt the need, and entertained the prospect. Augustine's 'restless heart' made it an indelible part of Christian consciousness. It is a constant theme of poetry, from Virgil's *Eclogues* and Dante's *Commedia* to W. B. Yeats and T. S. Eliot. Even Camus and Sartre affirmed the desire while denying a proportionate object. Hence the cheated lover quality of existentialist *angst*, which treats this life and world as arousing the desire for a complete fruition we then seek in vain. From a theological perspective, such thought is valuable not as an accurate diagnosis, but as a symptom whose articulation is evocative rather than precise. The symptom is of the *imago dei* – which may not even know itself as such – confusedly sensing that created objects cannot fully satisfy the human aspiration for the good.[109]

From hope's perspective, the desire for fuller or perhaps even perfect happiness may be taken up and clarified by the theological specification of a proportionate object in God.[110] As a natural desire it is somewhat raw and confused as to its object, and therein lies its very suggestiveness as a kind of intimation – though not a proof – of the divine. As the eighteenth-century journalist and poet Joseph Addison put it:

> Whence this pleasing hope, this fond desire,
> This longing after immortality?
> Or whence this secrete dread, and inward horror,
> Of falling into naught? Why shrinks the soul
> Back on herself, and startles at destruction?
> 'Tis the divinity that stirs within us;
> 'Tis heaven itself, that points out an hereafter,
> And intimates eternity to man.
> Eternity! thou pleasing, dreadful thought!¹¹¹

Whether put poetically or in plain prose, a desire for happiness which 'reaches beyond our grasp' is of vast relevance to hope. To the extent that even a virtuous and happy life does not totally satisfy the desire – i.e., to the extent happiness is inevitably cramped and imperfect in this life – the theological virtue of hope meets human aspiration halfway. Hope suggests that those who desire fuller happiness do not desire in vain, but are experiencing and attending to a moral-spiritual clue of sorts that is poised between their questions and a real answer that is only to be found in God. 'There are many who say, "Who will show us some good?" Lift up the light of thy countenance upon us, O Lord!' (Ps 4:6). This aspiration is not simply a medium of romantic escapism. As the third chapter will argue, it is laced throughout with moral and spiritual seriousness. A positive reading of the gap complements the negative reading and helps show that hope is attractive *even apart* from impediments to happiness. It makes clear that hope's appeal does not just hinge on dismay at life's sorrows, but is of interest to those whose lives are going well.

Given what has been said, the prospect of a kind and degree of happiness capable of overcoming the eudaimonia gap has significant moral and eudaimonic relevance. It suggests that if there were an object of hope which the gap did not outflank and contain, it would recognisably be 'good news' rather than just 'curious news' for us. In that respect, nature pays a kind of tribute to grace. But that view can only be articulated at the methodological border which divides philosophy from theology, and where reason cannot really go further without revelation. Just as Dante reached a stage where Virgil could lead him no farther and Beatrice became his guide, this marks the point where theology must carry the inquiry forward if we are to hope at all. Taking for granted now that there is space for hope to contribute to our predicament, the rest of this work will be openly theological, and seek to show just what hope contributes and how.

CHAPTER 2

The Theological Virtue of Hope in Aquinas

Preserve her, O Lord; teach her to place her hope and confidence entirely in
Thee ... keep her from both the sad extremes of presumption and despair.
Jonathan Swift, *Prayers for Stella*

Now tell me what is Hope, how much of it
Thrives in your mind, and where your Hope comes from.
Dante, *Paradiso* canto xxv

The proposal of theological hope is that the eudaimonia gap will finally
be overcome. As Scripture says: 'He will wipe away every tear from their
eyes, and death shall be no more, neither shall there be mourning nor
crying nor pain any more, for the former things have passed away' (Rev
21:4). But this will be a work of grace rather than of human effort. The
pagan and secular eudaimonists were in a sense right to think the gap is
inevitable and inescapable. There will be no secular *eschaton*, or none that
can transcend the gap. To put the point in Christian terms, we stand in
need of salvation.

In the previous chapter I mostly kept the theological brackets on to speak
in terms familiar to my philosophical interlocutors. Once those brackets are
taken off, key terms get a theological layering. Almost everything proper to
the eudaimonia gap is implicated in sin and its effects. Most impediments
to happiness can be described in terms of either personal or original sin
in their local and global causes and effects. It is bad news to us that these
impediments cannot be overcome even by our best efforts. By contrast, the
revelation that grace may effect salvation from the eudaimonia gap is good
news.[1] The proposal of Christian hope is that the eudaimonia gap – all the
falling short of a fallen world – has been conquered by Jesus Christ through
his life, death, and Resurrection. The risen Christ is the first member of a
'new creation' (Gal 6:15) in which the gap has no more power. As this suggests, Christian hope should not be confused with vague belief in a happy

afterlife. It is the personal, specific, and confident hope in *this* God or in *my* God: the Father, Son, and Holy Spirit, whose word is believed and whose love is trusted to bring about salvation.

To be 'saved' is to be 'made safe': among other things from the power of sin and the ultimate victory of the gap. This is a great part of what hope looks towards. As St. Paul says: 'the creation waits with eager longing for the revealing of the sons of God; for the creation was subjected to futility (*mataioteti*), not of its own will but by the will of him who subjected it in hope; because the creation itself will be set free from its bondage to decay and obtain the glorious liberty of the children of God' (Rom 8:19–21). That 'futility' (*mataiotes*) to which creation is now subject is a good theological translation for what I earlier referred to in philosophical terms as the 'impediments' (*empodiai*) to happiness.[2] Virtuous efforts can lessen but not overcome the eudaimonia gap. No amount of moral, political, or economic progress, and not even the best reforms in health care, social justice, or education can liberate us from the 'futility' to which creation is subject, or can remove the 'sting of death' (1 Cor 15:56). As the Nicene Creed makes clear: 'we look forward to the resurrection of the dead, and the life of the world to come'. The only road truly and fully beyond the gap is eschatological.

Jürgen Moltmann's Theology of Hope

The previous chapter sought to make room for theological hope, and this chapter will explicate Aquinas on hope to press it into service. But many sympathetic to theological hope would regard this as unnecessary and ill advised. Isn't a very rich and persuasive theology of hope already available to us through the very different and enormously influential work of *the* theologian of hope, Jürgen Moltmann? If so, why retrieve Aquinas' theology of hope, which was written hundreds of years ago within a different social context whose questions were not ours? Moreover, Moltmann himself refuses to grant Thomistic hope the more modest role of a valuable prototype from which important insights may be retained. As Moltmann reads him, Aquinas 'liquidated' theological hope of its meaning and nothing should be retained from the Thomistic wreckage.[3]

But Moltmann's own theology has increasingly come into question. As Gordon Graham notes, Moltmann's *Theology of Hope* is 'one of the best-known works of theology in this century and *at one time highly influential*' (italics mine). Like many others, Graham thinks that Moltmann's work has now crossed the threshold that divides the live option from the period piece. Moltmann's hope was 'formulated largely in the light of a perceived challenge to Christianity from an alternative Marxist analysis of history and society'. But due to the collapse of the Soviet Union and 'the changes that China underwent in the 1990s' – due, in short, to 'the demise of communism', a Christian hope whose main interlocutor is the Marxist analysis of society 'must now seem somewhat passé'.[4] But given Moltmann's impressive work and iconic status in all matters pertaining to hope, a consideration of his work and legacy is in order.

Moltmann's body of work and set of interests are enormous, and he has shifted position on important issues from the early 1960s to the present. For my purposes what matters is the general shape of his theology of hope. A professor of systematic theology at Tubingen from 1967 to 1994, Moltmann took an interest in social and political ethics prompted by Bonhoeffer, a dialectic interpretation of God inspired by Hegel, and a commitment to biblical theology drawn from von Rad and Kasemenn. The first of a major trilogy which includes *The Crucified God*, Moltmann's 1964 *Theology of Hope* was an immediate sensation that put eschatology back on the map after decades of neglect. In it the Jewish Marxist philosopher Ernst Bloch (whose *Principle of Hope* was finished in 1959) was clearly the major non-theological influence.

Bloch sought to reclaim and expand the role of hope in Marxism and proposed that religious messianism was something like a disguised Marxist dream. The utopian yearning behind such hope had the kind of motivating power which could propel the masses towards revolution. What was needed was to rescue utopian hope from religion in part by translating it into Marxist political terms and showing that those terms represented it more credibly. Marxism could then appropriate the utopian hope previously monopolised by messianism and pursue a communist utopia whose futuristic technology, Bloch suggested, would eventually rid us of death itself. The result is that 'true Genesis is not at the beginning but at the end'.[5]

Moltmann inherited from Bloch an overwhelming obsession with the future and the yoking of hope to the cause of revolution. He translates utopia back into the eschaton and restores genuine messianism. This saves hope from what Moltmann sees as the weak spot in Bloch's Marxism: its secular inability to redeem tragedy or the lost past, or to overcome death. Only the God of hope may do this through the cross and resurrection of Jesus Christ. But for Moltmann, this verdict is far from triumphalist and not even very cheering. He believes that the cross and resurrection turn the Marxist 'not' into a Christian 'not yet'. But at the same time they smuggle a contradiction into God and reality. In the crucified and risen Christ there is found death, sin, suffering, and dissension, and these are put in continuity with life, righteousness, glory, and peace.[6] Moltmann regards this as an intolerable contradiction, but might that tension be largely conceptual rather than ontological? After all, when Christ rose from the dead, surely he was not still undergoing the crucifixion? But according to Moltmann, Christ is at present both risen *and* crucified, so the contradiction is real. In this dialectic the 'not' of the cross co-exists with the 'already' of the resurrection in a state of mutual contradiction which obscures and destabilises the meaning of the present. One result is that Moltmann brands 'the visible realm of present experience as a god-forsaken, transient reality that is to be left behind'.[7] But how can it be left behind?

Escape cannot be found with reference to God or eternity as a point of stability. For Moltmann, there is no 'eternity of heaven' relative to which our flux may be measured, or into which post-mortem souls may ascend. There is only 'the future of the very earth'.[8] The one great gain of history is the raising of Christ, which contradicts 'the laws and constraints of this earth'.[9] But despite this contradiction, the evils named are still with us, and so the resurrection of Christ is still mostly future. The 'not yet' of his and our future is the goal of hope.

Moltmann says his first experience of God came as a prisoner of war from 1945 to 1948. Afterwards he felt keenly the post-Holocaust guilt of the German nation. His perpetual groping for the future and view of the present world as something to 'contradict' plainly owe much to this. At the same time, Moltmann insists that his theology is not just a post-war period piece. Everything he says about hope and eschatology is rooted in his doctrine of God. He insists that God is not 'extra-worldly'. Rather, 'the "God of hope" is a God with future as his essential nature' who encounters us in the present exclusively in 'his promises for the future'.[10] Scrapping patristic, medieval, Reformed, and early modern models of God, Moltmann denies the traditional doctrines of divine aseity, freedom to create, and impassibility for a God who is Hegelian enough to need ongoing evolution and development. The problem of evil is met with an eschatological theodicy in which *The Crucified God* does not explain suffering away, but lovingly endures it in solidarity with the afflicted. According to Moltmann, God is not just bound by time and suffering; God is not yet fully God, but like creation itself is a work in progress. Both God and creation are not 'static', but 'dynamic', and both evolve towards greater perfection. Moltmann denies being either a monotheist or a pantheist, and advocates instead a 'panentheistic view' in which God and the world are distinct but co-extensive, mutually dependent, and evolve in their journey together.[11]

Hope will only attain its object when the work of contradicting sin and death is complete and the dialectic of cross and resurrection reaches its final synthesis in both God and creation, so that the promise of the resurrection is fulfilled and God becomes 'all in all'. This is the object of hope, and it will happen in our historical world rather than in a transcendent heaven. Since God and the fulfilled eschaton belong to our time and world while contradicting the evils present in them, Moltmann's hope is neither otherworldly nor quietist, but a powerful agent for change in the world. Echoing Marx's priority of praxis, Moltmann insists that 'the new criterion of theology and of faith is to be found in praxis'.[12]

Moltmann's ethics flow directly from his eschatology. Christ's resurrection is the promise of our future resurrection, and the proper response to promise is mission.[13] We do not just await the eschaton; we may anticipate it by radical commitment to social justice and 'revolutionary social change'.[14] Talk of revolution echoes Bloch and his Marxist sources, and was later praised by many liberation theologians.

The revolution Moltmann foresees is not figurative. His goal is literally utopian: the 'new creation is to be realized in concrete utopias which summon and make sense out of present initiatives for overcoming the present negatives of life'.[15] What will Moltmann's utopias look like? According to him, the freedom and equal dignity of the persons of the Trinity entail the freedom and equality of humans as *imago dei*. Add God's identification with the suffering as a fellow victim who is crucified in and with the world's victims, and the ideal revolution will upend the complacent status quo and practise solidarity with victims by securing their equal rights and maintaining their dignity.[16] Initially Moltmann thought the political means should mirror the humanistic Marxism of Western Europe, duly baptised. He later came to believe that a more effective political theology for Europe would be a form of democratic socialism with teeth.[17] Such a revolution would seek to overcome economic and political alienation. It would be violent or not depending on the best proportionate means for securing 'the humane goals of the revolution'.[18]

Moltmann does not claim that the kingdom of God will come through political revolution, like the zealots of Christ's day. But he does think that revolution can anticipate the future kingdom and be a form of God's presence pushing history towards the eschaton.[19] This is precisely what his theology of hope looks like in action. Action or *praxis* becomes the 'new criterion' of theology and the ideal form of *praxis* is 'revolutionary social change'. The result is that an eschatological praxis of social reform which ideally aims at wholesale revolution is *the* act of hope. Looking towards the eschaton while climbing the barricades, Moltmann explodes the stereotype of hope as quietist and otherworldly.

In Moltmann's theology, bits of Hegelian metaphysics displace traditional monotheism and make room for panentheism. We part from the likes of Augustine, Aquinas, Luther, Calvin, and Barth for something closer to the theology of Whitehead and Hartshorne; and we abandon the doctrine of God found in historical councils and creeds from Nicaea to the Westminster Confession.[20] All this is paired with a Marxist and Blochian view of and commitment to revolution. The striking thing is just how consistent and coherent the vision is if you accept the major premises. Moltmann's theology is so systematic that everything from his doctrine of the Trinity to his *praxis* of hope is well calibrated and mutually dependent. As his commentator Richard Bauckham shows, you cannot detach his theology of hope from his limited and evolving God, or abstract his eschatology from the influence of Marxist dialectic.[21] Moltmann's theology of hope 'detached' from any of these things ceases to exist. To embrace his hope you must therefore carry an enormous load of metaphysical, theological, and political baggage which many find either dated or too high a price to pay.

Even if the baggage were shouldered, doubts arise with Moltmann's use of hope at the level of detail. Ethically speaking, the role he assigns to hope is bloated: 'from first to last, and not merely in the epilogue, Christianity is eschatology, is hope'.[22] In Moltmann's theology, hope is the solution for every problem, and the means for deciding what might even count as a problem. It is telling that his one book of ethics is simply titled *Ethics of Hope*. Using a monolithic methodology, Moltmann offers solutions to every known ethical problem from medical ethics and ecology to just war simply by running every problem through his hope calculus. Much of what he says in his book is deeply wise, but why must hope do all the ethical heavy lifting in human affairs? Ethical monisms are rightly held suspect as too implausibly a one-size-fits-all solution that oversimplifies in theory and lacks suppleness in practice. Even if this were not generally the case, framing Christianity as a hope monism would have a steep uphill climb given the impressive biblical and theological precedence accorded to charity in the tradition (as in 'the greatest of these is charity', 1 Cor 13:13).[23] There is the added problem that reactions against hope historically gain traction when hope's partisans claim too much territory and provoke a humanist push-back. Given Moltmann's iconic status in this field, his hypertrophic enlargement of hope is a wider cause for concern.

A major staple of ethics is action theory, and here Moltmann's hope is likewise unbalanced. For him, *the* act of hope is social reform and revolution in pursuit of freedom, rights, and equal dignity. What hope does is whatever revolutionary social justice does in pursuit of the eschaton. I am so far from wishing to deny the social and political consequences of hope that the last chapter of this book will be devoted to them. But surely the action of hope should not be so narrowly identified with social reform and political *praxis*. Indeed, to make activism and politics the bulk of hope's action is to make hope off-limits to many who very much need it: particularly, many who are very old, disabled, sick, powerless, mentally ill, imprisoned, debilitated, or dying. For such people will very often not be in a position to stage protests, run campaigns, write pamphlets, petition rulers, seek office, run organisations, and mount the barricades of revolution.

Hence in a strange twist, Moltmann's lopsided focus on hope as social and political praxis in favour of the oppressed leaves many oppressed people with few or no ways to *practise* hope. The consequence is that those who most need hope may be least able to express it. Here Aquinas' treatment strikes me as far more supple and many-sided since it makes space for spiritual and ascetic agency rather than just funnelling hope towards a Marxist conception of *praxis*. For Aquinas, one major action of hope is prayer construed as trustful waiting for and conscious dependence on God in trials.[24] This is exactly the kind of hopeful agency the severely incapacitated need, and Aquinas, unlike Moltmann, makes hope a meaningful option for them.

Moltmann's shift to a panentheistic God who suffers alongside victims looks like a rhetorical boon for theodicy, but it could threaten to make our grounds for hope weak. For Moltmann, the world is 'the history of an experiment of salvation'.[25] But since he rejects the traditional belief in God's eternity and omnipotence, does God retain the power to ensure that the experiment will be a success?[26] If not, then how can we be sure that hope's 'not yet' will triumph over the historical 'not'? We might have to take a wait-and-see approach to the eschaton, desperately hoping for the triumph of the Lamb while having no idea whether he is on the losing side.

Moltmann answers that our hope in God to redeem creation and become 'all in all' is warranted by the resurrection, which 'points beyond itself to an *eschaton* of the fullness of all things'.[27] But Moltmann is strangely coy when it comes to the credibility of the resurrection itself. From Jesus' demonstration that he could eat to St. Paul's catalogue of eyewitnesses to the risen Christ, the New Testament itemised 'many proofs' (Acts 1:3) for the resurrection as a historical event.[28] Both believers and nonbelievers have generally grasped the stakes here. St. Paul makes it all-important: 'If Christ has not been raised, then our proclamation has been in vain and your faith has been in vain ... we are of all people most to be pitied' (1 Cor 15:14, 19). Bernard Williams wrote that 'the intelligent unbeliever knows this as well as the Christian does', and that 'the moment Christians start shuffling on the historical claims for the Resurrection, they might as well shut up shop'.[29]

But given his view of history, Moltmann believes proofs of the resurrection are vain and tries to make the event transcend history. The resurrection 'is an event of *eschatological* novelty, which transcends the whole order of historical occurrence'.[30] It is so novel that it eludes everything we ordinarily mean by history and by event. Its only analogue will be the future eschaton which we have not seen, and so the resurrection cannot be believed as a historical event unless we already assume that the future eschaton will occur. Hence whether Christ rose from the dead is therefore only 'subject to *eschatological* verification'.[31] Of course, this tale of the resurrection implies that Christianity is ultimately not a historical religion.

Moltmann denies divine aseity, eternity, and omnipotence, the very attributes which previously made eschatological victory a Christian certainty. This opens up the question of whether his disempowered Trinity can make history a divine comedy rather than a divine tragedy. Moltmann's solution is Christ's resurrection, which justifies the promises of eschatological hope. But due to its radical novelty, we can only affirm the resurrection if we posit an eschatological future which when it does arrive will retroactively validate the resurrection. So we may believe that eschatological victory awaits only if the resurrection is affirmed, and we may affirm the resurrection only if we believe that eschatological victory awaits. Since the credibility of the resurrection derives from eschatological hope rather than from belief in the historical event, and since eschatological hope itself is justified by belief in the resurrection, Moltmann's theology of hope ends up in a vicious circle.[32] Strictly speaking, and even on his own chosen theological grounds, he cannot justify a confident expectation of God's final eschatological victory.

There is nevertheless a great deal to value and keep in Moltmann's theology of hope. His biblically saturated rhetoric of hope is perhaps unequalled in this century. Few have ever captured the *pining* quality of hope so well, or so perfectly balanced the serene assurance of hope with its feverish pursuit of the future. In addition, Moltmann refuses hope's equivalent of cheap grace at all points by his emphasis on social *praxis* and by grounding hope in the resurrection of Christ rather than in baptised optimism. But Moltmann fails to justify the confident hope both he and I want. His eschatology destabilises history in such a way that the credibility of the resurrection and therefore of eschatology becomes a question without an answer. His time-bound, limited, panentheistic God therefore cannot ensure an end of history in which life, righteousness, glory, and peace win out in the end. But if we cannot affirm the full coming and final victory of the kingdom, hope loses its certainty and confidence, turning into a theological maybe with nothing to prevent an agnostic eschatology. Hope certainly could be retained under this theological regime, but it would be the sort of hope that is often indistinguishable from anxiety. So even if for the sake of argument we waive the problems of its wider metaphysical, theological, and political baggage, Moltmann's theology of hope can be shown to be dialectically in trouble merely by immanent criticism.

Since Moltmann's own critiques of Aquinas have been widely discredited and laid to rest elsewhere, nothing in his theology of hope prevents the kind of Thomistic retrieval I propose.[33] But equally, nothing prevents theologians of hope from retaining valuable *bricolage* from Moltmann's own account and paying him an important debt of gratitude. Apart from the real gains mentioned earlier, Moltmann along with his friend Wolfhart Pannenberg helped rescue eschatology from the image of embarrassing conversation-stopper which the demythologisers had given it. His ground-clearing work was necessary for any serious discussion of theological hope to win a hearing, and any work on theological hope is deeply indebted to Moltmann by that very fact.

Aquinas on Grace

In what follows I will set forth Aquinas' model of theological hope. Drawing on and refurbishing a theology of grace inherited from Augustine, he regarded hope as an infused or 'supernatural' rather than an acquired or 'natural' virtue. I do not propose a wholesale justification of this theology of grace – a task that would require enormous space. But to make intelligible the sense in which hope is a virtue for Aquinas, I will provide a background sketch.

As its name suggests, grace is fundamentally a *gift*. Specifically, it is a gift of God which is unmerited and cannot be bought or won. Conceptually, it is indexed to God's charity, with the beneficent bounty and open-handed generosity this implies. The sensibility of grace, if not all the theological ruminants, is unmatched in Isaiah's prose:

> Ho, everyone who thirsts,
> come to the waters;

and you that have no money,
come, buy and eat!
Come, buy wine and milk
without money and without price
(Is 55:1).

The tradition Aquinas inherited agreed that grace was essentially a participation in the divine nature and goodness. He quotes the Vulgate: 'He has given us most great and most precious promises; that by these you may be made partakers of the divine nature' (*divinae consortes naturae* [2 Pet 1:4]). This claim was the starting point for reflection. But the scholastics were great system-makers and gloried in fine-grained distinctions. So the starting point is quickly parcelled into further distinctions which are then put to work in moral theology.

Aquinas believed that grace as a participation in the divine nature contributes to happiness. But how? The initial distinction is that the agent is raised up and rectified through 'elevating grace' (*gratia elevans*) and 'healing grace' (*gratia sanans*).[34] Grace as *elevans* directs us to a perfect end that exceeds our natural powers, and therefore it is *super*natural. Grace as *sanans* helps renovate the tainted moral psychology that is the result of original sin. Since fallen nature cannot do this itself, that also is a supernatural work.[35]

In keeping with the Christian tradition that evil is not created, Aquinas thought that humans were created by God wholly good and so unfallen. He calls this state 'integral nature' (*natura integra*).[36] By it we could readily attain the good proportionate to human nature. Humans were also and further created in a state of grace known as 'original justice'.[37] This gratuitously and supernaturally elevated them to friendship with God. Original justice is therefore a *gratia elevans*. By it the body and passions were harmoniously subject to reason, which was itself harmoniously subject to God, our creator and lord. In the original harmony of this grace, humans were preserved from sickness, hurt, and death. Aquinas quotes from Paul: 'By sin death came into the world' (Rom 5:12).[38] The familiar ills of the eudaimonia gap were by hypothesis absent in integral nature and original justice. Though raised in *gratia elevans*, humans did not need *gratia sanans*.[39]

Integral nature is not itself original justice. When nature was integral, humans were capable of acquired virtue and natural happiness. Original justice further made humans capable of the good of infused virtue and supernatural happiness beyond our unaided trying. Integral nature and original justice concretely overlapped, but were distinct. The consequence is that grace is not built into the definition of human nature (a view that might render us quasi-divine). Despite this qualification, humans were created in grace and called to supernatural beatitude. So while integral nature and original justice are distinguishable, they were never meant to be separated. One implication is that purely natural happiness or *eudaimonia* falls short of the human calling in the divine economy. The happiness of, say, the *Nicomachean Ethics* and of eudaimonism may be possible and relatively good. But viewed from a background of integral nature, original justice, and later redemption, it has a wistfulness similar to Dante's Limbo of the virtuous pagans.

Aquinas distinguished natural *eudaimonia* from supernatural *beatitudo* – or broadly speaking, Nicomachean happiness from Gospel happiness. This does not imply that there are two ends: a natural one equivalent to pagan happiness, and a supernatural one equivalent to Christian beatitude. As I read him, Christian or supernatural beatitude in this life consists in the exercise of 'infused' or supernatural virtues. But these perfect capacities, such as the intellect and will, which are and remain natural. The consequence is that those in grace do not receive a new nature beyond the human form they already have. If they did, grace would abolish our humanity and install a new nature. Instead, human moral psychology is modified by supernatural causation to receive certain attributes and do what we as humans by ourselves cannot do.[40] On this reading of Aquinas, there are not 'two ends'. Rather, natural and supernatural happiness represent two modes of fulfilling what is in fact one end, understood under the appropriate formality.[41]

When humans fell in sin, both original justice and integral nature were lost. Grace was forfeited but nature itself remained (though it became wounded, or no longer 'integral'). The passions, appetites, intellect, and will are thrown partly out of joint, there is a certain 'downward appetite to mix with mud',[42] and human life becomes vulnerable to fortune. At the same time, sickness and death itself torment human existence. The 'impediments' to happiness are now present, and what I have called the eudaimonia gap becomes a painful *datum*. But human fallenness only goes so far. Unlike the later Jansenists, Aquinas insisted that human nature remains essentially good. We retain the natural inclination to the good, and we lose none of our natural capacities.[43] Nothing like total depravity is in view.

Aquinas' account to this point suggests why grace is needed. Though humans were created in grace, the loss of original justice meant losing friendship with God. The threat of damnation then became terribly real. So the subsequent offer of redemption is very good news indeed: nothing less than being 'saved'. From the theological perspective, the eudaimonia gap my philosophical interlocutors regret emerges from a Fall they lack resources to name. By elevating us back to friendship with God, grace as *gratia elevans* makes perfect beatitude possible again. By partly rectifying the results of original sin, grace as *gratia sanans* begins a process of internal healing and transformation that culminates in the eschaton.[44]

For Aquinas, grace is essentially a participation in the inner life of the Trinity. As a partaker in the divine nature, the effect of this grace is to justify us anew before God, remitting the guilt of sin, and making us at peace with God.[45] Since justification was merited by Christ's Passion and applied to us as a gift, it is gratuitous. But for Aquinas, justification is not just a legal declaration of pardon. As creator, God's love causes the good that is loved, and is not just a response to a good already there.[46] Love involves willing the beloved's good. Humans are loved by God not just in having natural good willed to us, but, beyond this, the supernatural good of friendship with the Triune God. As creative and therefore causal, God's love effects within us the supernatural quality required for that good to be participated. Grace is thus a tangible 'gift' freely given (*dono gratis dato*): that of participation in the divine nature construed as a quality bestowed upon the agent as a free gift.[47]

That gracious quality cannot just be a transient act, motion, or passion. If it were, justification and grace would fleet in and out of existence, and not be durably predicated of the agent. This would render absurd scriptural language about the 'heart of stone' being replaced by the 'heart of flesh' (Jeremiah 32:39). But neither can grace be a substantial change of the agent, otherwise we would cease to be human. So what kind of quality is the *donum* of divine participation?

Aquinas regarded the grace of justification as a life-changing disposition or *habitus* infused into the agent by God.[48] In that sense it is called 'habitual grace'. As a habit it is an accidental rather than a substantial quality, meaning that our humanity is not collapsed into divinity. Since it is a gift rather than an achievement, it is 'infused' (that is, 'poured out') rather than 'acquired'. In that respect it is supernatural or beyond the capacity of unaided human nature to attain. But the fact that it is a habit *of the agent* makes it a genuine principle of operation for him or her, and not just a displacement of human by divine agency (which would make grace morally irrelevant).

Habitual grace is holistic rather than piecemeal: the whole person, not just scraps of a person, is the object of redemption. As a *habitus*, grace characterises the agent. It is not just an amorphous energy, but inheres in the various human capacities as derivative habits that are supernaturally perfective of those capacities.[49] In the form of the theological virtues, grace as faith perfects the intellect, and grace as hope and charity perfects the will. In the form of the infused virtues, the four cardinal virtues perfect their familiar capacities, but the mean of virtue is derived from revelation rather than just reason, and the cause of virtue is supernatural infusion rather than natural acquisition.[50]

Taken comprehensively, justification and habitual grace denote the 'general rectitude of order' by which the person as a whole is ordained to God.[51] Habitual grace is therefore called *gratia gratum faciens* ('grace making one graced or pleasing' [i.e., to God]), which in post-Tridentine theology came to be called 'sanctifying grace'. In Aquinas, it is distinguished from 'graces freely given' (*gratiae gratis data*) for the justified to help lead others to God (i.e., charisms).[52] It is also distinguished from the grace of *auxilium* ('help' or 'aid') construed as discrete supernatural motions given by God to either prepare the agent for the infusion of habitual grace, or subsequently to actualise the habit of grace into a supernatural act of faith, hope, charity, and so forth. This *auxilium* maps onto what post-Tridentine theology called 'actual' graces.

Habitual grace both elevates the agent to a supernatural life and partly heals our disordered moral psychology. It therefore does double duty as both *gratia elevans* and *gratia sanans*. Pervading the whole person, habitual grace effects 'a certain regeneration or re-creation' that is a gift of divine mercy. The providential work implied is of course indexed to salvation history, and does not just emerge mid-air. In Aquinas' telling, the willing death of the obedient Christ satisfies for sin and for the first humans' pride and disobedience.[53] The merit of Christ's Passion is applied to Christians through baptism in which the 'old man' is buried with Christ and the 'new man' reborn in grace emerges.[54]

Being justified and partly healed, those in habitual grace are called the 'regenerate', and habitual grace is often referred to by Aquinas as our 'newness' (*novitas*): the spiritual or regenerate life of the 'new man' who now forms a member in the body of Christ. This is contrasted to our 'oldness' (*vetustas*), or the sinful remainder we are being healed from. Such considerations led Aquinas to distinguish between imperfect supernatural happiness, in which perfection is incomplete; and perfect supernatural happiness, which is proper to the fully healed and perfected saints. These two are further distinguished from natural happiness, which is always imperfect since fallen nature cannot attain perfect *eudaimonia*.[55] This is a theological way of saying that the eudaimonia gap cannot be closed by fallen nature: a point argued in the previous chapter non-theologically. Aquinas obviously does not use the phrase 'eudaimonia gap'. But while he often describes our predicament as one of sin, both personal and original, he sees the predicament of sin as coextensive with what I have described more neutrally as the eudaimonia gap.[56] (When in my own account by this point I refer to the gap, I am simultaneously referring to *sin*: to a status quo configured by human fallenness, and to the sinful responses and their effects to which our lack of beatitude tempts us, yet without compelling us.)

The claim that supernatural happiness consists in graced activity raises the question of how habitual grace will be put into action. To answer this Aquinas posits *auxilium* or 'helping' grace as an activating motion of God given to actualise the habit of grace.[57] Prior to the Fall, humans would only have needed *auxilium* to actualise the habit of grace, making it exclusively a *gratia elevans*. But post-Fall, humans additionally require such help because fallen nature is not yet fully healed. Like a broken leg that is set but not fully mended, fallen nature is partly but not fully healed by habitual grace. Concupiscence and ignorance leave us with weak spots vulnerable to temptation. Aquinas stiffly resists anything like Pelagian moral theology. Even when regenerate, postlapsarian nature requires supernatural *auxilium* or help as a *gratia sanans*, as indicated by the Lord's Prayer.[58] These involve our own agency as well. Though derived from God as primary agent, such *auxilia* graces are applied through instrumental causes such as prayer, the sacraments, the Scriptures, spiritual experiences, and friends.

The correlation of habitual and *auxilium* grace led Aquinas to follow Augustine in affirming the seven gifts of the Holy Spirit as major players in the moral-spiritual life. Because conformity to grace and participation in the divine nature are imperfect in this life, supernatural habits such as the theological and infused moral virtues are participated in imperfectly. We are still afflicted by 'folly, ignorance, dullness of mind and hardness of heart', and so forth.[59] Accordingly, gifts of the Holy Spirit opposed to these burdens are given to put cooperation with grace on a surer footing. Each gift is a discrete supernatural habit which inheres in a particular theological or infused moral virtue. So located, each gift makes one amenable to the promptings of God's *auxilium* as it moves one to act out of a particular infused virtue. For instance, the gift of fear makes one more amenable to infused temperance, the gift of piety makes one more amenable to infused justice, and so forth. These gifts provide a greater interior affinity with the inspiration of the Holy Spirit, and allow one to cooperate with God's *auxilium* in a better manner: with greater promptness, facility, and naturalness. Bernard Lonergan argues that this model, which emerges later in

Aquinas' career, is 'a very adequate answer to the objection that external intervention is violent, or as we should say, unnatural'.[60]

Granted that the habits of grace can be put into act with God's help, the way is open to saying that God cooperates with human agency in bringing about supernatural acts. As this suggests, Aquinas believed that human and divine agency were non-competing. God as providential first cause works with and through secondary causes. As creatures, humans are secondary causes with whom God may work by cooperating with our free will. The agent's contribution to an act of faith, hope, or charity does not begin where God's contribution ends. Instead, God's contribution is precisely what enables the agent's own.[61] The act of an infused habit is thus fully one's own, and fully dependent on God. The fortunate conclusion is that the Christian is not doomed to be a mechanically shoved grace puppet whose agency becomes otiose.

To explain human and divine contributions to supernatural acts, Aquinas further distinguishes between operative and cooperative grace. The operative occurs when the agent is moved but 'God is the sole mover'. The cooperative occurs when God works with the agent, so that 'our mind both moves and is moved'.[62] Each occurs within both habitual and *auxilium* grace. Habitual grace is operative insofar as the person is supernaturally elevated, partly healed, and justified – all of which are God's work. But habitual grace is cooperative in that it gives the capacity to perform acts of infused virtue, and so is the principle of human merit. Likewise, *auxilium* grace is operative insofar as God initiates the process of conversion, and in that God gives the convert further *auxilia* by which he or she perseveres in habitual grace. But *auxilium* grace is cooperative insofar as God works in and through the agent so that he or she may perform supernatural acts throughout the life of Christian discipleship.[63] As an act flowing from that habitual grace which is the principle of merit, such an act is meritorious of reward from God.

The topic of merit is important to theological hope.[64] One of the vices Aquinas opposes to hope is presumption, which is a bloated parody of hope, as rashness is a bloated parody of courage. By it one presumes to receive 'pardon without repentance, or glory without merits'.[65] The requirement of merit is one way hope resists morally flaccid complacency by acknowledging the need to pursue, for example, social justice and personal transformation. Yet Aquinas insists that we do not merit condignly or 'strictly speaking', by putting God in our debt. Instead we merit congruently or 'with qualifications', in that God chooses to reward us freely. In that respect we may merit the increase of infused virtues by using them well. We may also merit eternal life in the mightily qualified sense that the transformation required for perfect beatitude is one which grace effects through free will rather than despite it. Whatever may be said of other models of merit, Aquinas does not make it a smokescreen for crass 'works righteousness'. His stress on merit does not fall on God owing rewards as a debt of justice, but on reward as something God elects to do as fitting.

Charity as 'the form of the virtues' is the primary principle of merit and of sanctification. For Aquinas, the agent is sanctified by the presence and increase of habitual grace. Since happiness consists in virtuous activity, supernatural happiness will consist in the activity of supernatural virtues. These both express grace and are rewarded by God with the bestowal of further grace. In our concrete moral and spiritual development, sanctification *is* beatitude, and vice versa. Aquinas believes that grace is meant to be truly transformative of character, neither to bypass human agency nor to leave it unregenerated. This befits a virtue ethics model of happiness that is internally rather than externally related to the character one has. But while the share of supernatural happiness that can be had in this life is real and admirable, it falls well short of the perfect beatitude that eschatology promises. Christian *beatitudo* does not simply escape the eudaimonia gap with Stoic immunity. The gap will only be adequately overcome in future glory, and so hope becomes deeply important.

Aquinas' Starting Place for Theological Hope

Grace elevates us to a new kind of happiness. But our share in that happiness in this life is still imperfect and at risk. This makes it intelligible to view human life as a journey or pilgrimage. Following tradition, Aquinas construes human identity as hope-shaped. The Christian is traditionally called *homo viator*: the 'human wayfarer' or pilgrim who is 'on the way' (*in via*) and who seeks to arrive in the heavenly homeland (*in patria*). Hope is thus a time-indexed virtue concerned with finishing the job by sustaining the wayfarer 'on the way' amid the impediments to happiness familiar within the eudaimonia gap.

'So faith, hope, and charity abide, these three' (1 Cor 13:13). Hope in God's covenant promises set the religious tone in Israel for hundreds of years. Set against the desolation of the cross, Easter morning ensured that Christianity bore within itself a supremely confident and triumphal hope.[66] The early Church stressed hope so confidently that death was often welcomed simply as a gateway to eternal life.[67] By contrast, later patristic and medieval theology took a more cautionary approach, warning against presumption and urging the need for ascetic patience. Peter Lombard's *Sentences* was the paramount scholastic work within Aquinas' context. A pioneering effort to distil and adjudicate the tradition of Latin theology for which Augustine was the greatest authority, the *Sentences* defined hope vaguely as an 'expectation of perfect happiness', but left its practical role unclear. As so often happens in treatments of the theological virtues, Lombard gives the impression of dragging in hope as an afterthought and making it a mere pendant to faith and charity.[68] By contrast, Aquinas took an unusual amount of interest in hope, studying it both as a passion and as a virtue.

The Nature and Object of Theological Hope

Much has been said about Aquinas' model of theological hope in the introduction. There I aimed to give a snapshot of Thomistic hope that brought the main contours into view so they could be taken in at a glance. The following will examine the technical details with the focus required to make his account intelligible. The object of any hope for Aquinas is a 'future good possible but arduous to attain'.[69] Theological hope shares this characterisation, but makes it more specific. In it the future good sought is perfect happiness, and this is to be found in God, making such hope 'theological'. Since God is not a body, such hope seeks an intelligible good and properly resides in the will rather than the passions. Volitional hope may overflow into and stimulate the passions, often giving rise to feelings of hope.[70] But the passion of hope itself – which Aquinas thinks conspicuous among animals, inexperienced youth, and drunkards – should not be confused with hope as it appears in the will.[71]

Theological hope is proper to the will as the virtue or good habit which enables one to rely on God to reach ultimate beatitude. For Aquinas, the will integrates all of our desires, passions, and aims over a lifetime. As a rational appetite for the good, it has to adjust over time to changing circumstances and challenges that call for a reaffirmation of one's commitments. Hope disposes the will to do this well when it comes to circumstances that challenge one's pursuit of God as future, possible, and arduous. As such, hope enables us to respond virtuously to the eudaimonia gap. With respect to the gap's positive side, hope believes that perfect happiness is *possible* but *future*. At the same time, sudden tragedy, crushed dreams, and mounting disappointments can shake our confidence, raising the prospect of despair. So with respect to the gap's negative side, hope believes that finally getting beyond the gap is possible but very much *arduous*. As a virtue, hope disposes the will to persevere in its commitment despite these challenges. This disposition is not just indexical, but relational: hope is the needy love and trustful reliance on God as the saviour and friend who will help one successfully complete the journey. Aquinas explains this action of hope in terms of final and efficient causality.

The Final and Efficient Causes of Hope

The fullest and most mature work of Aquinas on hope is in the *secunda secundae* of the *Summa theologiae*. Because of this, and the fact that he uses different terminology for hope elsewhere, my explication of Aquinas will largely focus on hope as it appears in its final form there. In the *secunda secundae*, at the twilight of his career, Aquinas summarises, extends, and tidies up his previous work on hope. I complained earlier that Lombard had left the practical role of hope vague. But the same could be said of almost all theologies of hope up to Aquinas' time. Unlike charity or courage – to take just two examples – identifying act-types proper to hope had proven difficult. The question of what it concretely meant to enact hope was therefore muddled. Aquinas found this unsatisfying, and sought to examine hope with unprecedented scholastic precision.

He began by distinguishing between two senses in which God is the object of theological hope. 'Hope', Aquinas writes, 'regards two things, viz. the good which it intends to obtain, and the help by which that good is obtained'.[72] The first is hope's final cause or end, consisting in God as the source of one's eternal happiness. The second is hope's efficient cause or means, and consists in God's help (*auxilium*) to attain the final end. From the perspective of final causality, 'Hope denotes a certain stretching forth of the appetite towards an arduous good'.[73] From the perspective of efficient causality, 'Hope attains God by leaning on his help'[74] through relying on God's 'omnipotence and mercy'.[75] Hope's basic action therefore consists in seeking God as final cause, and relying on God as efficient cause to that end. I will examine each of these in turn, beginning with hope's final cause or end.

The final cause of hope is 'eternal life, which consists in the enjoyment of God Himself. For we should hope from Him for nothing less than Himself'.[76] This comes about through the beatific vision of the divine essence, that blissful contemplation of God 'face to face' which is the activity of happiness in its supreme perfection. If the final end which hope seeks is God as one's eternal happiness, does this mean that hope is indifferent or hostile to earthly goods and happiness? Bent on a heavenly promised land, does hope deflate human life and social concerns with a reductive *contemptus mundi*? Many in the tradition helped build the stereotype of the hopeful as having their head in the clouds and one foot in the grave. Aquinas is certainly not among them. He emphatically believes in the essential goodness of creation. Beyond this, he thinks we may enjoy a rich if limited happiness in this present life, and that we should 'rejoice in hope' at the approach of eternal life.[77]

The result is that hope, for Aquinas, does not fit into a narrative meant to make this life and world look bleak. Taking the Lord's Prayer as the model prayer of hope, Aquinas says that we should pray for temporal goods, but do so 'in reference to eternal happiness'.[78] Earthly goods from one's daily bread to the most pressing goals of social justice are fully *compatible* with theological hope insofar as they are virtuously sought. Just as importantly, they may *participate* in theological hope as 'secondary final causes' ordered to our 'ultimate final cause'. Just what this looks like is the topic of the last two chapters of this volume.

The second part of hope's action is its efficient causality.[79] Aquinas believes the hopeful should lean on God's grace as the 'help' (*auxilium*) that will sustain them in the Christian journey. The efficient cause of hope is necessary because even those in habitual grace need further graces or *auxilia* in their Christian vocation.[80] We are not a finished product, and Pelagian self-helpism will not get us there. Aquinas discerns two senses in which we need hope's efficiency: the first ontological, and the second moral. Ontologically, habitual grace as a potency is 'actualised' by *auxilium*. Hence the post-Tridentine relabelling of *auxilium* as 'actual' grace. In this respect, *auxilium* functions as 'elevating grace' or *gratia elevans*. Morally, habitual grace as a regeneration in Christ is ongoing and is helped along by *auxilium*. Even the regenerate is described by Aquinas as *homo infirmus*: a 'sick human' not fully healed from concupiscence and in need of continual help and forgiveness. A frank look at the moral failings of Christians favours this view. In this respect, *auxilium* functions as 'healing grace' or *gratia sanans*. The *auxilium* of hope's efficient cause is therefore both ontological and moral, needed both because we are creatures and because we are sinners.[81]

Hope's efficiency returns us to the subject of cooperative grace. Agents do not just passively receive God's *auxilium*; they must entrust themselves to it, leaning and relying on God; not forgetting to do so, and not failing to act after doing so. This is the human contribution to hope's efficient causality, which arises from *gratia cooperans* in which God cooperates with the agent to enable supernatural action, engaging the will and informing human capacities.[82]

Leaning on grace as hope's efficient cause: this is how Aquinas puts what we would describe in plainer terms as asking God for help to do your duty or to become a better person, seeking forgiveness, praying for strength or for healing, relying on God to get you through tough times, and so forth. For this to be a genuine act of hope it must be conformable with and expressive of a life ordered to hope's final cause: to God construed as our ultimate end. By this grace Aquinas even says that one may 'attain' God in this life. 'Insofar as we hope ... by means of divine assistance (*auxilium*), our hope attains (*attingit*) God himself'.[83] God as end may be 'a future good' of the next life, but by prayerfully leaning on God's *auxilium*, hope attains God as present in this life.[84]

Hope is a crucial meeting place for all the infused habits and the whole supernatural life. By hope we pray for, trust in, and rely on God's *auxilium*.[85] With such extensive and immediate reliance on God, why would we ever need to lean on anything creaturely in the supernatural life? Aquinas answers that it is because God frequently works through instrumental causes to confer grace: a theme which resonates with his view that the causal relationship between the creator and creature is non-competitive and that creatures themselves can be made into blessings.[86] The greatest instrumental cause of grace is Christ's humanity and his Passion. Other instrumental causes include the sacraments, the prayers of the saints, good friendships, and even the physical benefits that help us on our journey.[87]

The Relation of Hope to Faith and Charity

Aquinas takes pains to explain the difference and relationship between hope and its fellow theological virtues, faith and charity. They are 'theological' in that God (*theos*) is their object and sets their mean, they are infused by grace rather than acquired by habituation, and they are divinely revealed rather than humanly discovered.[88] While the object of each is God, they differ in the aspect of God each regards. The object of faith is God *qua* first truth. By it the intellect is perfected through learning revealed truths about God and matters important for salvation.[89] The object of hope is God *qua* one's own good or beatitude. By it the will is perfected by clinging to God for one's own sake. The object of charity is God *qua* goodness as such. By it the will is still more perfected by clinging 'to God for his own sake'.[90]

Following scholastic practice, Aquinas sees hope and charity as tracking two kinds of love: 'love of concupiscence' (*amor concupiscentiae*) and 'love of benevolence' (*amor benevolentiae*).[91] By the former we wish good to ourselves, and by the latter we wish good to another. It is by concupiscent love that 'we are said to love wine, or a horse, or the like' – i.e., in an interested sense, or for one's own sake. It is by benevolent love that 'we love someone so as to wish good to him' – i.e., in a disinterested sense, or for the beloved's own sake.[92] Benevolent love is a necessary but not sufficient condition for friendship, which also requires a mutuality founded on a shared good.[93]

Hope corresponds to concupiscent love, and charity to benevolent love. This is because hope seeks God not as good simply, but as one's own good specifically.[94] Charity does the reverse. Nevertheless, Aquinas does not see the two loves as opposed. For him, concupiscent and benevolent love are both good, though the latter is more perfect. It is anachronistic to read into Aquinas' distinctions the oppositions between selfish and unselfish, or egoistic and altruistic. For him, the two loves do not stand to each other as good to bad, permissible to meritorious, or suspect to innocent. They stand to each other as lesser good to greater good, with the lesser being fully good in its own way.[95]

Aquinas regards self-love as good, though to remain that way it must be subordinated to the love of goods greater than oneself. These range from the local and national good to the good of one's species to the good of the universe and the good that is God.[96] So while concupiscent love seeks one's own good or perfection, this need not occur *at the expense* of still greater goods.[97]

Aquinas uses these two loves to help explain Christian conversion.[98] To do this, he speaks of the 'order of generation', or the sequence in which faith, hope, and charity arise. Since we cannot seek what we do not believe exists, faith is prior to hope and charity.[99] But charity is the 'form' of the supernatural virtues, and habitual grace is only present when one has charity. The consequence is that faith without charity is 'unformed' and not of itself salvific.[100] Because *auxilium* grace precedes conversion, preparing us 'as matter for form' for the influx of habitual grace, unformed faith is supernatural and disposes to such grace. What might this look like? Among the articles of faith are promises of everlasting life which dispose to hope. If we believe in this promise, we are very much disposed to desire the good promised: one which from the perspective of the eudaimonia gap is utterly wonderful and felt to be miraculous. The will may accordingly stir towards that good, giving rise to motions of interested or concupiscent love under the influence of *auxilium* grace. From this, unformed hope may come about.[101] At that point the will shall be deeply invested in what faith makes it possible to believe.

The initial result may be a spiritual twilight period where the agent hovers between seeking happiness on the eudaimonia gap's terms, and seeking a surpassing beatitude made possible by grace. Whether over the years or in a sudden Damascus experience, the agent may grow disposed to God in a very new and different way. As with Augustine, one may not immediately let go of the old lifestyle, but one may begin to see and entertain a different and attractive possibility. In Aquinas' terms, one would then have unformed faith and hope, though not yet charity.[102] Yet at a certain point, the agent may decide the prospect is worth it and commit to the new relationship with God. From that commitment charity is born.

A fine example of this process is told with a novelist's eye by the Venerable Bede in his *Ecclesiastical History of the English People*. There the Anglo-Saxon King Edwin is deliberating with his nobles about whether they should 'follow the new teaching' which many of them find compelling, and convert to Christianity. At that moment one of the king's counsellors delivers the speech quoted at the beginning of this book. It is a historically important speech which helps decide the council and changes the course of our history. In it we overhear people disquieted by the familiar ills of the eudaimonia gap, and who are tantalised by a more hopeful prospect. Yet that prospect requires a break with the old life and commitments that may be costly. In this passage Bede captures the sense in which unformed faith and hope precede and stir towards conversion and the influx of charity.

Hope seeks the end of perfect beatitude in God, and so it loves with *amor concupiscentiae*. God offers this end not as something owed, but as a free gift of charity. Eternal life is therefore the consequence of *amor benevolentiae*. The kind and degree of benevolent love on offer are astounding, as St. Paul notes: 'While we were yet helpless, at the right time Christ died for the ungodly. Why, one will hardly die for a righteous man – though perhaps for a good man one will dare to die. But God shows his love for us in that while we were yet sinners Christ died for us' (Rom 5:6–8). To believe that God loves one with such extraordinary benevolence presents a new consideration – namely, that God is lovable in a still higher way than that of concupiscent love, lovable not just as one's own good, but utterly lovable, as goodness itself. This disposes the hopeful to reciprocate benevolent love back towards God.[103]

For Aquinas, love of God as meeting one's own needs creates space in us to receive God's benevolent love and to then embrace that supreme charity with grateful awe and moral wonderment. Like the prodigal son, one meets with a goodwill beyond one's deserts and beyond all reckoning. To this the proper and glad response is to reciprocate benevolent love back towards God in our own creaturely way. One appreciates that God is not just a means to one's own happiness, but supremely good and worthy of all our love.[104] In that respect the process is similar to the benevolent love which people spontaneously show to those who do them some great kindness. Consider the man beaten by thieves and rescued by the Good Samaritan. If the two later met, would anyone be surprised if the erstwhile victim showed the Samaritan benevolent love in return, caring about him for his own sake rather than, say, as a ruse to get more money out of him?

Aquinas regards unformed hope as an *amor concupiscentiae* for God that disposes one to a response of *amor benevolentiae* for God. In scholastic jargon, faith and hope precede charity in 'the order of generation', but charity precedes both in 'the order of perfection'.[105] The response of benevolent love is essential to enjoying the love of friendship (*amor amicitiae*) with God. Friendship requires but does not just consist in mutual benevolence. Beyond goodwill, a friendship must be *about* something. There must be a *communicatio* or something held in common that characterises the friendship and enables a real relationship. But what will constitute the *communicatio* on which friendship with God is built? Surely it is far-fetched to picture God and humans as conventional friends. Their ontological and moral distance raises questions about what they will have in common, and what the friendship will be about. Aquinas answers that the *communicatio* is the divine nature itself and the supernatural happiness bestowed upon those who partaker in it.[106] The friendship based on this communication is charity, and the corresponding participation in the divine nature is the essence of habitual grace.

Charity as friendship with God begins with the reception of habitual grace and all of the other infused habits it enables. At that point, unformed faith is formed, making the act of faith justifying and salvific.[107] Unformed hope also becomes formed, so that one not only longs for future beatitude, but personally trusts in God to get there.[108] In addition, faith, hope, and charity are complemented by the infused moral virtues and the seven gifts of the Holy Spirit that are infused with habitual grace. Amid such graces, the 'greatest of these is charity', which Aquinas regards as the 'mother and root' of the infused habits, hope included. Put more technically, the different infused habits pursue their own proximate ends, but charity further directs these ends to its own ultimate end of union with the divine friend.[109] Charity is also the 'greatest' theological virtue in that it alone will remain in heaven. Faith and hope will both pass away, since clear vision makes faith unnecessary and perfect possession leaves nothing to hope for.[110]

It is important to note that hope is not just a duet between God and oneself. When charity informs hope, it gives to it an ecclesial and social dimension. Hope may be a self-regarding love, but charity regards the friend as another self. Hope informed by charity therefore hopes for the beloved neighbour as for another self, giving hope a social dimension I will later examine at length.[111]

Transformed by the infusion of grace, charity, and the infused habits, the convert is 're-born' or regenerated in Christ, becoming the 'new human' (*novum hominem*) who walks in 'newness (*novitas*) of life'.[112] This in turn is a new kind of happy life (supernatural *makarios* or *beatitudo*) that differs from natural happiness or *eudaimonia*. Very broadly, it is the happy life of the Gospels as distinct from the philosophers: the way of life proper to those living not merely the acquired virtues but their infused counterparts. This *beatitudo* is the 'newness of life' in question, and like *eudaimonia* it is constituted by virtuous activity – in this case, the practice of the infused virtues. This takes concrete form in the 'New Law' of the Gospel, pre-eminently in the beatitudes of Christ's Sermon on the Mount.[113]

The Opposed Vices of Despair and Presumption

Following tradition, Aquinas identifies despair and presumption as the two vices opposed to hope. Full treatments of them will follow in later chapters, but a brief word is fitting here to make hope's operation clearer by showing what hope is not, and what it opposes. Like hope itself, despair regards an arduous good. But unlike hope, despair considers that good impossible to attain. This breakdown of hope is both cognitive and conative. Cognitively, it is due to the 'false opinion that God refuses pardon to the repentant sinner, or that He does not turn sinners to Himself by sanctifying grace'.[114] Conatively, this horrible error leads the will to give up and quit the journey in what Pieper calls an 'anticipation of nonfulfillment' which the agent takes to be final.[115]

Despair does not emerge from nowhere. Following Pope Gregory the Great's *Moralia in Job*, Aquinas sees sloth or *acedia* as its typical cause. Sloth is one of the most complex moral concepts in the tradition. In English and many other languages it suggests idleness, laziness, and inertia. But acedia proper is far more complex.[116] Keeping to the Gregorian account, Aquinas describes acedia as 'sorrow at divine goodness'. Crucially, this sorrow is not simply an emotion. Derived from the Latin word for 'bitter', acedia is a habitual state of disgust or repugnance in the will. Aquinas states that the object of loathing is 'the divine good within us'.[117] Specifically, sloth is the will's repugnance to charity's fellowship with God, a kind of nausea towards grace. The reason why the slothful feel sorrow and repugnance towards the spiritual life is that they resent the costly demands of discipleship and would prefer to be left alone by God in a contented mediocrity.

Sometimes this is because the spiritual life demands physical effort – as with fasting, works of justice and charity, getting up early for church, or fighting off drowsiness in prayer. Hence the stereotype of sloth as physical laziness. But this is a symptom, not the essence of sloth. Properly speaking, acedia flows from a spiritual laziness which breeds loathing with the spiritual life due to the effort required for virtue and holiness. The result can be a sort of generalised spiritual depression, what Aquinas calls a 'sluggishness of the mind' which resists beginning 'good works'.[118] Acedia is directly opposed to the spiritual joy of charity, but indirectly it exercises a vicious trickle-down effect into hope. As a spiritual sadness that demoralises the agent and increasingly makes the religious life a source of loathing, acedia is a kind of gateway vice to despair:

> [T]he fact that a man deems an arduous good impossible to obtain, either by himself or by another, is due to his being over downcast, because when this state of mind dominates his affections, it seems to him that he will never be able to rise to any good. And since sloth is a sadness that casts down the spirit, in this way despair is born of sloth.[119]

Presumption by contrast is a bloated likeness or parody of hope. It comes in two forms, both of which ruin hope's relationship to grace.[120] The first is the roughly Pelagian kind which declines to seek grace for help and healing, assuming that sheer effort will suffice for salvation. Aquinas regards it as the evil fruit of vainglory, and recalls the biblical admonition: 'You humble those who presume of themselves'.[121] The error here consists in that peculiar kind of self-reliance which sees it as unnecessary to seek and rely on God's grace.

Just possibly, the stress on grace might seem to enable moral laziness with a wink and a nod. If we are dependent on God for what matters most, why not opt out of the moral struggle and abdicate responsibility for transforming oneself and the world, vaguely expecting God to do everything in a way that lets one conveniently withdraw from the process? Such worries lurk behind criticisms of hope as otherworldly and disengaged. But Aquinas condemns this as an equal and opposite form of presumption. What looks like heroic trust in God may be driven by a moral laziness which blots out God's justice so as to complacently secure 'pardon without repenting or glory without merits'.[122] By leaning inordinately on God's *auxilium* while refusing to cooperate with what *auxilium* prompts them to do, such agents fail to merit and decline to be transformed. This kind of presumption 'removes or despises the *auxilium* of the Holy Spirit' by which we repent and perform the acts of the infused virtues.[123] The contemporary forms taken by presumption and despair, and the resources for overcoming them, are the topics of Chapters 4 and 5.

Hope's Gift, Certainty, and Beatitude

The moral threat of these vices makes abundantly clear hope's continued vulnerability and need for firming up if we are to carry on well with the journey. Aquinas says that one major resource for keeping hope strong is the particular gift of the Holy Spirit aligned with it: the gift of fear. This is said to make the agent more amenable to the promptings of grace as they stimulate the virtue of hope.[124] Like all habits of grace, hope is a potentiality that is actualised through *auxilium* as a discrete supernatural motion. Fear as a habit is nested in the overarching habit of hope, and its role is to make the hopeful more docile and pliable to the motion of *auxilium* prompting hope into action against various resistances, such as temptations to presumption.

Religious fear strikes many as archaic, monstrous, and unsuited to the lived experience of hope. In the fifth chapter, I will address such concerns, but for now it must be stressed that Aquinas believes that fear does not reduce hope to quavering. As the next chapter will discuss, he thinks that hope fosters joy at nearing the goal, and that we should legitimately 'rejoice in hope' (Rom 12:12). The fear he endorses does not render this schizophrenic. Aquinas distinguishes a variety of fears to clarify which he associates with the gift. All fear is a dread of losing what one loves: 'fear is born of love, since a man fears the loss of what he loves'.[125] When the beloved is not infallibly and permanently possessed, fear in some form is a proper effect of love.

But what kind of fear is this when the object of love is God as willed by theological hope? Fully virtuous fear is not servile fear, according to which the prospect dreaded is simply punishment.[126] Aquinas' ideal of the gift is filial fear, where what is feared is separation from God.[127] So hope's proper fear is not a cringing dread of punishment. In its purest form, it is dread of whatever might estrange us from God, and this makes it fully compatible with the charity by which we cling to God.[128] What has been said so far is purely schematic. In the fifth chapter, I will provide the details for a renovated model of fear that I think is spiritually healthy and a genuine aid to hope.

Fear itself is complemented by the peculiar kind of 'certitude' which Aquinas ascribes to hope. This kind of certitude is not that of speculative certainty. It is not, that is, the firm belief that one's salvation will transpire as a future event. Hope's certitude belongs to the will's analogous but distinct kind of certainty: one which clings with complete trust to the means necessary for salvation.[129] This implies complete certitude about the divine means but enough scepticism about ourselves to rule out a self-deceived moral infallibilism. Such certitude strikes precisely the balance needed to disqualify presumption while precluding despair.

Following Augustine's example and long tradition, Aquinas fits the beatitudes into the framework of the virtues and the gifts. In his theology, the beatitudes are not discrete habits; they are the acts of the seven gifts of the Holy Spirit. Since each theological virtue has at least one gift assigned to it, each has at least one beatitude associated with it by means of the gift. To hope's gift there accordingly belongs a particular beatitude. Following Ambrose, Augustine, and received tradition, Aquinas believes the beatitude which puts the gift of fear into action is poverty of spirit. It helps to void the pride, vainglory, and greed which feed presumption, acedia, and despair. In the sixth chapter, I will discuss how spiritual poverty enables the agent to overcome the threat posed by 'worldliness' to hope.

I regard the main outlines of Thomistic hope as persuasive and worthwhile. It assures us that the aspiration for a fuller good is not in vain, and it encourages us with the anticipation of perfect beatitude. By sustaining us amid tragedy, injustice, and the inevitable approach of decline and death, it defends us from despair. By rooting us in acknowledged dependence on God while demanding merits that contribute to this world, it removes us from presumption. In doing so, hope offers a more attractive solution to the eudaimonia gap than either pagan or secular resignation: one that makes a key contribution to this-worldly happiness while disposing us to full beatitude in eternal life. In what follows, I will assume the general contours of this account as a given while striking out on my own and describing the hopeful life in contemporary terms. This will involve engaging with relevant interlocutors and important issues, portraying the life of hope, and describing practices by which it is expressed and sustained.

The Quietist Negation of Hope

I have claimed that the theological virtue of hope makes an important contribution to the happy life. Yet theological hope itself has had a great many 'cultured despisers' who disagree. For Nietzsche, Christianity with its hope for heaven mandated a life-denying and miserable way of life. It was the 'vampire' that sucked the blood out of the Roman Empire and ensured that 'the whole labour of the ancient world was in vain'.[130] Rousseau saw hope as a distraction from human progress and earthly well-being.[131] For Swinburne and many *fin de siècle* pessimists, hope was the heavenly bribe Christianity offers to make people buy into a life of gloomy asceticism. The great tragedy of post-Greco-Roman civilisation is that the offer was accepted: 'Thou hast conquered, O pale Galilean: the whole world has grown grey from thy breath'.[132] Such critiques vary in quality from mere abuse to the pardonable disgust felt for models of hope which wrongly blackened this life and world to make heaven sound like the only good worth having. But for the most part, such criticisms come from thinkers whose attack on hope itself is just one file in a brief meant to discredit Christianity itself: to 'crush the infamous thing' (*Ecrasez l'Infame*).[133] Much of what has been said already will have made clear that Christian hope in anything like the Thomistic form neither entails nor condones these follies. The last chapter of this book will address many of the social concerns at greater length. But in this section, I want to address concerns about the object of hope which are driven neither by purely social or by anti-Christian purposes. Many with no stake in 'crush[ing] the infamous thing' have grave and intelligent concerns about hope's nature and main interest.

In this section, I will seek to clarify the nature and object of hope, addressing misconceptions about its final cause or eschatological end, and engaging some prominent interlocutors. Most of it will address Timothy Jackson's argument in *Love Disconsoled* that hope sullies *agape*'s 'purity of motive' with a mercenary interest, that it distracts from neighbour-love and the joys of this life, and that hope's object is unnecessary anyway since *agape* and the possibilities of this world suffice for the good life.

Many would agree with Iris Murdoch that 'In the moral life the enemy is the fat relentless ego'.[134] Over the centuries, quite a few have claimed that theological hope subtly joins the enemy through its apparent self-preoccupation and self-regard. Hope loves God as one's own beatitude, fulfilment, and perfection. To some, this makes it a 'selfish' virtue far removed from the disinterested love of God and neighbour. Darlene Weaver has argued powerfully against this view.[135] But many still see the self-regarding love which Aquinas called *amor concupiscentiae* as a kind of boil which must be lanced by the other-regarding love of *amor benevolentiae* in some form. This suspicion of hope's self-regard was carried to its extreme by the seventeenth-century French Quietists who advocated a *l'amour pur* for God so disinterested that it did not even prefer salvation to damnation. All that mattered was to unite one's love with God's will, whatever that had in store. From where Quietism sits, 'every request for oneself is self-interested, contrary to *l'amour pur* and to conformity with the will of God'.[136] What the scholastics called *amor concupiscentiae* is to be wholly 'quieted' by disinterested love which voids self-regard altogether through abandonment to the divine will. Karl Barth said of self-love that 'God will never think of blowing on this fire, which is bright enough already'.[137] But the Quietist goal was to extinguish that fire completely. As Bossuet wrote in his critique of François Malaval and Madame Guyon, this theology requires 'the exclusion of every desire and every request for oneself, abandoning oneself to the most hidden wishes of God, whatever they should be, either for damnation or salvation'.[138] Though the two emerge in starkly different contexts and have very different qualities overall, there is a definite parallel between the Stoics' resignation to fortune and the Quietists' resignation to Providence. Both commend resignation to a power of necessity before whose lofty cause hope is made to seem morally immature and narcissistic.

Quietism sought *l'amour pur* as a mystical ascent beyond selfishness into pure divine love. Put abstractly, this sounds inspiring. But as a matter of policy, its results are horrid. Such a theology instrumentalises the self, abdicates any meaningful moral patient status, and, by construing the person as nothing but a burnt offering to the divine will, it raises dark questions about the character of God so understood. By treating one's neediness before and dependency on God as morally and spiritually trifling, Quietism undermines our very status as creatures. What else is a creature but a dependent and needy being before its creator? To treat that neediness as though it were not there is to performatively subvert the creaturehood which Christians theoretically profess. Quietism claims to void self-seeking, but ironically it does so by a peculiar self-promotion: one which assigns to its members the role of a spiritual and even mystical elite who effectively say to God: 'I express no needs and ask you for nothing; I love you disinterestedly'. It is indicative that this clashes so deeply with the ethical style of the Prodigal Son parable. Not only does the son's repentance begin with the recognition of his own abject neediness: one can hardly imagine him progressing to a high-minded *l'amour pur* in which grateful dependency is simply abolished.

The theological virtue of hope is implicitly negated by Quietism. Hope loves God *secundum quid*: for one's own sake as one's perfection and beatitude. Charity loves God *simpliciter*: for God's own sake regardless of what we get in return. Aquinas explicitly states that hope and charity as loves are related as imperfect to perfect. I fully agree with this, and reject any theology of hope which seeks to dethrone charity's primacy among the virtues. Nevertheless, imperfect goods are still *goods*. All things being equal, there is no reason why lesser goods should be discarded for not being the best. This especially holds true when the lesser good both disposes to reception of the greater and complements it when the greater has been received. Precisely this was suggested in the previous section in terms of the relation between hope and charity. But for those who think that anything less than *l'amour pur* is suspect, hope cannot even occupy this modest role. Hence the most telling critics of Quietism such as Bossuet focused less on its mystical vagaries and more on its subversion of hope.[139] In such theologies – historically marginal and yet recurrent – faith and charity abide, these two; but if I have hope I am a noisy gong or a clanging cymbal.

Timothy Jackson's Critique of Theological Hope

In a very different context, confessional background, and overall theology, somewhat related suspicions emerge in Timothy Jackson's *Love Disconsoled*. Though Jackson concedes the permissibility of a vague and uncertain hope for future beatitude, he insists that it is not permissible to believe in or assign it any importance. 'Love's priority', according to Jackson, 'implies the moral irrelevance of an afterlife'.[140] He rejects any hope that believes in and seeks future beatitude because it corrupts the motives of charity and because it 'tempts us to hate life or love death'.[141] Jackson gives a place to self-love in his ethics, so this is not Quietism.[142] But there is a family resemblance between the Quietist *l'amour pur* which finds hope a pollutant and the Jacksonian 'purity of motive' assigned to charity relative to which theological hope is a threat.

Arguments similar to Jackson's occur in Christian history at infrequent intervals, but he makes by far the best case for them in the contemporary literature. As a Christian theologian, Jackson is not a 'cultured despiser' whose critique of hope is meant to discredit Christianity. He is someone who knows and loves the faith from the inside (even playing the role of Christian apologist in a debate with Christopher Hitchens). Jackson is also a prominent ethical thinker who deserves Jeffrey Stout's accolade for plumbing the 'ethical significance' of Christian claims with 'a degree of eloquence and insight uncommon in recent Christian ethical writing'.[143] His case for the prosecution is the most sophisticated and sustained attempt for centuries to debunk theological hope on Christian grounds, and this makes him an important part of the *status questionis*.

Jackson is a former and devoted student of both Paul Ramsey and Richard Rorty. They represent the two poles or tensions in his thinking: on one hand, a Christian *agape* which makes charity bedrock; on the other, a postmodern *askesis* which unmasks false consolations. As it happens, Jackson thinks these can be admirably reconciled: that the love whose type is Ramsey should be disconsoled by the *askesis* whose type is Rorty.[144] The 'false consolations' of Boethian invulnerability and Pauline immortality cloud the nature of *agape* and therefore should go. This is done with a pragmatism which Rorty thought unmasked Christian love as false and cruel, but which Jackson thinks unwittingly helps to clarify *agape*.[145] The idea is that Rortian and pragmatic critiques cut deep enough to expose consolation as a wish-fulfilment fantasy while failing to damage *agape* itself. Christian charity thus both survives and indirectly benefits from this *askesis* through having the blemish of consolation removed.

Rortian scepticism is in turn chastened with a Christian moral realism and agapism which Jackson thinks acknowledge fallibility and vulnerability just as well as postmodernism while having better resources than Rortian irony for keeping solidarity alive.[146] His test case is the *kenosis* and Passion of Christ which expose false consolations while nevertheless showing that the commitment to charity is intrinsically worthwhile.[147] What Christians require is a 'strong *agape*' committed to Christ's command to 'love one another as I have loved you'. Jackson thinks that God is perfectly loving, that *agape* is its own reward, and that Christians may lead the good and happy life in this world. Nevertheless, the disconsoling *askesis* reveals that we need a 'strong' *agape* able to carry on in the knowledge that tragedy and injustice will not be rectified by heavenly consolations. Contrary to Julian of Norwich, all manner of things shall (very possibly) not be well. Though the last word in our lives and world may be tragic rather than comic, Jackson tells us to refuse both pessimism and despair, on one hand, and the opiate of consolation, on the other. Once again looking to Christ's Passion as the exemplar, Jackson instead commends a 'willingness to stick it out apagically even to the edge of doom'.[148] Here as elsewhere, Jackson's rhetoric suggests the image of strong *agape* in a heroic last stand against meaninglessness, nihilism, and tragedy.

According to Jackson, one of the addictive false consolations is the belief in personal immortality. 'Love of neighbour in time and for her own sake, calls on us to uncouple Christian charity from several notions to which it is traditionally attached: for instance, immortality as heavenly reward'.[149] Rorty, Sklar, Nussbaum, and others have convinced Jackson that both philosophy and theology are too consolatory. Appeals to immortality and future restoration may look consoling, but the suspicion is that they unwittingly function as a 'poisonous opiate' that plays down the degradation of victims and deadens us to the work of *agape*.[150] Jackson believes that Rorty, Nussbaum, and others have buried moral consolations among the philosophers, and that he is called to bury spiritual consolations among the theologians: to cast out the remaining 'Job's Comforters'. His disconsoling *askesis* is used to unmask a variety of false consolations, but most relevant here is his 'denial of the necessary immortality of love'.[151]

In language that recalls the Quietist search for a *l'amour pur*, Jackson states that a main reason for rejecting belief in the afterlife is 'a threat to purity of motive'.[152] Jackson's concern is that *agape* will be polluted by the motive of a heavenly bribe, reducing the strong *agape* he wants into a kind of spiritual commercialism where eternal bliss is up for sale and can be bought through acting charitably in this world. So while eternal beatitude is not strictly impossible as a gracious, unmerited, and unforeseen gift of God, Jackson thinks that in practice the consideration of heaven tends to spoil charity with mercantile motives.[153]

Representing all dangers of belief in heaven and the superfluity of it to charity is a single sermon by C. S. Lewis. Jackson makes Lewis the spokesman for traditional Christian hope, seeks to discredit him, and then behaves as if centuries of Christian tradition concerning hope have thereby been discredited. The following is the crucial claim of Lewis:

> We must not be troubled by unbelievers when they say that this promise of reward [heaven] makes the Christian life a mercenary affair. There are different kinds of reward. There is the reward which has no *natural connexion* with the things you do to earn it, and is quite foreign to the desires that ought to accompany those things. Money is not the natural reward of love; that is why we call a man mercenary if he marries a woman for the sake of her money. But marriage is the proper reward for a real lover, and he is not mercenary for desiring it. A general who fights well in order to get a peerage is mercenary; a general who fights for victory is not, victory being the proper reward of battle as marriage is the proper reward of love. The proper rewards are not simply tacked on to the activity for which they are given, but are the activity itself in consummation.... The Christian, in relation to heaven, is in much the same position.... Those who have attained everlasting life in the vision of God doubtless know very well that it is no mere bribe, but the very consummation of their earthly discipleship.[154]

This is a clear denial of Jackson's claim that the proper motive of heaven is external to charity, and therefore that charity's 'purity of motive' is besieged by hope. On Lewis' view, the end of heaven is internal to charity precisely because heavenly beatitude, properly understood, is the perfect communion with the God whom charity loves. This claim strikes me as sensible, and Aquinas says much the same thing, arguing that hope informed by charity seeks perfect beatitude through union with the divine friend.[155] Since communion with the friend is the proper or internal reward of friendship, there is no reason to depict heaven as an external or mercenary reward that pollutes charity.[156] Jackson counters that 'it is unclear that endless life is such an inherent "consummation" of Christian discipleship – what I have called "putting charity first" – that its absence would undermine the meaning of that discipleship'.[157] But the question Jackson has set up is not whether absence of theological hope undermines charitable discipleship, but whether it smuggles an impure motive into it. Lewis gives an argument for why it does not, and Jackson replies by changing the subject. Even if Lewis' sermon did demonstrate the evils Jackson fears, what would that prove beyond the fact that this one sermon contained errors? How would any broader criticism against theological hope have been made unless Jackson demonstrated that these errors were characteristic of hope in the Christian tradition over the centuries? But the spadework for such a vast genealogy is not even begun.

While Jackson is certain that hope is mercenary, he never pauses to consider what hope seeks. Denunciation of hope requires him to characterise its motives somehow or other, and he ends up talking as if the main goal of hope is immortality in the abstract. The desire for heavenly consolation, according to Jackson, is essentially the itch for 'endless life' and 'literal deathlessness'. But traditional hope does not seek 'literal deathlessness' as such. It seeks the perfect and irrevocable consummation of a loving relationship with God where there is perfect unity of motive, mutual benevolence, and everlasting enjoyment of the lovers in each other: for 'now we see in a mirror dimly, but then face to face. Now I know in part; then I shall understand fully, even as I have been fully understood' (1 Cor 13:12–13).[158] To depict motivated hope towards this end as nothing more than spiritual survivalism bribing its way into an impersonal immortality is to distort the rich, interpersonal character of Christian eschatology and theological hope. Yet this is what Jackson repeatedly does.[159] The result is that hope as a 'theological' virtue which aspires to God (*theos*) is never examined and never appears.

Influenced by the Rortian notion that false consolations are the midwives of cruelty, Jackson argues that hope undermines vulnerability and therefore makes cruelty more likely. He states that the greater 'the moral role played by immortality-as-endless-life, the harder it is to acknowledge human vulnerability; and the less we admit vulnerability, the easier it is to be cruel'.[160] The will-to-*agape* with its mission to end cruelty is thus at odds with theological hope, cruelty's implied accomplice. Jackson follows up by saying that: 'The risk of false comfort, as Rorty and Sklar point out, is a tendency to cruelty.... So, in quasi-Rortian fashion, charity tends to change the subject when the topic of heaven arises'.[161]

Jackson does not say what cruelty he envisions, let alone give evidence for hope's production of it. But the accusation is incongruent even granted his own premises. Jackson portrays hope as tainted by the effort to buy heaven through acts of charity.[162] Clearly it would be suicidal to practise cruelty on these terms. The hopeful as Jackson depicts them would see cruelty as the thing most to be feared, and beneficence as their ladder to paradise. This may be a reductive view of charity, but obviously it leaves no room for cruelty and loudly demands the opposite. Jackson's critique of hope contradicts itself. If he is right about the motives of the hopeful, he is wrong about the cruel tendencies of hope, and vice versa.

Jackson is not a Sadducee. He insists that heaven is unnecessary, but not impossible. Charity in this life suffices, but: 'all things being equal, we would prefer a lasting communion with those we care for'.[163] The result is that we may vaguely hope for an afterlife without believing in one, since 'love's willing the good for others insures only the present plenitude of the self'.[164] Theological hope is therefore replaced with agnostic hope conceived of as a vague wish. But Jackson forbids this thin hope to believe that its object exists. Moreover, he does not allow agnostic hope to have any action-motivating or action-guiding role in our lives: 'Love's priority implies the moral irrelevance of an afterlife'.[165] Agnostic hope is therefore not a virtue at all, even considered on its own terms.[166] Indeed, Jackson regards 'any virtue' as 'dubious' if it is unable to 'accept the finality of death'.[167] There is even a depressing hint that the goods of the afterlife, if they do exist, may perhaps be irredeemably lost through 'self-consciously grabbing at them'.[168] Having no place in virtue, action, or the moral life, theological hope emerges not as a shrunken virtue, but as a dangerous vice.

So in the end what is the place of agnostic hope? It is not a virtue, it does not affect deliberation, and it is no way action-motivating or action-guiding. Jackson answers that hope in the afterlife is permissible as a vague 'wish' or *utinam*. As such it overlaps with what Elizabeth Anscombe in *Intention* calls the 'idle wish', writing that 'a chief mark of an idle wish is that a man does nothing – whether he could or no – towards the fulfilment of the wish'.[169] Anscombe would agree with Jackson that his agnostic hope conceived as an idle wish is 'morally irrelevant'. But then we are right to ask whether Jackson has done justice to hope in any biblical or Christian sense by making its role so trifling.

The role of hope in salvation history is certainly not modest. From beginning to end, the Old Testament is saturated in divine hope. 'Hoping against hope' (Rom 4:18), Abraham founds the Chosen People and becomes their paradigm of piety. Amid slavery in Egypt and the Babylonian captivity, Israel is sustained by a hope in God's deliverance that refuses to quit. The Book of Psalms, the great prayer book of Judaism and Christianity, is one of the greatest utterances of hope ever made. The psalter voices unshakeable confidence in God, pictured throughout in hope-specific metaphors – as a refuge or fortress to shield us, or an eagle that will lift us up – all this despite injustices, deportation, and tragedy. 'Yea, though I walk through the valley of the shadow of death, I will fear no evil: for thou art with me; thy rod and thy staff they comfort me' (Ps 23:4, KJV). Such words cannot be understood, let alone prayed, once hope is subtracted from faith. A spirituality of disconsolation, far from being their end, is precisely the problem they set out to cure. The ardent messianic hopes of the Minor Prophets and of Christ's contemporaries emerge from and heighten these sensibilities.

The New Testament gives an even larger place to hope, and based on the Resurrection makes it quality triumphal. Christ hung on the cross, and we too will suffer: *but the tomb is empty*. The victory that is the 'assurance' (Acts 17:31) of final victory has been won, and this is a unique bulwark for our hope and discipleship amid life's trials. Hence the Letter to the Hebrews describes hope as 'the sure and steadfast anchor of the soul' (Heb 6:19) and 1 Thessalonians speaks of the Christian persevering in part through donning 'for a helmet the hope of salvation' (1 Thess 5:8).[170] Plainly there is no pretending that Jackson's faint and uncertain hope is the lawful heir or successor concept to this tradition of hope. No one, for instance, would be justified in calling Jackson's agnostic hope a 'sure and steadfast anchor of the soul', or be well advised to put it on as a 'helmet' for salvation. Jackson himself insists that his form of hope is 'morally irrelevant'. By any reasonable standard this fails to do justice to biblical and Christian hope as a moral category that helped fuel centuries of religious practice and kept the Chosen People going despite the crushing blows of history.

Based on salvation history and the Resurrection, Christianity prized a hope that was far more than a faint and muted *utinam*. Jackson is well aware of the possible counterexample the Resurrection poses to his overall theology. He puts the central question well: 'is not the empty tomb a central and ineliminable consolation'?[171] The Resurrection is the *crux experimentum* which would show that Christianity ends not in *disconsolation*, but in *reconsolation*. Jackson himself seems to doubt whether Christ historically rose from the grave, but 'Christ's own example on the cross suggests the possibility of obedience in the midst of doubt'.[172] As he admits, this makes his position 'admittedly more Joblike than Pauline'.[173] He does not deny that the Resurrection happened, though he rehearses the Bultmannian theory of 'the welling up of the Easter spirit' among the disciples whose Lord is bodily rotting.[174] But whether the tomb was empty or not is theologically irrelevant for Jackson. Why is this? He rightly insists that the cross exhibits the fullness of self-giving, self-sacrificing *agape*. With everything needed to teach and effect 'strong *agape*' in place as of the crucifixion, what place could the Resurrection have? Only the distracting one of undermining vulnerability and making us think about the afterlife again. Viewed from Jacksons' canon within the canon of strong *agape*, this would only invite backsliding, and so the topic of the Resurrection must simply be elbowed aside.[175]

Non-belief in the Resurrection pulls Jackson's theology in a sombre direction. For him, 'the best of biblical piety' is summed up by Abraham on Mount Moriah and by Job in the slough of despond.[176] This strain of piety reaches its agapic climax on Golgotha, and then it has nowhere left to go. 'Love on the cross' is the pioneer who has now crossed the last frontier. Jackson's theology therefore effectively *stops* on Good Friday; Easter Sunday holds no new triumphs for it. The 'disconsolation' of the cross is not succeeded by the 'reconsolation' of the empty tomb, but by agnostic silence.

A cynical critic might interpret this evading of the Resurrection as a lack of faith, as though Jackson were on the path 'that led an earlier generation by stages from Latitudinarian theology, to Deism, to Hume, to Holbach'.[177] Such a view would do injustice to Jackson. Nothing shows him to be gripped by the sceptical worries of someone whose faith is gradually being hollowed out by secularism. Jackson fully affirms the doctrines of creation, divine providence, and the Incarnation, and he claims that God *could* grant us an afterlife if this were spiritually necessary.[178] In this he differs from Philippa Foot and Rosalind Hursthouse, who affirmed the desirability of Christian hope, but not its possibility given their naturalistic limits. Since Jackson affirms Providence, his position is quite different: he believes in a God with the power, if not the will, to make 'these bones live' (Ezek 37:3).[179] The only reasons Jackson gives for actively doubting Christ's Resurrection or ours are entirely moral, and have to do with preserving *agape* from pollutants such as hope. But Jackson has failed to show that theological hope renders us mercenary, that it denigrates the world, or that it makes us morally apathetic or cruel to our neighbours. Moreover, his own agnostic hope fails to do justice to the robust place given to hope in the biblical and Christian tradition. Jackson has therefore given the churches no compelling reason to take an eraser to parts of the Apostles' and Nicene Creeds. The profession 'I believe in the resurrection of the dead, and the life of the world to come' has not been unmasked as a Job's Comforter.

Hope's Contribution to Charity

Jackson puts hope in the dock and *agape* in the judge's seat pronouncing a verdict of guilty. I have tried to prove hope's innocence, so to speak, and therefore have focused on the harm it does not do to charity rather than the good it might do. But the whole image of antagonism between these theological virtues should be overcome. Though I believe with Aquinas that charity is the form of the virtues and the greatest of virtues, I also believe that hope benefits charity itself and gives it a larger field of operation. This is important to the topic of hope's relation to charity that Jackson raises. Like Aquinas and the traditional generally, Jackson believes that *apape* is characterised by willing the good of the beloved.[180] Hope can contribute to this in concrete ways. An example would be that when I look at my wife, child, or neighbour, I do not see someone bound for Sheol or for annihilation, but for glory. I do not see them merely through the prism of Mount Moriah, the despond of Job, or even Christ's Passion abstracted from the Resurrection. Chastened by the costly reminder of the cross, I nevertheless see them through the eyes of Easter morning. I would will their good in any case, but the presence or absence of hope alters the kind and degree of good I may will for them. Through the mediation of charity one may hope, pray, and labour for the eternal good of the beloved: hope that they shall see God face to face and enjoy perfect and irrevocable happiness in God's presence forever.[181] This is an expression of charity which hope alone makes possible.

Hope therefore allows us to believe that greater good can be done to the beloved than would otherwise be the case. All of our lives are undeveloped to some point, and our share in supernatural happiness in this life is imperfect. Every one of us, I have argued, is on the wrong side of the eudaimonia gap by a long way. But consider those whose lives are radically undeveloped, maimed, or ruined, and who for various reasons do not have a realistic chance of being appreciably mended in this world. They are either descending on a eudaimonia arc, or they never really ascended it in the first place. From the perspective of happiness, they are more and more has-beens or tragic might-have-beens. Without hope, charity can only will them goods of virtuous activity, accomplishments, freedom, health, and overall happiness that it is impossible for them to receive. By contrast, hope believes that their story does not end where the eudaimonia gap leaves it: that God 'will wipe away every tear from their eyes ... neither shall there be mourning nor crying nor pain any more, for the former things have passed away' (Rev 21:4).[182] Charity would not be hamstrung without this hope. Most of the good we will and do for others on a daily basis we could still do. Yet this contribution of hope to charity is a real addition rather than a threat. In the fourth chapter, on presumption, I explain why virtuous hope for our neighbour's eschatological good also sternly dissuades from indifference to our neighbour's earthly lot.

Jackson argues that hope as a false consolation has 'a tendency to cruelty'.[183] But how does this claim fare when we consider how the consolation of hope is usually given? The hour when such comfort is most sought and most given is the deathbed, the funeral service, the cemetery, and the period of mourning. Suppose a mother and father standing beside the coffin of their dead child, or the child at the coffin of a dead parent. The pastor or loved one who comforts them with the promise of the Resurrection is not engaging in a practice with a 'tendency to cruelty'. To suggest so would be a bizarre mockery.

To an extent, the bereaved understandably grieve for their own loss, but they may rightly grieve that further and genuine goods they will the deceased now seem impossibly out of reach for them. The parents mourn the development, accomplishments, happiness, possible marriage, and children that their son or daughter will never have. The child mourns the healing, reconciliation, and development their parent is now debarred from. The good which charity wills, mortality foils. Hope not only consoles the bereaved with the possibility of reunion; it consoles them *as* charitable with the prospect of still willing the beloved good (not the same goods, but still *good*).

In grave suffering or at a deathbed, the good which *agape* wishes the beloved the strong agapist cannot affirm as a credible option for them. The consequence is that the presence or absence of hope alters the expression of charity itself. Unlike hope-filled charity, strong *agape* ends in the territory of melancholy resignation. The fifth chapter of Jackson's *Love Disconsoled* is perhaps the central one in the book, and the quotations that mark its beginning strike the representative note. From *The Iliad* Jackson quotes: 'There is nothing alive more agonized than man of all that breathe and crawl across the earth'. And from the Book of Job: 'Human beings are born to trouble just as sparks fly upward'.[184] Jackson's chosen exemplars of the moral and spiritual life are Job in his dark night, Kierkegaard's Abraham on Moriah, and Christ emptying himself as a slave and as the Suffering Servant crying out: *'Eloi, Eloi, lema sabachthani?'*[185] Despite living before Christ, Job and Abraham are Jackson's success stories of love disconsoled: those who chastened the mercy and reconciliation of *agape* with the *askesis* of disconsolation.[186] 'The greater the love', Jackson frankly states, 'the more it will be disconsoled and disconsoling, yet without despairing of the works of love in caring for others'.[187] His theology is a very accurate test case of what happens to charity when deprived of hope, and it invites comparison with Dodds' phrase: 'God's in his Heaven, all's wrong with the world'.[188] Like Kierkegaard's knight of infinite resignation, the strong agapist keeps going even while outflanked by the eudaimonia gap. Strong *agape*, which is hopeless *agape*, is not precisely Stoic. But as Jackson himself admits, his kind of *agape* invites Stoic comparisons.[189]

The good of perfect happiness which charity rightly wills the beloved, which is gravely absent in many and fully present in none, is a good which hope proposes as possible. As such, hope gives greater scope to charity by letting us believe that the full, lasting, and complete happiness we want for the beloved can be attained by them, and therefore is something we may pray for and will to them in earnest rather than just idly wishing they could have in some counterfactual state that can never be. Obviously this is not an excuse to avoid willing them such good as is possible now. It is the opportunity not to *stop* willing them good insofar as mortality and the gap limit them. It is to say that the eudaimonia gap does not transcend charity, but is ultimately transcended by it.

Hope also empowers charity in terms of our relationship with God. Jackson admits that we would like for our loving relationship with God to continue after death, even if we cannot affirm this.[190] Hope makes it possible to believe that charity can attain full fruition and achieve perfect and unimpeded communion with the beloved. This helps resolve a pressing problem – namely, how do you avoid demoralisation if you affirm a God of perfect love who for no fault of your own probably plans your imminent annihilation? This dismal thought is baggage which strong *agape* must shoulder. Jackson believes in God's immediate providence over human beings as a corollary of creation *ex nihilo*.[191] It follows that if I die and there is no afterlife, I cease to exist, and my ceasing to exist is not something God simply watches, but something in which God as my creator is involved.

If I cease to exist, God withdraws the creative causality which holds me in being, and *therefore* I no longer am. For absolutely no reason – or none Jackson is willing to suggest – God would ontologically withdraw from me as a creature and literally annihilate me.[192] Surely from the perspective of a loving charity, this is a disturbing thought. Jackson takes aim at the theodicies of Robert Adams and John Hick, arguing that justice does not require God to confer immortality.[193] But even if we grant this, Jackson has already admitted that God has the power, if not the will, to keep me in existence. So why, granted the power, does the God who is love lack the will to refrain from destroying me? What is it about arbitrary and ultimate abandonment that *befits* a relationship of loving charity? Jackson is silent on these points, and here strong *agape* threatens to cancel itself out. On one hand, we are to abandon hope to make our charity freer and truer to itself. On the other, to do this, we must make God's charity darker, less intelligible, and more subject to doubt. As though they were in an odd competition, our *agape* puts on muscle to the extent God's *agape* threatens to atrophy.

Hope comes to the aid of charity here by promising that the divine friend is not planning my imminent annihilation, but wishes to continue, increase, and perfect our loving relationship in a covenant love that is unbroken by death. Jackson sees Job as an exemplar of disconsoled love, yet Job is not pleased to consider the loss of a loving relationship with God.

> Oh that you would hide me in Sheol, that you would conceal me until your wrath is past, that you would appoint me a set time, and remember me! If mortals die, will they live again? All the days of my service I would wait until my release should come. You would call, and I would answer you; you would long for the work of your hands.
>
> (Job 14:13–15)[194]

Hope allows this expression of love to believe that God will remember us and continue to call to us, not casting us away, but still 'longing for the work of your hands'. In terms of charity to both God and neighbour, theological hope is therefore not a parasite or deadweight, but something which makes a real contribution to Christian love itself.

CHAPTER 3

Rejoicing in Hope

For nothing in the present life is so firm that the soul could be secure and at rest; hence, it says in Genesis 8:8 that 'the dove found no place where her foot might rest'.

Thomas Aquinas, *Super Epistolam ad Hebraeos*

We have been born anew to a living hope through the resurrection of Jesus Christ from the dead, and to an inheritance which is imperishable, undefiled, and unfading, kept in heaven for you.... In this you rejoice.

1 Peter 1:3–6

Hope to joy is little less in joy
Than hope enjoyed. By this the weary lords
Shall make their way seem short.

Shakespeare, *Richard II*, Act II, Scene 3

In the previous chapter, I closed by arguing that hope provides legitimate consolation and that it cooperates with charity, so that Stoicising critiques of hope which take it for a Job's Comforter are mistaken. But while the comforts of hope are legitimate, they are not monolithic. The journey of hope is obviously fraught with hardships and has plenty of room for lament. At the same time, the hopeful life can put on festal robes, and is not just a matter of wearily running down the clock to the eschaton. The theological virtue of hope, I wish to demonstrate, has a liturgical rhythm of sorts: a 'feast day', triumphal, and jubilant side to complement its 'fast day', lament, and consoling side. Encouraged by Christ's Resurrection and the hope of beatitude whose first fruits appear even now, the Christian should habitually 'rejoice in hope' (Rom 12:12). That neglected practice and its moral importance is the topic of this chapter.

The Restless Heart and the *Desiderium* for Ideal Happiness

My earlier treatment of the eudaimonia gap mostly focused on problems that impede happiness. On top of this 'negative' side of the gap, I also noted a 'positive' side: one comprised not of ills that frustrate happiness, but of the desire for a fuller share in it. In that respect, the gap refers not to evils we do not want, but to a good we reasonably want more of. Theological hope validates and even encourages this desire, suggesting that it is not childish, vain, or absurd, but fully reasonable and in the dramatic sense 'comic' since God's generosity makes it capable of fulfilment. 'What no eye has seen, nor ear heard, nor the heart of man conceived, what God has prepared for those who love him', (1 Cor 2:9). This positive reading of the gap complements the negative reading and presents hope as attractive even to those who are not badly oppressed by impediments to happiness: to the overall virtuous and happy during ordinary and generally enjoyable periods of life. It is a second and more positive occasion for hope which is commonly experienced and which I will briefly sketch.

Drawing on the work of Michael Himes and C. S. Lewis, William Mattison III has given an admirable gloss on Augustine's theme of the 'restless heart'. Mattison suggests that we have a 'seemingly unquenchable desire' for the 'complete satisfaction of our longings'.[1] The restless heart is a staple theme of Christian tradition. But Mattison notes that the desire is extremely common even among nonbelievers; Jean Paul Sartre and Albert Camus are his favourite examples. Like Tennyson's Ulysses, each of us may say: 'I am become a name/ For always roaming with a hungry heart'. Mattison describes the 'seemingly unquenchable desire' this way:

> We always hunger for more, and never seem to be fully satisfied ... human persons never do sit back in this life and say, 'there is nothing more to do, or nothing further I could enjoy'... even those of us who live satisfying and rewarding lives would have to admit that our lives are not complete. We long to be closer to others, to work on important life projects, to continue to improve ourselves, to understand more.[2]

The value of this account is that it does not make the ongoing unexhausted desire for happiness rest on a childish malcontent with the happiness one does have. Of course, a 'restless heart' based on the inability to appreciate the good before you would be mere querulousness, like the greedy birthday child for whom no number of presents is enough. But the unexhausted aspiration that is of moral interest is not a dull insensitivity or lack of appreciation for the present good. It is a very qualified insatiety that is fully compatible with appreciation and gratitude for the happiness one does have while seeing possibilities for further and better personal and social goods that are important and not just whimsical.

This side of the eudaimonia gap may weigh on the virtuous and happy without implying overall disenchantment with the happy life they have. Mattison describes it as a certain 'lack of satisfaction, or ongoing restlessness, even in the presence of genuinely good things'.[3] The happy live well, but they do not 'just sit back' and stop aspiring. They still eat and drink, engage in relationships, leisure activities, and personal and social projects. Provided they are virtuous, these activities may be constituents in happiness, but the fact that more constituents are always sought suggests that a further and ongoing share in happiness is looked for. If we think of the constituents of happiness as being like bricks that build a house, we see that the house is never exactly finished: there is always more to do, more to pursue.

To put the point in Augustinian and Thomistic terms, we are never *perfectly* happy. We never attain what Aquinas describes as 'the perfect good, which satisfies appetite altogether'.[4] As noted earlier, Aquinas thought that desire for the perfect good was proper to the human condition – that it was a natural desire. Even if the moral psychology behind this it is doubted or denied, the aspiration is remarkably common, and a theologian writing about hope should have something to say about it or risk irrelevance to lived experience.

Mattison's claim is that even amid genuine happiness, there is a remainder of restlessness construed as disquiet. Augustinian language of the *cor inquietum* is loaded, suggesting pensiveness or dissatisfaction. But suppose we tweak the remainder of restlessness so that it does not necessarily refer to these, but to the ongoing openness or appetite for fuller and completer good. Dialectically, this would allow us to waive the controversial questions of whether the remainder of restlessness entails disquiet and whether it supervenes upon a 'natural desire' for a perfect happiness which 'satisfies appetite altogether'. I do not want to undermine those further claims, but they involve debates in moral psychology which would take us too far afield. All that must be taken from the 'restless heart' theme here is the more modest claim that even the virtuous and happy continue to desire and pursue an ideal of good they never fully exhaust and to that extent never fully attain. This unexhausted desire is crucial to how we experience the positive side of the eudaimonia gap.

The happy and virtuous do not stop wanting to know more, to understand things better, to improve more, to love better, to mend our world, to accomplish more, and so forth. The implication is that the good they have and may achieve is not as complete or ideal as they would like. Good agents quite properly have an ongoing desire to continually move towards this 'more' and 'better' and 'improved' position, to chase a fuller and more perfect good. Yet they never seem to have arrived completely and finally (even the dying have dying well left to accomplish), and so they do not just retire their intellectual and moral agency, but keep pursuing things and engaging in projects. This ongoing appetite for an ideal of happiness or completion that we never fully attain and never truly exhaust I will refer to semi-technically as the *desiderium* to help distinguish it from other desires and to avoid repetitious paraphrase. It is to this *desiderium* that hope positively speaks, since it implies that the 'more' and 'better' and 'improved' good we pursue is not an ideal ultimately beyond our grasp, but the very thing we were made to enjoy: what 'God has prepared for those who love him' (1 Cor 2:9).

Theological hope elevates and heals this desire in grace, playing the role of *gratia elevans* and *gratia sanans*. Given what hope promises, it alters the way we experience the *desiderium* in our lives. Since we are *in via* to the attainment of that ideal good *in patria*, the unexhausted desire for happiness rightly takes the form of joyful anticipation: what Scripture calls 'rejoicing in hope' (Rom 12:12). Crucially, I want to show that this does not entail undervaluing this life or world: that the desire for heaven is not *in competition* with our appreciation of earth.

Historically, a strong aspiration for an ideal good or even complete fulfilment is expressed in various ways in countless songs, romances, paintings, films, philosophies, religions, 'mystery traditions', and even political theories. The very difficulty of articulating this *desiderium* makes it elusive, and gifted poets generally take its portrait better than those limited to dryer technical vocabularies. Matthew Arnold is a good example of someone who affirms the desire for a fuller and perhaps perfect happiness entangled with the desire for ultimate meaning:

> But often, in the world's most crowded streets,
> But often, in the din of strife,
> There rises an unspeakable desire
> After the knowledge of our buried life;
> A thirst to spend our fire and restless force
> In tracking out our true, original course;
> A longing to inquire
> Into the mystery of this heart which beats
> So wild, so deep in us – to know
> Whence of lives come and where they go.[5]

Arnold affirms the *desiderium* while disbelieving it has a proportionate object. Brazening this out leads him to a 'wistful, soft tearful longing'.[6] In Arnold and in the English Romantic poets, the *desiderium* is experienced as though calling to us 'from an infinitely distant land' charged with the suggestion of beatitude. Just what might satisfy the *desiderium* and how is frequently left hazy, often because the poets have sought fulfilment in the *desideratum*, but the expected level of bliss proved elusive. Wordsworth's relationship to nature is perhaps the most famous example. Reflecting in later years on his youth, he wrote in *Tintern Abbey*:

> For nature then . . .
> To me was all in all. – I cannot paint
> What then I was. The sounding cataract
> Haunted me like a passion: the tall rock,
> The mountain, and the deep and gloomy wood,
> Their colours and their forms, were then to me
> An appetite: a feeling and a love,
> That had no need of a remoter charm,
> By thought supplied, or any interest
> Unborrowed from the eye. – That time is past.[7]

Such poetry helps to articulate the kind of longing which many people have felt, for similar or different objects, and which invites phrases like 'To me was all in all' or 'Haunted me like a passion'. Poetry like this enriches our sense of just how happy someone can conceive of being while recording, importantly, that the object of longing and the longing itself have an elusive relationship. Both phenomena are deeply relevant to hope.

So that the *desiderium* does not sound vague, I will glance at a few examples of how it plays out in widespread and recognisable forms of obvious personal, social, and moral importance. Perhaps the most popular target for the *desiderium* from the medieval rise of courtly love to Hollywood films today is an exalted ideal of romantic love. 'If at that moment I had been questioned of anything whatsoever, I should have answered simply *Love*, with a countenance clothed in humility'.[8] These are Dante's words after getting his first coveted greeting from Beatrice, but countless people who fall in love treat it with the same quasi-mystical fervour, believing the *desiderium* has found its proportionate object in the romantic beloved.[9] Others envision a future Utopia as a state that will either confer perfect collective happiness or at least a supreme degree of happiness impossible to us now. In contrast to the Yahoos who represent humanity construed as disgusting, stupid, and uncivilised, Swift in *Gulliver's Travels* describes the noble Houyhnhnms whose life is one of sober occupations and 'sweet reasonableness'. H. G. Well pictures a future utopia of flawless hygiene, perfect health, refined hedonism, and scientific curiosity.[10] Some project the desire for complete happiness backward, and imagine that a proportionate object must have existed in the past. Nostalgia is the flip-side of Utopia: the feeling that the golden age has passed, whether it is the Garden of Eden, the Elysian Fields, a preferred century, one's own childhood, or 'the Age of Innocence'. One especially popular form of this nostalgia since the late eighteenth century has been a bucolic vision of the unspoiled rural village or local community enjoying something like premodern *Sittlichkeit*.[11]

Many writers within the fantasy genre express essentially the same vision with an invented world. A variation of the projected *desiderium* is the common if implicit belief that one can get temporary hold of Arcady in some favoured hour or season such as a wedding, a honeymoon, or a holiday. The most common candidate is perhaps Christmas depicted as 'the most wonderful time of the year': one that is or at least should be a momentary paradise and ceasefire with the eudaimonia gap. Hence the increased misery and exaggerated disappointments of those for whom the 'magic' fails. The shared feature in all these projections is an imaginary, proposed, momentary, or past setting in which it is thought that the *desiderium* for an ideal good could or should find its proper object, fully or at least to an enormous degree. The heart will not be restless if only it can rest *there*.

Importantly, the basic impulse behind the *desiderium* not only finds romantic and escapist outlets, but takes shape in politics and activism. The ideal might not be imaginary but practical and fuel serious proposals for moving towards a real rather than counterfactual utopia. Consider the wild euphoria with which many greeted the French Revolution before the Reign of Terror. In Wordsworth's poem, 'French Revolution', he contemplates the imminent overthrow of 'meagre, stale, forbidding ways/ Of custom, law, and statute'. Believing like many that he is witnessing the earthly dawn of *Liberté, Egalité, Fraternité*, he gushes:

> Bliss was it in that dawn to be alive ...
> When Reason seemed the most to assert her rights,
> When most intent on making of herself
> A prime Enchantress – to assist the work,
> Which then was going forward in her name!
> Not favoured spots alone, but the whole earth,
> The beauty wore of promise
> What temper at the prospect did not wake
> To happiness unthought of? The inert
> Were roused, and lively natures rapt away![12]

(This is, of course, early Wordsworth; he later famously changed his tune.)[13]

Similarly if less lyrically, countless communists and socialists have seriously envisioned and worked to bring about their ideal of perfect human brotherhood and material happiness.[14] The 2008 American presidential campaign aroused similar euphoric hopes in many people: the tears and raptures, the hymn-like chanting of 'Hope' and 'Yes, we can!' showed that the *desiderium* had been roused in many and was tinged by much utopian and even, at times, some messianic sentiment. Plainly the *desiderium* for an ideal good at which 'The inert' are roused 'and lively natures rapt away' is not just fodder for science fiction, nostalgia, romanticism, and fantasy. It takes political and social forms through rallying cries and proposals for a just society, local or global. Many forms of environmentalism vary the theme through a vision for ecology.[15]

The point of such examples is to show that the *desiderium* is not a scholastic abstraction, but a living, widespread, and recognisable reality that takes context-specific forms. For present purposes, what matters is not so much *what* has been imagined or proposed as a supreme good, but *that* there is recurrent appetite for such proposals at all.

The Normative Status of the *Desiderium*

The lofty hopes which the *desiderium* kindles make it alluring but dangerous. It often spurs the idolatry by which agents make a finite good their ultimate end. So much is obvious, but there is another danger which usually goes unremarked. Ardent aspirations can end in burnout and give way to the disillusionment and cynicism that feed sloth and despair. 'These violent delights have violent ends/ And in their triumph die'.[16] As bloated hopes, youthful dreams, and grandiose aspirations either wither or are gratified but fail to deliver the expected degree or duration of beatitude, a mounting sense of disappointment often leaves agents hard-bitten. When this happens, subsequent offers of a supposedly ideal good may look like snake oil, making it seem prudent to see through the new con at the risk of being taken in once again.

Since theological hope promises perfect beatitude, the disillusioned will tend to cynically reject it as the biggest fraud of all. They become like the art critic who saw so many dull paintings of rivers under the moonlight that when he saw a real river under the moonlight he scorned it as 'conventional'. Cynicism of this sort is facile optimism or naïve hopefulness stood on its head. So idolatry is not the only danger posed by the *desiderium*.

Many idolaters become disgusted with their false gods, but do not know where else to go, and like any number of Graham Greene characters, they sink into inertia and despair.[17] As this suggests, the *desiderium* often fuels monomaniac hopes, and must be dealt with cautiously. Aquinas rightly notes that 'both children and drunkards are strong in hope'.[18] The danger being identified is that childish and drunken hopes may result in hope's equivalent of a hangover: pervasive disenchantment. The *desiderium* must therefore be chastened with a reasonable ascesis and not be uncritically endorsed, or bad habits of hope could inoculate the agent against good habits of hope.

Nevertheless, the proper response of theological hope is not to cynically debunk the *desiderium* as such even when it is drunken or astray. Immense longings, dreams, and aspirations may flow into adolescent or idolatrous outlets, but they may also lead to great reform movements or heroism, being the raw materials for magnanimity. By contrast, setting one's sights low may rule out the embarrassment of adolescent excess, but the effort to be mediocre may be punished by its own success: one which Aristotle describes as the life of pusillanimity.[19] An alarming number of people do ignore the common good, neglect self-improvement, and devote the majority of their leisure to a dreary flickering of the mind over endless cable television, video games, and social media. Part of our ethical job, I take it, is to encourage greater aspirations rather than to make it seem mature and urbane to settle for almost nothing.

The longing for an ideal good can produce mixed results, but the solution is not to anaesthetise the desire, but to hold it up to the light: to recall the *desiderium* to people's attention when it lies beneath a hard shell of boredom, cynicism, or disenchantment; to validate the appetite itself while reserving judgment about what it has fed on in the past; and to chasten and direct it to its proper object in God as the source of perfect beatitude.

As this account suggests, the *desiderium* is marred by sin. But hope's response is 'a bruised reed he will not break, and a smouldering wick he will not quench' (Is 42:3). For the Christian, the *desiderium* is not ultimately a 'melancholy' one doomed to frustration, as it is for Sartre, Camus, Arnold, and countless others. Lewis sees the *desiderium* providentially as a kind of intimation or signpost pointing us to a transcendent object. On his telling, the great joys that excite the desire awaken the longing for heaven, even if we do not know this or cannot describe matters this way. This makes such experiences 'the scent of a flower we have not found, the echo of a tune we have not heard, news from a country we have never visited'.[20]

Theological hope supernaturally elevates the *desiderium* to the end of friendship with God, and therefore helps to clarify the desire itself. In contrast to muddled aspirations and general wanderlust, hope specifies a proportionate object for the desire. The consequence is that one gains a life-changing sense of direction. One is no longer *homo erro*: the human wanderer who does not know whether or where the ideal good can be found. One is *homo viator*: the human wayfarer encouraged by the knowledge that the ideal good can be found, who knows where it lies, and who is sustained by the resolution to make the journey and the encouraging belief that one is 'on the way' (*in via*).

Of course, someone who lacks theological hope is not necessarily miserable or vicious. I am not advocating a radical Augustinian approach, and I agree with Aquinas that natural *eudaimonia* is true, rich, and admirable, if limited. I believe that a good but flawed life can be carved out in the eudaimonia gap. But even if such a happy life is available – say, roughly on Aristotle's terms – it faces serious problems of its own, and theologically speaking it is not *all* we may hope for.

It may serve to recall Aristotle's own attitude to what I have called the eudaimonia gap: 'We must not follow those who advise us, being men, to think of human things, and being mortal, of mortal things, but we must, so far as we can, immortalize, and strain every nerve to live in accordance with the best thing in us'.[21] This lofty aspiration could serve as the motto of magnanimity, and that particular virtue is certainly the best tutor of the *desiderium* at the natural level. But, as I argued earlier, Aristotle's view leads to a certain resignation because the Aristotelian agent *qua* rational can envision a superlative degree of *eudaimonia* he or she *qua* mortal cannot fully attain and enjoy. 'We are happy, but only as men', he says wistfully.[22] Yet this is a passing concession, not a nervous collapse. Aristotle lacks angst, focusing on the *eudaimonia* within reach rather than grousing about the loftier kind we can conceive of but not attain. The Christian may meet Aristotle here halfway, acknowledging the richness of natural *eudaimonia* and avoiding the scorched-earth rhetorical strategy which holds that either your heart rests in the Triune God or you are a complete wreck. Just because the pagan cup does not run over does not mean it is entirely empty. Yet the gap in *eudaimonia* remains, and I argued in the first chapter that this is an acute problem.

Granted such points, hope changes the stakes for happiness. To the nonbeliever, hope suggests that happiness is no longer a matter of 'so far as we can', but 'so far as we could want': proposing that God as the divine friend and perfect good will completely satisfy the *desiderium* as its proportionate object. To the idolatrous who think to find total completion through falling in love, finding the perfect career, traveling the world, building utopia, or whatever it may be, hope chastens without demoralising. The desire for ideal good which these finite goods aroused need not be killed, but converted (which obviously may involve pains of its own). As Augustine says: 'Seek what you seek, but it is not where you seek it'.[23] Moreover, if the desire for perfect happiness has God as its object, then the lack of total satisfaction that is our earthly lot can itself be seen as a gift. Rather than proving that the *desiderium* is vain, the inability of the desire to find a proportionate finite object reminds us of where it will *not* be found. In this respect, theological hope provides an error theory for diagnosing much of what is wrong about idolatry, misguided nostalgia, and utopianism.

If matters ended there, hope might lead us to reject all earthly goods and worldly endeavours as nothing but harp-strumming by the waters of Babylon. Many of Christianity's 'cultured despisers' would salute this view, since it is part of their polemic to unmask hope as a self-deceiving hatred of life. Rousseau claims that the 'pure and simple religion of the Gospel' presents life as a 'valley of sorrows' to be wearily endured while awaiting death and heaven. And St. Paul frankly admits that those whom God has called are disproportionately poor, uneducated, and lacking in worldly success (1 Cor 1: 26–27). Rousseau fastens onto this point to twist his knife: 'True Christians are made to be slaves, and they know it and do not much mind: this short life counts for so little in their eyes'.[24] This stock polemic has an ancient pedigree. The familiar tale, tweaked and varied by Celsus, Voltaire, Gibbon, Hume, Nietzsche, Russell, and others, generally proceeds in this way. Christians are fixated on heaven because the world has not been kind to them. Having missed out on happiness here, they console themselves with the wish-fulfilment fantasy of the hereafter, and avenge themselves on the happy, healthy, and fortunate by declaring their worldly joys bankrupt. Instead of having to admit that they are failures, hope licenses Christians to convert their wretchedness into a moral trophy and promissory note of heaven while indulging the sweets of resentment towards the 'worldly' – that is, towards everybody else – by passive aggressive moralising and hints of divine punishment. The world-renouncing hope of Christians turns out to be nothing more than a case of cosmic sour grapes.

This polemic is itself a wish-fulfilment fantasy of what the pagan adversary wants Christianity to be, the better to dispatch it. In the fifth chapter, I will discuss the fact that hope acknowledges tragedy and tries to deal with it as arduous rather than just dispensing religious analgesics. But while most people who know the faith know this polemic for a caricature, some may suspect that there is a real point here which has been grossly stretched. Any theology of hope which props up a severe *contemptus mundi* reinforces the thrust of this polemic, and I will return to that topic in the final chapters. Fears that the hope debunkers have something of a point also help account for the neglect of hope by Christian ethicists who dread the jeer of 'pie in the sky'. What must be established is how the hopeful should regard created goods and earthly projects granted that they have in some sense redirected the *desiderium* from those objects and towards God as supernatural end. If we are not to be idolaters, must we be iconoclasts?

Aquinas indirectly addresses this point by noting that Scripture often depicts eternal beatitude 'by means of various goods known to us'.[25] The New Testament describes entry into eternal life in various images: as inheriting the kingdom, being with Jesus in paradise, eating the fruit of the tree of life, being given the morning star, entering into perfect rest and joy, being admitted into the heavenly city, going to a wedding feast, and so forth.[26] Rather than cooling off the *desiderium*, such images are meant to inflame it. Specifically, they are meant to evoke the desire for the heavenly kingdom by comparing it to created goods we know while stretching the concept of those goods to suggest a vaster fruition than we have ever met with. The propriety of these as icons of beatitude presupposes the goodness of the created things that are used as materials for building the icons. Otherwise, the image of heaven as a wedding feast, say, would be morally convertible with the image of heaven as a drunken orgy or something else unfitting.

Still more importantly, a certain analogy is presupposed between the created goods invoked in the imagery and the eternal enjoyment of God. For Aquinas, this follows from the analogous language used for predications of God. Making sense of Scriptural statements such as 'God is good' or 'God is wise', he writes: 'when we say, "God is good," the meaning is not, "God is the cause of goodness," or "God is not evil"; but the meaning is, "Whatever good we attribute to creatures, pre-exists in God," and in a more excellent and higher way'.[27]

The point is that absent some analogy between created and divine good, it would be meaningless to say 'God is good' or 'wise' or 'loving' or 'righteous', and so forth. Saying this just means 'God is the cause of' gets embarrassing quickly. God is the cause of cockroaches and of the dull-witted. Yet we would not say, 'The Lord is a cockroach' or 'God is a dull-wit' the way we say, 'the Lord is kind and merciful' or 'God is good'. Aquinas concludes that divine predications are therefore analogous rather than univocal or equivocal, 'although they fall short of a full representation of Him'.

> God prepossesses in Himself all the perfections of creatures, being Himself simply and universally perfect. Hence every creature represents Him, and is like Him so far as it possesses some perfection; yet it represents Him not as something of the same species or genus, but as the excelling principle of whose form the effects fall short, although they derive some kind of likeness thereto.[28]

When Scripture speaks of heaven or beatitude as a marriage feast or bejewelled city, I take it this way. The bliss of a wedding or the exquisite beauty of a jewel possess a created good or perfection which in a finite way reflects the God who 'prepossesses in Himself all the perfections of creatures, being Himself simply and universally perfect'.[29] The images Scripture uses have a privileged place here, but the logic behind that use is more generally applicable to the finite goods and experiences which awaken the *desiderium* in us.

Hope chastens the *desiderium* by teaching that the fullness of good cannot be found in an idealised romance, career, holiday, subject, cause, society, and so forth. But in line with divine predication, I suggest that such finite goods have an analogous rather than equivocal or univocal relationship to the perfect good found in the vision of God. Ruling out the sour-grapes model of hope noted earlier, this suggests that goods which must be renounced *qua* idols may, all things being equal, be retained by the hopeful *qua* icons. As a far-off reflection of their creator, the fitting response of the Christian hopeful to these created goods is neither to overindulge nor to disdain them. As Aquinas suggests, the proper response is to *refer* them to eternal happiness.[30] As I will shortly describe, this goes beyond thanksgiving and praise to include the adoration of God: something possible if the created good is treated as a kind of local theophany, a reflection of the God for whom hope longs. The 'referring' of created goods to eternal happiness also demands that some ascetic restraints be put in place. It indirectly implies that the goods we pursue, and the manner in which we pursue them, should be the *sort* that are 'referable' to eternal life. Given the errancy of concupiscence, reasonable asceticism retains an important role.

More generally, created goods may be ordained to the end of hope. Insofar as they offer opportunities for virtuous activity, they are the occasion of such happiness as we may have in this life.[31] A loving relationship, a zealous cause, a captivating career, a thrilling subject, fascinating travels, and the like may therefore still offer the prospect of magnificent good, if no longer of perfect good. Pursuing and enjoying such goods may be 'referred' in hope to our overall movement towards perfect beatitude, making them constituents in the present happy life.[32] Put more technically, the finite goods and virtuous activities referred by hope to our eternal end are incorporated into imperfect beatitude as materials for and constituents of it, and when perfect beatitude is attained, it will consummate rather than simply abrogate the happiness which preceded it.[33] As the Vatican II document *Gaudium et Spes* stated when addressing a related point: 'after we have obeyed the Lord, and in his Spirit nurtured on earth the values of human dignity, brotherhood, and freedom, and indeed all the good fruits of our nature and enterprise, we will find them again, but freed of stain, burnished and transfigured'.[34] The life of grace and supernatural virtue is one of real if imperfect happiness that both prepares us for eternal happiness and constitutes its very beginning. 'For it is one thing', Aquinas says, 'to hope that the tree will bear fruit, when the leaves begin to appear, and another, when we see the first signs of the fruit'.[35] Owing to hope, the end of perfect beatitude therefore has an internal rather than an external relationship to imperfect beatitude. Christians may therefore see their earthly desires and projects in a unique way, affirming their goodness while denying their ultimacy considered in themselves, and seeing the partial fruition attained in and through them as the first fruits and reflection of something greater.

The greatest statement of this vision is undoubtedly Dante's relationship with Beatrice in the *Vita Nuova* and especially his Divine Comedy. Centuries of Dante criticism have stressed that the perfection which Dante saw in Beatrice he regarded as a *signum* of divine perfection.[36] To take but one episode: in the earthly paradise at the top of Purgatory, Dante beholds a heavenly pageant with Christ appearing in the form of a Griffin pulling the cart of the Church.[37] Like us, Dante is not able to see Christ face to face; he is not yet ready for the beatific vision. Nevertheless, he is able to see the reflection of Christ in the eyes of Beatrice, whom he has long loved, and who first really awakened his *desiderium*. He therefore stares into her eyes for some time, seeing Christ mirrored there. But it is not as though anyone else's eyes, a clear pool, or any mirror handy could have reflected Christ to him in quite the same way. It matters that Dante sees Christ in *Beatrice's* eyes, looking lovingly at her, but further and ultimately looking with love at Christ. For us who see through a glass darkly, created goods from a human relationship or admirable pursuit to zeal for the good society may likewise reflect God's goodness and be part of our movement to God. The influence which hope exerts on the *desiderium* therefore chastens idolatry without collapsing into misanthropy, seeing created goods and earthly projects in iconic terms and as steps on hope's journey. In both of these senses, they may be referred to hope's ultimate end: the beatific vision of God.

Hopeless Death and Technological Hedonism

Hope also offers something important to those less prone to idolatry than to despair. Because hope informed by charity trusts in God as one's perfect friend, the hopeful may joyfully anticipate beatitude in the spirit of the Psalm verse: 'I believe that I shall see the goodness of the Lord in the land of the living' (Ps 27:13). The hopeful see their existence differently from those without hope, believing there is an ultimate meaning and transcendent point to their lives and world. Committed atheist though he was, George Orwell is an intriguing interlocutor on this point. He noted that much modern technological hedonism stems from losing that ultimate meaning and transcendent destiny which were spiritual bulwarks of Western civilisation for centuries. Orwell does not want to retrieve theological hope or belief in the Christian heaven, but he cautions his fellow socialists that 'its disappearance has left a big hole, and that we ought to take notice of that fact'.[38] He rebukes most socialists for thinking that material prosperity is our final end, for assuming 'that all problems lapse when one's belly is full. But the truth is the opposite: when one's belly is empty, one's only problem is an empty belly. It is when we have got away from drudgery and exploitation that we shall really start wondering about man's destiny and the reason for his existence'.[39] Orwell therefore suggests that the average comfortable person finds it worrisome to think about 'man's destiny and the reason for his existence' since the post-Christian answers to these ultimate questions are frequently bleak. Moreover, questions about life's nature and meaning are hag-ridden by even more bothersome questions about death's nature and meaning. Theological hope is particularly relevant here.

Serious considerations of death are plentifully recorded in Western history, from ancient Egypt to the modern period. Questions about what dying will be like, whether I will continue to exist, where I will go, and whether I will meet my loved ones again are obviously common, and often produce those Hamlet-like anxieties about 'what dreams may come' (if any). No less important is the sense that the answers to these questions determine not just any possible future life, but deeply affect what I make of the present life. As St. Paul suggestively remarks in the person of the hedonist: 'If the dead are not raised, "Let us eat and drink, for tomorrow we die"' (1 Cor 15:32).[40] So the questions concern not just what if anything awaits after death, but the long retroactive shadow which death casts on one's whole life and which partly determines how we read life's meaning. Consider the following Old Testament passage in which the wicked reason thus:

> Short and sorrowful is our life, and there is no remedy when a man comes to his end, and no one has been known to return from Hades. Because we were born by mere chance, and hereafter we shall be as though we had never been; because the breath in our nostrils is smoke, and reason is a spark kindled by the beating of our hearts. When it is extinguished, the body will turn to ashes, and the spirit will dissolve like empty air. Our name will be forgotten in time and no one will remember our works; our life will pass away like the traces of a cloud, and be scattered like mist that is chased by the rays of the sun and overcome by its heat. For our allotted time is the passing of a shadow, and there is no return from our death, because it is sealed up and no one turns back.
>
> (Wisdom of Solomon 2: 1–5)[41]

The concerns expressed here are surprisingly contemporary: the worry that one was never purposed, but is a product of blind chance; that everything we are and do has no permanent significance; that we will be ultimately forgotten and 'dissolve like empty air'; the anxiety that in the end we simply do not matter. Mortality in such reflections is not just a fate, but a hermeneutic. Like a final chapter in a book or final act of a play, its meaning partly determines the meaning of the whole novel or play. The meaning of death partly determines the genre of our life as agents seeking happiness amid the eudaimonia gap. Is that gap an arduous challenge the protagonists finally overcome, so that our genre, in the end, is ultimately comic? Or is death the gap's final triumph, so that our genre is in the end somewhat tragic? As St. Paul suggests, the way we read death may deeply affect the kind of life we choose. The Wisdom of Solomon passage quoted here ends with the wicked saying that hedonism is the best option given the ultimate meaninglessness and shortness of life: 'Let us take our fill of costly wine and perfumes.... Let none of us fail to share in our revelry, because this is our portion, and this our lot' (Wisdom of Solomon: 2:7, 9).[42]

I noted earlier Orwell's claim that loss of hope in heaven 'has left a big hole'.[43] He suggests with some plausibility that technological hedonism and flashy amusements are adopted in part as existential narcotics to help us forget that the hole is there. Hence the modern ideal of happiness, Orwell suggests, is a 'strip-lighted paradise' of pleasure resorts and perpetual entertainment with a *summum bonum* half-jokingly conceived of as 'relaxing, resting, playing, drinking and making love simultaneously'.[44] Orwell thinks the net effect of our 'strip-lighted paradise' is to abolish the 'patches of simplicity' in which questions about the meaning of human existence and destiny are likely to occur. The unconscious aim to stifle reflective thought and the pondering of ultimate questions is aided by radios and other media which are never turned off and whose job is that of a spiritual anaesthetic. Orwell regards much of this as 'simply an effort to destroy consciousness' and to return one to a womb-like state of contented passivity. This technological hedonism tends 'to weaken (man's) consciousness, dull his curiosity, and, in general, drive him nearer to the animals'.[45] Orwell diagnosed this trend in the 1940s, long before it was magnified by the invention of cable television, 3-D movies, video games, the Internet, and smartphones – to say nothing of emerging technologies such as virtual reality headsets. Certainly his concern is anything but dated. The tech fetish with its offer of infinite distractibility has in recent decades grown alarmingly bloated. As has been quipped, the great offer today of multinational corporations to our youth is: 'Let them eat iPhones'.[46]

Though very much an atheist, Orwell suggests that into the spiritual vacuum left by hope's retreat has settled an existential drift which leads people to distract themselves from a sense of emptiness through tawdry amusements, refined hedonism, and expensive tedium. As W. H. Auden teasingly put it:

> The lights must never go out,
> The music must always play,
> Lest we should see where we are,
> Lost in a haunted wood,
> Children afraid of the night
> Who have never been happy or good.[47]

I have already insisted that absence of theological hope does not necessarily doom one to the splendid vices, that the pagan cup can be partly filled according to the mode of acquired virtue. But the pagan cup can also be drearily chipped and empty, and from the Christian perspective, the aforementioned trends look like a very banal return to the bad news. Orwell suggests that with the loss of hope in heaven 'one of the props of Western civilisation has been knocked away'.[48] Of course it would be wrong to characterise contemporary society as nothing more than technological *vanitas* writ large. But the trend which Neil Postman called 'amusing ourselves to death' is alarmingly common.[49] It is entangled with the cult of youth and beauty which seeks to infinitely forestall aging with cosmetics and surgery, and the consumeristic lifestyle which Nicholas Boyle describes as making 'life in the shopping mall' the supreme good.[50] Such escapist efforts to forget death are partly the cause and partly the result of the bread-and-circuses flashiness of the 'strip-lighted paradise'.

I suggested earlier that the desire for a fuller, more perfect, or ideal happiness is material with which hope can work. The question 'why do people choose banality?' rather than aim for higher goods is of course a very old one. Plato in the *Gorgias* asks with sincere bewilderment: 'How can a grown man leave the city's business and spend his time whispering with two or three youths in a corner, never saying anything that matters?'[51] But there is the further problem that the sort of vulgarity which Orwell identifies pollutes the aspiration for happiness with a narrowness of vision that makes the options for happiness seem few and crude. Hence in addition to explicitly religious appeals and more temperate habits, a major resource for disposing back towards hope consists in intellectual, aesthetic, and cultural influences which expand people's iconography of happiness and which suggest more and better possibilities for fulfilment.

Western culture historically teems with an iconography of happiness: a few examples would include Virgil's *Eclogues*, Dante's *Paradiso*, the great paintings of Fra Angelico and Michelangelo, Tallis' *Spem in Alium*, Bernini's *Ecstasy of St. Teresa*, Milton's *L'Allegro*, Shakespeare's great comedies, Bach's Brandenburg Concertos, Handel's *Messiah*, Holst's *Jupiter*, the stained-glass windows of Notre Dame, the great works of the Romantic poets, Dickens' *Christmas Carol*, and biblical imagery of divine ecstasy and heavenly beatitude. There is here an embarrassment of riches which makes any chosen examples almost arbitrary. Serious exposure to such advertisements for beatitude helps to expand our iconography of happiness beyond the limited options of the 'strip-lighted paradise', and goes a long way towards making perfect happiness at least thinkable. Exposing ourselves and our children to these and innumerable such resources can help prepare the way to making the vision of hope intelligible and deeply moving.

Orwell may be wrong to wholly blame the 'strip-lighted paradise' on the loss of hope. But hopelessness certainly creates in many a sense of emptiness and quiet despair which reinforces the widespread combination of existential boredom and technological hedonism: the itch to find distraction in a 'kingdom of noise'. The infusion of hope therefore makes a real difference to the twilight of the gods spiritual surliness that lurks under the technological glitz of much post-Christian culture. Hope restores the sense that one's own destiny and that of one's world have a transcendent meaning and purpose: that one was *meant* to exist, is infinitely loved, and is purposed for beatitude.

A Life of Hopeful Rejoicing

Hope encourages the *desiderium* for an ideal of happiness that is never fully exhausted and never fully attained. It helps resolve not just the negative side of the eudaimonia gap, but its positive side by negotiating the appetite for something fuller, more just, more beautiful, and happier than ever seems within earthly reach. Unlike what we might call the Stoic suggestion – which Quietism and Jackson's strong *agape* recall – hope invites us to respond to the eudaimonia gap by desiring more, not less: to believe in and look forward to perfect happiness through loving union with God. Fixing our eyes on final bliss and glory, hope imparts an attitude of joyful expectancy which gives rise to what the New Testament calls 'rejoicing in hope' (Rom 12:12).

Rejoicing about what you do not yet have calls for comment since the joy may look premature. The distinction turns on how intention qualifies our concept of possession. Aquinas notes that an agent may possess an end either in reality or by intention: that is, by having a good now, or by anticipating having it later. Those who lead a life of infused virtue possess the end of supernatural beatitude 'in reality' now, if only imperfectly, and to that extent they are happy.[52] At the same time the hopeful 'possess' the end of perfect beatitude right now in the highly qualified sense in which an intention already possesses its end. Aquinas remarked:

> Happiness is the last end of human life. Now one is said to possess the end already, when one hopes to possess it; hence the Philosopher says that 'children are said to be happy because they are full of hope'; and the Apostle says (Romans 8:24): 'We are saved by hope'.[53]

While hope does not properly possess the end it intends to enjoy, its intention of the end confers anticipatory joy. Everyday examples bear out the general phenomenon: for instance, people who hope to go on holiday. They may delightedly linger over the brochures and enthuse to friends about the possible trip. But those hoping to go on holiday are not just thinking of the enjoyment they hope for; they are enjoying now the prospect of the holiday's anticipated enjoyments. Hence it is not unusual to find that afterward people look back not just to the holiday, but to the anticipation which preceded the holiday, saying something like: 'The vacation was wonderful, but I'm sorry it's over. It gave me something to look forward to'. That delighted *looking forward to* captures the qualified sense in which the enjoyed object was possessed in intention by hope before it was possessed in reality full stop. Moreover, such hope can be deeply sustaining and help to prevent demoralisation, and this is especially true when the object of hope is highly important to us. As Jane Austen notes of Fanny, who is eagerly awaiting her brother's return from overseas in *Mansfield Park*: 'Upon the whole, it was a comfortable winter to her; for though it brought no William to England, the never-failing hope of his arrival was worth much'.[54]

The beatifying vision of God, which is theological hope's object, is not just 'worth much', but worth all: it is the 'pearl of great price' (Matt 13:45). Unsurprisingly, the quality and intensity of anticipatory joy for this *summum bonum* may be very great. The Psalmist's words capture the sensibility well: 'I rejoiced when they said unto me, let us go to the house of the Lord' (Ps 122:1). I have suggested that hope's rejoicing contributes very much to the happiness of this life.[55] The implication is that the regenerate do not just have partial beatitude now; their hope of perfect beatitude intensifies the partial beatitude they do have, and alters its whole tone.

This rejoicing side of hope has been ignored in theological ethics. Even in the life of the Church, it is mostly unconscious and passed down the generations almost exclusively through feast days, liturgy, and hymns, but with little comment besides. The result is that theology has abandoned people at just that point where their aspirations are strikingly receptive to hope: namely, in their desire for happiness experienced as a frequent restlessness for a 'something more' that is hard to articulate, but is often coloured with transcendent associations.

Yet hope's rejoicing is not decorative, but morally crucial. Sloth paves the way for despair, and sloth often comes from keeping hope buttoned up. Aquinas notes that 'just as despair is contrary to hope, so is sloth contrary to spiritual joy. But spiritual joy arises from hope'.[56] Not to celebrate hope is to risk a spiritual vacuum into which acedia easily settles. It is similar to the married couple who fail to actively express their love and become vulnerable to marital boredom and burnout. In the sixth week of Easter, in the Liturgy of the Hours, a concluding prayer asks: 'May we look forward with hope to our resurrection, for you have made us your sons and daughters, and restored the joy of our youth'.[57] Traditionally, hope has been associated with 'the joy of youth', a spiritual analogue to the hopefulness of youthful vitality. By contrast, acedia and despair have been seen as the supernatural equivalents of decay and bitterness. Hence the contrast between cynical youth who are spiritually senile, so to speak, and elderly people who retain hope's spiritual youthfulness. The latter might say with St. Paul: 'Though our outer nature is wasting away, our inner nature is being renewed' (2 Cor 4:16). As Josef Pieper writes:

> It seems surprising, however, how seldom the enchanting youthfulness of our great saints is noticed; especially of those saints who were active in the world as builders and founders.... Nothing more eminently preserves and founds 'eternal youth' than the theological virtue of hope. It alone can bestow ... that strong-hearted freshness ... that resilient joy, that steady perseverance in trust that so distinguish the young and make them lovable.[58]

This 'joy of our youth' must be clarified. We need to know what kind of joy it is, and we need to know how it relates to our agency. Some conceptual explicitness about joy and rejoicing, and their relevant distinction, is therefore required. Aquinas himself distinguishes between joy proper (*gaudium*) and delight generally (*delectatio*). Each shares the object of a good anticipated or obtained, but *delectatio* usually refers to physical pleasure, though it can be generalised to mean any kind of pleasure. By contrast, joy or *gaudium* refers exclusively to rational delight of will and mind (*delectatio rationis*) in a good we regard and embrace.[59] The two often flow into and stimulate each other even while they remain distinguishable. But the point is that spiritual joy, for Aquinas, does not just mean a religiously induced good mood; but a considered satisfaction of mind and will in one's spiritual good.

In partial contrast, rejoicing is something we *do*, and therefore it constitutes a moral-spiritual practice. It would be foolish to over-determine the forms this practice may take, but some content to the idea must be given. Aquinas did not say much about this, but he said enough to make clear his tendencies. Rejoicing in hope, considered as a practice, is pictured by him as an intellectual-contemplative exercise, or what he calls a *consideratio*. His recipe is to ponder the great events of salvation history with the main canvas for the mind's eye being the life of Christ. As this rightly and importantly makes clear, Christology is essential to hope. The Incarnation is his point of departure. He writes:

> Hope seems to proceed from the consideration (*consideratio*) of Divine favours, especially the Incarnation, for Augustine says: 'Nothing was so necessary to raise our hope, than that we should be shown how much God loves us. Now what greater proof could we have of this than that God's Son should deign to unite Himself to our nature?'[60]

The ground of hope is God's charity for us, and, as often happens when Aquinas wants a moving or lyric description, he cedes the floor to

Augustine. In a well-known verse, John Keats spoke of how when 'new wonders' cease, then 'crude and sore' we begin 'the journey homeward to habitual self'. Though Aquinas said little about how he takes the *consideratio* to work, he plainly wants us to see the Incarnation as a 'new wonder' again; to get beyond the habitual self's mere rote assent to doctrine and to rediscover this proof of God's charity with contemplative clarity and moral surprise. 'The end of all our exploring', T. S. Eliot wrote, 'Will be to arrive where we started/ And know the place for the first time'.[61] We are to ponder afresh God's shocking generosity, to spiritually gape in awe, and to rediscover in the Incarnation overwhelming grounds for our hope. Once this is in place, the theme may be varied and celebrated to any height by seeing in Christ's life and the divine economy the many tendrils of this 'great proof' of how much God loves us, the consideration of which 'raise(s) our hope'.

One variation on the theme is the Eucharist construed as the enduring presence of the Incarnation. Since it belongs to friends to 'dwell together', Aquinas states that the Eucharist is 'the sign of supreme charity, and the uplifter of our hope, from such familiar union of Christ with us'.[62] The life of Christ itself varies the 'how much God loves us' theme with minuet-like precision, from the first healings to the last words of forgiveness on the cross. The Passion greatly expands the theme, moving from generosity to mercy, and shows that even when we are wicked, we are actively loved: 'God shows his love for us in that while we Resurrection were yet sinners Christ died for us' (Rom 5:8). St. Paul clearly means us here to feel moral surprise tinged by gratitude and humility, adding, 'Why, one will hardly die for a righteous man' (Rom 5:7), let alone the wicked.

I discussed the centrality of the Resurrection to hope in the previous chapter. There I argued that the Easter mystery vindicates the grounds for hope and imparts to it a unique sensibility. Aquinas adds that a major part of why Christ rose from the dead was to make hope credible for us, and to sustain it: 'since through seeing Christ, who is our head, rise again, we hope that we likewise shall rise again'.[63] The Resurrection also shows that God's charity for humanity does not stop with death, but is so great that it will *overcome* death.[64]

The Ascension is unjustly side-lined in theological ethics. Aquinas rightly insists that it is meant to 'uplift our hope: hence (Christ) says (John 14:3): "If I shall go, and prepare a place for you". For by placing in heaven the human nature which He assumed, Christ gave us the hope of going there'. The Ascension further uplifts our mind 'to heavenly things'.[65] This seems correct. We can hardly neglect thinking about where Christ now is, or what this suggests about the reality of what we loosely call 'heaven', for ourselves, our loved ones, and our neighbour generally.

It is of great moral importance that the practical consequence of a hope rooted in Christology is to rejoice. Since rejoicing obviously contributes to and validates the presence of happiness, the imperative to rejoice implies that earthly happiness is compatible with and fitting to the Incarnation and to eschatological hope. This was not a foregone conclusion, since the hope of heaven could be taken to imply dissatisfaction with earth, and the ritual enactment of dissatisfaction could then be morally demanded. Lament, not rejoicing, would then become the basic attitude of hope to life, and conscientious misery might seem like the witness of a good conscience. But while lament has an important place in hope, the object of lament is not life itself, but the sin-damaged alternations to life which I identify with the eudaimonia gap. The gap, not creation and humanity (which God called 'very good'), is what hope laments as a 'valley of tears'. To say otherwise would be to brew Manichean remedies. It would also imply that the Incarnation was kenotic in the sense of disgusting: that by taking on human life God had in effect donned a filthy hair-shirt. The words of King Lear here apply: 'that way madness lies'.[66]

These considerations are Christological staples of hope. The Incarnation makes clear that hope rests primarily not on what we do, but on what God has done for us. This is then worked into the hope-uplifting 'proof' of how much God loves us. An element of awed gratitude and moral surprise is therefore proper to hope and a fitting ingredient in its rejoicing. The 'considerations' that are material for spiritual rejoicing may be pondered and expressed in various ways: through private prayer, the reading of Scripture, liturgical participation, and so forth. Often these will give rise to a spiritual joy which is both a preventive and curative remedy for sloth, and an important part of keeping hope strong. Hope's rejoicing therefore both expresses the hope we already have and allows it to grow still further. As Von Hügel says on a related point: 'I kiss my son not only because I love him, but in order that I may love him'.[67]

Such 'rejoicing in hope' may be spontaneous, but it also requires regular scripts, so that the habit of hope is delegated not just to occasional moods, but to arranged times and liturgical seasons. Two magnificent examples are Gaudete Sunday in Advent and the *Exsultet* proclamation of the Easter Vigil. Such occasions of rejoicing, being scheduled for the entire Church, are the product of commitment rather than passing fancy. As such, they reinforce the status of hope as a virtue of the will rather than something whose exercise is left to mood or chance. Such consistency and regularity are important. Hope may be a gift of grace, but as a habit of the will its maintenance requires an organised set of attitudes and trained habits which must be kept strong through consistent expression.

Aquinas' model of *consideratio* is cerebral in style and not very embodied in its form of expression. Partly to complement this approach, and partly because it is independently important, a second and more embodied form of rejoicing in hope merits discussion: the practice of praise and thanksgiving. This takes us back to a scriptural mode for expressing hope. The New Testament sometimes addresses what Christians should do in leisure time and when they are joyful. For James, the matter is quite simple: 'Is any one among you suffering? Let him pray. Is any cheerful? Let him sing praise' (James 5:13). Having said substantially the same thing to the Colossians, Paul writes to the Ephesians: 'And do not get drunk with wine, for that is debauchery; but be filled with the Spirit, addressing one another in psalms and hymns and spiritual songs, singing and making melody to the Lord with all your heart' (Eph 5:18–19).

Aware that people look for a release from stress and weariness through wild parties, drunkenness, and a rowdy night life, Paul does not just dissuade from 'debauchery', but tries to fill the void with devotional music, divine praises, and thanksgiving. It is the Christian answer to the *bacchanal*.[68] The Psalms constantly suggest that such praise not be muted, self-conscious, and officious; but a true instance of rejoicing that invokes festive tones. 'O come, let us sing to the Lord; let us make a joyful noise to the rock of our salvation! Let us come into his presence with thanksgiving; let us make a joyful noise to him with songs of praise!' (Ps 95:1–2). 'I will go to the altar of God, to God my exceeding joy; and I will praise you with the harp, O God, my God' (Ps 43:4). 'Sing aloud to God our strength; shout for joy to the God of Jacob!' (Ps 81:1).[69]

Such rejoicing is not a substitute for the hedonistic partying that offers an escape from routine, boredom, and stress. The reverse is true. A debauched night life is a dreary substitute for the spiritual rejoicing in which the heart intent on God openly delights in the fact. Such expressions depend not just on the inclination to rejoice, but on the *decision* to rejoice. But while this is initiated by the will, the expression often then overflows into the passions, and this further stimulates the will's original movement.[70]

Obviously, such rejoicing may take numerous forms depending on the context, culture, and individuals in question. But whether it is a community of monks singing the liturgy of the hours, a parish singing hymns during Mass, Evensong at King's College, Cambridge, or a family gathered around the piano, the practice gives concrete form to the 'consideration of divine favours' by which we rejoice in hope. If this positive side of hope is not regularly willed and expressed, the danger is that hope will start to look like a weary holding operation in a war of attrition against despair.

The triumphal entry into Jerusalem, with its hosannas to the Son of David, is an excellent paradigm for hope's legitimate rejoicing. 'As (Jesus) was now drawing near ... the whole multitude of the disciples began to rejoice and praise God with a loud voice' (Lk 19:37). As they advance on the journey, the hopeful also believe that the risen, ascended, and glorified Christ is 'now drawing near', and therefore they rejoice. Luke adds that the disciples rejoiced and praised God 'for all the might works they had seen' (Lk 19:73). Likewise, the hopeful do not just abstractly look forward to heaven, but root their anticipation and trust in what Aquinas describes as the '*consideratio* of divine favours': namely, in the 'mighty works' the Church has seen, especially the Incarnation, Passion, and Resurrection of Jesus Christ. This spiritual rejoicing which hope gives rise to is the opposite of Timothy Jackson's love disconsoled with its sombre resignation. Jackson rebukes the consolations of the hopeful and seeks to silence the hosannas of the children with Rortian irony. I suggest that we would do better to adopt a vision which resists these cold counsels and repeats the happy defiance: 'If these were silent, the very stones would cry out' (Lk 19:40).

CHAPTER 4

Presumption and Moral Reform

Their vanity was in such good order, that they seemed to be quite free from it, and gave themselves no airs; while the praises attending such behaviour, secured and brought round by their aunt, served to strengthen them in believing they had no faults.

Jane Austen, *Mansfield Park*, chapter 4

Indeed we also work, but we are only collaborating with God who works, for his mercy has gone before us ... it goes before us so that we may live devoutly, and follows us so that we may always live with God: for without him we can do nothing.

Augustine, *De natura et gratia*, 31

Reverent dread is a lovely truth ... whereby man is wakened from the sleep of sin.... This dread helps us as an entry, to seek comfort and mercy of God, and enables us to have contrition by the blissful touching of the Holy Ghost.

Julian of Norwich, *Showings*, Part III, chapter 74

Luther notes in one place that we can fall off a horse either from the right side or from the left.[1] Jackson falls away from hope by putting on disconsolation as self-consciously as a monk putting on a hairshirt. But we may equally fall away from hope by indulging the false consolations that are its counterfeit. I take it that the comforts and rejoicing of hope rightly show a certain confidence. Christian wayfarers believe they know where perfect beatitude may be found and they trust in grace to get them there. This is preferable both to secular resignation to the eudaimonia gap and to strong *agapism* with its peculiar kind of Stoic resignation. The danger, however, is that consolation may be subverted into presumption. The confidence of hope needs to be balanced by a continuing sense of creaturely dependency and ongoing moral accountability. Otherwise, we may come to believe either that grace and a Saviour are not needed, or that God will save the world in a way that lets us abandon it.

In this chapter, I will examine hope's relationship to presumption, a peculiar vice of false and bloated hope which colonises and subverts moral agency, and which is often confused with theological hope itself; giving the virtue a bad press. Aquinas regards presumption as inordinate hope, or an exaggerated mimicry of hope. Of course, one cannot hope too much in God, but one can hope in the wrong way. In particular, Aquinas sees presumption as the breakdown of hope's 'efficient cause': the grace on which the hopeful lean.[2] This breakdown may occur in two ways. The first, roughly Pelagian kind is when one refuses to seek God's grace out of self-reliance or self-righteousness. Here the agent refuses to lean on God at all. The second, lazy and complacent kind is when one refuses to repent or perform good works in the belief that salvation is guaranteed and easy. Here the agent in a sense leans on God too much.

With respect to the first, I will examine the influential work of the secular pragmatist Jeffrey Stout. He explicitly wishes to forge links with Augustinian Christians, broadly construed, for joint academic and political ends. Stout argues that the virtue of piety, by which we acknowledge our indebtedness, is an important piece of common ground that can help Christians and secular democrats work together. But while he frames piety as shared moral space, he redefines the virtue entirely in secular terms of gratitude and self-reliance, insisting that to repent, to seek grace, to defer to God, and to own the need to be 'saved' is unworthy of the self-respecting democratic agent. To the extent Christians follow Stout's proposals; the virtue of hope will be subverted by a contemporary analogue of Pelagian presumption.

As an example of the second kind of presumption, I will examine the phenomenon of 'moralistic therapeutic deism'. The phrase was coined by some notable sociologists who researched in depth the spiritual lives of young people today as they themselves described it. The yellowed, crumbling, and hackneyed script according to which religious practice is increasingly hollowed out by secular non-belief turns out, as we might have expected, to be far too simple. Instead, it appears that the rising generation has increasingly fashioned for itself a self-satisfied and morally flaccid pseudo-Christianity which maps fairly well onto complacent presumption. I will contrast this pervasive trend with the Christian summons to repentance, and defend that summons against Nietzsche's subtle criticisms of repentance as a form of life-denial and self-hatred. The chapter will conclude with a good word for hope's unpopular gift of fear, suggesting that it is a key resource for overcoming presumption in all of its forms.

Emersonian Piety and Self-Sufficient Presumption

An essential point of Pauline and Augustinian Christianity is that salvation is not proportioned to our unaided moral trying. If it were, we would not need grace, mercy, or a Saviour. One major task of theological hope is to get our dependency on grace right to help us to complete the journey. This makes hope very much a 'virtue of acknowledged dependence' which commends childlike trust in divine grace to be saved. The sensibility is captured by the Psalmist: 'Some trust in chariots or horses, but we trust in the name of the Lord' (Ps 20:7). The doctrine of creation *ex nihilo* entails that all that we have and are is in its most basic sense derived rather than discovered. Emphasising our moral and ontological neediness relative to God, Stanley Hauerwas goes as far as to say that what 'it means to be a Christian' is '*always* to be a beggar'.[3]

But many find childlike trust and any hint of supplication to be scandalous, believing it results in a moral agency of feudal grovelling and spiritual infantilism. In such worries we detect the ghost of Pelagius, and a resistance to the Augustinian legacy of orthodox Christianity. On this subject our most bracing and influential critic is undoubtedly the pragmatist Jeffrey Stout. In *Democracy and Tradition*, he describes his own ethics as 'Pelagian' in an extended sense. Since he does not believe in God, he is not a textbook Pelagian. But he sees the inner logic of both Pelagianism and Montanism as kindred to his own ethics.[4] Moreover, his constant praise for 'the self-reliant heart', a 'self-reliant posture', 'self-dependence', and 'self-respect' shows a family resemblance to Pelagianism which no amount of atheism can wholly blot out.[5]

Harold Bloom called Emerson *the* founding prophet of the American religion, and suggested that most of those who think of themselves as orthodox Christians are in reality Emersonians at heart: that the creed of self-reliance, self-help, self-esteem, and can-do optimism has bitten so deeply into the American identity that it has hollowed out Augustinian Christianity and refashioned it in its own image.[6] Stout regards this as hyperbole concealing a half-truth, suggesting that 'many Americans who call themselves Christian are in fact more Emersonian than Augustinian in outlook'.[7]

The cultural trappings of Emersonian self-reliance may be American, but the undergirding Pelagian ethos has widespread parallels throughout the Western democracies. Indeed, Stout sees Emerson and the pragmatists as heirs to a radical tradition of democracy and even romanticism whose roots lie in England. In his telling, the 'best shortcut through this complicated thicket of intellectual history is to say that Emersonian theorists of virtue sought to democratise a Burkean conception of piety that came to them by way of Wordsworth'.[8] Historically, *pietas* is not a devotional concept; in that sense, it is not especially 'pious'. It owes much to Roman ideas about what the acknowledgement of one's parents and community should look like. Aquinas rightly sees Cicero and Augustine as historical exemplars of such thought, and identifies the sources of our life, upbringing, and nourishment as piety's objects.[9] Edmund Burke greatly valued *pietas* in what he took to be this classical sense, and scolded revolutionaries and radical democrats for their apparent *impietas*. Stout counters that democratic reformers retained the virtue of *pietas* and even improved the concept by purging its 'fossil and unhealthy air' – for him, this means the air of feudalism and Christianity – which burdened *pietas* with the doctrines of hierarchy, creation, and original sin.[10]

The democratising of piety which Stout hails began in England with Thomas Paine and William Hazlitt, duly cast as proto-Emersonians. As this historical trail suggests, Stout's arguments for pragmatism, democracy, and piety are not parochially American, but are part of a transatlantic conversation 'in which', as he argues, 'every society with democratic aspirations' faces similar questions, and often supplies similar answers.[11]

Emersonian piety rejects feudal deference to authority and tradition, and insists on equal discursive rights in deliberating about the good. It is democratic in spiritual no less than in political matters, excluding any need for redemption or the Church with its priestly and sacramental mediation. But Stout insists that this does not leave piety bankrupted. It still does crucial moral work as 'the virtuous acknowledgement of dependence on the sources of one's existence and progress through life'. These sources range from one's country, local community, and the discursive traditions from which one emerged, to the parents, teachers, friends, and fellow citizens to whom one is indebted.[12] Because piety is to be democratic, Stout thinks it must be broadly Pelagian. Grace is therefore cut from the sources of dependence list. One major reason is that Stout fears that what starts as the perceived moral need for grace, forgiveness, and a Saviour ends with a community that prizes authoritarian gatekeepers of grace and forgiveness, and so with Christian citizens prone to serf-like deference to premodern traditionalism and clerical authority.

Stout's overall project is bound up with a major goal (some might call it an obsession) of his career: to halt the anti-liberal momentum he ascribes to the work of Alasdair MacIntyre, Stanley Hauerwas, and John Milbank. Again and again, he polices their hyperbolic rhetoric and resists their claim that modern democracies are individualistic, atomistic, and averse to virtue, community, and tradition. Against this view, he argues that modernity can be virtuous – in an important respect by being pious – but that its piety will have to be 'cleansed' of religious subservience by 'democratic self-respect'.[13] Such virtue can and does significantly bind modern communities together in a genuine solidarity focused on the common good.

For Stout, Walt Whitman strikes the characteristic note: 'Long enough have the People been listening to poems in which common humanity, deferential, bends low, humiliated, acknowledging superiors'. But now 'Erect, inflated, and fully self-esteeming be the chant', and then the people 'will listen with pleased ears'.[14] But Stout insists that this attitude is not 'impious' since piety, properly understood, only demands 'the *fitting* or *just* response to the sources of our existence and progress through life' (italics mine).[15] Piety is not to be expressed through deference or obedience since 'Gratitude, not loyalty or deference, is, for the tradition of Emersonian perfectionism, the better part of piety'.[16]

The secular strain is by this point evident, but the stress on gratitude is held by Stout to motivate the pragmatist to acknowledge an indebtedness to religious sources of social and moral vitality. With Dewey, Stout therefore rejects 'militant atheism' with its ingratitude to religion.[17] In this tale, Emersonian piety is cast as a *via media* between militant atheism and Augustinian orthodoxy: purged of the former's arrogant disregard of moral debts, and of the latter's feudal scraping and sin-sleuthing mistrust of self. But this still leaves unclear just how Emersonian piety will relate to its Christian cousin.

Augustine wrote that 'true virtues cannot exist except in those who possess true piety'.[18] Stout notes that this has often led Augustinians to claim that the secular premises of modern democracy are impious given that they do not acknowledge the true God. (By 'Augustinians' he simply means 'non-Pelagians' who affirm original sin and the need for grace, using the label very broadly.)[19] A default social expression of this viewpoint is to reject secular democracy as a creature of impiety and to withdraw into a traditionalist sect or Christian subculture. Stout sees MacIntyre, Hauerwas, and Milbank as the contemporary leaders of this Augustinian withdrawal. A major part of his strategy is to exonerate Emersonian piety from Christian suspicions by stressing that it has much more in common with Augustinian piety than has been allowed: enough for the two sides to work together building up a society far richer than a MacIntyrean ruin.

Emersonian piety insists on gratitude to the benign 'sources of one's existence and progress through life'. Since many of these sources for many people are religious, Emersonian piety acknowledges – and to that extent *validates* – its Christian cousin. For this and other reasons, Stout suggests that Augustinian Christians and secular democrats can work together profitably if not always easily in the wise ordering of civil society.[20] Christians owe Stout a debt of gratitude for the seriousness with which he takes their presence and their arguments in discussions about ordering civil society. Few secular philosophers have read contemporary theologians so deeply, or engaged with them more sincerely. At the same time, the sense in which Emersonian piety 'acknowledges' its Augustinian opposite is studiously vague, and it might turn out to make little difference.

In Stout's account the 'militant atheist' is depicted as a boor who refuses gratitude towards the real good Christianity has done out of blind zealotry. He distances himself from this atheist by asserting that the secular pragmatist is happy to acknowledge debts to religious traditions and communities as sources of moral vitality.[21] This is not merely a sop: it is meant to help convince the Augustinian that the secular pragmatist is a workable ally. The mutual if limited recognition of virtuous aims and dispositions between the two parties will, it is hoped, secure mutual trust and cooperation over large areas. Yet there is a latent irony here: namely, that Stout gives us no idea what it is about Christian piety that he or anybody else *should* respect and be grateful for. The account threatens to slip into a polite fiction. At times Stout praises the courage or social justice of individual Christians or historical Christian movements. But insofar as they are thanked or admired, it is not for qualities he regards as specifically Augustinian (these are invariably condemned), but for qualities which overlap with Emersonian thought and practice. In effect, the Emersonian 'acknowledges' Augustinian 'sources of existence' just insofar as they are equally describable as Emersonian sources of existence. The move is almost a parody of Chesterton's quip that 'Christianity and Buddhism are very much alike, especially Buddhism'.[22]

The one specifically Augustinian trait Stout gratefully acknowledges is the impulse against idolatry whose inner logic he thinks should ultimately lead theism to negate its own God as the last idol left standing.[23] So the great benefit of Augustinian Christianity turns out to be its suppressed power to advance atheism. The idea that such left-handed compliments are the grateful tributes which Emersonians make to Augustinians – one which is supposed to mark them off from the 'arrogant disregard' of militant atheists – is audacious, to say the least, and the Augustinian might be excused for preferring the candour of militant atheists to such play-acting. The consequence is that Stout's piety does no substantive work in bringing secular democrats and Augustinian Christians together. They may still come together over issues of justice, the common good, civil society, and so forth, a point to which I will return in the last chapter. But the suggestion that piety should be redefined along Emersonian lines that would put Christianity out of business is neither a goodwill gesture, nor a serious basis for cooperation. It has, rather, the sly unwholesome air of a hostile takeover.

The fact becomes obvious when Stout defines piety such that Augustinian qualities are made out to be not just superfluous, but unworthy and pathological. Traditional Christian doctrines are forthrightly described as 'blight'.[24] Like Paine, Hazlitt, Emerson, and Whitman, Stout disdains the feudal, deferential, undemocratic, clerical, and sin-obsessed qualities he sees as proper to Augustinian Christianity. Moreover, habitual deference to an authority over oneself is deemed undemocratic and unfitting. This is not due to the belief that no existing authority is wise or good enough to merit this response, but to the belief that such deference *itself* wrecks the habit of democratic agency.[25] Even if the God of Abraham, Isaac, and Jacob were conceded to exist, nothing suggests that Stout's pragmatist would accept subservience to this unelected and undemocratic hierarch. The whole tenor of Emersonian piety would still point in the opposite direction to 'take my yoke upon you' (Matt 11:29). Quite possible the Emersonian would view an actually existing Lord God rather as the American revolutionaries viewed the actually existing King George III.

Moreover, Stout thinks that belief in a debt which one lacks the power to repay is a 'mark of sadomasochistic pathology', and insists on the need for a 'piety cleansed of sadomasochistic tendencies by democratic self-respect'.[26] The comment is in fact a barely concealed attack on the theology of Christ's atonement, itself deemed not just unnecessary, but unbefitting the virtue of piety. By the canons of pragmatic piety, then, belief that Christ died for our sins is 'masochistic self-abasement'.[27] It matters very much that Stout makes these points while charting the boundaries of the virtue of piety as such, and not as giving suggestions for how piety should best be expressed while conceding that it could lack some of the recommended qualities and yet remain a true if lesser instantiation of the virtue in question. And indeed, it would be absurd to characterise a habit of 'sadomasochistic tendencies' and 'masochistic self-abasement' as a virtue. The result is that Stout does not merely omit the matter of Augustinian piety, he banishes its form. Even if the God of Christianity existed, Stout says nothing to suggest that Augustinian piety would be anything more than a splendid vice.

Such characterisations are not themselves astonishing. They sometimes read like softened Nietzsche scorn; they recall Swinburne's talk of 'the pale Galilean'. What is astonishing is that Stout describes traditional Christianity as sadomasochistic while simultaneously striking a pose of phantom gratitude for it and scolding the 'militant atheist' for neglecting to give thanks for what he himself deems 'blight on the human spirit'. But why should the militant atheist – why should Stout – give thanks for this appalling burden? They are the very chains which both of them want struck off.

While emphasising its common role for pragmatists and Augustinians, Stout frames piety entirely in Emersonian terms. He does this by slanting piety exclusively towards gratitude and self-reliance, and by insisting that deference and dependence shown towards God are unnecessary and detrimental to piety's fitting and virtuous expression.[28] But if what is essential to piety is what Emersonians like about it, then to the extent Christians accept Stout's redefinition of piety it will be easy for the Augustinian bits of the virtue to appear to Christians like awkward add-ons with no meaningful role to play. The Augustinian traits will then increasingly look like what Stout and his fellow Emersonians say they are: 'ossified poetry'.[29] At best they will then be superfluous curiosities, like a Baroque gargoyle on a modernising building. Such an object may receive all the lip-service due to elaborate 'ossified poetry', but it hardly fits in with the newer architecture, and during renovations the case can easily be made to have it discreetly removed. Through his reformulations, Stout has eased the way for Christians discreetly to remove the Augustinian encrustations from piety, leaving only its pragmatic core.

The likely result is clearly foreseen by Stout himself: that a great many who 'call themselves Christians' will become 'in fact more Emersonian than Augustinian in outlook'.[30] In both Bloom and Stout's opinion, this phenomenon of the anonymous Emersonian is a good thing and is well under way. As Stout writes of the 'alienated theologians' who start to think Emersonian thoughts: 'most of them are moving in the direction of heresies that I embrace, so I welcome their company'.[31]

One can hardly blame Stout for welcoming this trend given his own commitments, but his explication of the virtue of piety is a concealed exercise in exclusion-by-stipulative-definition, and as such dubious. Stout can hardly expect broadly Augustinian Christians to let him redefine piety along Pelagian lines while simultaneously describing it as common ground and pretending to validate their theological integrity. He would resist any effort to redefine piety such as to tacitly beg the question in favour of

Augustinian sources. Can he be surprised if the theological border police cry foul when he claims to establish as common ground a virtue of piety which from their perspective looks rather like the vice of presumption?

The debate between Pelagianism and Augustinianism is ancient and ongoing. In the past generation of theological ethics the greatest flashpoint of this debate, for better or worse, has been the running dispute between Jeffrey Stout, on one hand, and Stanley Hauerwas, Alasdair MacIntyre, and John Milbank, on the other. As this suggests, more is at stake than one scholar's attempt to retrieve *pietas* from the history of ideas antique shop. Stout's attempt to justify Emersonian piety before a Christian audience is shaped to the needs of a political agenda. It is part of his aim to shift the citizenry away from the anti-liberal animus, 'premodern traditionalism', and 'terminal wistfulness' he ascribes to MacIntyre, Hauerwas, and radical orthodoxy – a bog into which Stout thinks a generation of Anglo-American Christians has sunk, to the detriment of contemporary democracy.[32]

Works like Augustine's *City of God* offer a rival genealogy of morals, one in which self-reliance is diagnosed as 'prideful self-assertion, a wilful rejection of a human being's actual status as the fallen creature of a perfect Creator'.[33] From the perspective of theological hope, Emersonian self-reliance encourages the vice of presumption born of vainglory by condemning the Christian practice of seeking and depending on divine grace for forgiveness and redemption. What Stout calls piety is, in part, a blunt refusal of grace. His own prominence and influence suggest that what Christians might call Pelagian presumption is doing very well for itself at present; in part through re-descriptions that aim to detoxify the brand and get religious citizens to buy into the project. Meanwhile, Christians are not encouraged to ask whether this would constitute self-betrayal since the terms of the discussion have been defined in advance to conceal the presence of that threat. As a result, just how great a breach is being demanded of them is never raised for consideration. Since presumption as a concept has largely disappeared from the present moral landscape, the transition may hardly seem notable to those making it.

Stout's formulation of piety acknowledges one's ongoing dependence with gratitude. Considered as a creature of avowedly secular ethics, and not as a coy subversion of Christianity, it is a lucid and sophisticated body of moral thought. I will return to the constructive possibilities of piety in the last chapter. But for now, consider that in more popular and less academic forms, the ideal of self-reliance has widespread, duller, and crasser mutations. For instance, exaggerated self-reliance is often cast as essential to a middle-class, upwardly mobile, and social-climbing Anglo-American way of life. Consider Arthur Miller's spokesman for worldly success in *Death of a Salesman*, the diamond tycoon Uncle Ben. He holds himself up as an exemplar of self-reliance and success, boasting: 'When I was seventeen I walked into the jungle, and when I was twenty-one I walked out. And by God I was rich'.[34] In a society for whom self-reliance is often wed to a bloated careerism, the temptation to the 'self-made' mentality with its self-righteousness, self-satisfaction, and presumption is hardly idle.

Augustinians such as Richard John Neuhaus and Peter Berger think the inroads of Emersonians and other preachers of self-reliance have been exaggerated. They feel that many Western countries, and particularly America, are more deeply Christian than is often acknowledged.[35] But other thinkers, no less 'Augustinian' in Stout's broad sense, believe that America and other Western democracies are much less Christian than they appear. Already in the 1970s, the German philosopher Josef Pieper suggested that a vague theism which is ultimately Pelagian operates as a kind of default middle-class creed in Western society. He warned of:

> the typically liberal and bourgeois moralism that is antagonistic not only to dogma as such, but also the sacramental reality of the Church: solely on the basis of his own moral 'performance', an 'upright' and 'decent' individual who 'does his duty' will be able to 'stand the test before God'.[36]

This corresponds to what Aquinas meant by the sin of presumption in its self-reliant form. Bloom and Stout think countless Augustinians are really Emersonians at heart. Pieper somewhat relatedly claims that the religious trends of the Western middle class, despite Christian cultural trappings and occasional churchgoing, comfortably accommodate the vice of presumption. Even if Pieper exaggerates its scope, the phenomenon is recognisable and widespread. As William Mattison and others have noted, many who self-identify as Christians believe religion is an implicit contract or bargain whose inner logic precludes the need for grace.[37] God delivers various commandments, it is up to Christians to follow these rules by their own moral efforts, and if they more or less keep their side of the bargain they will 'go to heaven when they die'. God plays the role of lawgiver and judge; the earlier roles of Saviour and giver of grace, even where verbally retained, are made obsolescent. The fact that so many half-churched people mistake this for Christianity shows how widespread the vice of presumption is among those who lack the theological vocabulary to name it.

From the Thomistic perspective, these self-reliant trends gesture toward the shade of Pelagius. They all involve the refusal to acknowledge our creaturely neediness and spiritual dependency on God combined with a failure to lean on hope's 'efficient cause': the grace we require to reach salvation.[38] The remedy to this is a conscious reliance on God's grace: to overcome presumption by getting hope's 'leaning' right. This requires a frank admission of one's fallibility and poverty before the creator as well as recourse to God for needed grace, forgiveness, and mercy through prayer and sacrament.[39]

A virtue of acknowledged dependence like no other, hope's reliance on God is naturally expressed through petitionary prayer. Aquinas sees the Lord's Prayer as the paradigmatic expression of hope.[40] It shows awareness of our neediness and dependency on God. Moreover, it asks God to provide what we do not presume we can get by ourselves. Whether it is the petition for our daily bread, for forgiveness of our trespasses, or for the grace to overcome temptation, the Lord's Prayer replaces self-dependence with dependence on God, unmasking any illusions of self-sufficiency and construing the self as a sinner in need of continual strength, healing, and grace.[41] Where this habit of hopeful trust and divine reliance is regularly and sincerely expressed, the Pelagian mutations of contemporary culture will find it hard to make inroads and the triumphalism of Bloom will ring false.

'Glory without Merits'

Just as agents can lean too little or not at all on God, so they can lean on God too much and regress into a spiritual infantilism that shirks accountability and moral work. The appearance that hope commends this behaviour has often caused it to be thought a morally deflationary force: a heavenly consolation which makes this sinful world look like a dissolving phantasmagoria before the in-breaking eschaton. Those who think this way may come to see earthly progress as a waste of time. They may also show apathy towards the suffering, seeing their pains as momentary trifles compared to the pleasures of eternity. They may view God as exclusively merciful and not just, so that grace makes no costly demands and sin has no consequences.

In his work, which I have already discussed, Timothy Jackson rightly warns against this phenomenon. Yet this false consolation is one of presumption rather than hope. As Aquinas trenchantly put it, what the presumptuous presume to get is 'forgiveness without repentance, or glory without merits'.[42] The type is recognisable: soft-pedalling God's justice and inflating self-worth, such agents assume salvation is not just possible, but guaranteed. They go from being wayfarers on the journey to tourists on holiday, neglecting good works or impenitently keeping up sinful habits in the belief that God will write these off as trifling indiscretions. From the virtue perspective, such presumption fails to see the connection between character and happiness, regarding the two as extrinsically related and assuming that God will bestow beatitude despite our agency rather than with and through it. This is the opposite of the view set forth earlier that happiness or perfection, both natural and supernatural, consists in virtuous activity.

Timothy Jackson is instructive here. At times he regards hope for the afterlife as a bribe, at other times as a distraction.[43] He accuses hope of 'a troubling denigration of this world' and claims that it undermines charity by playing down human vulnerability.[44] If 'all shall be well' for the suffering in heaven, may we not let *agape* slacken on earth? Jackson is right that a certain kind of stress on the afterlife can lead people to take earthly misery lightly, letting the tasks of charity and justice sag by framing tragedy as a momentary inconvenience. By raising this point, he brings up concerns that parallel Aquinas' own concern over the presumptuous expectation of 'glory without merits'.

St. Paul wrote that 'the sufferings of this present time are not worth comparing with the glory that is to be revealed to us' (Rom 8:18). Relativizing suffering with respect to the eschaton is a staple consolation in the tradition. As St. Teresa of Avila said: 'In light of heaven, the worst suffering on earth will be seen to be no more serious than one night in an inconvenient hotel'.[45] Joseph Fitzmyer reads the Romans passage quoted earlier as saying that hope enables a deepened patience with suffering.[46] Aquinas says much the same, and surely this view is right.[47] Hope does not just empower patience when suffering; it alters the quality of patience itself. Patience without hope is prone to a melancholy resignation which can lead to demoralisation, burnout, and cynicism. By contrast, hope alters the quality of patience markedly by opening it up to a confidence and anticipation otherwise unavailable.

Such traditional staples of consolatory literature are meant to comfort the afflicted, but read in the wrong way they might comfort the apathetic. If my neighbour's misery is just one night in a bad hotel, perhaps I do not need to worry that much about it. Doubtless this line of thought has been abused in various times and places by the morally apathetic who are quick to gild the lily and slow to help. The danger comes from those who use eschatology to emphasise the fleeting nature of the world and then offer bland assurances that 'this too will pass' to desperate neighbours, dressing up as consolation what is really the refusal to help.

Such complacency disposes agents to look on fellow human beings lacking proper food, shelter, medicine, and education, reflect that they will go to heaven shortly, and then enjoy the truly false consolation of not having to help. Such presumption is the compliment which laziness pays to heavenly rectification in the effort to excuse an absence of earthly exertion.[48] Hence the importance of retaining the vice of presumption in our moral bestiary so as to prevent cases of mistaken identity between it and the virtue of hope. Had that distinction been more clearly and forcefully retained in Christian ethics, the atmosphere of moral quietism which so often taints the image of hope would either never have existed or would be widely exposed as an elementary mistake.

It is against this background that hope's relationship to merit – discussed in Chapter 2 – should be viewed. Christ admonishes his followers to 'lay up for yourselves treasures in heaven, where neither moth nor rust consumes and where thieves do not break in and steal' (Matt 6:20).[49] In relation to this directive, Aquinas suggests that the measure of eternal beatitude is importantly related to the measure of present merit and charity.[50] St. Paul is applied to for support: 'he who sows sparingly will also reap sparingly, and he who sows bountifully will also reap bountifully' (2 Cor 2:6). How is this not spiritual commercialism? Aquinas explains the matter as follows: 'every virtue obtains its meritorious efficacy from charity, which has the end itself for its object'.[51] God is charity, and the degree of beatitude in God is 'distinguished according to charity … which the more perfect it will be in any one, the more will it render him capable of the Divine clarity, on the increase of which will depend the increase in perfection of the Divine vision'.[52] The proposal is that all who partake in the vision of God attain perfect happiness, and in that respect they all share the same happiness. But those who have grown more in charity and the infused virtues are able to see and enjoy more in the beatific vision. A rough analogy would be two people whose appetite is perfectly satisfied by the same meal, but one of whom had cultivated a more refined palate and who detected ingredients and appreciated nuances which the other missed.

I argued in the second chapter that hope's desire for the enjoyment of God does not make it a mercenary virtue.[53] The pursuit of merits in the interest of beatitude does not alter this. If the concept of merits were divorced from that of charity, the scheme would indeed be crass. Merits would just be stocks purchased for the heavenly investment fund, and the purest selfishness could mimic the externals of charity while lacking its love. Every good act could be calculated simply to advance one into a finer niche of paradise. This economic view of the spiritual life is not what theological hope proposes. God through charity is one's friend, and the object of hope is perfect beatitude through union with God. Merit implies that the degree to which one will be able to enjoy that friendship depends in part on the extent to which one has grown in that friendship by engaging in the activities proper to it: those which deserve approval from God and which transform one into the kind of being capable of divine enjoyment.[54] Here as elsewhere it is important to make clear that the object of theological hope is not an impersonal paradise or vaguely conceived heaven for which God is the necessary ladder. The object of hope is a perfect communion with God which constitutes our supreme perfection as rational creatures, and this end is obviously intrinsic rather than instrumental to friendship with God.

Hope alters our perception of time in a unique way. Morally, it imparts to the time we have, the time that is ours, a sense of urgency and momentousness. The quality is conveyed by Christ's saying: 'We must work the works of him who sent me, while it is day; night comes, when no one can work' (John 9:4). Time is obviously finite, and any moral theory can make room for the thought that the conditions of agency, and therefore of moral operation, are determined by the time that will be ours. But hope adds the sense of a personal and infallible moral verdict being passed by omniscience on what we have done with our time – a verdict reinforced by the accountability proper to omnipotence. Hence the wealth of admonitions to vigilance in Scripture. Christ will come 'like a thief in the night'; we are to 'keep our lamps lit'; the unprepared may be told, 'Fool, your soul is required this very night'. The stakes could not possibly be higher in such passages, and their sense of time morally charged towards the future tense is the work of hope.

Dickens gives a particularly striking depiction of time's moral quality from the perspective of hope, or rather (since the episode is one of backward-looking defeat) hope inverted into despair. Seeing belatedly the spiritual ruin wrought by time's wastage, the ghost of Jacob Marley laments his lack of good works, and stresses the nexus of hope, time, and merit. Scrooge has congratulated Marley for having been a good man of business, when he is brought up with a shock:

> 'Business!' cried the Ghost, wringing its hands again. 'Mankind was my business. The common welfare was my business; charity, mercy, forbearance, and benevolence, were, all, my business.... Why did I walk through crowds of fellow-beings with my eyes turned down, and never raise them to that blessed Star which led the Wise Men to a poor abode! Were there no poor homes to which its light would have conducted *me!*[55]

As in the parable of Lazarus and the rich man, Marley grasps only too late the stakes between hope and merit: ' "Oh! captive, bound, and double-ironed", cried the phantom... "Not to know that any Christian spirit working kindly in its little sphere, whatever it may be, will find its mortal life too short for its vast means of usefulness. Not to know that no space of regret can make amends for one life's opportunity misused! Yet such was I! Oh! such was I!" '[56] Illustrators can make the scene look cartoonish, but Marley's tone of despair convinces and his warnings make the first puncture in Scrooge's own impenitence.

Hope's relationship to merit rules out the view of time as a spiritually neutral medium. From the perspective of hope, time is a precious and non-renewable resource that affords our only opportunity for moral and spiritual labour, growth, and desert with a view to future judgment. This does not imply that recreation and refreshment therefore have no place.[57] But it does suggest that mere idleness and the excessive killing of time are not just minor foibles, but foolish waste and ruinous husbandry.

Through the mediation of charity, hope's relationship with merit is other-regarding and not just self-regarding. Charity as love of neighbour as oneself is extended to hope for neighbour as oneself.[58] With charity, we may hope for our neighbours, and not just for ourselves. This makes our neighbours' plight relevant to our hope for them. To neglect our needy neighbours and not to come to their aid temporally and spiritually is to abandon them and tempt them to despair.

As the last chapter will discuss at greater length, the consequence is that hope, reinforced by charity, is invested in social justice and love of neighbour generally.[59]

'Forgiveness without Repentance'

Whereas Pelagian presumption does not lean upon God enough, complacent presumption errs by leaning on God too much: in a self-righteous and self-satisfied way. As just discussed, Aquinas believes this happens if you expect 'glory without merits'. But it may also happen through expecting 'forgiveness without repentance'. Aquinas sees spiritual narcissism as the source of this impenitence. 'Such presumption', he writes, 'seems to arise from pride, as though man thought so much of himself as to think God would not exclude him from glory ... however much he might be a sinner'.[60] The presumption is that God is so loving and merciful that no contrition for sin or purposed amendment of life is necessary for salvation.

The belief that one is all but guaranteed to go to heaven unless one is spectacularly wicked is not uncommon. It underlies the therapeutic spirituality of millions who take their simplified Rousseauan catechism from charismatic gurus and talk-show hosts – often while still thinking of themselves as thoroughgoing Christians. The New Age publishing industry, with its seasonal crop of spiritual 'masters' and best-sellers, explicitly markets such narcissism to Christians by aping their theological vocabularies. The 'power of positive thinking' movement with its countless successors and imitators is thinly veiled presumption originally served up by a Christian pastor.[61]

The most recent diagnosis of such trends has come through the work of sociologists Christian Smith and Melinda Lundquist Denton. Based on lengthy sociological research and thousands of interviews, their thesis is that the majority religion of America's youth is not Christianity in any historically recognisable form at all. Instead, it is 'Christianity's misbegotten step-cousin, Christian Moralistic Therapeutic Deism'.[62] While their research net was cast in the United States, the spiritual trends they identify are widespread in late modern Western democracies. According to the authors, the largely unreflective creed of today's youth amounts to the following:

1. 'A god exists who created and ordered the world and watches over human life on earth'.
2. 'God wants people to be good, nice, and fair to each other, as taught in the Bible and by most world religions'.
3. 'The central goal of life is to be happy and to feel good about oneself'.
4. 'God does not need to be particularly involved in one's life except when God is needed to resolve a problem'.
5. 'Good people go to heaven when they die'.[63]

The important sociological claim is that such beliefs are common among churchgoers as well as the unchurched. This is not just the 'spiritual but not religious' penny catechism, but the way countless self-described Christians speak. Religion so understood 'is about providing therapeutic benefits to its adherent'. It involves 'belief in a God who created the world ... but not one who is particularly involved in one's affairs – especially affairs in which one would prefer not to have God involved'.[64] Hence it does not require, or even suggest, the need for 'repentance from sin, of keeping the Sabbath, of living as a servant of a sovereign divine, of steadfastly saying one's prayers, of faithfully observing high holy days, of building character through suffering'.[65] The journey to heaven itself becomes a therapeutic, consumer-centred transaction.[66]

Such transcendence on the cheap is a good inoculant against repentance. Once breezy self-satisfaction becomes the meaning of life, why would a loving God demand costly moral reform? Part of God's job will be to *protect* clients from a Damascus experience. The eschatology of this religion is very economical. 'Good people go to heaven when they die', and the criterion for being 'good people' is notably modest. This is a far cry from Aquinas' view that the goal of hope is 'an arduous good'. The account of Smith and Denton may be exaggerated, though they have been criticised less for exaggerating the trend than for worrying about it.[67] But to the degree they are correct, contemporary 'religious lives' are increasingly a parade-ground exercise in presumption.

Moralistic therapeutic deism is not theologically inquisitive enough to ask what sin might mean. From its zone of spiritual atrophy, repentance looks like an ascetic thought too many. Precisely because its moral imagination is so bare, and its conscience so inarticulate, it cannot even be bothered to issue a ringing *non serviam*. Beneath its polite exterior lurks an impenitence so self-assured that it need not raise its voice in defiance. It is a kind of distinctly postmodern pharasaism: one made to suit the spiritual preferences of modern consumers.

Complacent presumption obviously takes many other forms than this. What they all have in common is the failure to repent of sin, and therefore the absence of true conversion. This failure differs markedly from weakness of will or *akrasia*. The special token of impenitence is not that it succumbs to temptation after resolving not to, but that it never resolves to renounce sin and relevantly give one's life to God in the first place. The Council of Trent defined contrition with sufficient generalisation as a 'sorrow of soul and detestation for the sin committed, together with the resolution not to sin again'.[68] The failed repentance of King Claudius in *Hamlet* shows how the first ingredient does not always issue in the second. But often impenitent presumption is sufficiently settled, dazed, and self-satisfied never to get even that far: never to be gnawed by serious moral disquiet at all. If the presumptuous do become bothered by a dim, uneasy feeling that the activity of sin may be a problem, the last line of defence, as Aquinas indicates, is to bank on 'forgiveness without repentance'. The result is a certain irony: the embrace of a false mercy which leads not to loving reconciliation with God, but to a thick shell of impenitence that rules it out by refusing what reconciliation requires. This becomes more or less inevitable when God's justice is discreetly shelved or kept in soft focus.

'If thou be stung with conscience of sin', Tyndale wrote, 'and the cockatrice of thy poisoned nature hath beheld herself in the glass of the righteous law of God, there is none other salve for remedy, than to run to Christ immediately, and to the Father through him; and to say, Father I have sinned against thee'.[69] But take that glass away or blur it sufficiently, and the sense of wrongs needing to be righted will fade, obscuring the need for reconciliation. As this suggests, recovery of a sense of sin is required to correctly diagnose presumption as such, and to make repentance an intelligible option.

The Nietzschean Critique of Christian Repentance

But some thinkers believe that repentance and remorse entail self-hatred and a 'self-deception' which cut so deep as to threaten self-erasure. Nietzsche is Christianity's most forceful critic here. In his musings on the 'eternal recurrence' he depicts repentance as a loathsome denial of life that conceals an existential death-wish. His probings merit attention here because they indirectly serve to highlight some of the questions and problems involved in hope's recourse to grace in repentance. The backdrop is Nietzsche's theory of the 'eternal recurrence' which appears consistently and over many books, especially in *The Gay Science* and *Thus Spoke Zarathustra*. It appears as the cosmological theory that the world and all events in it, past, present, and future, forever recur in an infinite number of identical cycles without the slightest variation: 'all things recur eternally, and we ourselves too; and we have already existed an eternal number of times, and all things with us'.[70]

Nietzsche often writes as though he believed in this theory literally. Scholarly opinion is divided here, though, with Nietzsche's admirers scrounging for metaphorical explanations to gloss away what looks like an embarrassing cosmological thesis.[71] But the moral work to which Nietzsche puts the tale is clear. Whether or not the world is an endless rerun, he does seriously believe that the relationships between everything in the world are essential to what the world is, and that all events and things are fully interlocked, so that if anything had happened differently, we would have a different world. He further thinks that the events and experiences of each person are essential to who each person is. Nietzsche does not distinguish between the essential and contingent features of a person. Every event and experience that goes into shaping me is properly constitutive of who I am.[72] If any event or experience in my life had been different, I quite literally would not be myself, but someone else. Strictly speaking, I just would not exist; someone else (perhaps remarkably like me) would. I can therefore only accept *my* life if I will that my past be just what it was. The atomism implicit in this is perhaps not very interesting. What does arrest the reader is the problem Nietzsche wants us to face: that we do not seem able to affirm our lives as a whole, or regard our lives as a whole. Partly out of guilt, we engage in self-division and therefore self-deception.

The lesson of the eternal recurrence is that I must want my life to be exactly what it has been, in this and all possible worlds, or else I cannot affirm my own existence. To make us face the necessity of doing this, Nietzsche invites us into a thought experiment:

> What, if some day or night a demon were to steal after you into your lone-liest loneliness and say to you: 'This life as you now live it and have lived it, you will have to live once more and innumerable times more; and there will be nothing new in it, but every pain and every joy and every thought and sigh and everything unutterably small or great in your life will have to return to you, all in the same succession and sequence' ...
> Would you not throw yourself down and gnash your teeth and curse the demon who spoke thus? Or have you once experienced a tremendous moment where you would have answered him: 'You are a god and never have I heard anything more divine'?[73]

Nietzsche's demon tries to shock and awaken us from our small-mindedness, forcing us to stop wobbling and take a yes-saying attitude towards our lives as a whole. To affirm your life, he thinks, you must embrace the 'eternal recurrence' – minimally as a thought experiment. Doing so allows you to pursue 'the ideal of the most high-spirited, vital, world-affirming individual, who has learned not just to accept and go along with what was and is, but who wants it again and again just as it was and is through all eternity'.[74] But ecstasy at eternal recurrence will not always be easy, for a variety of reasons. For most people, these will include moral reasons. To take life in Nietzschean stride is to welcome many things morality abhors.

> Life is *essentially* appropriation, injury, overpowering of what is alien and weaker; suppression, hardness, imposition of one's own forms, incorporation and at its least, exploitation.... [Exploitation] belongs to the essence of what lives, as a basic organic function; it is the consequence of the will to power, which is after all the will to life.[75]

The 'life' we are to say 'yes' to embraces much that morality says 'no' to. Guilt is therefore one reason the eternal recurrence might lead us to 'gnash our teeth' in despair. But this is a danger only if we accept that morality *does* bind us: a view for which Nietzsche's response was contempt. He insisted that morality in any of its forms – from Socrates and Christianity through to and beyond Kantianism – polluted our attitude to our own past with self-reproach and remorse. The remorseful person wishes he or she had acted otherwise. By Nietzsche's lights this is suicidal, since it means willing my own non-existence and signals backsliding into a 'no-saying' attitude to life. Nietzsche therefore sees quite clearly that acceptance of the eternal recurrence 'requires freedom from morality'.[76] Accepting the recurrence requires an attitude to the past which a Christian moral taxonomy would call impenitence, and it rules out the recourse to grace and mercy proper to theological hope. Nietzsche's 'yes-saying' attitude is not theological enough to be presumption proper, but it shares the basic hallmark: a moral grammar of self-satisfaction and the refusal to admit guilt or error.

Nietzsche's claims are highly arguable and fatalistic, from his atomistic view of the self to his odd assumption that the only reasonable responses to the eternal recurrence would be ecstasy or despair (why not indifference or resignation?) They are also wildly unsociable. Ruling out in advance the possibility of regretting past actions makes it impossible to apologise or make reparations, and so all but rules out reconciliation between injured parties. Disdaining the moral high ground, Nietzsche often claims the aesthetic. But even aesthetically, his prescribed attitude will strike many as boorish. Imagine, for example, a King Lear who never admits to having been a fool, who never learns from his mistakes, and who stays glad to have disowned Cordelia, with their poignant reconciliation scene scrapped for one last, dying snarl of self-righteousness. But perhaps Nietzsche's biggest problem is immanent. He seems not to have noticed that embracing the eternal recurrence unwittingly demands a certain will to powerlessness that the *Übermensch* will surely find tiresome.[77]

Leaving such problems aside, the important question Nietzsche's account raises for mine is whether hope, by demanding repentance of the sinful past, might ask us to take an attitude towards our past selves that motivates implicit efforts at self-erasure. The theologian might reject Nietzsche's overall account while believing it raises an analogous problem for hope. The precise form this problem would take is whether contrition, with its wish that I had acted otherwise in the past, might cut deeper than we realised by smuggling in the tacit wish not to be who I am now. Might repentance implicitly threaten to rupture my identity as an agent over time, so that far from an act of local moral surgery, it 'goes all the way down'? Put differently, the question is: can I repent and in some sense break from my past while still accepting my past as constitutive of myself? Or is repentance an act of implicit self-violence in which I try to retroactively edit portions of my past out of my moral identity, creating rupture and inviting self-deception? This is a problem which is too little noted, but which Nietzsche indirectly brings into focus.

He thereby brings up a problem in the near neighbourhood of hope. Remorse plays an important part in Christianity. 'And Peter remembered the saying of Jesus, "Before the cock crows, you will deny me three times." And he went out and wept bitterly' (Matt 26:75). Very grave remorse may even tempt one to despair, as appears to have happened with Judas. So as not to despair, an agent might reject the moral demands that are preconditions for remorse, opting for something vaguely resembling presumption. Nietzsche rejected moral demands with furious defiance and great conceptual clarity. But we can easily imagine agents who simply forget about moral demands, perhaps through 'a pleasantly undemanding and unreflective way of life, a dazed but adequately efficient consumerism'.[78] This is Bernard William's description of Nietzsche's 'last man': a figure perhaps intimated in the moralistic therapeutic deist.

In the Gospels, the Pharisees are often shown policing a moral theology like the one Nietzsche loathed. When the woman caught in adultery is treated as someone to be stoned, the assumption of her persecutors is that her past *should* make her despair, and that those who will kill her are the agents of despair. But part of hope's point is to allow for a *tertium quid* that escapes the horns of morality's despair/presumption dilemma in a style similar to that suggested by Christ (John 8:11). Hope offers the possibility of reconciliation by (1) falsifying the presumption which refuses repentance, while also and crucially (2) falsifying despair through affirming the possibility of gracious forgiveness and subsequent reconciliation. In Pauline terms, hope employs 'grace' to overcome the despair/presumption dilemma posed by the 'law's' possible construal of our past.

To ask forgiveness, I must admit wrongdoing and show remorse, wishing that I had acted otherwise and intending to do so now. In Nietzsche's terms, this means willing my own non-existence since if I had acted otherwise in the past, I would not be who I am now. But apart from the arguable atomistic view of identity implied, penitently admitting past errors does not require me to try and erase my past on pain of despair. Unlike the eternal recurrence, eschatology implies that while the past cannot be changed, it can be redeemed – that I have been given the gift of time enough for reconciliation.[79]

Grace makes it possible to repent of my past and at the same time accept it as constitutive of who I am. By showing contrition I continue to identify with that past – to 'own' it as mine – rather than feigning a rupture that invites self-deception or threatens my identity over time.

This makes reconciliation possible in a way that denial of guilt would not. In subsequently receiving forgiveness, I may even accept that past insofar as it became an opportunity for enhanced plenitude: as the occasion for increased self-knowledge, corrected hubris, renewed fervour, praise, and gratitude. In Dante's *Paradiso*, past sins even occasion a 'smile' in the blessed: not because they are prurient or take the cost of redemption lightly, but because the sin as memory's object is now seen wholly through the formality of God's goodness and its redemptive effects, and in this they rejoice.[80]

Aquinas is right to think that it is not hope but presumption to reckon upon 'forgiveness without repentance'. Nietzsche is not interested in forgiveness, but his polemic against repentance brings unnoticed problems to the fore. Hope often tugs us towards repentance in search of forgiveness. But such reconciliation with God does not require irreconcilability with one's past and one's self. The remorse and self-reproach which hope require do not lead to self-hatred and self-erasure, but to the encouraging thought that I do not need to deny my faults to escape despair, and therefore that presumption is not the only or best way to affirm my life. This makes hope's rear-guard action against presumption a Good Friday moral space of sorts, where we attend to what our sin has cost, and refuse the presumption which rates Christ's blood cheaply. But the whole point of this exercise is to lead us back to that Easter Sunday space that is proper to hope in its native rather than its remedial mode.[81]

Eschatology and the hope of forgiveness allow me to accept the repented past as part of myself and even see it as the occasion for grace and mercy. The memory of that past may cause regret, but it also occasions gratitude at the mercy we have received and renewed appreciation for the love which welcomes rather than disowns the prodigal. At least in that respect, the sin I repent of is a *felix culpa*.

The Gift of Fear

The fear of the Lord was once the beginning of wisdom, but many now think it a vulgar expedient. This is probably due to the belief that the object of fear is simply punishment, and this is felt to be backwards. Aquinas had a more nuanced view of fear and its object. He believed with Augustine that fear was the gift of the Holy Spirit specially associated with the virtue of hope, and saw in it a valuable resource for overcoming presumption. But the recent literature has treated fear as an embarrassment. The awkward result is that hope's gift has been left dangling, making the virtue look like an otherwise solid building with one staircase leading to nowhere. In important respects, this has left research on hope 'closed for repairs'. Rather than trying to hush the gift up, I will suggest that fear taken in a nuanced way is spiritually valuable and does not render piety grotesque.

Earlier I noted that Aquinas followed Augustine in assigning each of the seven gifts of the Holy Spirit to one or more of the seven infused virtues. The purpose of each gift is to make the agent amenable to the grace of the Holy Spirit who prompts the use of the virtue with which that gift is associated. As hope's gift, the job of fear is to facilitate and remove barriers to hope's action. Presumption is a major barrier to hope, and the tradition to which Aquinas belonged saw fear as particularly good at unsettling and ruffling undue complacency.

Aquinas regards fear in any form as a dread of losing what you love: 'fear is born of love, since a man fears the loss of what he loves'.[82] When the beloved good is not possessed with total security, fear of some kind is a reasonable effect of love itself. Aquinas therefore distinguishes kinds of fear according to the kinds of love to which they correspond. Servile fear dreads punishment and therefore is based on self-love. Filial fear dreads separation from God and so is a fear based on love of God.[83] Initial fear, which is proper to spiritual beginners, mingles these two. Such fear dreads both punishment ('fear him who can destroy both body and soul in hell', [Matt 10:28] and separation ('I never knew you; depart from me' [Matt 7:23]).

It requires a certain frankness to admit that the Christian conscience has historically seen fear of damnation as a valuable but secondary moral stimulant: important, but very much a minor player compared to charity and related virtues.[84] Whether it is a nagging but inarticulate fear that your sins and injustices will eventually 'catch up to you', or the explicit prospect of a wretched afterlife, such fear has historically been seen as a bracing tonic against presumption.

Aquinas believes that the more we grow in charity, the more filial fear displaces servile (as in 'perfect love casts out fear' [1 Jn 4: 18]), so that we get beyond initial fear. His ideal of the gift is thus filial fear, whose object is not punishment, but separation. Given its object, such fear is perfectly compatible with (indeed, is a consequence of) the charity by which we love God. It is expressed through recoiling from the sins that might separate us from God, and by entrusting ourselves to God for the grace needed to do just that. The first aspect curbs presumption's complacency, and the second curbs its self-reliance.

Fear of any kind might seem unsuitable to hope, but Aquinas suggests why they pair well: 'God is the object of both hope and fear, but under different aspects'. Specifically, 'the consideration of His justice gives rise to fear, but the consideration of His mercy gives rise to hope'.[85] He goes on to say that presumption errs by striking justice out of the divine nature, thereby hoping in God under the aspect of a false mercy. Not only does this raise 'cheap grace' worries; it props up a theology which makes God something of an enabler.[86]

In therapeutic deism and kindred opiates, God will keep out of 'affairs in which one would prefer not to have God involved'. If that were true, one problem it would raise is that God does not take us seriously: does not love us enough to hold us accountable, or to will our improvement. God becomes like a slovenly and indulgent parent who does not mind if the children are wicked or stupid so long as they are having a good time. Not only does this theology make God thoroughly uninteresting and of questionable goodness, it yields a very low anthropology: a vision of the human race as determinedly mediocre, with no place for exemplars, heroes, saints, or reformers.

Presumption shuts the door to charity, which wills the real rather than just the apparent good of the beloved. By contrast, fear makes charity conceivable by taking justice seriously, therefore making it possible to believe in a God who will not cheapen or corrupt us, but who truly wills our improvement and our good. Hence while perfect charity casts out fear, fear is the 'beginning of wisdom' that helps facilitate charity. By insisting that God is just, fear casts out presumption's habit of relating to God casually and cheaply. As such it facilitates charity's thicker and richer relationship with God.

The gift of fear is the work of grace. But various practices and considerations may dispose to it. Considerations of 'the last things' figure prominently here, from the liturgies and sermons of All Saints, All Souls, and Christ the King, to Shakespearian soliloquies about damnation, ornately sculpted cadaver tombs, Renaissance paintings of the Last Judgment, and that prolonged exercise in *memento mori*, Mozart's *Requiem*. The contemplation of such liturgical and cultural items, and meditations on time, death, judgment, and the afterlife, help cultivate the vigilance and watchfulness proper to fear. They also make it less possible to avoid consideration of what used to be called *the soul*, but which is not called anything anymore, having long since been deposed from ethical reflection.[87]

But what about those distant from such spiritual formation? Here we encounter a dilemma. The gift of fear requires conversion, but the belief that fear is part of the Christian package can be a stumbling block to conversion. At the same time, if we treat fear like unseemly 'baggage', we risk proposing a truncated Gospel that dissolves into presumption. So how might we present fear to those tempted to regard it as feudal grovelling?

Appeals to the fittingness of justice may help to make fear look less scandalous: less a mere recourse to arbitrary violence. Many who deny a God who *could* hold agents accountable in a transcendent sense nevertheless see the *fittingness* of such accountability in principle, since it would imply that reality was ultimately just. In Jim Crace's recent novel *Harvest*, the squire and rustics of a hamlet in an obscure and forgotten corner of pre-industrial England provide a test case. Two strangers, a father and a son, squat and cause problems on the squire's land. Showing insolence, they are brutally treated by the villagers and sentenced to the pillory for a week. This soon breaks the elderly father's neck, and the hamlet folk find his corpse – half-gored by a loose pig – next to the raging, cursing, despairing son. The monstrousness of the situation dawns on the narrator, Walter Thirsk. Like the author, he is non-religious. Yet he reflects:

> None of us had the expertise to make repairs, although we knew we had to … to what? To make amends? So we did what little could be done – mostly wiping off the blood, closing the wounds enough to hide the grinning white of bone.… But I could sense the thunder and the lightning closing in on us. A mighty storm of reckoning was on its way, if there was any justice in the world. The air was cracking with the retributions and damnations that, in my heart of hearts, I knew that some of us deserved.[88]

As it happens, the village and its people do end up ruined by an enclosures act which scuttles their farms, turns them adrift, and rents out the land to the more lucrative enterprise of sheep-farming. In the episode, there is no settled belief that punishment really is on its way, but there is a sense that punishment is deserved even if there is no one to mete it out. It is a kind of half-articulate, pagan piety. It is not sure if reality is just and therefore in some sense to be feared by the unjust. But this attitude sees it as *fitting* for reality to be just and therefore believes that 'some of us deserve' punishment even if there is no one to render it. The recognition of such fittingness is not the fear of God. But it helps make the fear of God as an idea meaningful, and opens up space from which it might be accepted.

Another approach to fear is partly aesthetic. We may be made more amenable to fear through forms of education that have the power to shape vision, attitudes, and taste. This approach involves awareness of what Edmund Burke and others call 'the sublime'. To regard the sublime is to make mental and imaginative space for appreciation of awe-inspiring objects that make you feel existentially dwarfed. In the language of Burke,

Kant, and others, this makes it a discrete aesthetic category apart from 'the beautiful'.[89] Typically the beautiful describes forthrightly pleasing objects such as gardens, sunsets, roses, jewels, peacock tails, snowflakes, a lovely face, and the like. It includes the orderly, harmonious, gracious, smooth, sweet, delicate, and elegantly varied. The sublime denotes objects which primarily stimulate awe, wonder, and fear; and secondarily stimulate admiration, reverence, and respect.[90] Characteristic objects include thunderstorms, the ocean abyss, a dark chasm, ancient monuments, the night, fireworks, a lion's roar, great waterfalls, and anything captured by the phrase 'terrible as an army with banners'. As instances of his related category, 'the Great', Joseph Addison describes: 'a vast uncultivated Desert, of huge heaps of Mountains, high Rocks and Precipices, or a wide Expanse of Waters'. All of these produce a 'Stilness and Amazement in the Soul'.[91] Rather than being pleasant, cheerful, and safe, the objects of the sublime tend towards the gigantic, the overpowering, the untameable, the unexpected, the obscure, the arduous, and the frightful or ominous. Representative is 'that sort of delightful horror' which comes from reflecting on infinity and eternity.[92] One need not be a romantic, still less 'Gothic', to make aesthetic room for this category. To say nothing of the Bible itself, elements of the sublime are found in figures such as Homer, Virgil, Dante, Michelangelo, JMW Turner, Shakespeare, Mozart, and Beethoven.[93] Moreover, the universe itself includes many sublime as well as beautiful objects, to keep to this terminology. To attend only to one category at the expense of the other is an aesthetic provincialism.

Awareness of the sublime is not fear of the Lord, but appreciation of awe-inspiring and unnerving goods shapes an aesthetic and affective disposition that makes religious fear more intelligible. It teaches that fear may suitably be felt for objects deemed worthy of a certain veneration. Where such an appreciation is present, the transition from servile fear to initial fear to filial fear may be smoother. One will be primed to attend to the *goodness* present in certain objects which instil awe and fear.[94] By contrast, where such an appreciation is lacking, the agent may be predisposed to regard religious fear as 'rather in bad taste' – as nothing but a cringing, demeaning, and prudential desire to keep safe before a threatening deity acknowledged to have power but not yet goodness.

Closely related to this is the religious category which Rudolf Otto called the 'numinous' and described as a divine quality which excites awe, dread, or fear (*tremor*).[95] Examples are numerous in the Bible, where theophanies tend to arouse wonder and dread.[96] After his vision of the angels ascending and descending on the ladder to heaven, Jacob rises from sleep saying 'how dreadful is this place' (Gen 28:17). When Isaiah sees the Seraphim and the glory of the Lord in the heavenly temple he cries out: 'Woe is me! For I am lost … for my eyes have seen the King, the Lord of hosts!' (Is 6:5). Ezekiel saw 'rings' in his theophany which 'were so high that they were dreadful' (Ezek 1:18). At the sight of the glorified Christ in his exile on Patmos, John says, 'When I saw him, I fell at his feet as though dead' (Rev 1:17). As Otto notes, such holy dread is common to Christian experience outside Scripture, and indeed to religions generally.[97]

According to Otto, the numinous is experienced as supremely majestic, overpowering, unapproachable, urgent, and wholly other. This gives rise to an awe that may be accompanied by shuddering, fear of divine wrath, and a sense of creaturely smallness and utter dependency combined with a perceived unworthiness in need of 'covering' before this mighty presence.[98] Otto calls this the *mysterium tremendum*, but he adds that it is also *mysterium fascinans*, having a glory, wonder, or majesty which arrests, fascinates, attracts, and compels.[99] Mozart's *Rex tremendae* is a magnificent example of such compounded *tremendum* and *fascinans*.

Though the two must not be crudely equated, Aquinas identifies certain sublime and numinous qualities in the gift of fear itself. He quotes with approval Pope Gregory's comments on the passage in Job ('The pillars of heaven tremble, and are astonished' at God's word) to the effect that: 'The heavenly powers that gaze on Him without ceasing, tremble (*contremiscunt*) while contemplating: but their awe (*tremor*), lest it should be of a penal nature, is one not of fear but of wonder (*admirationis*)'. Rather than fearing punishment, the angels are here said to 'wonder at God's supereminence and incomprehensibility'.[100]

The gift of fear expresses a recoiling from sin combined with awe at the 'supereminence and incomprehensibility' of the God to whom one adheres. The first aspect corresponds to the main work Aquinas ascribes to fear. Whether it is servile, initial, or filial, fear checks pride and presumption with the intended benefit that 'a man be converted to God and adhere to him'.[101] In its aspect of over-awing pride it is analogous to shuddering before the sublime and to Otto's *tremendum*. But Aquinas also affirms an element of wonder or amazement (*admiratio*) in religious fear similar to appreciation of the sublime and to Otto's *fascinans*.[102] This second aspect of fear is said to remain even in heaven; hence the trembling of the angels in Gregory.

An episode in the *Paradiso* illustrates this religious *admiratio*. When Dante looks on the apostles James, John, and Peter in *Paradiso*, he sees them as 'mountains' (*monti*) too vast for his gaze to fully take in. The effect is to make him feel tiny and compressed under an immense spiritual 'weight' (*pondo*). Before their greatness he feels overwhelmed and humbled yet not disrespected or humiliated – he is after all being loved and welcomed into heaven – and he delights to revel in a goodness greater than himself.[103] What a critic might mistake for servile cringing would to the participant be an experience of awe in which revulsion from sin comes naturally. To regard God would by hypothesis raise this *admiratio* to its highest pitch. This consideration is an important corrective to Stout's Emersonian conflation of humility and obeisance with humiliation and self-disrespect. Why before the Holy of Holies should our only possible reaction be feudal grovelling or Promethean defiance? Why rule out the kind of humbled awe which Dante and others movingly capture?[104]

Aquinas suggests why this *admiratio* of fear would fittingly remain in heaven. Though directed exclusively towards God, the formality of such fear corresponds to appreciation of the goodness of sublime, numinous, and fearful goods. I have suggested that such appreciativeness helps smooth the transition from servile to initial to filial fear. When loss of the personal and divine good is no longer possible, and fear of punishment and separation are forgotten in a draught of Lethe, it will be fitting for the appreciative quality in fear to remain. For the 'supereminence and incomprehensibility' of God which inspired that *admiratio* will remain, and such wonder is perfectly compatible with a secure and perfected charity. A spirituality which includes elements of the numinous will obviously foster that awe, wonder (*tremor, admiratio*) and sense of humility which dispose to and often supervene on fear proper.

In my consideration of fear I have treated Burke and Otto as valuable *bricolage*. Parts of their overall accounts have dated, but I have gone the way of a *bricoleur* by retrieving important insights from their accounts while not committing myself to carry every satchel of their philosophical baggage. These insights explain much that is common in religious experience and that is relevant to the gift of fear. Though they often overlap in practice, experience of the sublime and even of the numinous need not be a motion of the gift of fear. But any vision and spirituality which includes these categories will foster attitudes and passions which dispose to it, honing spiritual reflexes against presumption.

Rejoicing in hope must be distinguished from presumption in its various forms, from Emersonian self-reliance and Pelagian self-helpism to the spiritual smugness of therapeutic deism. Theological hope with some help from fear is good at exposing and overcoming presumption in these guises. Growth in hope requires a sharp turn away from self-reliance towards reliance on God's grace and mercy, and the renunciation of self-satisfaction for moral labour, admission of sins, and personal transformation in pursuit of the arduous good. Those are precisely the qualities of character that preserve the rejoicing in hope commended earlier from a false rejoicing in presumption.

A critique of presumption is another way of getting at the point that grace is meant to transform our character, neither bypassing human agency nor leaving it unregenerate. It is a central concern of virtue ethics to regard the kind of person one is and the sort of character a community needs to have. As Tyndale points out: 'An adder … is hated of man not for the evil it hath done but for the poison that is in it'.[105] Failing to grasp this crucial point, the presumptuous expect the fruits of perfection while showing no interest in being perfected. Plainly this conflicts with any view of happiness as constituted by a virtuous way of life.

The Emersonian pragmatist and moralistic therapeutic deist cut themselves off from these sensibilities of fear, and dramatically shrink the sources of awe, wonder, and admiration. They regard Dante's mountains as molehills, and listlessly ask what is so amazing about grace. Such approaches resist anything like the gift of fear and reinforce presumptuous tendencies. To the extent our aesthetic and religious education can make room for ingredients like the sublime and the numinous, hope's gift will become increasingly intelligible.

Religious fear has notoriously been misused at times, and I have no interest in reviving crude excesses. But while past ages may have gone too far in one direction, I do not think that a good reason to go too far in the other. The model I have advocated seeks to restore a sense of balance. When the fear of the Lord is treated as an embarrassing conversation-stopper, the vice of presumption arrives like a thing expected, and the Gospel is subverted. By contrast, an appropriate model of fear configures an aesthetic and spiritual vision apt to regard presumption not just as vicious, but as boorish. Far from being a blemish on hope, fear properly understood turns out to be a crucial means for keeping hope strong and the Gospel intact. Fear is, as advertised, a gift.

CHAPTER 5

Despair and Consolation

For God alone my soul waits in silence; for my hope is from him. He only
is my rock and my salvation, my fortress; I shall not be shaken.

Psalm 62:5–6

Not, I'll not, carrion comfort, Despair, not feast on thee;
Not untwist – slack they may be – these last strands of man
In me or, most weary, cry *I can no more.* I can;
Can something, hope, wish day come, not choose not to be.

Gerard Manley Hopkins, *Carrion Comfort*

Earlier I described the negative side of the eudaimonia gap with its impediments to happiness, calling on philosophical interlocutors to round out my account and avoid the appearance of theological question-begging. I claimed that natural happiness is genuine and worthwhile but far from perfect, and that its imperfections are deeply unsettling. Hope, I suggest, vastly improves the situation by assuring us that it is possible and not just desirable to overcome the eudaimonia gap with its formidable impediments. As Lady Julian wrote: 'Sin is behovable, but all shall be well, and all shall be well, and all manner of things shall be well'.[1] Hope and the life of grace are not proof against misfortune and the cross, but Christians rightly regard outrageous fortune differently from 'those who have no hope' (1 Thess 4:13), recalling that Christ himself endured the shame and will one day make all things new.

Imperfect Happiness and the Hope of the Beatitudes

Theological hope is not a moral and spiritual anaesthetic. I believe that Aquinas was correct to say that hope does not detach us from earthly goods, but consciously refers them to our eternal end. Hope is therefore invested in earthly projects and cannot adopt Stoic apathy to insulate us from human vulnerability and tragedy. The hopeful are 'on the way' to a

139

destination free from the eudaimonia gap's limits, but meanwhile, they are not there yet, and so remain vulnerable. Moreover, through charity we hope for our neighbours. Ultimately, we hope for their eternal good, but proximately, we hope for their temporal good as referred to the eternal. This implicates us in our neighbours' vulnerability as well. On top of whatever harm comes our own way, we are called to 'bear each other's burdens, and so fulfil the law of Christ' (Gal 6:2). The view that hope opts out of the cross is both mischievous and mistaken.

As this suggests, the pursuit of imperfect supernatural beatitude will include virtuous commitments which come with a cost. It could involve cutting back hours spent pleasantly gardening to volunteer in a grimy soup kitchen, or forgoing a desired vacation to donate the money to a crisis pregnancy shelter. Such activities contribute to happiness in one way while sacrificing different activities which might contribute to it in another. This is not to declare gardening and vacations morally bankrupt on the basis of a supernatural high ground. Leisure and commonplace activities may express a good deal of virtue in their own right. Yet the agent may often forgo these to pursue activities that exhibit different virtues, typically, infused virtues such as faith, hope, and charity.

Christians will be apt to think these activities contribute to happiness in a deeper and more lasting way than their alternatives, and to believe that they direct us to a higher end. Even some non-Christians lend support to this view. A striking instance emerges from late antiquity. The Roman Emperor Julian 'the Apostate' is second to no one in history for his hatred of Christianity, going so far as to bathe in bull's blood to efface his baptism. But while he extolled pagan virtue, he certainly saw the appeal of one Christian virtue missing from the canonical pagan list – *agape* or charity. Julian saw both the benefit of charity to the common good and the religious sales appeal it lent Christianity. 'These impious Galileans', he wrote, 'not only feed their own poor, but ours also; welcoming them into their *agapae*, they attract them'.[2] Though a declared anti-Christian, Julian encouraged the formation of pagan charities that would mimic the philanthropy which made Christianity appealing. Soup kitchens for Zeus do not survive. What does survive is the frank admission from a hostile source that the defining virtue of Christianity wrought major benefits for the human condition.[3] Granted that Julian was just cynically leveraging charity for its selling power, this confirms that the most distinctively Christian of all virtues, despite being based on supernatural premises, was widely recognised as making lives better and happier even by those who rejected the premises.

Such recognitions often look like the tribute which nature pays to grace, and they are not uncommon. The philosopher Philippa Foot provides some curious examples. Like Rosalind Hursthouse, she insists that virtue contributes to happiness while admitting that the demands of virtue are costly. She writes: 'Joy is of the essence of the good life, but is of course compatible with prolonged suffering. In this connection I think also of an old Quaker woman of whom I have read, who after much persecution and suffering spoke of her "joyous life" preaching the Word'.[4] Foot is anxious to protest her atheism. Yet she is repeatedly mystified by the happiness of Christians who practise virtues which get them into trouble even while suggesting that these virtues simultaneously add a 'depth' to their happiness that would otherwise be lacking. In the first chapter, I cited her example of the young German Letter-Writers whose anti-Nazi activism landed them in prison, and whose Christian hope sustained them in the shadow of execution. Foot says this case 'puzzled me for years', since while on paper the Letter-Writers occupy a position like Aristotle's 'man on the rack', they nevertheless foil theoretical predictions of wretchedness. 'Readers of these letters', Foot writes, 'have been struck by the extraordinary sense of happiness they radiate, which has perhaps to do with the fact that practically all the writers were devout Christians (with hope in) God'.[5]

In the Letter-Writers' case, the virtue of hope appears to be the greatest contributor to happiness amid obvious tragedy. In the persecuted Quaker woman's case, the virtue of charity appears to be the mainstay in her 'joyous life preaching the Word'. In both cases, many possible and important constituents in the happy life are missed while other constituents believed to be even more important are added. As Newman put it, such happiness gains in perfection, depth, and merit what it may lose in comfort, money, leisure, and security: 'just as a face worn by tears and fasting loses in beauty, or a labourer's hand loses its delicateness'.[6] Aquinas like many others suggests that faith, hope, and charity contribute richly to happiness and lead to increased love, joy, reconciliation, peace, mercy, communion, goodwill, and so forth.[7] These are real gains, but they obviously come at a cost.

I take imperfect supernatural happiness in this life to be genuinely happy but bittersweet. For one thing, the context for such happiness is the eudaimonia gap, though I have suggested that hope allows one to face the gap more satisfactorily. For another, such happiness motivates edifying projects which tax many of our ordinary enjoyments even while they open up deeper possibilities for perfection, community, love, and fulfilment.

The happy life which the hopeful enjoy is an 'arduous good' rather than something easy. But natural happiness (roughly, the philosopher's *eudaimonia*) is necessarily imperfect because its possessors do not seek or hope for perfect happiness at all. By contrast, supernatural happiness (Christian *beatitudo*) is incidentally imperfect because its possessors believe perfect happiness is possible and that they are on the way there. Typically, the former experience imperfect happiness with a certain resignation, whereas the latter do so with resilient hope. This obviously impacts the *way* in which each views the limitations on their happiness.

Hope admits that supernatural happiness is doomed to imperfection in this life. It therefore encourages eschatological patience at the brute fact of imperfection, restraining the utopian excess that may lurch into disillusionment, consequentialism, or tyranny, depending on the direction in which it is pulled. But while hope justifies patience with imperfection, it does not motivate a truce with the eudaimonia gap. Hope does not justify the thought that such imperfections will have their way in this life, and so we should just leave them unmolested and await a future heaven. As I have suggested, hope motivates the effort to overcome impediments to happiness in this world in preparation for the fully unimpeded happiness of the next, disposing earthly possibility towards eternal actuality as 'matter' disposed for the full influx of 'form'.[8]

Hope therefore encourages realism if this is taken to mean patience enough to admit that imperfection cannot be got rid of wholesale. Such patience prevents an overly imminent eschatology or a lapse into zealotry which expects the kingdom of God on earth. But hope also motivates efforts to overcome imperfection insofar as this is possible, disposing towards the perfection for which we hope. The result is a *zealous patience*. On one hand, the hopeful know that final victory over the gap awaits the eschaton. Hence failures to increase individual and social happiness will rightly be met with lament rather than despair. On the other hand, the hopeful are zealous to overcome imperfection and will engage in costly and difficult border skirmishes with the eudaimonia gap, seeking to improve individual and social happiness where we may.

What does hope's attitude of zealous patience towards the eudaimonia gap look like in practice? Obviously, forms of it vary, but I suggest that the best illustration comes from the beatitudes in the Sermon on the Mount. Working in the mode of hope and based on eschatological promises, the beatitudes contend with the eudaimonia gap *in via* while acknowledging that final victory will only come *in patria*. The tradition of reflection on the beatitudes spans nearly two millennia, and its contemporary literature is vast.[9] In a later chapter, I will engage biblical scholarship on the topic, but at present my focus is on Aquinas. My interest here is the exemplary way in which the beatitudes illustrate the bittersweet nature of imperfect supernatural happiness. As discussed earlier, Aquinas associates each beatitude with one of the seven gifts of the Holy Spirit; understanding the gift as a habit and the beatitude as that habit's act. Each gift is assigned to one of the seven infused theological and cardinal virtues, and the purpose of the gift is to make the agent docile and pliable to the grace of the Holy Spirit who prompts the exercise of that virtue.[10]

As their name suggests, the beatitudes are concerned with beatitude or happiness.[11] Each beatitude declares happy those who pursue some arduous task such as poverty, mourning, meekness, hungering for justice, and so forth.

Their reference to future reward takes up the Old Testament pledge of the Promised Land and ordains it to the eschatological kingdom. Like hope, each of the beatitudes therefore seeks a 'future good possible but arduous to attain'. Aquinas therefore speaks of 'the beatitudes of the present life, *which are based on hope*' (*beatitudines praesentis vitae, quae sunt spei*, emphasis mine).[12] But how are they based on hope? He believes that each beatitude corresponds to gifts which inhere in all manner of infused virtues, only one of which is hope. But if each beatitude shares hope's object of 'future good possible but arduous to attain', why not just say that the beatitudes as a set correspond to hope's own gift, making a tidy and intuitive alignment?

Aquinas takes this option off the table by insisting that the beatitudes contain 'the total formation of the Christian life', and plainly this involves much more than hope and fear.[13] Yet there is supposed to be some sense in which all of the beatitudes are 'based on hope'. How are these competing territory claims to be unravelled? Aquinas seems never to have spelled this out clearly. But based on his overall scheme of infused habits and theory of causality, I suggest the following. Aquinas' action theory allows certain, more determinate ends to be referred to and in a qualified sense to be contained by other, more general ends. His example is that an army's ultimate end in 'fighting well' is 'victory'. At the same time, certain proximate or more immediate ends will be ordained to that ultimate and more comprehensive end. His example is 'The right ordering of this or that regiment' as a proximate end ordained to the ultimate end of victory.[14] As such, the proximate end is contained in the ultimate as a 'species' is contained in its 'genus'. Yet the proximate end is a genuine end in itself. If the ultimate end of victory were not attained, the proximate end of 'the right ordering of this or that regiment' still might have been attained. In this respect, the proximate is contained in the ultimate end, but the integrity of the proximate end itself remains. My suggestion is that the ultimate end of hope is likewise the 'genus' relative to which the proximate ends of the beatitudes are the individual 'species'.

Aquinas believes that each beatitude has a proximate end which corresponds to that beatitude's gift. For instance, poverty of spirit pursues the end of fear, and purity of heart seeks that of understanding. From these proximate ends the beatitudes derive their species. The ultimate ends they seek are the rewards for those beatitudes. Poverty of spirit is rewarded with the kingdom of God, and purity with seeing God. However, 'all these rewards' Aquinas states, 'are one in reality ... eternal happiness', given that the kingdom of heaven, 'which is eternal life, contains all good things'.[15] But since we cannot comprehend the perfect good, the rewards of the beatitudes are described by 'various goods known to us' so as to make eternal happiness colourable to us, and not a bare concept too empty to stimulate desire.

The ultimate end of each beatitude is thus eternal happiness, and each beatitude pursues this ultimate end as the eschatological reward for arduous tasks such as mourning and hungering for justice. Every beatitude has its own proximate ends as 'species', but the ultimate end of the beatitude as a 'genus' is hope's own – perfect happiness pursued as a 'future good arduous but possible to attain'. In that respect, the virtue of hope could profitably be seen as the *form of the beatitudes*.

If the hopeful life is concretely expressed by the beatitudes, this suggests that beatitude is what hope made it out to be all along: an 'arduous good'. Acts like renouncing wealth in solidarity with the poor, curbing with meekness the urge to vengeance, hungering after justice, and doing the hard work of peace-making are all costly and entangle us in people's brokenness. A happy life which takes such acts on board will gain here but lose there, entangling itself in others' needs and hurts while providing its own set of enrichments. The beatitudes are nothing if not arduous.[16]

This suggests that the hopeful life is far more *human* than is made out by those who suspect it of otherworldly withdrawal. Leo Tolstoy is symptomatic of the fault line here. He advocated celibacy and reviled marriage as a state of 'slavery, satiety, repulsion' which entangles one in a life of 'ugliness, dirtiness, smell, sores'.[17] His proposal is that ordinary human life – which marriage and childrearing carry on – is simply disgusting. We should 'transcend it' in a state of antiseptic mysticism that is only tenuously organic. Neo-Platonic, Stoic, and Manichean flights from vulnerability and embodiment often make similar noises, proposing a mystical aloofness inured to the world of pain, dirt, disease, and smells.[18] At its worst, this is plain misanthropy. But while the worst is seldom reached, elements of misanthropy often pour their drainage into Christian thought and practice. The Stoic invulnerability advocated by Boethius and the wholesale interiority advocated by Thomas à Kempis are symptomatic.[19] By contrast, through tethering hope to the beatitudes, any 'high-minded' disgust and renunciation of the human are ruled out by the hopeful. Hunger and thirst for justice, solidarity with the poor, peace-making, and the like are a plunge into rather than an escape from the world of dirt and frailty.

The hopeful are therefore vulnerable to the eudaimonia gap and their virtuous commitments implicate them in their neighbours' vulnerability. Their share of supernatural happiness can only be imperfect, falling well short of the beatific vision. The point helps to save hope from an overly realised eschatology liable to presumption.

But equally, the hope of the beatitudes offers gains which disarm the eudaimonia gap of its greatest weapon: the threat of despair. This consideration is best explained with reference to the three 'sets' into which Aquinas divided the beatitudes. The first is spiritual poverty, meekness, and mourning. This set corresponds to eternal happiness by way of removing obstacles to it: specifically, the obstacles to genuine happiness posed by the temptation to grub for merely 'sensual happiness' in a life of wealth and hedonism. The second set is justice and mercy, and it corresponds to eternal happiness primarily through disposing to it in a life of 'active happiness'. The third set is purity and peace-making, and it corresponds to eternal happiness as a beginning of that 'contemplative happiness' whose consummation is the beatific vision. With respect to eternal happiness, the first two sets refer to merits and the last set to the reward. With respect to this life, each set contributes at varying levels to the imperfect happiness of this life while readying us for the perfect happiness of the next.[20] This corresponds well to what I argued earlier both about happiness beginning in this life and about its demand for merits and transformation.

For Aquinas, the various rewards of the beatitudes denote eternal happiness itself under different characterisations.[21] With great ingenuity, he suggests that the reward correlated to each beatitude corresponds to the good mistakenly sought in some vicious behaviour opposed to that beatitude. The beatitudes thereby become a way of recognising apparent happiness and driving it out for genuine happiness. For example, the intemperate seek comfort from life's toils in 'the pleasures of the world'. They are therefore told that by a mourning which repents of hedonism they 'shall be comforted' in a better way by the spiritual life. The violent fight to gain a secure possession for themselves. They are told that by a meekness which curbs violence they will find an equilibrium which confers spiritual security in this life and will 'secure the land' in the heavenly kingdom. The unjust take what belongs to others because they think this will fill their emptiness. They are told that by hungering for justice they will 'be satisfied' by moral and spiritual goods which more adequately address the desire for fulfilment. The apathetic avoid their needy neighbours 'lest they be busied with other people's misery. Hence Our Lord promised the merciful' that they would 'obtain mercy' and forgiveness in this life, and 'be delivered from all misery' in the next.[22] The insight is that sinful behaviour aims to fulfil a real need. The beatitudes seek to fulfil rather than debunk the need while exposing false solutions as counterfeits.

The rewards of the beatitudes may only be fully attained in the next life, but I agree with Aquinas that the rewards are partially attained in this one. To recur to earlier examples, despite their great losses, Foot's Letter-Writers and embattled Quaker woman all give evidence of being comforted, reconciled, fulfilled, and spiritually secure or at peace. When the latter spoke of her 'joyous life preaching the Word', the joyful life in question was *this* one. To a significant degree, it was made enjoyable by the sort of rewards ascribed to the beatitudes.

From the viewpoint of hope, imperfect supernatural happiness is a halfway house which improves on imperfect natural happiness but is itself incomplete. The hopeful believe they know enough about the limits of natural *eudaimonia* to see supernatural *beatitudo* as a trade up, and they rightly rejoice in hope during their earthly sojourn. They overcome the Ecclesiastes mood with its sting of futility and refuse the melancholy resignation which the eudaimonia gap on naturalistic grounds invites. But the gap still afflicts the hopeful, and costly moral work and reform is required of them. Moreover, the length of their journey, the sufferings they will face, and the timing and nature of their death are all frightful unknowns. As a 'rational appetite', the will has a symbiotic relationship with the intellect's reflections on these uncertainties, and so may become dismayed. As Dante says when facing the 'deep and rugged road' which Virgil has laid before him: 'one who unwills what he willed' may 'change his purpose with some new second thought/ completely quitting what he first had started'.[23] In this respect, part of hope's role is to brace the will before the many and daunting challenges of our *status viatoris* lest the agent despair.

The Stoic Hope Option

The virtue of hope is not morally and spiritually invincible. We are threatened by temptations to presumption, sloth, and despair: threats usually occasioned by the world's contingencies. The resulting moral vulnerability is an ineradicable hazard of the imperfect happy life. Only those who have attained the fullness of perfection – who have been finally and permanently 'saved' – are spiritually and morally indefectible. Yet this only comes when *homo viator* emerges as *homo comprehensor*, and to vary the proverb of Aeschylus, call no one safe until he is dead. Given this ongoing vulnerability of the hopeful I disagree with John Bowlin's characterisation of hope as a 'Stoic' virtue which is proof against fortune. In his *Contingency and Fortune in Aquinas' Ethics*, Bowlin argues in elegant and spare prose the intriguing case that Aquinas is rather less of an Aristotelian, and rather more of a Stoic, than Thomist scholarship grasps.

According to Bowlin, Aquinas takes from Aristotle the point that the virtuous agent really is morally caught in the world of 'contingency and fortune'. Luck therefore has moral consequences. Important goods such as a fine education, decent upbringing, a healthy social context, and the intelligence for contemplation are good in themselves. They are also important for acquiring and practising virtue even though they come by fortune's lottery. The virtues in many respects are ways of cultivating these goods, using them well, or dealing well with their absence or with the complications they involve. To that extent the shape the virtues take is determined by conditions posed by our pursuit of goods in the world of fortune. Considering what prudence, courage, or justice traffic in, the virtues require a serious role for fortune in the moral life.[24] But Bowlin rightly notes that Aquinas is not satisfied with the kind and degree of happiness available on Aristotle's terms. Compared to the happiness of Adam in Eden or the bliss that awaits in heaven, one may generously acknowledge happiness *in via* while reserving the right to 'express theologically charged discontent with the virtue and happiness available to us *in via*'.[25]

At this point, Bowlin sees Aquinas adding Stoic supplements to his overall Aristotelian account. Conceding that fortune still matters, Bowlin suggests that the infused virtues induce 'Stoic modifications' unknown to the acquired virtues, and that these 'eliminate fortune's authority over virtuous habits and actions, and by implication, its influence over the happiness of the virtuous'.[26] How does this happy immunity take place?

Earlier I noted Aquinas' habit of distinguishing proximate from remote ends. Applied to this topic, proximate ends are the immediate goals of a virtue, and typically these have to do with attaining some good in the world of fortune. For instance, the immediate goals of justice might include apprehending murderers, abolishing slavery, or implementing a just wage. Infused virtues and especially charity further direct these laudable goals to our ultimate end of attaining and adhering to God. This implies two different levels at which virtue may succeed. The proximate ends of virtue fail much of the time. The murderer may go uncaught, slavery may continue, the campaign for just wages may flag. Aquinas' Aristotelian side requires us to say that such misfortunes involve real loss and occasion grief. But in a different respect, the virtuous effort may be a superb success. The rejected social reformer or dishonoured prophet may still attain the ultimate end of infused virtue by referring themselves to God with firm adherence.[27] Agents outmanoeuvred by fortune may still have gotten closer to God and grown in sanctification through their virtuous efforts. As Bowlin sees it, infused virtue is therefore immune to fortune where it matters most: in our ultimate ordination to God. In this account, infused virtue is therefore double-edged: Aristotelian enough to feel the sting of tragedy, but Stoic enough to survive anything. (Among other things, this helps account for martyrdom as both a triumph and a loss.) Bowlin's exegesis here is for the most part excellent, his narrator's voice is lively, and he engages with a wide set of sources, making the book far more than an insular Thomist affair.

The next point in the argument is that agents with infused virtue still lack the perfect and unimpeded attainment of God, and so they long for a 'happiness that transcends fortune's reach'. The result is that the over-all attitude of the virtuous towards fortune 'must be hope'. The moral work this hope does has less to do with anticipating future reward than with conferring present invulnerability. Since the world of contingency can only foil the proximate ends of infused virtue, the ultimate end is said to be perfectly safe for those who refer proximate ends to God in hope. As Kierkegaard put it: 'spiritually there is only one who can slay me, and that is myself'.[28] The consequence of morally disarming fortune in this way certainly sounds fortunate: 'Success is guaranteed, the difficult good achieved, in the very act of hoping'. Bowlin states that 'This is, of course, a Stoic rendering of Christian hope' since it insists that 'there is no chance that fortune might interfere with the hopeful' in their pursuit of the ulti-mate end.[29]

With this claim we pivot from 'Stoic modifications' to something like Stoic triumphalism. Bowlin seems to endorse what Jackson thought the most damning indictment of hope: the spectacle of it conferring a thick shell of moral and spiritual invulnerability. With supremely confident lan-guage like 'Success is *guaranteed*' and '*there is no chance* that fortune might interfere with the hopeful' (emphasis mine), he conjures the image of a super-powered hope which appalling tragedies can irritate but in no way threaten.

Bowlin is surely correct when he ascribes to Aquinas the view that infused virtue may attain its ultimate end even when the proximate fails. And through its eschatological promise and reliance on grace, hope provides unique resources for dealing with proximate defeats by assuring us that the defeat is not total, and that the conditions of defeat are not permanent. Hope is therefore apt to sustain and comfort us when fortune goes awry: to help us persevere and grow even amid tragedies, injustices, failures, dry spells, discouragement, personal decline, and a general sense of *tedium vitae*. But Bowlin does not pause to consider our lack of guarantees here. At some point, we may begin to view the arduous journey as impossible or fail to rely properly on grace for our strength. This exposes us to the threats of sloth and despair.

Earlier, I discussed Aquinas' view of sloth or *acedia* as a spiritual disgust or 'sorrow about spiritual good' that makes the will resistant to grace. Typically, that sorrow results from inertia about the spiritual life and the sense that the demands of discipleship are too burdensome, making the whole affair an object of loathing.[30] This state often settles into the spiritual vacuum which results from the failure to 'rejoice in hope'. At the same time, bad fortune may pose its own temptations to *acedia*. Particularly when hope is feeble, the sheer accumulation of sad knocks may foster a melancholy outlook which makes divine help look unreal and future beatitude seem unlikely. Gregory the Great personifies sloth encouraging the Christian to despair: 'What reason do you have to be happy, putting up with so much grief?'[31] In this respect, Aquinas sees *acedia* as a gateway vice to despair. The arduous good may start to look like an impossible good when a person is overly downcast: 'because when this state of mind dominates his affections, it seems to him that he will never be able to rise to any good.... In this way despair is born of sloth'.[32]

Hope is equipped to help agents persevere through despondency, as courage braces us to persevere in frightful conditions. But like courage, hope is vulnerable to contrary temptations posed by our entanglement in the world of fortune. Granted, the ultimate end of infused virtue may be attained even when proximate ends are foiled. But the defeat of proximate ends often consists in misfortunes which tempt to sloth or despair, and in that sense misfortune threatens the agent's ordination to the ultimate end. Whether by sudden tragedy, the dashing of youthful hopes and dreams, the mounting of disappointments, or the slow attrition of the years, the blows of fortune try our hope. In its capacity of rational appetite, the will knowingly regards these troubles which frustrate the yearning for happiness and whose configuration over time is fraught with bewildering uncertainties. The result may be a demoralisation, brooding, and dejection that collapse into sloth and despair. Hope therefore remains vulnerable, and in the absence of renewed considerations and commitments it may fail.[33] Since misfortune is a characteristic medium for temptations to sins against hope, it follows that the hopeful are not invulnerable to fortune – any more than they are invulnerable to temptation or sin. It is simply not the case that 'there is no chance that fortune might interfere with the hopeful'.[34]

The Stoic hope option with its serene invincibility turns out to be a harmful obscuration. It thrusts the sombre threats of sloth and despair off-stage, making the hopeful feel overly secure and perhaps exposed to presumption. The unwitting effect is to make despair easier to fall into when suffering becomes weighty. Should misfortune tempt to sins against hope, agents who believe that misfortune lacks this power will have to conclude that *they* are to blame. Their Stoic armour-plating means that nothing external or contingent could have posed the moral hazard, so the push against their hope must be due to an internal breakdown. Just for having to flex its muscles against temptations to sloth or despair, the virtuousness of their hope will look doubtful. Prone to excessive self-condemnation, the appearance will be that their hope is weak or lost. They will be hope's equivalent of scrupulous people who think themselves morally indistinguishable from adulterers just because their pulse quickened when someone attractive entered the room. For if 'Success is guaranteed', and 'there is no chance that fortune' can afflict hope, what else could be to blame for temptations to sloth and despair but one's own flaccid or defunct hope? And since Stoic hope does not acknowledge moral vulnerability as basic or counsel leaning trustfully on God's grace when that vulnerability is tried, what source of help and strength might agents run to when they panic that their hope is weak? No source of help has been identified since the need for help has not been acknowledged. The ironic result is that by exaggerating hope's strength, Bowlin makes it weaker. Stoic hope neglects the ongoing moral vulnerability of the hopeful and therefore loses an essential quality of hope born from our neediness: namely, the doggedness and tenacity required amid the challenges that make the road long and the journey hard.

The Consolation of Hope

Aquinas says despair occurs either when one thinks that God will not give the grace needed for beatitude, or when one thinks forgiveness is impossible.

The latter kind of despair is perhaps rarer today, but the scrupulosity which views past sins as unforgivable still ravages some consciences. An example is Scobie, the protagonist of Graham Greene's *The Heart of the Matter*. He persists in an affair in the belief that his mistress will have a nervous breakdown if he leaves her. At the same time, he keeps the adultery secret from his wife to spare her trauma. In the end, hiding his guilt leads him to receive the Eucharist in mortal sin since abstaining would rouse his wife's suspicions. He continues this routine with no intention to repent. Thinking he is either unforgivable, or that he will never get the grace to repent, he concludes that he is such a moral bungler and blasphemer that the best thing to do would be to free everyone – God included – from the damage he causes them. He commits suicide in the belief that he is damning himself for the greater good.[35]

George Orwell believed the story was ridiculous, even granted the religious premises. Who in their right mind, he asks, would knowingly go to eternal damnation 'with a stiff upper lip' out of 'pure gentlemanliness … merely to spare the feelings of a couple of neurotic women?'[36] But Greene does at least capture the sense in which a despairing train of thought is itself warped, and he imparts despair's sense of being boxed in, of there being no escape. Many 'haunted by their past' are grievously battered by a moral self-loathing that may give rise to the horrible thought 'I don't deserve to be forgiven; I can't be forgiven'. As Stanley Hauerwas suggests, the possibility of such despair makes it necessary to 'learn to be a sinner' in the sense of learning to *identify* as a sinner, as someone who refuses self-righteousness, confesses faults, and requests forgiveness. This requires a lengthy *ascesis* involving self-knowledge and humility. It also requires avoiding the strange pride which inflates self-importance by treating one's sin as a cosmic crisis that even divine mercy cannot cope with. Perhaps most importantly, it requires the self-condemning and scrupulous to practise what St. Francis de Sales calls 'meekness toward oneself'; and this may require a different kind of *ascesis*.[37]

Probably a more common temptation to despair arises from doubts about whether God will provide the strength to persevere, or whether tragedy and suffering will break us in the end. But what does it *mean* to say that God will give us strength? Presumably it means something supernatural is going on; that the strength in question is a work of grace. What we need is a quasi-technical account of this: *quasi*, because we cannot speak as though from God's point of view; but *technical* to the extent that some content to our moral agency must be given. Aquinas' account may here be pressed into service. As discussed earlier, he viewed hope's causality roughly in means/ends terms: the 'final cause' or end is perfect beatitude, and the 'efficient cause' or means is helping grace or *auxilium*.[38] This may blandly be translated 'help', but the operative sense of *auxilium* is military, and was especially used to describe *auxiliary* troops or reinforcements who relieve a beleaguered army. The sense of 'help' is that of the cavalry coming to the rescue, and *auxilium* ascribes something like this to God's grace. Whereas habitual grace imparts a steady disposition to act, *auxilium* grace denotes God 'acting' upon us by a movement of grace that actualises the habit's potential.[39] Hope, as a virtue of habitual grace, therefore looks to God and relies on grace for continued help. This involves relying on God when discouraged or tempted to give up. What might this recourse look like at the level of detail, and what kind of consolation might we expect? Here I will build on and elaborate certain mechanics of Thomistic hope set forth in the second chapter.

As a virtue of the will, hope's bracing effect will boost volition. Its comfort will involve considerations that encourage the agent and help to reaffirm the commitment to carry on with the journey. Being the work of a supernatural virtue, the help we lean on is the *auxilium* which actualises the habit of hope. But since hope is the agent's own virtue, *auxilium* will work cooperatively, buoying up the will to recommit to hope rather than simply bypassing agency. I suggest that our agency will be engaged in several related forms: (1) the contemplation of what reasons we have to hope at all; (2) the consolation or encouragement that perseverance is possible with divine *auxilium*; and (3) the recommitment to the journey of hope combined with fresh reliance on divine help. This suite of movement, in which human agency has recourse to divine grace, we may perhaps call the 'prayer of leaning'.[40] I will briefly discuss each of its three parts.

Aspect (1) is the contemplation or *consideratio* of reasons for hope, and these centre on God's role as saviour throughout salvation history, particularly in the Incarnation and in the saving work of Christ.[41] The Resurrection of Christ is a particularly potent source for hope since it demonstrates that the eudaimonia gap, with the temptations to despair it poses, will ultimately be overcome. That subversion of the gap is nowhere better put than in *The Exsultet* proclamation of the Easter Vigil. There the candlelit assembly, liturgically skulking since Good Friday's 'pitch of grief', suddenly hears the joyous reversal: 'exalt, let them exalt' and 'be glad, let earth be glad', for Christ 'broke the prison-bars of death and rose victorious from the underworld'! This crescendo of the liturgical year announces an epistemology of the Resurrection according to which the Easter mystery will fully overcome the gap, demoting death itself from conqueror to conquered. The Pauline taunting of death, unforgettably set to music in Handel's *Messiah*, captures hope's ultimate subversive power: 'O death, where is thy sting? O grave, where is thy victory?' Only through hope in the Risen Christ can such audacity manage not to be ridiculous. Such considerations are warrants of God's power and mercy, and lend credence to divine promises for the eschaton. At the same time, hope's 'taunting' never turns into a cheap levity which forgets the tragedy of sin or costliness of redemption. The fact that Christ still bears his wounds even when raised – that even in apocalyptic imagery he is the 'lamb standing as if slain' (Rev. 5:6) – suggests that the Resurrection does not require forgetting or trivialising the forces of sin and death which mar human life until the eschaton, and which Christ took on in his Passion.

The *consideratio* of hope's basis and promises disposes to (2) the proper consolation of hope, which we might describe as the consolation of possibility. The intellect's belief that the ultimate good can be had with divine help may impinge upon the will, buoying it up with a sense of good prospect. As such, hope's proper *consolatio* may be subjectively experienced as a sense of encouragement, expectation, possibility, trust, invigoration, confidence, and resilience.[42] As the Psalmist says:

> The Lord is my light and my salvation;
> whom shall I fear?
> The Lord is the stronghold of my life;
> of whom shall I be afraid?
> Though a host encamp against me,
> my heart shall not fear;
> though war arise against me,
> yet I will be confident.
>
> (Ps 27: 1, 3)

As the Psalm makes clear, the psalmist is beset by enemies ('evildoers assail me to devour my flesh', Ps 27:2). So this is not cheap optimism, but confidence under fire. Obviously, the spiritual *consolatio* depends on the theological *consideratio*. 'I will be confident' hangs on the theological reasons for believing 'The Lord is my light and my salvation'. For Christians, principal reasons include the Incarnation, Passion, and Resurrection of Christ.

This consolation of possibility may or may not include emotional comfort. The conviction 'I can do all things in him who strengthens me' (Phil 4:13) is apt to encourage us in a way that involves feelings of hope which solace the afflicted. But properly speaking, hope's *consolatio* belongs to the will. So while 'sensible consolations' may arrive like water in the desert, they are not guaranteed, and are not even the goal. The goal, of course, is the *auxilium* grace of God, sought as 'our refuge and strength, a very present help in trouble' (Ps 46:1). The fact that hope's consolation does not always bring emotional comfort provides a comfort of its own: namely, the belief that spiritual dryness is not *proof* of divine abandonment.

The possibility of extreme dryness or desolation is one reason why it helps to describe hope as a virtue of the will which helps one to keep going not just until, but amid, the loss of characteristic enjoyment. However frightful the condition doubtless is, those who do not *feel* hopeful can still *go on* hoping. The examples of Christ in Gethsemane and of saints who endured the 'dark night' are instructive here.[43] When things grow dark and the will is dismayed by an ever-widening eudaimonia gap, hope may or may not offer emotional consolation. But the belief that the journey is possible with God's help is itself a consolation because it shows there to be possibilities other than despair.[44]

What I have loosely called the consolation of possibility disposes to (3) the renewed commitment to persevere in the journey while having prayerful recourse to God for the grace depended on in consequent exertion. In relation to this, Aquinas alters the linguistic picture of *auxilium* from a cavalry charge to the loving aid supplied by a 'friend in need'. To do so, he characterises the relationship between human petitioner and divine helper in terms of Aristotelian friendship. Aristotle sees the friend as someone to petition for help in time of need: most especially in weakness and old age.[45] Likewise, the Christian who is the friend of God through charity plays the role of the needy, hapless friend who petitions God for required grace or *auxilium*. Unsurprisingly, the representative way in which this is done is through the Lord's Prayer. As noted earlier, Aquinas sees this prayer as the preeminent expression of hope. It makes petition (*petitio*) or prayer (*oratio*) to the divine friend from whom the Christian asks for the *auxilia* needed to reach the kingdom.[46] From hope's perspective, it is therefore not enough to commit to persevere on the journey. A Pelagian could do that. To be an act of hope at all, and the particular act I have called the 'prayer of leaning', the agent must commit to persevere on the journey while seeking the grace to do so, and then act in the confidence that God will help us – or, put more strongly – will save us.[47] Expecting to receive aid from God 'as a helper strong to assist', the wayfarer is thereby emboldened to keep going.[48]

Possibilities for a Hopeful Death

If this is required during the ordinary trials of life, it is *a fortiori* required during great pain, tragedy, decline, and the violent and fearsome shock of dying. Death and dying have a peculiar relationship with hope. On one hand, they are a kind of spiritual border over which the hopeful must cross to fully attain what they hope for. On the other, they have the power to throw hope into grave doubt and threaten us with final despair. Late medieval theology in the Latin West insisted, with some plausibility, that we are especially prone to despair as death approaches and we face what Newman calls 'That sense of ruin, which is worse than pain/ That masterful negation and collapse/ Of all that makes me man'.[49]

Dying was never easy, to put it mildly. But today's social and medical context poses unique challenges. Death has gone from an inevitability prepared for beforehand and given public liturgical meaning afterward to a monstrosity we can make no sense of. Moreover, with the late modern 'triumph of medicalised death', the site of dying moved from the security and familiarity of the home to the mechanised and alien hospital. In a trade-off of agency, the main actor in death is no longer the dying but the doctor, who as William May puts it, goes from being a 'caretaker of the sick' to 'the enemy of death': 'The patient', he writes, lies 'helpless between two rival powers [death and medicine] that fight out their battle across relatively defenceless terrain'.[50] That inarticulate helplessness sums up countless people's experience of dying today. Of course, this context also provides medical support we would hardly do without, and is full of benevolent carers. Nonetheless, the contemporary experience of dying has become not just traumatic, but, what's worse, *unintelligible*: a landscape without signposts, an event without meaning, in which bewildered agency often frays. This setting can reinforce the demoralisation and brooding that tempt to *acedia* and the horror of despair.[51]

One excellent resource for addressing the temptations to despair posed by dying is the late medieval idea of the 'art of dying' (*ars moriendi*). It is beyond my scope to address this important topic in full, but I do want to give some sense of what role hope has within it. I am also less concerned here with the historical *ars moriendi* literature (fascinating as it is) than with the concept that dying could be an 'art' at all.[52] In contrast to the disempowerment and passivity frequent to 'medicalised death', the goal here was to foreground the agency of the dying: to say that dying is something we *do*, not just something that happens to us. To reflect this, the dying person in the tradition is ascribed an active role: that of *Moriens*, or the die-er, for whom dying becomes a 'work': something that fits into a project of the hopeful, somehow, rather than simply abolishing all projects.

That astonishing notion of dying as an 'art' validates agency but also makes demands on it, since it takes skill to practise any art, and practice to develop a skill. Hence the best guides in this tradition, such as Erasmus and Jeremy Taylor, focus less on the deathbed as the make-or-break moment and more on the lifelong cultivation of the skills to practise an art of dying.[53] This is *asceticism* in the original sense of spiritual and moral exercises analogous to an athlete's training.[54] The skills, of course, are the virtues, and it comes as no surprise that hope is a pre-eminent virtue in the *ars moriendi*.

Like all virtues, hope requires practice to develop. In part it must be developed with an eye to one's death. That way dying, when it approaches, will not pose considerations entirely novel – and therefore all the more dismaying – to the life and vision of hope cultivated up to that point. Ideally, dying should be taken account of long before it approaches, and should not catch us wildly off-guard in a way that shocks toward despair.

The spiritual practices by which we cultivate hope toward dying are not esoteric, and many are exercises which hope would in any case motivate. They might include liturgical celebrations of the Resurrection, prayers for the dead, meditation on death and last things, self-examination with a view to the coming judgment, visits to the dying, recollection of divine mercies, 'rejoicing in hope' with a view to future beatitude, and entrusting oneself to God for strength. To make these part of an *ascesis* preparing for death one would attend to the eschatological elements within them which cultivate awareness and attachment to eternal life (hope's 'final cause'), and which express trust and reliance upon divine grace to reach it (hope's 'efficient cause'). To paraphrase Jeremy Taylor, the best way to enable a hopeful dying is by a hopeful living.

Such spiritual-athletic practices forearm hope against the threat of despair posed by death. At the same time, many require more lucidity than we can bank on while dying. What then? There remains the 'prayer of leaning' described earlier which expresses the virtue of hope in a primary way by seeking and relying on God as one's ultimate goal and divine friend. Requiring little more cognition than it takes to cry for help, it is available to many who cannot practise elaborate spiritual exercises at death, and may occur in and through prayers of petition, reception of sacraments, and so forth. The Book of Psalms is of course the paradigm for relying on God this way. Without slurring over tragedy, the psalms voice total confidence in God as one's rock, refuge, and fortress despite horrors and at death: 'Yea, though I walk through the valley of the shadow of death, I will fear no evil: for thou art with me; thy rod and thy staff they comfort me' (Ps 23:4, KJV).

In addition to one's own agency, the role of the Church as the communion of the hopeful is crucial. A hopeful death is not just about 'doing' various practices as a lone ascetic, but being situated in the ecclesial context that sustains and gives hope meaning. The minister and fellow Christians must validate and encourage hope in the dying, especially when the mind is at the end of its tether. But even so, many cannot consciously practise an art of dying due to mental deterioration.[55] As Michael Banner notes, 40 per cent of people in the United Kingdom and the United States will not experience a lucid and 'clearly heralded death as commonly occurs with cancer'. Prior to death they will instead 'slip into protracted dotage and feebleness', perhaps through Alzheimer's or some other form of dementia. Banner argues that this 'trajectory toward death', marked by 'growing dependency', 'protracted long-term care', and reduced lucidity, will not 'allow us to assume the dying role' of the traditional *ars moriendi*.[56] Empirical studies and social anthropology have shown that recognisable forms of agency (of a type that 'ordinary people' tend not to register) remain even in those with severe dementia and kindred illnesses.[57] But the overall point is a useful reminder that we cannot assume that the dying will always be able to practise an 'art', leaving a gap in the *ars moriendi* itself.

In such cases of greatly impaired agency, the role of the Church is all the more important. Being comatose or seriously demented does not remove one from the body of Christ, and one's death is an event in that body of which Christ is the head. As a baptised infant is placed in the faith of the church, the comatose or demented may be placed in the hope of the church, particularly through ongoing care which treats them as intended for future glory, and through loving prayers on their behalf. Allen Verhey has stressed the need for patients rather than doctors to be the main actors at death.[58] But if we adopt a wider view of agency which mental incapacity requires – one which takes the communion of the saints seriously – then in a different respect we can say that the Church as a whole, the body of Christ in union with its head, is itself the primary actor at death.

Yet most can consciously enact the role of 'die-er' or *Moriens* to a significant degree. Sacramentally, the virtue of hope comes to a head in the last rites for Roman Catholics, and this is paralleled by prayers for the sick in the Book of Common Prayer. The last rites apply the sacraments of Anointing of the Sick, Penance, and the Eucharist in a hope-specialised way.[59] There the Eucharist collects a hope-specific name, *viaticum*, or 'food for the journey', in a way that tracks our hope-specific identity, *homo viator*. Moreover, the 'Commendation of the Dying' which follows *viaticum* is a treasury of readings and prayers for hope taken from Scripture and the psalms.

Ranging from the serene trust of 'The Lord is my shepherd' to Job's words of agony, they provide an overall script for a hopeful death which hovers at the borderline between fear, rage, lament, pleading, and feelings of abandonment, on one hand, and trust, confidence, assurance, and longing for God, on the other. They remind us that fellow travellers have been there before, and in the litany of saints, they recall that we are surrounded by that same cloud of witnesses. Taken together such texts give full expression to hope's basic act of steadfast reliance on God, and they give full scope to the tonalities of hope, from trust to lament to anticipation, making hope's exercise far from monolithic. In so doing, they express and pour many thoughts and feelings into a hope-shaped mould which absent such *ascesis* could readily drift towards despair.

From a Christian perspective, such prayers of reliance do what needs doing with a greater spiritual richness and psychological rawness than Kubler-Rossian stages of grief. The 'Commendation' or comparable texts should be worked into the life of hope, not just on the deathbed, but throughout the dying process. Keeping the Resurrection in view, contemplating scriptural exemplars of a good death, and finding words for one's struggles in the psalms gives a canonical script for hope to fall back on that helps the dying cope with outrageous circumstances and helps them overcome the temptation to despair. The final and supreme act for which the *ascesis* of hope trains us, and in which the virtue of hope culminates, is the act of surrendering one's life back to God in the hope that the grain of wheat dies to bear much fruit. In the lives of some saints, this act of self-bestowal has been serene, even ecstatic.[60] However, emotional comforts cannot be reckoned upon, and the consolation of hope as I have described it is far more complex. But as the example of Christ himself suggests, we can follow up 'Why have you forsaken me?' with the supremely reassuring 'Into your hands I commend my spirit'.[61]

The life of hope is a genuinely happy one, but its pursuit is arduous, and we ourselves remain vulnerable. Hope disarms the eudaimonia gap of its worst weapon, despair, but a hopeful life does not vacate the gap through Stoic opiates. How, then, are the hopeful to go on? What might life in the gap look like, poised between the 'already' and the 'not yet'? I suggested that the beatitudes help illustrate the policy of hope in conditions of imperfect happiness. That policy is complex and layered, but I singled out a few key aspects. First, the hope of the beatitudes acknowledges that the eudaimonia gap cannot be wholly overcome in this life or world. Utopianism may therefore be ruled out as a form of eschatological impatience. We cannot build a perfect 'city, and a tower whose top is in the heavens' (Gen 11:4).

Second, hope allows us to appreciate that beatitude truly can begin in this life. A conscientious commitment to misery is not baggage the Christian needs to carry. Third, hope does not motivate a truce with the eudaimonia gap, or the conditions that make for sin and grief. The beatitudes express hunger and thirst for justice, the extending of mercy, and commitments to peace-making, all of which help overcome impediments to people's happiness. The policy of hope as expressed by the beatitudes is therefore one of *zealous patience* with the circumstances of imperfection. It motivates a socially committed way of life that faces down utopianism, misanthropy, and despair by ardently seeking such beatitude as may be had in this life – individually and socially – as a very valuable but limited beginning.

The result is a bittersweet happiness that faces tragedy with hope rather than resignation. All of this requires the admission that we remain vulnerable, not just to suffering, but to the temptations of sloth and despair which suffering poses. I therefore disagreed with John Bowlin for characterising hope as transcending moral hazard through Stoic insulation from the world of contingency. In considering the threat of despair, I stressed the resilience, encouragement, and perseverance which hope makes possible. But this is not a Pelagian affair. It requires recourse to grace: for example, in what may be called the prayer of leaning. Such recourse is the basic act of hope when beset with difficulties, and I suggested that it involves several ingredients: (1) the consideration based on salvation history and particularly the life, death, and Resurrection of Christ that hope's goal is possible and that God will not abandon us. (2) The consolation of possibility in which renewed awareness that 'I can do all things in him who strengthens me' (Phil 4:13) provides the encouragement to persevere. (3) The agent's renewed commitment to persevere in the journey of hope while simultaneously having recourse to the grace or *auxilium* of God who is trusted as a 'helper strong to assist'.[62]

Hope also offers unique resources for facing death. It provides what Kenneth Burke calls a 'structure of encouragement': one which assures those in an end-of-life battle of attrition that 'a personal tomorrow still exists' for them and their loved ones in contrast to 'the disastrous feeling of "not worth while"' that fosters despair.[63] By calling to mind the grounds for hope, by making clear that our present situation is not permanent, and by relying on grace to sustain us, hope braces the will to persevere in the journey and precludes undue dejection, sloth, and despair. As Isaiah wrote: 'They that hope in the Lord shall renew their strength; they shall take wings as eagles; they shall run and not be weary; they shall walk and not faint' (Is 40:31).

CHAPTER 6

The Problem of Worldliness

Now we have received not the spirit of the world, but the Spirit which is from God.

1 Corinthians 2:12

She started singing, and the way she sang
Captured my mind – it could not free itself.
'I am', she sang, 'the sweet Siren, I am,
Whose song beguiles the sailors in mid-sea,
Enticing them, inviting them to joy!
My singing made Ulysses turn away
From his desired course; who dwells with me
Seldom departs, I satisfy so well.

Dante, *Paradiso*, canto XIX

In discussing finite goods and earthly projects, the way that hope resists presumption and calls for moral effort, and the social commitments of the beatitudes, I have argued that hope invests us in worldly goods, and even ordains them to our eternal end. In part this was to shake off the stubborn prejudice that hope insinuates quietism, misanthropy, and dualism. In part it was to illuminate the nature of hope itself. But even if hope were a leaven to the world, this would still leave unanswered the question of how the hopeful see their place within it. The New Testament says that 'here we have no lasting city, but seek one which is to come' (Heb 13:14). This raises obvious tensions in terms of the agent's identity as a sort of 'dual citizen' who seeks happiness first in the earthly city, but ultimately in the heavenly city. Since these cities often represent competing loyalties – most dramatically seen in martyrdom – this forces us to think through the relationship between those identities, and the prospects for social and ecclesial tension they involve.

Early Christians often do give the impression of having a foot in two worlds: a departing foot in this one, and an arriving foot in the next. To take just one biblical instance, the Letter to the Hebrews notes with

160

approval the worldly alienation of Abel, Enoch, Noah, and Abraham, all of whom 'acknowledged that they were strangers and exiles on the earth' (Heb 11:13). This is not credited to their own idiosyncrasies, but is represented as highly reasonable: 'They desired a better country, that is, a heavenly one' (Heb 11:13–16). The early Church reinforced such trends. The second-century *Epistle to Diognetus* famously said that Christians 'reside in their own homelands, but as if they were foreigners ... they are in the world but not of the world'.[1] The sense of a foot in two worlds helped fashion the image of Christians as pilgrims or wayfarers on the journey of hope from the earthly to the heavenly city.[2] As Peter Brown says, the early Church espoused a jubilant and confident hope which not only wanted to 'leap-frog' the world, but which even 'tended to leapfrog the grave (through) a heady belief in the afterlife'.[3]

Similar views emerge in the patristic, medieval, and later tradition where 'the world' becomes a foil to the Christian pilgrim or wayfarer on the journey of hope.[4]

This can create the impression that the hopeful are deeply alienated from earthly society. Honouring Caesar, paying taxes, or engaging in social charity would not necessarily alter this. Christians might, for important reasons, seek to benefit the earthly city; but this alone would not imply that they *identify* with it, or feel they really belong to it. The possible impression could be quite the reverse. As Gerhart Ladner says, in the historical tradition *homo viator* generally sees the earthly stop as a temporary inn: 'he will rest in it bodily, but mentally he is already somewhere else'.[5]

Must Christians be 'in the world' but 'not of it' in a way that alienates them from family, town, community, culture, and civil society more broadly? The *homo viator* motif to many seems to imply this. I will concede that the wayfarer model at its most Platonic is guilty as charged. But rather than discarding the model as such, I will suggest that Thomistic hope sustains a model of *homo viator* that does not entail a worrisome alienation. On the contrary, there are intriguing resources in that account for better understanding and sustaining the identification with one's country and with society.

At the same time, it would be foolish and self-deceiving to whitewash historical Christian tensions with 'the world'. There is *some sense* in which that locus has been held suspect in high places. Christ ominously told his disciples: 'If the world hates you, know that it has hated me first ... because you are not of the world ... therefore the world hates you' (John 15:18–19). Historical reflection on hope is likewise ambivalent or distrustful about 'the world'. This ambivalence may look like an embarrassment best dropped discreetly, but I will suggest that the tradition identified subtle problems we have neglected to our own loss. It may have addressed those problems with varying degrees of success, but I believe that the traditional ambivalence of hope concerning 'the world' (in some yet-to-be-defined sense) was not misanthropic or paranoid, but morally reasonable and eschatologically inevitable.

What made Christians in the past eager not to be 'of the world' in some morally charged way? Despair and presumption are usually seen as hope's opposites. But in the tradition that stretches from the New Testament, Church fathers, medieval scholastics, and Protestant reformers up to Vatican II, another great threat to hope was identified. More pervasive than despair and presumption, and a breeding ground for both, it has faded from moral consciousness along with the category used to mark it out. This threat to hope is the state of character known as 'worldly sin' or 'worldliness': a category which despite its contemporary neglect was a major figure in the older tradition.

Aquinas and others describe this pejorative sense of the world as the excessive attachment to external and this-worldly goods such as wealth, fame, reputation, social status, honours, power, and influence.[6] These motivations, and the social conditions they help to configure, are 'the world' which the hopeful are cautioned not to be 'of'. More than a single vice, worldliness is a complex state of character in which we judge our identity to be ultimately this-worldly and therefore shut the door to eschatological hope. Since worldliness is also a major cause of apathy towards the poor and the underprivileged, I will suggest that the topic is relevant to social ethics generally. Looking towards remedies, I will examine hope's overlooked beatitude, poverty of spirit, suggesting that its voiding of greed, vanity, ambition, and power-seeking is the best remedy to the worldly character. This beatitude was traditionally seen as the remedy to worldliness. It is therefore no surprise that when concern about the latter receded, the beatitude itself was left with little work to do. By putting worldliness back on the map, the importance of hope's specific beatitude should be made clearer.

Worldliness is vicious and dehumanising, as will be discussed. Hope's opposition to it frees the wayfarer to be 'of the world' with respect to virtuous earthly projects and the building of a just society. The consequence, I suggest, is that the hopeful are *contra mundum* in a way that actually allows them to be far more *pro mundo* than they could otherwise be. In the next and last chapter I will explain just what hope may contribute to the earthly city, and the investment which the hopeful have in their social and this-worldly identities.

Worldliness in the Tradition

Aquinas has many insightful things to say about worldliness, but on this subject he is less a pioneer and more a faithful transmitter of the received tradition. He also assumes that his readers are familiar with what the tradition says about worldliness and often just directs them to the pertinent biblical or patristic sources.[7] Since part of my goal is to retrieve worldliness as a coherent moral category, I will begin with a history of the concept to bring into sight what the tradition meant and what associations it called up for Aquinas and most Christians in past ages.

The New Testament consistently uses shocking language to describe 'the world'. In Luke's Gospel, 'the children of the world' are sharply distinguished from 'the children of the light'. John's Gospel calls the devil 'the ruler of this world' who must be 'cast out' (John 12:31). Later in the same Gospel, Christ says that the world cannot receive the 'Spirit of truth' (John 14:17). World-bashing receives its most blunt spokesman in James: 'Do you not know that friendship with the world is enmity with God? Therefore whoever wishes to be a friend of the world makes himself an enemy of God' (James 4:4). Perhaps most chillingly, the first letter of John states that 'the whole world is in the power of the evil one' (5:19) and that 'If anyone loves the world, love for the Father is not in him' (1 John 2:15).

Whatever is meant by 'the world' in such passages, it is obviously seen as a permanent and malignant setting to the Christian vocation. But it is not immediately clear why the world should be described so pejoratively. Did not God create the world and call it very good? More baffling, how is one to square 'for God so loved the world' (John 3:16) with 'love not the world' (1 John 2:15)? Scripture scholars have shown that the English word 'world' does duty for several different Greek words, helping cause this confusion. 'World' may translate the Greek words *ge, he oikoumene, kosmos,* or *aion.*[8] *Ge* and *he oikoumene* sometimes refer to the earth but more often to the human race, and are not used pejoratively. The former in the Septuagint is that earth of which Genesis proclaims: 'And God saw that it was good' (Gen 1:10). All the passages condemning 'the world' in Greek condemn either *kosmos* or *aion.* In John's Gospel, *kosmos* can refer either to the physical world or the human race, as in 'for God so loved the *kosmos*'. Or it can refer to a fallen order set up in rivalry to God, as in 'love not the *kosmos*'.[9] Outside of John the dominant pejorative is *aion,* a temporal term meaning 'epoch', 'period', or 'age'. This is 'the world' that Scripture usually rails against: 'the present *aion*' (Matt. 12:32), which fell into sin and represents an order opposed to the coming of God's kingdom or *basileia*.[10] Its dominant images are Babylon and Babel, and it is sharply distinguished with the new, everlasting 'world to come' (Matt. 12:32), in which the kingdom of God will establish undisputed rule.

The Risen Christ is the first fruits of this new '*aion* to come'. Christians are drawn into his regenerated life, and all creation groans for the coming glory (Rom 8:22), but the old *aion* and its fallen ways linger until the eschaton. There is thus an 'already' with a 'not yet'. This sense of inhabiting a twilight between the ages created the image of the Christian as a pilgrim or wayfarer who is on a journey of hope from the worldly to the heavenly *aion*.[11] To take just one biblical instance, 1 Peter describes Christians as 'pilgrims and strangers on the earth' (1 Peter 2:11).

The early Church reinforced these trends, as seen in the already-quoted passage from the *Epistle to Diognetus*.[12] Augustine famously contrasted the 'pilgrim City of God' with the 'City of the World', the two of which are divided by competing loves.[13] Such thought was ubiquitous in the patristic and medieval Church. From the *Moralia* of Pope Gregory the Great and the *Rule of St. Benedict* to medieval hagiography, 'the world' and worldliness become foils to the Christian pilgrim or wayfarer on the journey of hope.[14]

Inflate such language without discretion, and Christianity becomes Manichean, dualist, or quietist. Hence the need for identifying what precisely is being condemned under the labels of 'the world' and worldliness. Most of the tradition – and to my eye, the best and most nuanced of it – took its cue from the key passage in 1 John: 'all that is in the world, the desire of the flesh, the desire of the eyes and the boastful pride of life, is not of the Father' (1 John 2:16).[15] This passage had the benefit of specifying what was actually being condemned. In the high medieval period especially, this passage came to be understood as condemning the feverish pursuit of pleasurable vanities (the 'desire of the flesh'), preoccupation with wealth and possessions (the 'desire of the eyes'), and the lust for power, renown, and honours (the 'boastful pride of life'). This was a distinction which Aquinas expressed and reinforced.[16]

That line of interpretation helped to give rise to the familiar triad of 'the world, the flesh, and the devil' as the standard sources of temptation: a triad common in baptismal formulae, emphasised by Aquinas, and made familiar in English through the *Book of Common Prayer*.[17] A sampling of texts over different periods will give a sense of what was meant by 'the world' in this pejorative sense. Dante in the *Purgatorio* personifies the world and worldliness by a Siren whose perilous song tempts the pilgrim to forget *Paradiso* altogether. As one victim of the Siren tells Dante: 'our eyes, attached to worldly goods, would never leave the earth to look above'.[18] Chaucer in the *Canterbury Tales* describes two forms of being ensnared by 'the world'. One is an excessive and upwardly mobile ambition to climb the social and economic ladder. By contrast, his Oxford clerk is praised for not being 'so worldly as to seek office': that is, he does not abandon his impecunious religious and philosophical research for a lucrative secular post.[19] Chaucer's second form of worldliness is the pride and complacency resulting from established riches, noble blood, high rank, estates, expensive clothing, and the like.[20] The greedy social climber familiar to much middle-class mythology is thus distinguished from the 'high born' worldling surrounded by aristocratic splendour. In Spenser's *Faerie Queen*, Mammon rules over the 'court of Ambition'. Proclaiming himself the 'God of the world and worldlings', his baits are riches, renown, power, honours, and estate.[21] Note that prosperity, high position, and a good name are not themselves condemned in such passages; what is reproved is the excessive ambition, sinful misuse, and complacency taken in them. Many sources see 'pomps and vanity' as the special token of worldliness. In *As You Like It*, Shakespeare identifies it with the 'painted pomp' of court life with its strutting, intrigue, jealousy, and flattery, contrasting these vanities with the simplicity of rustics and the contemplation of hermits.[22] An excellent summary of this tradition was given by the Anglican theologian William Law in the eighteenth century. There he described the temptations of 'the world' in these terms:

> To abound in wealth, to have fine houses, and rich clothes, to be attended with splendour and equipage, to be beautiful in our persons, to have titles of dignity, to be above our fellow-creatures, to command the bows and obeisance of other people, to be looked on with admiration, to overcome our enemies with power, to subdue all that oppose us, to set out ourselves in as much splendour as we can, to live highly and magnificently, to eat, and drink, and delight ourselves in the most costly manner, these are the great, the honourable, the desirable things, to which the spirit of the world turns the eyes of all people.[23]

Aquinas himself believes that the cause of this worldliness or 'worldly love' (*amor mundanus*) is the inordinate pursuit of external, transitory, this-worldly goods.[24] By this worldly love a person 'hopes in the world as his end' rather than in God.[25] By its very orientation, serious worldliness calls the wayfarer's journey of hope to a halt. It should therefore be no surprise that it is a major breeding ground for presumption and despair.

As previously discussed, Aquinas sees presumption as the breakdown of hope's 'efficient cause': the grace on which hope leans.[26] One conspicuous way this occurs is when through overconfidence and self-satisfaction we begin to lose sight of our need for grace and so fail to rely on God for strength and mercy. Worldliness accelerates this state. The worldly desire wealth, status, influence, and acclaim, and are generally eager to take credit for their own success. As John Henry Newman says:

> When a man has been advanced in the world by means of his own industry and skill, when he began poor and ends rich, how apt will he be to pride himself, and confide ... in his own resources ... how will such an one be tempted to self-complacency and self-approbation! How apt will he be to rely upon himself, to rest contented with himself.[27]

That spirit of godlike self-reliance sums up vulgar and widespread forms of the American Dream and related expressions that are still common. Yet Newman's overall point must be qualified. The attainment of this-worldly success, status, reputation, influence, and prosperity neither constitutes nor necessitates worldliness or presumption. As Newman wisely acknowledges, 'It may be a duty' for those with the requisite vocation 'to accept these things' and to 'not so much put them away, as to put away our old natures'.[28] Material success does not necessitate presumption any more than beauty necessitates lust. But if it is unchecked by hope's acknowledged dependence on grace, prosperity can easily produce the spirit of self-reliance that constitutes presumption. The remedy to this Pelagian mind-set is an acknowledged dependence on God's grace: to overcome presumption by getting hope's 'leaning' right. This requires a frank admission of one's creaturely neediness and poverty before the creator as well as prayerful recourse to God for needed grace and mercy.[29] Hope's conscious reliance on God counteracts that worldly presumption which is founded on the illusion of self-sufficiency. A consequence is that the Christian wayfarer cannot truthfully construe him or herself as an elite being who stands over and above 'the world', but as a sinner who is always in need of healing and forgiveness.

In contrast to presumption, Aquinas sees despair as the breakdown of hope's 'final cause': the end of eternal happiness for which hope longs.[30] It may not at first be evident why worldliness is a source of despair. This is because the kind of despair it fosters has receded from most people's moral taxonomies. Aquinas himself saw it clearly. He suggests that despair can happen in two ways. Hope's object, as noted before, is a 'future good possible but arduous to attain'.[31] The first kind of despair believes beatitude is an *impossible* good. This is either because one's sins seem too great to be forgiven, or because one is so miserable that it seems one 'will never be able to rise to any good'.[32] These are both recognisable and horrible forms of despair. But alongside this is a second form which denies that happiness is a future *arduous* good. It occurs when a wayfarer decides that happiness can be had on easier terms than the costly discipleship of committed Christianity, and so abandons the journey.[33] It may seem odd to call this a form of despair since the agent still hopes for happiness. To clarify we must therefore distinguish between 'theological' despair, which despairs of God (*theos*) as the source of happiness; and total despair, which despairs of happiness as such. The despair which denies that happiness is arduous is of the former but not the latter kind since the agent still hopes for happiness in some form. Because *a* habit of hope likely remains in the agent, he or she will continue to look and act hopefully, giving the impression that despair is not present. I will call this 'gentle despair' to distinguish it from the more familiar 'total despair'.

Aquinas ascribes this gentle despair to preoccupation with created goods which absorb our affections and make spiritual goods seem remote, boring, and evanescent. He writes: 'love of those pleasures leads someone to have distaste for spiritual, and not to hope for them as arduous goods. In this way is despair caused'.[34] Aquinas' own example for this is sexual pleasure, but his general point is that overindulgence in created goods spoils our spiritual palate, so to speak. Whether it happens quickly or slowly gains ground over the years, worldliness breeds the 'here and now' mindset which makes hope's eternal end look increasingly vague, costly, and remote – a mere will o' the wisp. The result is that the 'arduous' demands of Christianity no longer seem worth it compared to the more immediate gratifications to be had on secular terms. The excessive gratifications found in money, possessions, social status, power, reputation, fame, and honours fill precisely this role for the worldly. Thus whereas despair is usually associated with devastating sorrow and dejection, worldliness causes a largely unnoticed and even 'optimistic' despair in which hope for fulfilment shifts from God to this-worldly idols.[35] It produces that 'distaste for spiritual goods' through a state of sloth or 'spiritual sadness' which makes the wayfarer want to forget hope altogether.[36] Though worldliness has been neglected in the literature on hope, the set of attitudes, values, and habits it causes plainly subvert hope as a virtue. If is fully grown, Christian wayfarers forget who they are and where they are going, forsaking the journey of hope. Their state is then analogous to the sailors in *The Odyssey* who joined the Lotus Eaters: 'those who ate this honeyed plant ... longed to stay forever ... forgetful of their homeland'.[37]

A caveat must be issued to prevent misunderstanding. To resist worldliness, the wayfarer need not adopt the strictest asceticism, condemn all joys and culture of the present life, and in general walk about like a crank. As Sir Toby says in *Twelfth Night*: 'Dost thou think, because thou art virtuous, there shall be no more cakes and ale?'[38] Augustine and Gregory the Great both speak of how the wayfarer may legitimately enjoy the refreshment of a few 'wayside inns' on the journey, and say that these inns correspond to the good and innocent comforts one finds in life 'on the way'. The danger comes if the wayfarer 'lingers at the inn', failing to progress on the journey or even mistaking the inn for a permanent home.[39] To recall an earlier distinction, whereas the world in the pejorative sense (*aion, kosmos*) calls for resistance while the world in the benign sense (*ge, he oikoumene*) does not, even in the benign sense enjoyment of the world calls for balance, temperance, and the correct setting of priorities.

Avarice, Vainglory, and Ambition

Just what are the specific temptations of worldliness that tempt the wayfarer to gentle despair, and what are the remedies in the tradition for countering this? Pruning a very fertile and tangled body of reflection, Aquinas reduces worldly ends to four. They are wealth, power, fame, and honours.[40] Excessive attachment to wealth produces the vice of avarice, which Aquinas regards as immoderate love of money and the possessions money can buy.[41] This can be expressed in different forms, but most representative are hoarding and prodigality. The hoarder or miser loves the sheer accumulation of wealth and possessions. But perhaps more common today is the prodigal, spendthrift, or wastrel: that paragon of consumerism who craves the thrill of excessive shopping and buying.[42] Though the pursuit of power is distinct from the pursuit of wealth, the two are obviously related since getting and keeping wealth and resources typically requires local and international exercises of power, domination, and coercion.[43]

The worldly ends of fame and honours are more complex than that of wealth. Aquinas distinguishes undue desire for fame (which he calls vainglory) from preoccupation with honours (which he calls ambition). The vainglorious desire for fame and the ambitious desire for honours both proceed from pride, which is the inordinate desire to excel or establish superiority.[44] Not content simply with excelling, both vainglory and ambition wish to be *seen* and *esteemed* as excelling. But unlike vainglory, ambition is fastidious about its audience. The ambitious want to be deemed excellent not by the masses, but by 'the people who matter'.[45] By contrast there is an indiscriminateness and latent vulgarity in vainglory, which seeks celebrity status, newspaper fame, or even sensationalist notoriety on almost any terms. Widespread contemporary forms of vainglory are easily seen in the thirst for acclaim which imbues much popular culture. To take one example, consider the wild acclaim, the disciple-like mimicry, and the name-brand merchandising enjoyed by countless movie, TV, sport, and music celebrities. Millions of youths regard them as their idols, heroes, and exemplars *not* because of any perceived moral greatness, but simply due to their charm, distinction, and glamor. The appetite for fame and the famous casts a wide and indiscriminate net, now exalting in the red-carpeted glitter of a Hollywood Oscars ceremony, now grubbing for the petty acclaim of reality TV. A mania for fame is a manifest deadweight to the virtue of hope. When solidly entrenched, it makes wayfarers reluctant to look beyond a world where they may be so petted and admired, or at least makes them one of the starry-eyed fans whose 'minds lick up shadows'.

Ambition refuses to be similarly garish. Whereas the vainglorious simply want notoriety and applause as such, the ambitious want approval and distinctions from 'the right people': those deemed excellent, exclusive, and judicious, who are seen as having the right expertise and taste.[46] Ambition often produces a familiar contemporary type: the driven social climber who is eager to move up the professional or corporate ladder, acts from enlightened self-interest, flatters those with influence, trips up rivals, and shuns the unimportant and out of favour. If and when this opportunist becomes successful and is thought reputable, an agreeable sense of security, status, and smugness settles in. He or she is now considered accomplished and *distingué*. At the social level this smugness is often expressed through the pride felt in belonging to a superior and exclusive club. The group may preen itself for intellectual, cultural, national, economic, or even religious pretensions. 'We' may be the Greeks versus the barbarians, the aristocracy versus the common people, the Elect versus the ungodly, the rich versus the poor, the intelligentsia versus the philistines, or white-collar versus blue-collar workers. The important thing is that 'we' are the important, the distinguished, those 'in-the-know'. Ambition to get in or move up, snobbery once one has arrived, and domination of those below are the general trends. The net effect is to cause the ambitious to feel ultimately and magnificently self-satisfied and at home in this world, making the prospect of the eschaton little more than a vague threat to their secure, this-worldly splendour.[47]

If unchecked by some ascesis, these worldly vices lead to innumerable evils. Blown up to the collective level, they readily take the forms of plutocracy, racism, classism, militarism, and elitism of all kinds. Moreover, they dispose to apathy towards the poor, the disabled, the underprivileged, the oppressed, and the ostracised. Since such people rarely have worldly advantages to offer, they are typically shunned or ignored by the worldly.

The domineering, greedy, consumptive, flashy, and arrogant complex of vice that produces the worldly character is very much with us today. Examples could be multiplied, but let one suffice. Modern consumerism has been a very fertile womb for worldly sin.[48] At an elite level, avarice and ambition motivate many of the jet-hopping executives whose multinational corporations thrive on systems of greed and acts of hubris for which it is very difficult to hold them accountable.[49] Corporate elites frequently and with impunity exploit domestic workers at home, promote the dirty little secret of sweatshops abroad, break unions, manipulate geopolitical affairs, and wreck ecosystems with industrial waste. This phenomenon is in fact one of large-scale avarice and ambition in contemporary garb. Moreover, corporate marketing specialises in appealing to and further inflaming the greed, vanity, and self-importance of average consumers to ensure and ulti-mately increase profits. The products include costly emblems of lifestyle and trendy items whose name-brand chic confers the prestige and status sought by both the vainglorious and ambitious.[50]

Whether it is about getting the latest smartphone, an Armani suit, or a car with bragging rights, the consumeristic drive for finery is not just avarice writ large. As one marketing manual astutely notes, the successful company will cater to the consumer's 'desire to feel special'.[51] Barry Schwartz writes that: 'Part of (consumers') satisfaction from achievements and possessions comes from the awareness that not everybody can match them'.[52] In other words, the winning formula in marketing is to appeal not just to consum-ers' greed, but to their vainglory and ambition – in short, to worldliness. In the era of globalisation, such structures of sin threaten not just the virtue of hope, but the moral character and well-being of billions of people, along with the health of the planet itself. My focus here is the effect worldli-ness has on hope and my primary resource is historical. Nevertheless, it is important to make clear that worldliness plays out today in widespread and recognisable forms that threaten hope and countless other goods. In the following section, I will gesture at alternatives and remedies.

Worldliness is not just a cause, but a symptom of what I have called 'gentle despair'. On one hand, seeking ultimate comfort in some combina-tion of wealth, power, fame, and ambition smothers eschatological hope in those who have it. On the other, those lacking hope for eternal beatitude frequently default to the above in their desire to 'drink life to the lees' in this world.[53] This state of gentle despair has been overlooked in favour of 'total despair' with its forlorn desperation. Since few inhabit the latter's psychological netherworld, despair is mistakenly thought to be found only in the severely depressed or suicidal. But while it may lack tragic sullenness and wear a trendy and smiling demeanour, the gentle despair caused by worldliness is a sepulchre none the better for being whited. By exposing it, we correct a false impression which makes despair look exceedingly rare and hardly a live threat to 'normal' people. Correlatively, we see that the existing hope deficit is both ruinous in itself and in its wider effects.

Blessed are the Poor in Spirit

Various 'unworldly' remedies have been advised in the patristic, medieval, and later Western tradition for overcoming worldliness. Spiritual contemplation and works of charity were often recommended as remedies to what the *Book of Common Prayer* calls the 'pomps and vanity of this wicked world'.[54] As a long-term solution, religious life with its vowed poverty, chastity, and obedience was long considered the 'unworldly' trump card. The later tradition complicated this view. As Newman helpfully observed, in the cloister itself we may find 'the evil in which the world lies, in your own hearts', making Christians 'the world to each other'.[55] Besides, most Christians are not vowed religious. So while the evangelical counsels may be an exemplary way of living out hope, more broadly applicable resources are necessary.

As an essential remedy for worldliness we may consider hope's beatitude of poverty of spirit.[56] Aquinas regards this beatitude as a negation of pride, pomp, and greed. The beatitudes in general represent values that are plainly at odds with 'worldly wisdom', declaring states such as poverty, mourning, and meekness as blessed. Yet Aquinas states that the Sermon on the Mount, which opens with the beatitudes, 'contains the whole process of forming the life of a Christian'.[57] Since one does not need to be a monk to be a Christian, this implies that the unworldly remedies of the beatitudes are applicable to all Christians, and not just a select circle of vowed religious. The first of the beatitudes is 'blessed are the poor in spirit', which Aquinas associates with the theological virtue of hope. He interprets spiritual poverty in part as the renunciation of arrogant ambition and domineering ('the voiding of a proud and puffed up spirit'). That renunciation makes it freeing rather than burdensome to refuse a life devoted to money and prestige. I regard this beatitude as an essential means for combatting worldly sin.[58] But first we must ask the preliminary question: how does Aquinas' interpretation of this beatitude fare at the hands of biblical scholars?

Most contemporary biblical scholars regard the poor of the beatitudes as continuous with the 'the poor' (*ptochoi*) of the Septuagint and 'the poor' ('*ny*) of the Hebrew Old Testament. To be poor in this biblical sense had economic, social, and religious connotations. As Robert Guelich puts it, '*the poor* in Judaism referred to those in desperate need (socioeconomic element) whose helplessness drove them to a dependent relationship with God (religious element) for the supplying of their needs and vindication'.[59] Beggars, orphans, widows, and the destitute are representative types. But often the poor are further conceived as victims of the rich and powerful: as the oppressed, the underpaid, and the exploited who hope not just for sustenance, but for vindication.[60] In Isaiah 61, the promise is made of 'good news to the poor (*ptochoi*)', the hungry, and those who mourn. Davies, Allison, Guelich, and Betz see the beatitudes as claiming the fulfilment of these promises through the good news of the in-breaking kingdom in which the first will be last and the last will be first.[61]

Guelich pithily sums up Matthew's poor in spirit as 'those who find themselves waiting, empty-handed, upon God alone for their hope and deliverance'.[62] Any biblical short list would include 'Mary and Joseph, Simeon and Anna, Zachariah and Elizabeth, the shepherds of Bethlehem, and the Twelve' who are contrasted with the swaggering court of Herod and the well-fed religious elite.[63] While Luke declares 'the poor' rather than 'the poor in spirit' blessed, the commonest reading is that Matthew and Luke both have in mind the *ptochoi* or '*ny* of the Old Testament whose typically low socioeconomic status went with the typically religious attitude of finding their 'only hope in God'. In that respect, both evangelists support the connection between spiritual poverty and hope that is at issue.[64]

The beatitude does not declare sheer literal poverty to be blessed. After all, poverty can co-exist with wickedness, and why would all four Gospels enjoin Christians to alleviate poverty if this meant revoking the beatitude of the poor? Possibly to untie such knots, Matthew's beatitude describes the blessed state as being poor 'in spirit'. Dale Allison interprets 'in spirit' as a mentality which often but not always accompanied literal poverty.[65] Similarly, Hans Dieter Betz describes it as the '*insight*' of those who correctly recognise – typically but not necessarily through the difficult conditions of literal poverty – that the human condition as such is vulnerable, limited, needy, and dependent on God.[66] The beatitude itself is therefore separable from degrading poverty even though it grates against a life of luxury and affluence: an important point. The consequence is that liberation from poverty does not itself exclude one from the beatitude, thereby making the duty to aid the poor compatible with remaining poor in spirit.[67]

What exactly is the 'mentality' or 'insight' which makes one poor 'in spirit'? Betz claims that the disposition which corresponds to the insight is 'humility' construed as a truthful reading of the dependent human condition with respect to each other and before God. This poverty-as-humility is 'opposed to hubris, arrogance, self-indulgence': to a self-dependent, self-inflated lifestyle which performatively denies one's creaturehood and misreads one's human condition.[68] Aquinas similarly says that by this beatitude a person 'does not, by pride, seek greatness either in himself or in external goods, namely honours and wealth ... this proceeds from poverty of spirit'.[69]

Where Aquinas does differ from Matthew is in his tendency to speak of poverty as a chosen state either of vowed poverty or of a humble detachment which refuses to seek wealth, status, honours, and privilege. By contrast, biblical scholars typically claim that Matthew has more in mind those who are simply landed with destitution, oppression, and abuse, and who respond heroically with hope in God.[70] Though he says nothing to rule out those born poor, Aquinas' examples of the poor showcase renunciants rather than the exploited. This is an important difference of emphasis since it means that Aquinas fails to accent the victimhood that the Bible generally ascribes to the poor. In that respect, his account is fittingly corrected by the biblical sources which foreground that important matter. At the same time, his stress on voluntarily renouncing wealth and privilege for those who have the luxury of this choice pushes Aquinas' poor towards Matthew's both 'in spirit' and in fact. Indeed, it opens up the possibility of a side-by-side and not just sentimental solidarity across socioeconomic lines that would otherwise be hard to come by. So while important differences remain at the level of interpretation and especially of emphasis, Aquinas' view of spiritual poverty is not simply incompatible with the biblical texts and in many respects nicely complements them. As Hans Dieter Betz says with evident surprise: Aquinas' treatment 'although imposition, was carefully grafted onto a text that provides such points of contact and that seems strangely open to such interpretation'.[71]

Following Augustine's long-received opinion, Aquinas associates poverty of spirit with the gift of fear and so with hope.[72] But what might this beatitude look like in practice? Aquinas does not propose one discrete act type, but holds that poverty of spirit can be expressed through multiple practices, though he does not say much about what these might be.[73] For tangible and detailed ways of living spiritual poverty, we should therefore look to other sources and possibilities.

In an entertainment and consumerist culture which hides death and dying, one much-needed expression of spiritual poverty is the practice of *memento mori* (literally: 'remember [that you have] to die').[74] The goal is to soberly reflect that the bloom of youth, the security and comfort of wealth, the glory of the famous, and the distinguished swagger of the honoured are all alike fleeting. Meditations on death, visits to the sick and dying, and sober thoughts in a graveyard are all advocated as disabusing us from painted pomp, and as reminders that 'All flesh is as grass, and all its glory as the flower of the field' (Is 40:6). This Ash Wednesday message against worldly *vanitas* is also meant to undermine disparities between the rich and the poor, the famous and the disregarded, by casting death as the great leveller who equalises the condition of all in the end. Should this produce the effort to resist the spirit of overweening pride with its itch for wealth, fame, and honours, it would surely count as an exercise in poverty of spirit.

A second and Christological expression of spiritual poverty is meditation on the poverty and *kenosis* of Christ coupled with the appropriate resolutions to amend one's life.[75] 'Though he was in the form of God', Christ 'emptied himself, taking the form of a slave' (Phil 2: 6, 7). The Gospels depict Christ as born in a manger, living in humble obscurity in Nazareth, making his entrance into Jerusalem not in a chariot but on a donkey, washing the feet of his disciples, and exercising his ministry in radical solidarity with the poor and homeless: 'The Son of man has nowhere to lay his head' (Matt 8:20). As the New Testament scholar Richard Hays notes, Matthew 24 depicts Christ not only as *among* but even *in* the poor: 'Jesus himself is present in the hungry and homeless'.[76] The implied message is that the way of worldly pomp, riches, and arrogance has been falsified by the kenotic way of Christ who is himself the 'way' (*via*) which the wayfarer (*viator*) must walk: 'the road under our feet'.[77] Humbling oneself as a child, taking the lowest place at the table, identifying with the poor, rejecting ostentation and swagger, and other ways of following the poor Christ are thus genuine expressions of 'blessed are the poor in spirit'.

The religious life of vowed poverty is often thought of as the ultimate form of such *imitatio Christi*. But for laypeople who do not renounce all their possessions, various sources advise 'great plainness and simplicity of life' as a remedy to greed and luxury, and to free up funds for charity. As William Law writes: 'avoid all superfluous shows of finery and equipage, and let your house be plainly furnished with moderate conveniences. Do not consider what your estate can afford, but what right reason requires'.[78]

Such simplicity is an excellent alternative to and witness against the consumeristic excesses named earlier.[79] Besides a lifestyle of simplicity, St. Francis de Sales recommends frequent almsgiving for those with means. Aquinas regards almsgiving as an act of charity rather than of spiritual poverty. Nevertheless, the detachment from wealth which poverty of spirit effects removes an obstacle to charity and so gives it added scope. St. Francis also counsels us to 'love the poor (in their) poverty'.[80] He notes that St. Louis, a thirteenth-century medieval king of France, had three poor men to dinner with him every day and visited the poor and sick: not with his crown on, but in plainclothes. The point is not simply to do good to the poor, but to be in community and solidarity with them. 'If you love the poor', he says, 'be often in their company', engaged in shared activities such as work, conversation, meals, and joint projects.[81] The poor are therefore being conceived not just as lay figures for pious works of supererogation. The proposal is to be among them as one's fellows and equals, and to see Christ in their midst: to *enter* the spirit of poverty.[82] Acts such as these are poverty of spirit in tangible form. They surely counter-witness to consumeristic excess in a deeper way than just mailing a check to a charity or practicing inner detachment from surrounding wealth.

Such considerations obviously do not directly address the larger questions of social justice and human development which have to do with the alleviation of systemic poverty, and are a central concern of Christian ethics in any age. But that is only because my subject differs. Nevertheless, while poverty of spirit is distinct from the virtues of justice, liberality, and charity, it plainly makes their operation freer. The avaricious treat wealth as their access point to happiness, with the consequence that reduced wealth looks very much like reduced happiness. From that perspective, 'sell what you have, and give alms' (Lk 12:33) can only look like a self-immolating *ascesis*. Poverty of spirit alters this perception. By subverting greed and pomp through its identification and fellowship with the poor, this beatitude allows the wayfarer to view works of justice, almsgiving, and liberality as constituents in a good life rather than just the conscientious sacrifice of one.

Poverty of spirit frees one from undue preoccupation with wealth and prestige by countering the greed which leads to avarice, on one hand, and the pride which leads to vainglory and ambition, on the other. The 'proud and puffed up spirit' which spiritual poverty voids is thus precisely the spirit of worldliness as interpreted earlier. Poverty does this through practices in which hope, fearing to be separated from the love of God, resists the worldly preoccupation with riches, power, fame, and honours.

The association of this beatitude with hope was a brilliant insight of Augustine and Aquinas.[83] I have argued that hope is threatened by worldliness and needs resources to push back. We now see where an essential resource lies. Aquinas argues that the beatitudes are the acts of gifts which make us 'amenable' to the work of their respective infused virtues. Though spiritual poverty is the act of fear, hope's own gift, the literature on hope has said little about how this gift and beatitude make us 'amenable' to a more hopeful life. I believe that the answer is now in plain view. Spiritual poverty makes us 'amenable' to hope by countering worldliness: that preoccupation with possessions and prestige which produces 'distaste' for hope's commitments, main interest, and end. It is no accident that the neglect of worldliness as a moral category has gone together with the neglect of hope's gift and beatitude. When worldliness receded in the rearview mirror, hope's gift and beatitude were left with little apparent work to do. Hence in most of the literature on hope the gift of fear and beatitude of spiritual poverty are duly acknowledged but play no serious role. The recovery of worldliness as a moral category is therefore important also for the meaningful recovery of hope's gift and beatitude.

I began this chapter by noting the tension that is often thought to exist between the hopeful and 'the world' understood as a site they are 'in' but are not supposed to be 'of'. This tension has deep roots in the tradition, and has sometimes roused suspicions that a Church/world dualism is germane to Christianity. But as I have explicated it, 'the world' in the pejorative sense refers not to the physical earth, the human race, or human culture. It refers to a particular group of evils distinguishable from others: those which people uninterested in heavenly beatitude frequently default to in their desire to get the most out of this short life. In the New Testament and much of the subsequent tradition, these evils are thought to be representative of unregenerate human life.

Certainly the excessive pursuit of wealth, fame, status, reputation, power, and influence are extremely common, as the examples provided earlier suggest. For that reason worldliness often complicates the integration of *homo viator* in standard social and political life. The more the values, attitudes, habits, and way of life of a society are 'worldly' in this specific sense, the more Christians will have to object to deeply ingrained habits of their own society. The risk, of course, is partial social alienation. Considered purely as a risk, such alienation is not unique to hope or any other Christian virtue. Principled stands that risk alienation often have nothing to do with Christian interests. Groups and movements as various as the Jacobins, abolitionists, suffragists, and pacifists have in different contexts and in various ways risked alienation and incurred different kinds of social backlash. The risk is not uniquely Christian, and such principled stands have often been an important agent of social change.

Theological hope with its *homo viator* model of identity has the power to make Christians resist vicious and idolatrous demands of the state, market, or society. To that extent it is a potentially subversive *contra mundum*. My proposal is that Christians should be 'in the world' but not 'of the world' in terms of worldly values and habits. In that respect, they should be not just wayfarers and pilgrims, but aliens and exiles. But many have gone further than this, believing that postlapsarian society is not just marred by worldliness and the fallen *aion*, but *identical* to them. Where this is believed, hope's *status viatoris* is used to negate society as such. Some prominent Christians and movements have talked this way, despairing of society as irreformable. To say nothing of heretical movements from the Gnostics to the Cathars, this would include figures such as Tertullian, Thomas à Kempis, and Leo Tolstoy, and the more radical fringes of Egyptian and medieval monasticism up to the latter-day Mennonites, the Amish, and contemporary sects and doomsday cults.[84]

Despair of society is sometimes coupled with an attempt at physical withdrawal from society. But even where this does not occur, the sectarian group may advocate a *moral* withdrawal. Physically, the group may dwell in the local city, town, or village, but it may abdicate responsibility and minimise participation in anything outside its own Church structures.[85] It treats society rather like a father who disowns his son but still has to live next door to him. Obligatory polite noises may be made when they cross paths, but beneath any civil front lies a deep moral abandonment.

As Ladner notes, this *contra mundum* reflex was sometimes carried to bizarre extremes. For example, in the later Middle Ages some pious cartographers drew whole continents not as geometrical shapes, but as 'demonic figures' since 'all that is in the world' is said to be 'of sin'.[86] Such thought and practice has paved the way for 'cultured despisers' from Celsus to Bertrand Russell to claim that Christianity is otherworldly, obscurantist, and a menace to social reform and progress.[87] But antisocial Christianity and anti-Christian hyperbole are both overly simplistic accounts. Just why that is, and what hope has to offer social membership, is the topic of the next chapter.[88]

CHAPTER 7

Hope and the Earthly City

The principles of our being and government are our parents and our homeland, that have given us birth and nourishment. After God, therefore, we
are debtors chiefly to our parents and our homeland. Consequently just as
it belongs to religion to give honour to God, so does it belong to piety to
give honour to our parents and our country.

Thomas Aquinas, *Summa theologiae* II-II 101.1

The expectation of a new earth must not weaken but rather stimulate our
concern for cultivating this one.

Gaudium et Spes, chapter 3

And the city has no need of sun or moon to shine upon it, for the glory
of God is its light, and its lamp is the Lamb. By its light shall the nations
walk; and the kings of the earth shall bring their glory into it, and its gates
shall never be shut.... they shall bring into it the glory and honour of the
nations.

Revelation 21: 23–26

Without aiming at an overall theory of social identity or Christian citizenship, this chapter will argue that the virtue of hope has unique resources
for reinforcing our identification with and commitment to the 'two cities'.
If hope is funnelled into mind-body dualism, Platonic or otherwise, this
happy result is less likely. But as long as we affirm that humans are body-
soul composites or psychosomatic unities, our prospects brighten. If we
are essentially embodied beings, our identity will be importantly shaped
by the time and place of our lives, making our earthly and social identities
true parts of ourselves from which we cannot escape. Taken alone, this
point does not get social hope very far, but it does prevent a wrong turn at
the outset. It entails that the effort to identify with a dualistic conception
of the self which transcends social space will be ruled out as strictly incoherent. The consequence is that the hopeful cannot cease to identify with
their local social identities by pretending to wholly transfer that identity

somewhere else, such as the Church. To the contrary, I will argue that the hopeful are called to be citizens of two cities, and that this requires showing *pietas* to our earthly homeland. I will also make the point that virtuous love and honour for our homeland differs sharply from jingoism or chauvinism, and that it creates space for social criticism to become that act of charity which Aquinas calls fraternal correction. Dante will be my model for such 'dual citizenship'. He shows a committed but also critical love for his home city of Florence while ardently aspiring to the heavenly Jerusalem. The chapter then moves to the crucial argument that hope refers social goods and earthly causes to our eschatological end. This ensures that hope is *invested* in our earthly identities and can be a powerful agent of social change. Since hope ultimately seeks full citizenship with 'the saints and the household of God' (I-II.63.4), I will close by examining how eschatological considerations bear on that further identity.[1]

Homo Viator as a Citizen of Two Cities

Few theologians or philosophers today believe in mind-body dualism: the view, most famously associated with Plato, which Gilbert Ryle called 'the ghost in the machine'. For very good philosophical reasons, most profess belief in a psychosomatic unity according to which a human being is essentially embodied and not essentially a mind, soul, or psyche which just happens to operate through a body before eviction or release at death. Philosophically, mind-body dualism is a moribund theory defended only by a few idiosyncratic Platonists and Cartesians. The hylomorphic accounts of David Wiggins, Robert Pasnau, Michael Loux, Peter Strawson, Peter van Inwagen, and others strike me as far more satisfactory. But while their rejection of dualism is hylomorphic, they are joined in that rejection by almost every other philosophical camp, including empiricists.[2] Theologically, I see the rejection of dualism as fully in step with the Incarnation and Resurrection of Christ, to say nothing of the general resurrection of the dead. If the agent is essentially a soul or mind, it is very difficult not to think of the body as 'baggage'. Aquinas himself goes very far in stressing our essential embodiment, stating bluntly that 'My soul is not I' (*anima mea non est ego*) and insisting that death breaks human nature apart.[3]

Full recognition of embodiment makes a crucial difference to the identity of the Christian hopeful. As essentially embodied beings, our identity is importantly shaped by local and temporal factors. Alasdair MacIntyre put the point well:

> For the Platonist, as later for the Cartesian, the soul, preceding all bodily and social existence, must indeed possess an identity prior to all social roles; but for the Catholic Christian, as earlier for the Aristotelian, the body and the soul are not two linked substances. I am my body and my body is social, born to those parents in this community with a specific social identity.[4]

The Platonist or Cartesian may have a view of embodiment according to which it really is possible for the *psyche* or *cogito* to essentially subsist apart from the spatiotemporal world and therefore not to be essentially entangled in social space. But Thomistic embodiment offers no such escapist fantasy since it takes as basic the body-soul composite with its local and social origins.

Not pretending to escape social space, the Thomist can accept that we are socially embedded in a robust sense. Long before the work of MacIntyre and others made this a truism, George Orwell noted that habits, attitudes, feelings, and agency itself cannot transcend social context. 'My taste in books and food and clothes, my sense of honour, my table manners, my turns of speech, my accent, even the characteristic movements of my body, are the products of a special kind of upbringing'. Though some of these social features may be altered, it is impossible to transcend the whole, and it would be insane to try. As Orwell says: 'I would have to alter myself so completely that at the end I should hardly be recognizable as the same person'.[5] The account of hope I am offering, which presupposes full embodiment and consequent entanglement in the social world, can fully accept Orwell's point. Even if some forms of alienation are necessary (though regretted); alienation can never go all the way down.

Moreover, the body-soul composite from the Thomistic perspective includes the natural inclination to sociability, and upon this sociability the virtue of justice is built. One aspect of justice is *pietas*, which demands that reverence and regard be shown to our parents as the primary sources of our 'birth and nourishment'. Piety is demanded by the fourth commandment of the Decalogue, and Aquinas says it is owed by extension to non-parental sources of life and nourishment. This brings it within shouting distance of Jeffrey Stout's notion of piety, though without the anti-Augustinian polemic. Aquinas adds that after our parents, *pietas* should be 'given to our native land (*patria*)'. This includes 'honour to all our fellow-citizens and to all the friends of our native land'.[6] From this perspective, not only is it impossible to escape one's social identity; the failure to acknowledge indebtedness to the community that gave one 'birth and nourishment' is unjust.[7] The implication is that the wayfarer truly is a dual citizen. *Homo viator* may seek eternal citizenship in the city of God, but he or she owes honour to the earthly city analogous to the honour shown toward parents.[8] Since disowning that city, like disowning one's parents, is perhaps the grandest gesture of refusing honour, the effort to renounce membership in the earthly city is from this perspective both incoherent and unjust.

Thomistic hope will insist that we wayfarers are dual citizens bound in piety to honour our native homeland. It will also be invested in the social body and refer it to our ultimate end. Utter and wilful alienation from our earthly homeland is therefore ruled out. Nevertheless, the hopeful may find much in their societies wanting. Obviously, this includes social expressions of despair and presumption. But as I noted earlier, hope and its beatitude of poverty motivate commitments opposed to 'worldly' ends which often have broad social acceptance.

To take principled stands against socially embedded forms of avarice, vainglory, ambition, and domineering is plainly to risk a fair degree of alienation. For instance, those who lack a lifestyle of affluence, who are not devoted to the youth, beauty, and glamor-obsessed entertainment culture, who do not wear pricy, name-brand clothes, do not drive impressive cars, and do not toady to the affluent or show partiality towards the influential will lack entrance to certain social niches, activities, and ways of life. This can be particularly painful for the young whose peers often cluster into enclaves based on affluence and domineering and who often regard the name-brand and entertainment culture as the very currency of social existence and acceptability. Moreover, those who do not regard life as an upwardly mobile and essentially competitive scramble up the social and economic ladder and who fail to 'play the game' according to the social Darwinian rules that often govern the workplace or office will likewise risk a certain alienation. They may conscientiously abstain from the undue *arrivisme* and enlightened self-interest that motivate innumerable activities, decisions, policies, and conversational staples which are the basic career and social conductors for that context. Suppose such people do not merely abstain from such activities, but positively object to them – however charitably or intelligently – as vicious; and that they adopt practices which cut against the social grain. In short, suppose they try to lead a hopeful life shaped by poverty of spirit and the beatitudes in a contemporary business school, political party, high school, sports league, law firm, sales department, or other ambitious workplace, to name but a few examples. Allowing for cheerful exceptions, those who pursue this way of life will characteristically be seen as grating against the ethos of their social context. There is no merit in being a crank, but such friction may be inevitable if we are not to be cowardly or hypocritical. Christ himself was accused of 'having a demon' (John 8:48), and in the Good Friday liturgy, he is commemorated as 'rejected of men, a man of sorrows' (Is 53:3). Without seeking it, the hopeful may find themselves on the outside of many social practices and institutions. A degree of social alienation is at that point lamentably a given.

As I have described hope's social commitments, such alienation is never a *desideratum*, but an unavoidable share in the cross. The hopeful really are bound by birth and nourishment to their native homeland and people. Given the importance of these social identifications, the order of charity makes one's *patria* a pressing object of both love and hope.[9] So apart from the contextual improbabilities it would involve, one cannot respond to alienation by wholly *transferring* one's social membership out of one's *patria* and into the Church, as Hauerwas is often accused of doing.[10] Membership in the earthly city remains and that membership is in countless respects a social good, whatever attendant ills it may bring.

Not only does this rule out Church/world or related forms of dualism, it makes a crucial difference to how the hopeful should deal with alienation. A bad response would be to sink into the retaliatory pride and resentment which lead to an undue martyr, saint, or hero complex. Many sects and movements, from the Gnostics and Donatists to contemporary Christian subcultures, are littered with a self-appointed spiritual elite who hold their society in such contempt that alienation becomes a moral trophy. As with Milton's poorly sketched Christ, these chosen ones regard the generality of their fellow citizens as 'a herd confused/ A miscellaneous rabble ... of whom to be disprais'd were no small praise'.[11] Taken this way, misguided hope and its exaggerated distance from the world give the illusion that one stands over and above the world as 'the Elect' above 'the ungodly'. By contrast, I have emphasised that *homo viator* does not stand over and above the world, but is still prey to temptation, and continually needs repentance and grace. When hope and poverty's stand against worldliness threaten a degree of social alienation, the fitting response is to lament rather than to indulge in 'the sweets of resentment'. To the degree such alienation exists, temptations to exaggerate its extent must be fought or a martyr complex combined with the view of society as a *massa damnata* may result.[12]

In addition, piety and social hope commend membership in one's society. This requires purposeful and persistent integration where possible. What Aquinas says about Christ's manner of life is instructive here. His question is why Christ was not a hermit or extreme ascetic. Why is it, given the counterexample of so many prophets and saints, that 'the Son of man came eating and drinking'?[13] Aquinas answers: 'it was in keeping with the end' of becoming human that 'Christ should not lead a solitary life, but should associate with men. Now it is most fitting that he who associates with others should conform to their manner of living; according to the words of the Apostle (1 Corinthians 9:22): 'I became all things to all men'. He concludes, 'And therefore it was most fitting that Christ should conform to others' in innocent matters since common ground increases love and fellowship.[14] This is a judicious model for the hopeful. Should their way of life lead to partial alienation from the social body, the fitting response is not to withdraw further out of resentful indignation or compensatory pride, but to renew the effort to integrate in areas where we may. On Aquinas' reading, Christ conformed to the local 'manner of living' in part by attending dinner parties and not refusing a glass of wine. The hopeful may do so by any number of social and cultural practices which express and reinforce membership in their people, from embracing the national cuisine and local traditions to quoting the nation's poets and celebrating its holidays.

Where *pietas* is present in earnest, such expressions should be perfectly genuine rather than feigned. Such sincere identification will be 'somehow bound up', as Orwell says, with cultural symbols, places, practices, and objects of love. For us in England, he suggests, this could range widely, from the plays of Shakespeare and a fondness for 'traditional English Christmas' to 'the pub, the football match, the back garden, the fireside and the "nice cup of tea"'. 'Above all', Orwell reminds his self-alienated English readers, 'it is *your* civilization, it is *you*. ... The suet puddings and the red pillar-boxes have entered into your soul. Good or evil, it is yours, you belong to it, and this side of the grave you will never get away from the marks that it has given you'.[15] Comparable remarks could be made for those belonging to any other culture. They obviously do not imply fantasies of superiority, but simply a love and sense of belonging. Indeed, when healthily cultivated, this aspect of *pietas* lets us better appreciate the love that others have for their own cultures. As Samuel Johnson – himself a stern critic of chauvinism – insisted: 'That man is little to be envied, whose patriotism would not gain force upon the plain of Marathon, or whose piety would not grow warmer among the ruins of Iona'.[16]

In a distinct and quite morally driven way, the hopeful may further integration in their society by labouring for its common good. Here the beatitudes are again important for how we see hope concretely lived. Entangling oneself in human brokenness and working for the common good further integrates the hopeful in a morally meaningful way, shows a tangible commitment to their society, and takes much of the sting from any remainder of alienation. The earlier-noted example of Christian charity in the late Roman Empire is an excellent example. Though pagan Romans felt that Christians were in many respects alien, Christian contributions to the common good greatly reduced that alienation both in fact and in pagan eyes.[17]

The enduring point is that service undertaken in charities, community projects, and the like benefits not just one's co-religionists, but one's neighbours and society as such. Conceivably one might do this with a bizarre aloofness, 'ministering' to neighbours without entering into any communal ties with them, treating them as bare receptacles for our own moral projects. Jonathan Swift is an instructive example. In addition to being a splendid satirist, essayist, novelist, and poet, he was an Anglican cleric and the dean of St Patrick's Cathedral in Dublin. As a 'religious duty' Swift regularly gave alms to the beggars outside his Cathedral. But he did so with a kind of wryness: 'His beneficence was not graced with tenderness of civility; he relieved without pity, and assisted without kindness; so that those who were fed by him could hardly love him'.[18] It is difficult not to read this with a shudder similar to the music lover's shudder at a false note, and that is the point. Swift's contributions did not integrate him into the community, but they should have. This is why his 'beneficence' strikes a false note, and teaches us how *not* to contribute to the community. The opposite behaviour, magnificently shown in the lives of people like St. Vincent de Paul, William Wilberforce, Elizabeth Fry, Martin Luther King Jr., Leonard Cheshire, and Dorothy Day, is to contribute to one's community in a way that integrates one in it in important ways, building personal ties and relationships instead of posing as a distant heavenly presence raining down manna on the mortals below.

While the hopeful may be alienated from their society in certain respects, they should remain deeply committed to it. A potential but limited alienation should co-exist with tenacity in trying to reintegrate and contribute to the social body of which one is a part. By insisting on membership in one's society, by integrating where we may, by contributing, and by practising a partially alienated presence that refuses antisocial flight, suspicions of misanthropic grandstanding and risk-free armchair criticism are to an important degree defused. Such *viatores* show enough solicitude and love for their earthly *patria* to stay put and identify with it even when friction may tempt to social withdrawal.

Understood in this way, such alienation as one must adopt can itself be a medium of outreach. Objecting to worldly values, practices, habits, and institutions may partly alienate, but this alienation is not the result of standoffish withdrawal or insolent cheek. To return to Swift, such alienation should not be the superior person's disdain for the rabble of Yahoos. Rather, it should operate as a summons to one's people to recognise vicious and dehumanising practices for what they are. That summons should be charitably expressed. Indeed, it should be a performative exercise in that fraternal correction which Aquinas saw as an act of charity.[19]

Unavoidable alienation will then be an act of communication with one's society rather than surly withdrawal or passive aggression. It will issue a summons to moral accountability, invite a joint pursuit of the common good, and signal the intention to lovingly persist in identifying with one's people even amid, and not just until, the onset of serious tensions.[20] Contrary to the suspicions of Christianity's cultured despisers, such qualified alienation communicates that the hopeful are not mere traitors-in-waiting or fair-weather friends of their society.

The cases of Dante and Rudyard Kipling are illustrative. Defending his home country from charges of injustice, Kipling wrote: 'If England was what England seems ... 'Ow quick we'd chuck 'er! But she ain't!' This suggests that devotion to one's country may be dropped if one judges it is on balance corrupt. But this is 'like loving your children only if they're good'.[21] Far more edifying is Chesterton's claim that 'The recognized reality of patriotism is for better for worse, for richer for poorer, in sickness and in health'.[22] Not only does piety commend this approach; charity and hope do as well. Charity, which wills the good of the beloved, does not cease to will that good just because the beloved is not ideal. The pattern is the reverse, as suggested in the biblical phrase: 'God showed his love for us in that *while we were yet sinners* Christ died for us' (Rom 5:8, emphasis added).

A corollary is that commitment to one's homeland or country persists even if one strongly disagrees with its political, economic, or other policies. Love of *patria* may prejudice us to approve of its policies, but such love is not premised on this approval and so can outlast it.

Some have called into question the wisdom of such identification. In *After Virtue*, Alasdair MacIntyre suggested that those who wish to continue 'the tradition of the virtues' should treat contemporary society roughly as St. Benedict's monks treated the dying Roman *imperium*. The crucial moment came when 'men and women of good will turned aside from the task of shoring up the Roman *imperium*' and sought 'new forms of community within which the moral life could be sustained so that both morality and civility might survive the coming ages of barbarism and darkness'.[23] In full agreement with this view, Stanley Hauerwas has suggested that the

modern nation-state has become less of a country than a corporation. The
United States is by his reckoning little more than a militaristic plutocracy,
so that the call to make the ultimate sacrifice for your country sounds a lot
like 'being asked to die for the telephone company'.[24]

But Nicholas Wolterstorff and Jeffrey Stout have pointed out that it is
necessary to clearly distinguish the civic people and one's homeland from
the overlapping nation-state and political institutions.[25] The love of home,
land, neighbour, and a shared way of life which shapes cultural expressions
and local practices is prior to any specific economic, political, or bureau-
cratic arrangement. (Consider, for example, the distinction between 'the
United Kingdom' and 'England'.)[26] Obviously the two exert much mutual
influence and concretely overlap in many ways. But we should distinguish
them roughly the way we distinguish between a person and an office. Even
if everything MacIntyre and Hauerwas say is true – and I think a great
many of their specific criticisms are warranted – the social bond with
one's fellow citizens must not be confused with the sprawling institutional
bureaucracies that govern economic and political life. Refusal to cooperate
with certain policies and practices of the latter does not require repudia-
tion of one's commitment to the former. Recognising this fact also helps
to disentangle piety from jingoism. That disentanglement in turn makes
clear that love and honour of one's country neither requires nor condones
injustice to those outside national boundaries.

In contrast to Kipling and others who pronounce 'chuck 'er' over a
corrupt homeland, there stands Dante's committed membership in his
native Florence. Beatrice in the heavenly court vouches for Dante that
'There is no son of the Church Militant/ with greater hope than his'.
Though second to none in hope for the heavenly *patria*, Dante tenderly
loves his earthly *patria* ('my sweet fold where I grew up a lamb'). Though
he is in exile, Dante does not forget Florence, and pines to return to the
font at which he was baptised. He denounces the city severely at times
(Florence has, he insists, 'become as venal as a whore').[27] He also refuses
to bootlick to the corrupt elites who alone could recall him to Florence,
instead remaining a 'foe to the wolves that prey upon it now'.[28] But crucially, such social criticism and partial alienation flow from the anxious
piety of a loving son, not from the aloof disdain of a disowning one. In
short, Dante is personally *invested* in Florence. Zealous for membership
both in his native city and the heavenly city, Dante is an exemplary case
of *homo viator* as a committed dual citizen. He refuses the temptation to
renounce either citizenship just because the dual commitment involves
real tensions.

Worldly values and habits which vitiate hope cannot be acquiesced in, and such dissent typically comes at a social price. But if the hopeful affirm that creation is good; that they are essentially embodied, social, and local creatures; and that piety, natural love, and charity for homeland are important; this friction should co-exist with persistent identification with one's people, and a desire to see and affirm the good that is among them. The reasonable attitude to civic membership is therefore one of virtuous ambivalence. A judicious balance must be struck between affirming and denouncing, integrating and alienating. When alienation is unavoidable, it should be expressed in terms of fraternal correction and therefore in the temper and mode of charity, making alienation itself, to the extent it is necessary, a mode of communication and outreach. By contrast, a wholesale alienation which quits on the earthly city is a failure of hope to respond to the demands of piety and charity. The piety I am discussing has the resources to work with non-Christians in pursuing the common good for the earthly city, just as Stout wanted Christians to do. But it can do this without having to collapse its theological form and pour itself into an Emersonian mould.

My purpose here has not been to construct a theory of Christian citizenship or social membership as a whole. My task has been far more modest. I have wanted to make clear that exaggerated alienation is not proper to hope, insisting that committed membership can co-exist with unavoidable and partial alienation. By ruling out an excessive *contemptus mundi*, I have also tried to assure non-Christians that antisocial withdrawal is not hope's default social mode, but something the hopeful themselves have good reasons to resist.

Dominic Doyle's Christian Humanistic Hope

Granted that the hopeful amid ambiguities may continue to identify with the earthly city, just what stake does the virtue of hope have in that city, and what might hope do for it? As previously stated, theological hope does not abandon created goods and earthly causes, but refers them to our eschatological end. The most thorough contemporary attempt to unpack this is undoubtedly Dominic Doyle's recent book, *The Promise of Christian Humanism: Thomas Aquinas on Hope*.

An Associate Professor of Theology at Boston College, Doyle's work addresses the question 'does belief in a transcendent God help or hinder human flourishing in this world?' Put differently: can Christian hope sustain a true humanism, a true vision of human flourishing? Using Aquinas' theology of hope, Doyle argues that it can. The eschaton may be the final goal, but Christianity is a true 'humanism' because its promotion of 'the human person's religious transcendence' does not detract from but conduces to 'justice and flourishing in the present life'. The latter is ordained to the former by theological hope since, as Aquinas states, hope is able to take up temporal goods 'secondarily and as referred to eternal happiness'. In this respect, hope 'provides crucial grounds for Christian humanism'.[29]

The first third of the book looks at Christian humanism and rebuts objections from atheistic sceptics who regard Christian hope as morbid. Here Doyle turns to the work of Charles Taylor and Nicholas Boyle, both of whom advocate a humanism friendly to religious transcendence. On Doyle's telling, Taylor shows us that 'religious transcendence sustains the affirmation of ordinary life' rather than cheapening it. One consequence is that hope as carrier of 'religious transcendence' does not demand a flight from the world or high-minded scorn for ordinary life and daily routines. Hope comes to the aid of 'ordinary life', not least because its 'religious transcendence' helps sustain that life during suffering and at death.[30]

Nicholas Boyle argues that human life in order to flourish must be extended across time 'in contrast to the market culture's emphasis on the instantaneous point of consumption and its concomitant denial of finitude'. Consumerism fosters habits and a vision of instant gratification which grinds down an agent's ability to locate him or herself as extended across time, causing a trauma of dislocation which may end in despair.[31] When the social iconography is dominated by the shopping mall and Hollywood, and the social roles conferred by Church, the local community, and one's homeland weaken, selfhood and membership are largely sucked into the market culture. This outrage visited upon our humanity may cause a discontent which agents do not know how to escape – precisely because the terms in which they conceive of happiness have been defined for them in advance by consumer culture, which shuts out alternatives. The result, Boyle insists, is a bleak fracturing of selfhood and solidary in desperate need for hope.[32] Taken together, the works of Taylor and Boyle are said to show that 'religious transcendence' is not just compatible with humanism, but is a cure for its discontents.

But religious transcendence is not itself theological hope. Having gotten us this far, Taylor and Boyle are succeeded by interlocutors whose humanism is less shy about Christ. Jacques Maritain and John Courtney Murray rightly take centre stage here, and Doyle adopts their view that the Incarnation marks an enormous difference for humanism, since it ensures 'the intimate union between humanity and God'.

The Incarnation shows God's care for humanity, and even God's willingness to *join* the human estate, raising our dignity to otherwise inconceivable heights. Moreover, the life of grace in which the *imago dei* partakes actualises rather than violates human nature. As St. Irenaeus said: 'Christ became human so that humans might become divine', and 'the life of the human person ... is the vision of God'. Faith and reason, Church and society, are therefore not intrinsically at odds. To the contrary, Christian humanism exists to validate and ordain these to God, disproving the 'atheistic humanist claim that belief in God harms the human'. How are these ordained to God? For Doyle, the answer is found in theological hope.[33]

To his great credit, Doyle, in contrast to much Thomist scholarship, is able to translate Aquinas out of in-house scholastic language and to engage questions of widespread and obvious interest. He shuns arguments from authority, ably takes up contemporary problems, and in general his exegesis of Aquinas is succinct, lucid, and attractive. But oddly for a book subtitled 'Thomas Aquinas on Hope', there is almost no mention of what Aquinas saw as hope's moral entourage. Hope's opposed vice of despair is addressed only once in a brisk gesture.[34] Nothing is said about the vice of sloth, the vice of presumption, or hope's gift of fear. The challenges and vices which Aquinas saw hope responding to do not make an appearance, and the gift with whose aid he thought hope would triumph is cast adrift. The consequence is that Aquinas does not always sound very much like himself. At times it is almost a case of 'Hamlet without the Prince'.

Ignoring hope's opposed vices might leave the impression that hope faces no stiff resistance, and therefore that it operates from a position of ease. So is Doyle's hope, like John Bowlin's, serenely invincible and splendidly dexterous? Does Doyle confirm Timothy Jackson's suspicion that hope plays down our vulnerability, and does he promote that notorious Job's Comforter, belief in the 'facility of goodness' both personally and within history? This might have the odd result of making Aquinas the godparent of Whig hope, or something unnervingly like it.

Fortunately, Doyle is far more nuanced. Christian humanism does not come gift-wrapped in Stoic armour. Hope's good is agreed to be 'arduous'. Like the human condition generally, hope is caught in 'the suffering through which finite, fallen being must pass on its way to union with God'.[35] Doyle rightly notes that these test our faith, and teach that 'Christian life is less about giving "glowing accounts" of the cross and more about patiently bearing it'.[36] Hope's way to union with God is therefore 'cruciform'.[37] But in what sense is that so, and how will hope help us deal with this? The sense in which hope is 'cruciform' for Doyle is that the hopeful must operate in conditions of 'finitude, sin, and suffering'. This is certainly true, though left at that the diagnosis is generalised. The virtue of hope for Aquinas is a specialist tool dealing with specialised problems: particularly, despair and presumption, but also sloth and worldliness. Replacing these with 'finitude, sin, and suffering' generally leaves in soft focus moral items which Aquinas threw into bold relief, making it unclear what hope is designed to overcome, and to that extent, what hope is.

Doyle's constructive proposals for hope and humanism are original and intriguing. First, he draws on Aquinas to argue that theological hope refers created goods to our eschatological end. In his preferred vocabulary – 'Taylored', as he puts it, to accord with Charles Taylor – temporal hopes are 'secular hopes'.[38] By this Doyle means earthly and social hopes such as 'the struggle for justice within history'.[39] The result is a tidy alignment between secular hopes and humanism itself, since the latter is a pursuit for the human good. His normative claim is that secular hopes can readily 'participate in eschatological hope'. Put another way, humanism itself may partake of 'religious transcendence' in a social expression of grace perfecting nature.[40] This occurs when the hopeful ordain secular hopes as proximate ends to eschatological hope as their ultimate end. Importantly for someone ratcheting up social hopes, Doyle makes admirably clear that while we may hope *for* the created world we do not hope *in* it.

At this point Doyle strikes out in a quite original direction. He proposes: 'a legitimate development of Aquinas's account of the theological virtues'. This turns out to be fairly radical: an entirely new metaphysics of the theological virtues captured in this thesis:

> I argue that if hope be the motion that constitutes the transcendence advocated by Christian humanism, then faith and charity may be considered, respectively, the potency and the act of Christian humanism. This interpretation of faith, hope, and charity as the potency, motion, and act of Christian humanism helps articulate how the theological virtues, in distinct yet related ways, mutually inform Christian humanism.[41]

Faith is the potency because it 'shows the object' of the theological virtues, and by extension, of Christian humanism. Yet faith 'does not "move" towards it' and so it remains in potency.[42] Hope is the 'motion' by which we proceed towards God. It does not possess its object, and so hope 'has the imperfection of striving towards a goal that is not yet present'. This motion corresponds to 'the proper meaning of motion as reduction of potency to act'.[43] Charity is the 'act' of Christian humanism because it 'has the character of perfection in that it unites one to God'. In charity's '*actus,* becoming gives way to being, and there is no more essential imperfection that characterizes *motus*.[44]

To those for whom scholastic causation is an over-fine nicety, such musings may seem like 'noises off-stage' in an argument swept along by broader considerations. But Doyle takes this formula very seriously indeed, and effectively offers it as the metaphysical hardware for running his humanist software. As he sees it, the benefit of construing the theological virtues this way is to make them carriers of a Christian humanism which effects human flourishing. The job of theological hope here is to put secular hopes 'in motion' to the eschaton, so that hope bridges the human flourishing sought by humanism with the 'religious transcendence' offered by Christianity. Doyle sees this 'creative appropriation' of Aquinas as the finishing touch needed to complete the Christian humanism admirably begun but left unfinished in the work of Maritain, Murray, Taylor, Boyle, and the tradition as a whole.

The business of Christian humanism is therefore the pursuit and attainment of human flourishing or happiness in a life in which nature is being perfected by grace.[45] 'It is not simply a potency for that actual state of happiness; nor is it the completed and perfect act of happiness that has attained the goal. Rather, it is the passage from the potential for that act to the act itself; it is the process of actualizing the potency to be united with God'.[46] This 'passage' from the potency for happiness to the 'process' of actualising happiness through being 'united with God' corresponds to what Aquinas saw as the imperfect supernatural beatitude in this life moving towards perfect supernatural beatitude in the next.[47] Put more generally, Doyle sees faith, hope, and charity as the potency, motion, and act, respectively, of earthly beatitude in its movement towards the beatific vision.

As discussed earlier, Aquinas does not just see the life of virtue as *instrumental* to happiness; he thinks virtuous activity is *constitutive* of happiness. Perfection or happiness is constituted by activity (*operatio*) in accord with virtue, and this way of life is held to be characteristically enjoyable to the virtuous. At the natural level, the perfecting *operatio* comes through acts of the acquired moral virtues of prudence, justice, temperance, and fortitude, as well as the intellectual virtues. At the supernatural level, perfection occurs through acts of the infused cardinal and theological virtues, as well as the gifts of the Holy Spirit.[48] The virtuous life is the happy life, and all of the virtues contribute in their own way to it. Put in scholastic terms, the process of perfecting and so one's share in happiness occurs through virtuous actions which bring the agent's capacities from potency to act.[49]

Doyle renovates this account quite a bit. He suggests that faith is a potency which hope actualises, and adds that faith itself is not in act, with the result that it cannot be a constituent in imperfect happiness. Hope is a motion which partly actualises the agent, and charity is fully in act and therefore perfectly actualises the agent. So hope on Doyle's terms could be a constituent in imperfect happiness, and charity would be a fuller and more complete constituent. The consequence is that what Doyle calls Christian humanism, and which corresponds to Aquinas' imperfect supernatural happiness, is actualised entirely by hope and charity. In this account, the cardinal virtues will not themselves contribute to the happy life at all, and faith will only do so in terms of providing hope with the potency to move towards charity.

In Doyle's scheme, it appears that human flourishing, Christian human-ism, and the life of imperfect happiness in action *just are* the life of hope and charity. Because he says so little about what the life of Christian humanism concretely looks like, it is unclear what this hypertrophic enlargement of hope and charity in the moral life will amount to in prac-tice. It is also unclear what role the infused cardinal virtues will occupy in this new regime. That they are demoted is clear; what they are demoted to is not. By contrast, we know that faith is demoted from a contributor to happiness into the new role of potency for hope exclusively. But as Doyle presents matters, the cardinal virtues do not fit into the potency, motion, or act of Christian humanism at all; from that perspective, they have now become unemployed. This strikes me as a radical shrinkage of Aquinas' overall model of the virtuous and happy life.

The scheme of potency, motion, and act is used to suggest that hope takes up the secular or earthly hopes of humanism and puts them in 'motion' towards 'religious transcendence'.[50] In terms of what Doyle is trying to accomplish, this amounts to the claim that theological hope benefits and perfects humanism. Theological hope protects and sustains secular hopes, and these 'participate in eschatological hope' and indeed are 'the means of its realization'.[51] Doyle's general claim here is surely a legitimate development of Aquinas and a worthy thesis. But the claim does not require the separate and distracting effort to force faith, hope, and charity into a neat alignment of potency, motion, and act. Aquinas himself suggested a more internally consistent and coherent mechanism based on primary and secondary causality. In terms of hope's final cause, he wrote that 'hope regards eternal happiness chiefly, and other (i.e., tem-poral and created) goods, for which we pray God, it regards secondarily and as referred to eternal happiness'.[52] In the secondary and referred sense of final causality, we may hope and pray for our daily bread, a just social order, and so forth. In terms of hope's efficient cause, Aquinas applies the same logic of secondary causality: 'it is unlawful to hope in any man, or any creature, as though it were the first cause of movement toward happiness. It is, however, lawful to hope in a man or a creature as being the secondary and instrumental agent through whom one is helped to obtain any goods that are ordained to happiness'.[53] In the secondary and instrumental sense of efficient causality, we may rely on goods which help us on the journey, from forgiveness of sins and temporal necessities to social goods.[54]

As Joseph Merkt states, these points connect 'the secondary or created goods for which one should hope with the theological virtue of hope. Thus Thomas establishes a relationship between the material/political world and hope. He understands that in some ways the material/political world is a cause of hope and an object of hope'.[55] Aquinas' situating of primary and instrumental causality provided everything needed for Doyle to state his positive points about hope's contribution to humanism. Moreover, we are not told by him what is supposed to be *wrong* with Aquinas' account, leaving it unclear what difficulty is being got right.

Doyle's admirable project of Christian humanism did not require his idiosyncratic take on potency, motion, and act. That metaphysic cannot really be made to fit onto Aquinas' scheme of the virtues, and the old wineskin bursts when this new wine is poured in.[56] Yet there is a great deal to be grateful for in this book. Throughout it Doyle affirms an Incarnational vision in which grace perfects nature and the creator–creature relationship is non-competing. That vision is attractive, compelling, and a fine development of themes latent in Vatican II but rarely pressed into such thorough service. The general exegesis of Aquinas is firm and appealing, the humanist sources add valuable material, and the overall thesis and buoyant tone push against the stubborn prejudice that hope is otherworldly, aloof, and bored with the world. Most importantly, Doyle is right to take from Aquinas the proposal that theological hope does not abandon created goods and earthly causes, but refers them to our eschatological end. Along the way, many of hope's important bits fall victim to Doyle's scissors-and-paste, and the account is cluttered by a gratuitous metaphysics. But the overall thesis that Thomistic hope can benefit earthly society and perfect Christian humanism is well taken, and was far from a truism in the literature. Apart from that heavy-lifting, the convincing turn to Aquinas also helped to free theological hope from excessive preoccupation with Moltmann.

Hope's Ordination of the Earthly City to the Eschaton

Granted that we can incorporate the social body into hope as a secondary cause ordered to hope's primary cause, how is this to be done? The primary end of hope is eternal beatitude in God. The earthly city, then, cannot be hope's primary interest. Yet proximate ends, as has often been noted, may be referred to hope's ultimate end.[57] We may call this the 'referral thesis'. The referral thesis implies that earthly projects may become part of our overall project to arrive at the beatific vision. This occurs in many respects, two of which are relevant at present. First, how we conduct earthly projects figures importantly into whether we will attain the beatific vision, and in what way, quality, or condition. Here we may consult Christ's parable of the sheep and the goats in Matthew 24, followed by his parable of the talents in Matthew 25. More generally, much of what I have already said about acting hopefully such as to avoid despair and presumption lends concrete detail to this formal point.

Second, the referral thesis allows us to hope that our flawed earthly projects may be redeemed and perfected by divine mercy in the *eschaton*. The things we loved and cared for will be 'fulfilled' rather than 'abolished' in a pattern of glory perfecting grace as grace perfects nature. Were this not the case, it might suggest that everything we care about in the world is, *in itself*, a waste of time from the perspective of hope, and surely that is a thought too many. Instead, a cosmic fulfilment and reconciliation of earthly projects is envisioned: the swords will be beaten into ploughshares, Christ will make all things new, every tear will be wiped away, the leaves of the 'tree of life' will be given 'for the healing of the nations' (Rev 22: 2). Some of this imagery is almost mythological, yet it does what needs doing, and it would be deflationary to refuse a place for such evocations.[58] The referral thesis also makes sense of the view that it is good rather than distracting to pray for earthly needs and causes (most blatantly: 'give us this day our daily bread').

Moreover, through the mediation of charity we may hope for our neighbours' beatitude, and therefore for the beatitude of our fellow citizens, our earthly city, and the human race generally.[59] Since that beatitude is meant to begin in this life, though imperfectly, commitment to the common good and the happiness of our *patria* is incumbent upon the hopeful. As the Vatican II document *Gaudium et Spes* states:

> The expectation of a new earth must not weaken but rather stimulate our concern for cultivating this one. For here grows the body of a new human family, a body which even now is able to give some kind of foreshadowing of

the new age. Hence, while earthly progress must be carefully distinguished from the growth of Christ's kingdom, to the extent that the former can contribute to the better ordering of human society, it is of vital concern to the Kingdom of God.[60]

As *Gaudium et Spes* suggests, grace may pervade the earthly city itself. Society is the occasion not just for the exercise of natural virtues like prudence and justice; it also has ample scope for supernatural virtues such as charity. If heaven were eremitic, hope itself might lack any role here since it would then have nothing but incidental interests in social existence. But Christianity has always regarded the eschatological end itself in social terms: as a *patria*, a city, a communion of saints. Since the social body may be referred by hope to our ultimate end, society is part of hope's interests. This bears on the pursuit of justice. Martin Luther King Jr., for example, pursued both social justice and racial equality, on one hand, and the kingdom of God, on the other. Yet his hope for the kingdom did not just co-exist with his pursuit of justice; it helped motivate, sustain, and shape it. As William Mattison notes, hope allowed King to elude burnout amid setbacks, and to avoid becoming 'hateful out of impatience with those who were resisting his changes'.[61] King believed that the human brotherhood he fought for in this life would prepare people for the fellowship of God's kingdom, and at its best be a foretaste of that kingdom. The same basic pursuit is found in countless saints and reformers, from St. John Chrysostom and St. Vincent de Paul to William Wilberforce and Dorothy Day.

Social memberships provide the moral space for virtuous projects in and through which both individuals and societies are in part perfected. This is true both of natural and supernatural virtue, and that fact pertains to how the community's natural good relates to its possible supernatural good. Aquinas says that 'the acquired virtues dispose a person to receive infused moral virtue', and that the acquired virtues help 'preserve and foster' the infused virtues once habitual grace is infused.[62] While he is addressing the individual agent, the same formal relation would hold of the social body. Insofar as our social commitments conduce to natural virtue we are doing something worthwhile in itself, and we are also 'disposing' the members of the community towards the life of grace. To the extent our community tends towards virtuous social habits, these further conduce to the preservation and fostering of graced habits in the community.

Left at that, it might seem that the hopeful only contribute to the common good as a *preparatio evangelica*. They might undertake edifying projects of social reform or charity to soften up their audience for hearing the

Gospel. Natural virtue and happiness, though themselves trifling, would be fostered as a propaedeutic to supernatural virtue and happiness. But surely that view is appalling. Among other things, it would imply that the misery of victims would not *itself* bother us. Sympathy and concern would only arise if, apart from the fact of their suffering, we had independent reasons to think that this particular episode of suffering indisposed them to the Gospel. Thomas Merton's phrase 'the Moral Theology of the Devil' seems like an apt description of this view.[63] I will take it as uncontroversial that natural happiness or *eudaimonia* is intrinsically valuable: that it is a desirable perfection of created being. The more it is not just the privilege of a few but is widespread the more something worthwhile will have been done. Believing it is also possible by supernatural means to move from good to better, Christians may reasonably and charitably wish supernatural beatitude upon their neighbours and co-citizens. Indeed, granted their own eschatological premises, it would be horribly cruel *not* to. Yet this wish and prayer do not mean they want a just society exclusively to get everyone in it to heaven. Even where the supernatural good goes lamentably unacknowledged, Christians may rightly wish the natural good for its own sake, as far preferable to vice and misery. One important consequence is that when Christians and non-Christians work together to build a just social order, the latter need not regard the former's contribution as nothing but stealth proselytism. Christians would not be doing to their secular partners in pursuit of the common good what I earlier critiqued Jeffrey Stout for doing in his effort to redefine virtue in Emersonian terms while disingenuously claiming to validate Christian virtue.[64]

Social goods and social projects give plentiful occasion for infused virtues such as prudence, justice, and charity. These may be referred by the virtue of hope to our overall movement to the future good. As matter in and through which supernatural virtue may be exercised, social activities become constituents in a supernatural happiness that is on the way from imperfect to perfect. This is best grasped by looking at the formal relationship between imperfect and supernatural happiness, and then by considering how this bears on the good society.

The two phases of happiness, imperfect and perfect, are morally continuous in the sense that perfect supernatural happiness will consummate rather than abrogate imperfect happiness. Aquinas describes perfect happiness as a kind of fully grown 'fruit' relative to which imperfect happiness is not merely the 'leaf' which foretells the coming fruit, but as the early form of the fruit itself. A kind of 'imperfect inchoation of future beatitude' is possible 'even in this life. For it is one thing to hope that the tree will bear fruit, when the leaves begin to appear, and another, when we see the first signs of the fruit'.[65] The result of this continuity is that the virtuous constituents in imperfect supernatural happiness have an internal rather than external relationship to fully constituted and perfect supernatural happiness.

This will also true of *social* constituents in imperfect beatitude such as the building up of a just and charitable society. A project of justice, for instance, may be not just 'mine' but 'ours'. To the extent this virtuous activity is perfective and therefore happy-making, it will have made *us* rather than just *me* happy. Why is this? Not just because we both have been made more virtuous, perfect, and happy individually. To the extent our virtue and perfection occur in and through cooperative projects, our happiness is *shared*. I am presupposing here the fact of communal agency and identity: that agents may experience what John Hare calls a 'partial merging of identity' which results from 'an expansion of the normal boundaries' of agency beyond the purely individual. Like Charles Taylor and others, Hare resists the belief that identity and agency are strictly individualistic. There are group agents and group identities, and this accounts for the ascription of praise and blame, shame, guilt, pride, and merit, to whole groups and communities. This does not require the mistaken view that the individual is *absorbed* into the group. Rather, the individual has an essential self-identity which co-exists with various overlapping social identifications, and the individual's agency reflects the fact. Hare writes:

> It is not just in families and close friendships that partial merging of identity occurs. One can be ashamed and proud of things one's colleagues do. There can be partial merging of identity with entertainment and sports figures and with national figures, like the members of a royal family. It is also possible for individuals to merge themselves to various degrees into groups of smaller and larger size: clubs and colleges and countries. Socrates thought of the laws and institutions of Athens as like his parents in making him who he was.[66]

Insofar as I am a member of a group agent and identity, I may partake not just in group shame, pride, guilt, and the like. When I and the group engage in virtuous projects that are perfective of us as a social body, I may also partake in happiness socially. In that respect, the increase of virtue and happiness in the social body is an increase of these in me as well as others in the community. Christians will rightly see this as a goal for the Church, but the general point is not limited to the Church.[67] As an agent with a social nature, I have a personal investment in the virtue and happiness of any social body of which I am a part, including my *patria*. If it is becoming more virtuous and happy, then insofar as I partake in this movement I am becoming more virtuous and happy myself: but precisely *as* a member of the social body and not as an atomistic ego. This consideration helps lay to rest the common objection to hope, which I have already addressed, that hope is an essentially 'selfish' virtue indifferent to anybody else's happiness.

The great moral reform movement of the British abolitionists may serve here as an example. A group of mostly evangelicals and Quakers led by the able parliamentarian William Wilberforce, their 'Committee for the Abolition of the Slave Trade' formed in 1787 helped bring about the 1807 'Abolition of the Slave Trade Act'. One of the outstanding reform movements of history, it involved the social expression of justice, prudence, fortitude, and charity; and it helped make the citizenry more aware and more likely to support the hard moral work necessary to reach the desired goal.[68] Getting to this social good was an arduous process fraught with decades of setbacks, but the abolitionists persevered. As Wilberforce exhorted in one of his speeches:

> Let us not despair; it is a blessed cause.... Never, never will we desist till we have wiped away this scandal from the Christian name, released ourselves from the load of guilt, under which we at present labour, and extinguished every trace of this bloody traffic, of which our posterity, looking back to the history of these enlightened times, will scarce believe that it has been suffered to exist so long a disgrace and dishonour to this country.[69]

Years of tireless advocacy led to drastic changes in attitude and the moral resolve to end slavery (possibly at great national cost, since other world powers planned to keep exploiting cheap slave labour). Though earlier votes had been badly defeated, the final vote on the 'Abolition of the Slave Trade Act' passed in Parliament by a landslide of 283 to 16 votes. With victory finally declared, Wilberforce's colleagues rushed to cheer and offer him ecstatic tributes, while his own face streamed with tears.[70] The movement and its dramatic end capture well the phenomenon of social happiness as a shared participation in virtuous activities, moral perfection, and a significant degree of fulfilment.

The social body we hope for is deeply marred by sin and a flawed public order. Hope's participation in the beatitudes, which involves innumerable skirmishes with the eudaimonia gap, suggests that hope sets its moral sights very high. Because hope regards only a 'possible good' rather than an easy or guaranteed good, it is not a species of optimism. The consequence is that continued hope for society does not require the belief that things *will* get better, only the belief that important things *can* get better. Otherwise we would be forced to social despair.

We should work and hope for nothing less than a truly just, virtuous, and happy society. But since hope as a disposition of the will has as its object an 'arduous good', hope is not conditional on optimistic predictions. Jeffrey Stout rightly notes that the hopeful can affirm that 'You are still making a difference when you are engaged in successful holding action against forces that are conspiring to make things worse than they are. You are even making a difference when your actions simply keep things from worsening to the extent they would have worsened if you had not acted'.[71] The hopeful may affirm this while also believing that God's spirit is at work in the world, and with a reliance on divine help and a zealous patience which knows that much but not all may be mended before the eschaton. The paradox is that this ability to keep pursuing arduous goods after all the conventional optimists and political 'realists' have called it a day makes hope a magnificently dynamic force for social reform – as indeed the examples of Martin Luther King Jr., William Wilberforce, and others suggest.

The work that hope can do falls far short of the total social reform that can be done. Next to justice and charity, hope is almost a bit player. But hope does give to the other infused virtues an increased horizon, a trust in divine help, and a transcendent assurance. It may take up and refer the work even of infused justice and charity to the eschaton. Surely that kind of tenacious social hope is urgently needed in our present culture. The vice of despair has collective expressions: howls of pain that take form in the available outlets of pessimism, apathy, and cynicism. Amid economic worries, fraying solidarity, family breakdown, political bitterness, ecological decay, and global anxieties of all kinds, the danger of social despair is obvious. The virtue of hope regards an arduous and future good by definition. To the extent hope refers the social body to its final end, the hopeful may be daunted but will not despair over the many challenges of actually *moving* the social body towards the common good. At the social level, hope therefore provides resources for encouragement and resilience amid the failings which could otherwise prompt social demoralisation and despair.

The Heavenly *Patria* and the Beatific Vision

Gaudium et Spes speaks of social reform and work for the common good as a 'foreshadowing of the new age'. This would give them both immanent and transcendent importance. Social reform at its best may not just move towards the perfect friendship of the beatified communion of saints, but constitute a foretaste or premonition of it. As individual beatitude is imperfect in this life and perfect only in the next, the same relationship would obtain with social happiness. *Gaudium et Spes* states: 'after we have obeyed the Lord, and in his Spirit nurtured on earth the values of human dignity, brotherhood, and freedom, and indeed all the good fruits of our nature and enterprise, *we will find them again*, but freed of stain, burnished and transfigured (emphasis mine)'.[72] The beatified communion of saints 'will find', so to speak, the fullness of social fruition whose beginnings they helped set in motion on earth. Given this and our irreducibly social identity, it follows that even if 'here we have no lasting city (Heb 13:14)', it would be wrong to think that our earthly city is superfluous to who we are, either in this life or in the life to come.[73]

Hope construes the Christian as a wayfarer or *viator* on the most important journey possible. But plainly that journey begins, as epic poetry begins, *in medias res*. We are born entangled in a story that has already been going on for some time, and acquire at birth layers of social identity bound up with family, school, church, town, culture, nation, and so forth. The medieval maxim that grace perfects rather than abolishes nature implies, by extension, that the life of grace perfects and does not abolish social nature. Charity informs hope, and Aquinas says both that one's fellow citizens rank extremely high in the 'order of charity' (*ordo caritatis*), and that this order remains in the heavenly 'homeland' (*patria*): 'Nature is not done away, but perfected, by glory. Now the order of charity given above is derived from nature.... Therefore this order of charity will endure in heaven'.[74]

Hope perfects our sociability in part by gathering Christians together as a pilgrim people jointly seeking the kingdom. Yet even in the church our local social identities remain, and grace builds on these. So what might the perfection of this social nature by grace ultimately look like in terms that hope can aspire to, and work towards? It has been suggested that the resurrection of the body may include the resurrection of social identities as our 'larger body': that the nations, for example, will be 'healed' (Rev 22:2) in the eschaton, becoming fully and perfectly themselves, 'fulfilled' rather than 'abolished'.[75] If so, then while William Blake's *Jerusalem* tells an obviously apocryphal story of England's past, what it may get right is the bare idea that Christ will redeem the nations themselves with their created particularities. Scripture intriguingly states that something about the nations in their redeemed form will persist as an adornment or quality of the heavenly city itself: 'the glory and the honour of the nations' shall be brought *into* the heavenly city (Rev 21:26).[76] This helps to bury the view that hope, in the end, envisions the sheer destruction of our temporal and earthly identities, and therefore cannot be motivated to care much about them now.

Aquinas thought that the beatific vision of God's divine essence would perfectly satisfy the will of the rational soul created in God's image. Yet perfect love and friendship befit creatures with a social nature, and so he adds that the glorified saints will 'see one another and rejoice in God at their fellowship'.[77] As the communion of saints implies, perfect beatitude is social rather than individualistic. The Church Triumphant is not regarded by the Christian tradition as a long row of hermitages, but as a *civitas* united by perfect fellowship and love in the new creation. In Milton's sublime phrase:

> About him all the sanctities of heaven
> Stood thick as stars, and from his sight received
> Beatitude past utterance.[78]

In keeping with the New Testament, Aquinas says we are called to become 'fellow-citizens with the saints, and of the household of God'.[79] The communion of saints in glory is thus the consummation of the social body and its hopes as referred by theological hope to the eschaton.

In this work I have devoted rather a lot of space to social considerations both because they are important themselves, and because those committed to social justice often regard eschatological hope with unease or suspicion. I hope I have gone some way towards addressing such concerns. But it is also important to stress once more that hope, as a theological virtue, has God as its basic object and primary concern. In that sense, even a postmortem utopia would not suffice to satisfy hope. It is not only that the hopeful want to arrive 'at home with the Lord' (2 Cor 5:8), but that the presence of the Lord is required for them to believe themselves fully and perfectly at home. An afterlife paradise full of vernal delights but not the vision of God 'face to face' (1 Cor 13:12) could not, finally, interest them. God alone, the Father, Son, and Holy Spirit, is the proportionate goal of hope's striving.

Aquinas held that the beatific vision in which the saints behold God 'face to face' is not put on pause until the last judgment and the general resurrection of the dead. After death, the 'essence' of perfect beatitude is immediately attained by *homo comprehensor* or the glorified soul itself. Put that way, it might sound like all talk of valuing creation and affirming embodiment peels away in the end, so that we fall back on mind-body dualism. But Aquinas insists that as rational animals stripped of their bodies, the glorified saints await the resurrection to possess perfect beatitude 'in every way (they) would wish to possess it'.[80] Perfect beatitude is proper to our 'distinctively human capacities for knowledge and rationally informed love'.[81] But its 'stream of delights' (*torrens voluptatis*) is meant to be partaken of by the passions and the glorified body themselves, so that our embodied nature is a full participant in beatitude.[82] As St. Paul says: 'not that we would be unclothed, but that we would be further clothed, so that what is mortal may be swallowed up by life' (2 Cor 5:4).[83]

It may be asked whether we truly desire this state, and Christians often do scruple that they cannot find a conscious desire for heaven within themselves, or fear that it is weak and flickering compared with other desires at hand. A full treatment of this topic is outside my present scope. But in relation to it, I discussed earlier the *desiderium* for a fuller, ideal, or even perfect good; and sought to relate it to Scriptural images and concepts of beatitude. The New Testament depicts the coming kingdom using a wealth of imagery, such as a wedding feast, the Father's house, paradise, the wine of the kingdom, an entry into joy, the heavenly Jerusalem, the marriage supper of the lamb, and so forth. These images seek to direct the *desiderium* towards God through analogy with the enjoyment of created goods. As Aquinas says, Scripture suggests eternal beatitude 'by means of various goods known to us'.[84] His belief in analogous predications of God implies that a certain analogy is insinuated between the earthly goods and the heavenly good, however partial and qualified.[85] Bespeaking the goodness of creation, this qualification allows us to receive creation as a gift which reflects its maker instead of turning hope into a libel on human life, or slouching towards Manicheanism. It also allows us to follow the Scriptural example and speak of heavenly beatitude using the only language of desire and experience of delight we as finite beings have while fully admitting how inadequate these are to the reality they signify. In that way, created goods may be appreciated as icons rather than broken as idols, and we will not mistake as compliments to grace what are really just insults to nature.

Considered in this manner, life's great moments of overwhelming accomplishment or occasional ecstasy, our richest relationships and profoundest solidarities, the 'little glimpses' of something ineffable that are memory's great treasure, may all be read as a faint and far off *signum* of eternal happiness. Dante, it will be recalled, did not see Christ directly but indirectly, as mirrored in Beatrice's eyes. As with Scriptural imagery of the coming kingdom as a wedding feast or a bejewelled city, hope may relate to earthly projects and created goods not simply as distractions competing with God for our attention, but as suggestions, however modest, of the delight we may one day enjoy in God. Chastened by a reasonable *ascesis* that fences out hedonism, hope will then be enabled to accept life's small and great joys as 'local theophanies'. Considered as such they will be occasions for recollection and doxology which allow us to appreciate created goods both in themselves and, further, as conduits for divine contemplation and eschatological aspiration. Through hope, earthly goods and joys may give rise to the theological *a fortiori*: 'What must be the quality of that Being whose far-off and momentary coruscations are like this'![86] Ordinary and everyday joys surely also have an important place in this scheme.[87] We will also be greatly helped if we develop, through art and other resources, what I earlier called our iconography of happiness, as well as an awareness of the sublime. Where such contemplative practices are lacking, we easily come to think of heaven as officious or banal, and the fact that we so often do signals that we are in trouble, and need to cultivate remedies.[88]

Hope's tale fittingly ends with the homecoming theme in consummation. When the wayfarer's journey is complete, he or she is said to go from the arduous good of life 'on the road' (*in via*) to perfect rest and rejoicing 'in the homeland' (*in patria*). Since we live after the Incarnation and the Resurrection, hope's joyful anticipation of this perfect beatitude, true healing, and lasting peace is all the more credible. Death is not the final victory of the eudaimonia gap. Christ by his Passion and Resurrection has taken captivity captive (Eph 4:8), and he assures us that he is 'the living one; I died, and behold I am alive for evermore, and I have the keys of death and Hades' (Rev 1:18). The consequence is that no peace need be brokered with the eudaimonia gap by those of us who are still *in via*. No melancholy resignation to it should be counselled, and no thinly disguised despair should disconsole our love.

When the journey is finished, *homo viator* becomes *homo comprehensor*: one who has 'grasped' or 'laid hold of' (*comprehendit*) the perfect beatitude that comes through seeing the face of God. In common with his view of imperfect, earthly happiness, Aquinas regards the beatific vision as perfection, actuality, and activity (*operatio*). What is potential rather than actual is imperfect, and so happiness considered as perfection is a pure activity or operation. The beatific vision of God's divine essence is this perfect activity. In it we do not just know God through created effects; we know the very essence of God through the light of glory bestowed upon us.[89] This everlasting contemplation of goodness itself is the greatest possible perfection and activity of the intellect, and it produces utter and complete joy in the will. The beatific vision is thus perfect happiness considered both as perfection and as fulfilment. In it the eudaimonia gap is wholly overcome, and the *desiderium* for ideal, fuller, or perfect happiness at last and forever attains it proportionate object.

Notes

Introduction

1 Jean-Jacques Rousseau, *The Social Contract*, trans. Frederick Watkins (University of Wisconsin Press, 1986), p. 95.

2 One fine exception is Dominic F. Doyle, *The Promise of Christian Humanism: Thomas Aquinas on Hope* (Crossroad Publishing Company, 2012). I discuss this work in some detail in the final chapter of this volume.

3 I discuss these matters elsewhere. See David Elliot, 'The Turn to Classification in Virtue Ethics: A Review Essay', in *Studies in Christian Ethics* 29.4 (November 2016): 477–488.

4 I have borrowed this term from Seyla Benhabib, *Situating the Self: Gender, Community, and Postmodernism in Contemporary Ethics*. First edition (Routledge, 1992).

5 I owe this characterisation to Jeffrey Stout. See *Ethics after Babel: The Languages of Morals and Their Discontents* by Stout, Jeffrey (Princeton University Press, 2001), p. 163.

6 See Thomas Nagel, *The View from Nowhere*. New edition (Oxford University Press, 1989), pp. 3–12.

7 Church of England, *Book of Common Prayer*. Pew edition (Oxford University Press), p. 383.

8 Raymond Geuss, 'The Future of Theological Ethics', in *Studies in Christian Ethics* 25.2 (2012): 165.

9 Joseph Merkt, *Sacra doctrina and Christian Eschatology: A Test Case for a Study of Method and Content in the Writings of Thomas Aquinas* (The Catholic University of America Press, 1982), pp. 130–135.

10 Thomas Aquinas, *Summa theologica* (hereafter ST) II-II 17.1 (Unless otherwise noted, all translations come from the Fathers of the English Dominican Province: Christian Classics, 1981). On the definition of hope, see ST I-II 40.1–8.

11 Regarding the 'acquired' and 'infused' distinction, see John Harvey, 'The Nature of the Infused Moral Virtues', *Proceedings of the Tenth Annual Convention of the Catholic Theological Society of America* 10: pp. 172–221; John Inglis, 'Aquinas' Replication of the Acquired Moral Virtues: Rethinking the Standard Philosophical Interpretation of Moral Virtue in Aquinas',

Journal of Religious Ethics 27.1 (1999): 3–27; Bonnie Kent, 'Habits and Virtues (Ia IIae, qq. 49–70)', in *The Ethics of Aquinas*, pp. 116–130; and Angela McKay, 'Prudence and Acquired Moral Virtue', *The Thomist* 69 (2005): 535–556.

12 ST II-II 17.2.

13 ST II-II 17.1.

14 See Luigi Tomasi, 'Homo Viator: From Pilgrimage to Religious Tourism via the Journey', in William H. Swatos and Luigi Tomasi, *From Medieval Pilgrimage to Religious Tourism*, (Praeger, 2002), pp. 1–15.

15 Quoted and discussed by Christopher Janaway in Keith Ansell Pearson, *A Companion to Nietzsche* (John Wiley & Sons, 2008), p. 338.

16 Jeffrey Stout, *Democracy and Tradition* (Princeton University Press, 2004), p. 30.

1 The Eudaimonia Gap

1 Julia Annas, *The Morality of Happiness* (Oxford University Press, 1995), p. 46.

2 Augustine quoted by Aquinas in ST I-II.1.7

3 See Servais Pinckaers, *The Sources of Christian Ethics* (The Catholic University of America Press, 1995), pp. 134–168.

4 ST I-II.2.8.

5 See Servais Pinckaers, 'Aquinas's Pursuit of Beatitude: From the *Commentary on the Sentences* to the *Summa theologiae*' and 'Beatitude and the Beatitudes in Aquinas's *Summa theologiae*', in John Berkman and Craig Steven Titus, *The Pinckaers Reader: Renewing Thomistic Moral Theology* (The Catholic University of America Press, 2005).

6 For Aquinas, the general object of the will is good as such, and particular goods are sought as constituents in one's own perfection and happiness, though we may obviously be mistaken as to how to go about this, and get our priorities wrong. Yet the object of the will is not simply one's own happiness. As David Gallagher notes, Aquinas 'maintains that one's good is not limited to one's individual good but can include the good of other beings outside oneself'. Beyond one's own good, one is oriented even more to wider perfections of which one is a part, such as 'the good of the species, and yet more the good of the whole universe'. See David Gallagher, 'The Will and Its Acts', in Stephen J. Pope, *The Ethics of Aquinas* (Georgetown University Press, 2002), pp. 69–74, esp. p. 72.

7 ST I-II 2.8.

8 ST I-II 3.2.

9 ST I-II 3.2, 50, and 55.

10 It might seem that this model of happiness, by favouring high functionality, is inherently elitist. Elsewhere I give an argument for why it is not. See 'Defining the Relationship Between Health and Well-Being in Bioethics', especially pp. 12–15. Bits of this section draw on that article. I am grateful to

the publishers, Taylor and Francis Group, for permission to rework some of this material.

11 Jennifer Herdt, *Putting on Virtue: The Legacy of the Splendid Vices*. Reprint edition (University of Chicago Press, 2012), pp. 72–97.

12 Aristotle, *Nicomachean Ethics*, 1105b5. Unless otherwise stated, all citations of Aristotle are taken from *The Nicomachean Ethics*, trans. David Ross, revised by J. O. Urmson and J. L. Ackrill (Oxford University Press, 1998).

13 A burgeoning literature in childhood development, psychological science, and developmental psychology shores up many of these claims. Along with their bibliographies, see Darcia Narvaez, 'The Co-construction of Virtue: Epigenetics, Development, and Culture', pp. 251–278; Ross A. Thompson, 'The Development of Virtue: A Perspective from Developmental Psychology', pp. 279–306; and Dan P. McAdams, 'Psychological Science and the *Nicomachean Ethics*: Virtuous Actors, Agents, and Authors', pp. 307–336, in Nancy E. Snow, *Cultivating Virtue: Perspectives from Philosophy, Theology, and Psychology* (Oxford University Press, 2014).

14 ST I-II 33.4.

15 Thomas Aquinas, *Commentary on Aristotle's Nicomachean Ethics*, 1897–1898. Unless otherwise specified, all translations are from Thomas Aquinas, *Commentary on Aristotle's 'Nicomachean Ethics'*, trans. C. I. Litzinger. New edition of revised edition (Dumb Ox Books, 1993). See also Aristotle, *Nicomachean Ethics* 1170a6.

16 Jane Austen, *Persuasion*, Ch. 9. A fine discussion of this topic and Austen's moral views generally is to be found in C. S. Lewis, 'A Note on Jane Austen', in *Selected Literary Essays* (Cambridge University Press, 1969), p. 184.

17 Of course, the virtuous do not escape moral struggle, though, all things being equal, the tasks of virtue are far less of a struggle for them than for the continent and incontinent. See, for instance, ST I-II 91.6. Moreover, not all virtues are always enjoyable. Conspicuous here is fortitude, which confronts dangers and death, and which does not insulate us from fear and pain. Yet the courageous may take satisfaction in acting well and on behalf of a larger good, from one's country or community to God. See ST II-II.123.8.

18 As Nancy Snow notes, character traits such as generosity and benevolence have been found to enhance the 'attainment of objective goods' and 'allow us to meaningfully exercise our capacities and actualize our potential'. This tends to correlate with an increase in 'positive subjective states, such as enjoyment and feelings of heightened self-worth, vitality, and self-esteem'. Nancy Snow, 'Virtue and Flourishing', in *Journal of Social Philosophy* 39.2: 229. In a recent volume, Everett Worthington Jr., et. al., argue for a convergence between virtue ethics and positive psychology with its focus on positive emotions, happiness or well-being, and character traits. In the same volume, an intriguing entry by James van Slyke argues that research into 'mirror neurons' (by which we mimic others) supports the claim that character traits are formed in significant part through the imitation of role models. These two essays are very

helpful in light of situationist critiques of virtue ethics by John Doris and other experimental psychologists. See *Virtues and Their Vices* (Oxford University Press, 2016), pp. 433-458 and pp. 459–480, respectively.

19 This is different from saying that we pursue virtue as a means to which happiness is the end. As Jennifer Herdt puts it, 'The virtues are constitutive of, not instrumental to, happiness; they are part of happiness since they are worth choosing for their own sake' (*Putting on Virtue*, p. 328) rather than chosen for the sake of the enjoyment they characteristically do confer. She adds: 'The claim is not that *eudaimonia* is a consequence of achieving the good but that *eudaimonia* simply is the good. If something promotes my flourishing, I have a reason to do it, whether or not I happen to care about my flourishing' (p. 327).

20 ST II-II 179–182.

21 ST I-II 3.2. Aquinas observes that many lives are 'mixed', in that they feature elements of the active and contemplative life. So while he uses the active and contemplative ideals as thematic bookends, his account is elastic enough to accommodate a wide range of lifestyles. See ST II-II 179.2.

22 Ibid.

23 For a discussion of the Stoics on this point, see T. H. Irwin, 'Stoic Naturalism and Its Critics', in Brad Inwood, *The Cambridge Companion to the Stoics* (Cambridge University Press, 2003), pp. 346–348.

24 ST I-II 5.3.

25 For those engaging with philosophy, virtue ethics, and eudaimonism, the most helpful figure working in this area is Jean Porter, who has not only explicated, but refurbished Aquinas' account of happiness in light of contemporary moral psychology, the empirical sciences, and causation. See her *Moral Action and Christian Ethics*. New edition (Cambridge University Press, 1999), esp. pp. 138–166; and her latest and extended treatment in *Nature as Reason: A Thomistic Theory of the Natural Law* (W. B. Eerdmans, 2005), esp. pp. 141–221. For a more theological account of Thomistic happiness, see Servais Pinckaers, *Sources of Christian Ethics*. Revised edition (Catholic University of America Press, 1995), pp. 1–47 and pp. 134–167. For exegetical treatments, see Georg Wieland, 'Happiness', in Pope, *The Ethics of Aquinas*, pp. 57–68 and Kevin Staley, 'Happiness: The Natural End of Man?' *The Thomist* 53.2 (1989): 215–234.

26 Aristotle, *Nicomachean Ethics* 1099b.

27 Aristotle, *Politics* 1295a35.

28 Aristotle, *Nicomachean Ethics* 1101a10.

29 Annas, *The Morality of Happiness*, p. 367, italics mine.

30 J. L. Ackrill, 'Aristotle on *Eudaimonia*', in Amélie Rorty, *Essays on Aristotle's Ethics* (University of California Press, 1980), p. 24.

31 Aristotle, *Nicomachean Ethics* 1177a2.

32 Ibid.

33 Ibid., 1178a5.

34 Plato, *Apology* 40a-42.

35 Annas, *The Morality of Happiness*, p. 373.

36 Aristotle, *Nicomachean Ethics*, 1177a2-1178a5.

37 Ibid., 1177a.

38 Ibid., 1178a.

39 Ibid.

40 As Martha Nussbaum puts it: 'It is, as it were, the biggest and brightest jewel in a crown full of valuable jewels, in which each jewel has intrinsical value in itself'. *The Fragility of Goodness* (Cambridge University Press, 2001), p. 374. This allows one to say that other virtuous activities and *philia* also form parts of *eudaimonia* while being able to take Aristotle's privileging of contemplation in Book X seriously. See ibid., pp. 370–380.

41 *Nicomachean Ethics* 1178a25: 'The excellence of reason is a thing apart.... It (the contemplative life) would seem, however, also to need external equipment but little, or *less than moral virtue does*' (italics mine). The contemplative needs 'equipment' such as leisure, health, books, and a study, to say nothing of needing theoretical wisdom (*sophia*). The active person devoted to 'just and brave acts' and the other moral virtues needs a lot more equipment to work with in the way of money, tools, power, infrastructure, materials, social influence, and so forth, as well as practical wisdom (*phronesis*). These are even more dependent on the goods of fortune than modest contemplative needs ('for actions many things are needed, and more, the greater and nobler the actions are', 1178a).

42 See Nussbaum, *The Fragility of Goodness*, pp. 343–373.

43 Aristotle, *Nicomachean Ethics*, 1101a.

44 Ibid.

45 Put in eschatological language, Aristotle's is a fully rather than partly 'realised' *eudaimonia*: the happy life is an 'already' with no 'not yet'.

46 Aristotle, *The Nicomachean Ethics*, p. 265.

47 Ibid., 1177b30.

48 Ibid., 1101a10.

49 Ibid.

50 Within philosophy, any short list would include not just Foot and MacIntyre, but Martha Nussbaum, John McDowell, Rosalind Hursthouse, Annette Baier, Michael Slote, and Julia Annas. Within theology, it would include not just Stanley Hauerwas, but Servais Pinckaers, Jean Porter, Martin Rhonheimer, James Keenan, John Bowlin, and Jennifer Herdt (to name but a few). In this introductory paragraph, I have drawn on my article 'The Turn to Classification in Virtue Ethics: A Review Essay'. I am grateful to SAGE Publishing for permission to rework this material.

51 The hallmark of her later work is the return of teleology to ethics. She argues that our moral judgments as to whether something is good or bad for a person require a naturalism according to which terms like 'good' and 'bad' are known as such with reference to what benefits our species or life-form. The so-called naturalistic fallacy of G. E. Moore made this seem like a dead-end, but Foot draws on the logical work of Peter Geach to argue that Moore was mistaken, chiefly because he regarded goodness as an abstract property. In Foot's view, this is a false start since: 'In most contexts, "good" requires to be complemented

by a noun that plays an essential role in determining whether we are able to speak of goodness rather than badness'. *Natural Goodness* (Oxford University Press, 2001), p. 2. The adjective 'good' should not be construed as a predicative adjective, as in 'the horse is good' or 'friendship is good'. It should be thought of as an attributive adjective, as in 'a good horse' or 'a good friend'. This is because there is no 'good' in the abstract just as there is no 'small' or 'large' in the abstract. There are only good *particulars*, like a good horse or a good oak. And the measure of what makes them 'good' is whether they have all that they need to engage in the functions proper to a flourishing member of their kind. Aristotle makes a similar point in *Politics* 1254a. For Foot, morality-as-virtue and happiness-as-flourishing are inseparably related. Of course, the view pre-supposes that humans are distinctly rational. So while physical needs and ends set many parameters for human life, our mode of deliberating, foreseeing, and planning make it false to think that morality simply collapses into biology (Foot, *Natural Goodness*, pp. 25–38).

52 Ibid., p. 86.

53 Ibid., p. 97. She illustrates the point using the concept of *benefit*. For Foot, to say that virtue makes us happy in terms that work human nature into the discussion is to say that virtue benefits us as members of the human species. This conceptual tool is used to distinguish genuine from false happiness. As an example, she mentions Frederick and Rosemary West, serial killers who did not even spare their own children. Could they have lived a happy life, she asks? Suppose they claimed to enjoy their lives. Foot says it would still be preposter-ous to say that serial killing *benefited* them as human and social animals. Her conclusion is that virtues benefit human beings whereas vices do not: that the virtues are 'conceptually inseparable (from true happiness)' (ibid., p. 94).

54 Nussbaum, *The Fragility of Goodness*, pp. 330–331.

55 Among Aristotle commentators, Nussbaum argues for 1), T. H. Irwin argues for 3), and Annas says that the textual evidence in Aristotle is inconsistent.

56 Helmut Gollwitzer et al., *Dying We Live: The Final Messages and Records of the Resistance* (Wipf & Stock Publishers, 2009).

57 Foot, *Natural Goodness*, p. 96.

58 Ibid., p. 97.

59 Ibid.

60 Foot, *Natural Goodness*, pp. 95–96.

61 Ibid.

62 Rosalind Hursthouse, *On Virtue Ethics* (Oxford University Press, 1999), p. 167.

63 Ibid., p. 208.

64 Ibid., p. 172.

65 Ibid., pp. 171, 184, 265: perhaps pp. 232–233, 243.

66 Ibid., pp. 256–257.

67 Ibid., p. 261.

68 Ibid., p. 258.

69 Ibid., p. 264.

70 Ibid., p. 265.

71 Ibid.
72 For a thorough treatment of the teleological issues and debates, see Porter, *Nature as Reason*, pp. 82–124.
73 I owe this expression to Stout, *Ethics after Babel*, p. 336.
74 Immanuel Kant, *Critique of Judgment*, trans. Werner S. Pluhar (Hackett Publishing Company, Inc., 1987), pp. 349–350.
75 Immanuel Kant, *Critique of Practical Reason*, trans. Mary Gregor (Cambridge University Press, 1997), p. 95.
76 Ibid., pp. 92–95. See also John Hare's discussion in John Perry, *God, the Good, and Utilitarianism: Perspectives on Peter Singer* (Cambridge University Press, 2014), p. 94.
77 Immanuel Kant, *Groundwork of the Metaphysic of Morals*, trans. H. J. Paton (HarpPeren, 1964), p. 85. See the fine discussion by John E. Hare, *The Moral Gap: Kantian Ethics, Human Limits, and God's Assistance*. New edition (Oxford University Press, 1997), especially p. 72.
78 Kant, *Critique of Practical Reason*, p. 105.
79 Kant, *Critique of Pure Reason*, trans. Paul Guyer (Cambridge University Press, 1998), p. 681.
80 Kant, *Critique of Practical Reason*, p. 95.
81 See the discussion by Frederick C. Beiser, 'Moral Faith and the Highest Good', in *The Cambridge Companion to Kant and Modern Philosophy* (Cambridge University Press, 2006), pp. 606–607.
82 John Hare, 'Morality, Happiness, and Peter Singer', in Perry, *God, the Good, and Utilitarianism*, p. 102.
83 John Hare, *The Moral Gap* (Oxford University Press, 1997), pp. 69–70.
84 Ibid., p. 70. For the Schopenhauer reference, see Bernard Williams, 'The Legacy of Greek Philosophy', in Myles Burnyeat, *The Sense of the Past: Essays in the History of Philosophy* (Princeton University Press, 2007), p. 41.
85 Peter Singer and John Hare, 'Moral Mammals', in Dallas Willard, *A Place for Truth* (InterVarsity Press, 2010), pp. 169–194, especially p. 186.
86 Henry Sidgwick, *The Methods of Ethics*. Seventh revised edition (Hackett Publishing Co., Inc., 1981), pp. 411–417.
87 Ibid., pp. 496–510.
88 Singer and Hare, 'Moral Mammals', pp. 186–187.
89 Ibid.
90 For a discussion, see Hare, *The Moral Gap*, p. 100.
91 Sidgwick, *The Methods of Ethics*, pp. 504–509. Wrestling with the problem of despair, J. S. Mill went rather further than Sidgwick, saying we truly need 'the indulgence of hope with regard to the government of the universe and the destiny of man after death'. Such hope is 'legitimate and philosophically defensible' as a practical necessity without which we may be oppressed by 'the disastrous feeling of "not worth while"'. (J. S. Mill, *Three Essays on Religion* (1874), Essay III ('Theism'), Part V). This is tied up with the overall need for hope against demoralising fears that all may end in futility. In that respect, Mill made Coleridge's words his own: 'Work without hope draws nectar in

a sieve/ And hope without an object cannot live' (J. S. Mill, *Autobiography* (1873), ch. 5).

92 Hare, *The Moral Gap*, p. 103.

93 I say this not out of misguided triumphalism. Obviously in such a short space I cannot do full justice to Kantianism or Utilitarianism as moral theories, and certainly I do not aim here to refute them. My goal is simply to note worries in their literature similar to my own about a serious problem we jointly face. If anything, this should increase our philosophical solidarity.

94 Sidgwick did not commit one way or the other, and Mill accepted aspects of Christian hope while denying divine omnipotence due to the problem of evil. See the discussion by Hare, *The Moral Gap*, pp. 93–101.

95 This is not to say that existential angst is the only or the best response to the grim eschaton of physical cosmology. I agree with Jeffrey Stout that 'the highest achievable good, given whatever causal powers we have independent reason to believe in', is 'worth pursuing' (*Ethics after Babel*, p. 313). But the eventual loss of all good and all life projected by secular science, even if insufficient to drain moral motivation, is a melancholy thought to those committed to preserving life and the good.

96 These include life itself and the body; the goods of subsistence and health, such as food, drink, medicine, clothing, and shelter; the material goods that serve as equipment for one's activities, from money and transportation to the tools of one's trade; and the friendships and social relationships in which we carry out virtuous projects. It is in and through pursuing these goods that virtuous living is conducted: for example, the goods which prudence weighs, which justice distributes, which hospitality serves, and which temperance moderates. I discuss this at some length in 'Defining the Relationship Between Health and Well-Being in Bioethics'.

97 Lisa Sowle Cahill, *Global Justice, Christology and Christian Ethics* (Cambridge University Press, 2015).

98 Gordon Graham, *Evil and Christian Ethics* (Cambridge University Press, 2000). Graham argues at book length that atrocious evils cannot be adequately explained by secular humanism and naturalism; that there is a remainder of moral explanation best accounted for not by modernist thought or by 'postmodern eclecticism', but by the New Testament and traditional Christian belief in demonic agency. I myself would not balk at the theology presupposed here, but whether or not horrendous evil can only be adequately explained in this way, Graham is right that only religious hope can reasonably expect that the terrible marring wrought by many such evils can ever be mended. Not in this life, and not by any secular balm, may the victims of serials killers or of genocide find adequate redress and healing.

99 My claim is not that the eudaimonia gap, virtuously faced, inevitably weakens our overall motivation to pursue the moral good or happiness, but that it weakens the facility, the confidence, and the extent to which we can pursue what we reasonably desire as the adequate moral good and adequate happiness, for reasons suggested in this chapter. I have borrowed the term

'demoralisation' from Robert Adams. See his 'Moral Arguments for Theistic Belief', in C. F. Delaney, ed., *Rationality and Religious Belief* (University of Notre Dame Press, 1980), p. 125.

100 See the discussions by McKay, 'Prudence and Acquired Moral Virtue' and Kent, 'Habits and Virtues (Ia IIae, qq. 49–70)'.

101 For clinical evidence that hopefulness tends to increase life expectancy, helps with overcoming physical and mental illness, and is crucial but elusive absent religious beliefs in end-of-life palliative care, see the suggestive empirical data marshalled by Stan van Hooft, *Hope* (Routledge, 2014), pp. 66–80; David Clarke, 'Faith and Hope', *Australasian Psychiatry* 11.2 (1 June 2003): 164–168; Terry Bunston et al., 'Facilitating Hopefulness', *Journal of Psychosocial Oncology* 13.4 (16 May 1996): 79–103; Gottschalk La, 'Hope and Other Deterrents to Illness', *American Journal of Psychotherapy* 39.4 (October 1985): 515–524; Sheena Sethi and Martin E. P. Seligman, 'Optimism and Fundamentalism', *Psychological Science* 4.4 (1 July 1993): 256–259.

102 I would distinguish an accommodating interpretation from a pragmatic will-to-believe (or in this case, a will-to-hope). Accommodating interpreters do not decide to believe (or try to do so), they charitably consider reasons to believe, which is a more modest task. As Aquinas notes, when a person is favourably disposed towards believing, 'he thinks out and takes to heart whatever reasons he can find in support' of belief, yet without credulously dispensing with good reasons. See ST II-II 2.10. For a fine contemporary discussion of William James' 'The Will to Believe', see Adams, 'Moral Arguments for Theistic Belief'.

103 Raymond Geuss, 'The Future of Theological Ethics', in *Studies in Christian Ethics* 25.2 (2012): 165.

104 See Stout, *Ethics after Babel*, pp. 109–112.

105 For arguments agreeing with this claim from the perspective of a secular philosopher, see ibid., pp. 186–188. My proposals here presuppose the difference between secular and theistic ethics while suggesting that the difference is not so great that the two speak in equivocal terms and therefore have nothing mutually to say or offer.

106 William Morris, *The Earthly Paradise*, Prologue, l. 12, 978.

107 ST I-II 2.8.

108 Aquinas sees this as the perfection proper to human and rational animals, and sees it as analogous to the perfection by which members of any plant or animal species flourish. See Porter, *Nature as Reason*, pp. 145–163.

109 The moral psychology behind this view may of course be doubted or denied, and I will return to this point in the third chapter.

110 I would argue that this specification is the work of theological faith, meaning that what we are dealing with is not a 'natural desire for the supernatural', but rather a general and unspecified natural desire for perfect beatitude which can be supernaturally specified as having the Triune God for its object. See Porter, *Nature as Reason*, p. 158.

111 See Alister E. McGrath, *A Brief History of Heaven* (Blackwell Publishers, 2003), p. 169.

2 The Theological Virtue of Hope in Aquinas

1 This is not to say it *is* the Good News, or the totality of the Gospel. Yet it is one important aspect of the Gospel.

2 See Joseph A. Fitzmyer, S.J., 'The Letter to the Romans', in Raymond Brown, *The Jerome Biblical Commentary* (Prentice Hall, 1968), pp. 316–317.

3 Jürgen Moltmann, 'Christian Hope: Messianic or Transcendent? A Theological Discussion with Joachim of Fiore and Thomas Aquinas', *Horizons* 12.2 (September 1985): 333.

4 Graham, *Evil and Christian Ethics*, p. 205.

5 Ernst Bloch, *The Principle of Hope* (Basel Blackwell, three volumes, 1986), p. 1375.

6 Jürgen Moltmann, *Theology of Hope*. New edition (SCM Press, 2010), p. 18.

7 Ibid.

8 Ibid., p. 21.

9 Ibid., p. 32.

10 Ibid., p. 16.

11 Jürgen Moltmann, *God in Creation*. First edition (SCM Press, 2000), pp. 98–103. See also the helpful discussion by Richard Bauckham, *Theology of Jürgen Moltmann* (Continnuum-3PL, 1995), pp. 186–188.

12 Jürgen Moltmann, *Religion, Revolution, and the Future* (Scribner, 1969), p. 138.

13 Moltmann, *Theology of Hope*, pp. 195–196.

14 Moltmann, *Religion, Revolution, and the Future*, p. 5.

15 Ibid., p. 40.

16 See Moltmann, *Theology of Hope*, pp. 304–338; Jürgen Moltmann, *The Trinity and the Kingdom: The Doctrine of God*. Fortress Press edition (Fortress Press, 1993).

17 See Moltmann, *On Human Dignity: Political Theology and Ethics*. First edition (Fortress Press, 2007), pp. 168–180; see also the treatment by Gary Dorrien, *Reconstructing the Common Good: Theology and the Social Order* (Wipf & Stock Publishers, 2008), chapter 4.

18 Moltmann, *Religion, Revolution, and the Future*, pp. 38, 143.

19 Moltmann, *On Human Dignity*, p. 111; Jürgen Moltmann, *The Crucified God*. New edition (SCM Press, 2001), p. 337. See also the discussion by Bauckham, *Theology of Jürgen Moltmann*, pp. 103–106.

20 See Moltmann, *The Crucified God*, pp. 201–204; Jürgen Moltmann, *The Future of Creation*. Annotated edition (Augsburg Fortress Publishers, 2000), pp. 62–65. For a sympathetic discussion of Moltmann's panentheism, see Bauckham, *Theology of Jürgen Moltmann*, esp. p. 54. For a critical discussion, see David P. Scaer, 'Jürgen Moltmann and His "Theology of Hope"', *Journal of the Evangelical Theological Society* 13.2 (1 March 1970): pp. 69–79.

21 Bauckham, *Theology of Jürgen Moltmann*, pp. 1–28.

22 Moltmann, *Theology of Hope*, p. 16.

23 For an excellent overview and contemporary defence of Christian *agapism*, see Timothy P. Jackson, *The Priority of Love: Christian Charity and Social Justice* (Princeton University Press, 2009), esp. pp. 1–27.

24 See Thomas Aquinas, ST II-II 17 2, 4; *Super I Epistolam B. Pauli ad Corinthios lectura*, ch. 15.

25 Moltmann, *Religion, Revolution, and the Future*, p. 32.

26 Moltmann's rejections of theistic omnipotence may be found in chapter 6 of *The Crucified God*, especially at pp. 221 and 252.

27 Moltmann, *Theology of Hope*, p. 196.

28 See Scaer, 'Jürgen Moltmann and His "Theology of Hope,"' p. 73.

29 Michael Wood and Bernard Williams, *Essays and Reviews: 1959–2002* (Princeton University Press, 2014), p. 21.

30 Bauckham, *Theology of Jürgen Moltmann*, p. 42.

31 Moltmann, 'Resurrection as Hope', in *Religion, Revolution, and the Future*, p. 50.

32 At one point Moltmann does allow that while there are no historical analogies to the resurrection, there are 'analogies in the category of the Spirit and his effects'. He suggests that 'the experiential form of the resurrection is … the justification of the godless in a world of unrighteousness, the experience of faith, certainty in the midst of uncertainty, the experience of love in the midst of death'. See Moltmann, 'Theology as Eschatology', in Frederick Herzog, *The Future of Hope: Theology as Eschatology* (Herder & Herder, 1970), p. 163. But this could not be anything like an epistemic justification for adopting hope since these are the experiences of those who already have hope. In addition, Moltmann is clear that while these may be analogies of the resurrection, they are not analogies of the resurrection *considered as a historical event*. The circularity problem therefore remains where it was. It is also doubtful whether Moltmann intended this appeal to spiritual experience to justify our hope in the resurrection and eschaton at all. As his sympathetic expositor Richard Bauckham notes, Moltmann throughout his career continued to insist that 'the resurrection far transcends these analogies and can find an adequate analogy only in the future new creation. Belief in it is therefore inseparable from hope'. See Bauckham, *The Theology of Jürgen Moltmann*, p. 43. It seems that the only way Moltmann could escape the circularity is by appealing to a model of history and event which is incompatible with his eschatology and panentheistic theology. But this would be to forfeit his main project.

33 See Dominic F. Doyle, *The Promise of Christian Humanism: Thomas Aquinas on Hope* (Crossroad Publishing Company, 2012), pp. 45–48, 69–71; Jean-Pierre Torrell, *Saint Thomas Aquinas: Spiritual Master v. 2* (The Catholic University of America Press, 2003), pp. 325–327.

34 For a thorough treatment of these two aspects of grace, see Bernard Lonergan, *Grace and Freedom: Operative Grace in the Thought of St. Thomas Aquinas*, ed. J. Patout Burns, S.J. (Darton, Longman & Todd, 1971), pp. 41–54.

35 ST I-II 109.

36 ST I-II.85.1.

37 ST I-II 109.8.

38 For a historical-critical treatment of this verse which complements Aquinas, see Joseph A. Fitzmyer, *Romans* (Yale University Press, 1993), pp. 405–408.

39 My treatment of *natura integra* and original justice substantially follows that of Jean-Pierre Torrell, *Surnaturel: A Controversy at the Heart of Twentieth-Century Thomistic Thought*, ed. Serge-Thomas Bonino, trans. Robert Williams, revised by Matthew Levering (Sapientia Press, 2009). My interpretation of Thomistic grace is greatly indebted to Joseph Wawrykow's 'Grace', in R. van Nieuwenhove and J. Wawrkyow, *The Theology of Thomas Aquinas* (University of Notre Dame Press), pp. 192–221.

40 For example, charity as grace perfects the will, and infused temperance as grace perfects the passions. As infused and gracious virtues, this perfection is effected supernaturally. But *what* is perfected is and remains natural: the human will, appetites, and other natural capacities. See ST I-II 113.

41 My interpretation of grace and nature is indebted to Jean Porter, *Nature as Reason*, pp. 378–400, whose account, along with that of Wawrykow, I substantially follow. Good additional sources are Steven Long, 'On the Possibility of a Purely Natural End for Man', *The Thomist* 64 (2006): 211–237; and Staley, 'Happiness: The Natural End of Man?'. My goal here is not to adjudicate the nature-grace controversies, but simply to say where I stand so as to put my account of grace in context. Influenced by these thinkers, my view in brief is that to build grace into the definition of nature would seriously risk collapsing nature into divinity. Besides wrongly making humans naturally deific, such a collapse would leave unclear what Christ assumed in the Incarnation. It would also open up the door for a Jansenist interpretation of the Fall according to which in losing grace, we effectively lose nature. Moreover, if the natural human end were a graced end, then it would be exceedingly hard to say that humans were not the same species as anything else that shared a graced end. But this would result in baffling conclusions, such as that humans and angels shared the same *natural* species.

42 Paul Hammond, *The Poems of John Dryden* (Pearson Education, 1995), p. 235.

43 Ibid. Torrell, *Surnaturel*, pp. 174–178.

44 ST I-II 109.8. See also Wawrykow, 'Grace', pp. 193–196.

45 ST I-II 113.9. Aquinas regards this as God's greatest work, quoting Augustine's statement that: 'the justification of a sinner is a greater work than the creation of heaven and earth' because 'heaven and earth will pass away, but the salvation and justification of the elect shall endure'.

46 ST I 20.2.

47 ST I-II 110.1.

48 See Wawrykow, 'Grace', p. 194. Grace does involve the 'motions' (*motus*) of the Holy Spirit, but the representative sense of grace as a 'state' refers in Aquinas to habitual grace.

49 ST I-II 110.

50 The infused cardinal virtues are required since the supernatural end exceeds the proportion of the acquired natural virtues, and yet in order to attain the supernatural end, a life of justice, temperance, fortitude, and prudence is nevertheless required. The solution is for God to infuse cardinal virtues analogous to their acquired counterparts, but differing in that they are proportioned to the supernatural end. See ST I- II.110.4 and endnote 11 in the Introduction.

51 ST I-II.113.1.

52 ST III.1.

53 ST III.49.3.

54 ST III.47.2., ST III.69.1, 2, 4.

55 See Porter, *Nature as Reason*, pp. 156–162.

56 For instance, he thinks that contemplative happiness may be diminished or lost through forgetfulness, sickness, or busyness. Likewise, active happiness may be mostly lost through tragedy, and wholly lost through a lapse into vice (ST I-II 5.4). All of these evils are either sin or the results of living in a sinful world. Yet they may also be described in terms that my philosophical interlocutors and people generally would acknowledge as realities and as real problems. Aquinas uses both vocabularies, slipping from the philosophical to the theological depending on what audience he has in mind at a given point.

57 When it comes to the enormous variety of grace distinctions which follow, particularly *auxilium*, operative, and cooperative grace, I closely follow Wawrykow's 'Grace', pp. 192–218.

58 'For which reason', Aquinas says, 'it is becoming in those who have been born again as sons of God, to say: "Lead us not into temptation," and "Thy Will be done on earth as it is in heaven," and whatever else is contained in the Lord's Prayer' (ST I-II.109.9). In appealing to the Lord's Prayer as a locus for *auxilium*, Aquinas taps into Augustine's anti-Pelagian claim that even the regenerate need further graces to persevere in grace – otherwise we would not pray for them. In many places Aquinas describes the act of hope as leaning or relying on God's *auxilium* to see us through the journey.

59 ST I-II 68.

60 Quoted in Jennifer Herdt, *Putting on Virtue: The Legacy of the Splendid Vices* (University of Chicago Press, 2008), p. 91.

61 See Doyle, *The Promise of Christian Humanism*, p. 54.

62 ST I-II.111.2.

63 Ibid.

64 ST I-II 114.1. See also Wawrykow, *Westminster Handbook to Thomas Aquinas* (Westminster John Knox Press, 2005), pp. 92–95.

65 ST II-II 21.

66 See N. T. Wright, *Surprised by Hope: Rethinking Heaven, the Resurrection, and the Mission of the Church* (HarperOne, 2008), pp. 40–79.

67 Peter Brown, *The Cult of the Saints: Its Rise and Function in Latin Christianity* (University of Chicago Press, 1981), pp. 69–70.

68 Merkt, *Sacra doctrina and Christian Eschatology*, pp. 130–135.

69 ST II-II 17.1.

70 II-II.25.5.2.

71 ST I-II 40.6.

72 ST II-II 17.4.

73 ST II-II 17.3.

74 ST II-II 17.2.

75 ST II-II 18.4.

76 ST II-II 17.2.

77 ST I-II 5.3, *Super Romanos* 990.

78 ST II-II 17.2. For a full treatment of this subject, see Doyle, *The Promise of Christian Humanism*, pp. 119–144. In the final chapter of this volume, I discuss this book in some detail.

79 As Joseph Wawrykow notes, the place of hope as an efficient cause on which we 'lean' is a late development in Aquinas. See his *God's Grace and Human Action: 'Merit' in the Theology of Thomas Aquinas* (University of Notre Dame Press, 1995), pp. 130–134, 248–250. In Aquinas' early work the *Scriptum*, he had posited only one object of hope: God as final cause. Habitual grace was all that one required to attain salvation, making further graces or helps unnecessary. This accords with Lombard and most scholastic interpretations. But later in his career, Aquinas added the second object of hope: God as efficient cause operating by means of *auxilium* grace. The object of hope is now not merely God in heaven, but God in this life as a 'helper strong to assist' one in completing the journey (ST II-II 17.6). Hope in the *Scriptum* is a far more autonomous affair; God provides habitual grace and the agent largely takes matters from there. Hope in the *Summa* implies that even after justification God intervenes through the 'efficient cause' of ongoing *auxilia* or actual graces. The *Summa*'s hope is no longer just a matter of 'God as my beatitude', but much more of 'God as personal saviour'. By this point in his career, Aquinas has rejected the original formulation of hope as radically inadequate. Wawrykow has argued that the change was due to Aquinas' discovery of late writings of Augustine against semi-Pelagian tendencies which 'had passed out of theological circulation after the Carolingian period', *God's Grace and Human Action*, p. 132; *The Westminster Handbook to Thomas Aquinas*, p. 68.

80 ST II-II 17.1, 4, 5.

81 See Wawrykow, *The Westminster Handbook to Thomas Aquinas*, pp. 63–67.

82 The sensibility is captured well in a passage by the Carolingian theologian Paschasius Radbert: 'Christ is held by the hand of hope. We hold him and are held. But it is a greater good that we are held by Christ than that we hold him. For we can hold him only so long as we are held by him'. Josef Pieper, *On Hope* (Ignatius Press, 1986), p. 33.

83 ST II-II 17.1.

84 Thomas Aquinas, *Compendium of Theology*, ed. and trans. Cyril Vollert, and Richard A. Munkelt (Angelico Press, 2012), pp. 213–232.

85 Given that all of the infused virtues are actualised by *auxilium*, and given that all of these virtues *qua* cooperative require the agent to lean on that *auxilium* for God to cooperate with the agent, it follows that the acts of all

other infused habits depend in this crucial respect on hope. If trust in God's *auxilium* goes awry through either presumption or despair, the operations of the other infused habits break down. Hope is not the form of the virtues, but it is something like their bottleneck.

86 To explain this, Aquinas distinguishes between primary efficient causes and instrumental efficient causes. God is always the primary efficient cause of *auxilium*. In fact, hope's reliance on this is what distinguishes it from infused magnanimity. Like hope, magnanimity seeks an arduous good. But magnanimity does this 'in the hope of obtaining something that is within one's power', whereas theological hope regards the arduous good 'to be obtained by another's help'. In this respect Christian beatitude differs sharply from pagan *eudaimonia*. See ST II-II 17.5.

87 The scope of human life with its basic needs, relationships, efforts, and pursuits may therefore not just be ordained to God as final end, but may also be instruments through which God works to move us to that end. See Cessario, 'The Theological Virtue of Hope', in Pope, *The Ethics of Aquinas*, p. 236.

88 See ST I-II 62; 63.3, 4; 64.4.

89 ST II-II 4.2.

90 Doyle, *The Promise of Christian Humanism*, pp. 80–90.

91 For excellent treatments of the distinction, see Guy Mansini, '*Duplex Amor* and the Structure of Love in Aquinas', *Thomistica* (1995): 127–196, and William Mattison, 'Movements of Love: A Thomistic Perspective on Eros and Agape', *Journal of Moral Theology* 1.2 (2012): 31–60.

92 ST II-II 23.2.

93 ST II-II 23.1.

94 Along with ST II-II 17.8, see the fine discussion in Thomas Aquinas, *Hope, 2a2ae. 17–22. Latin Text. English Translation, Introduction, Notes, Appendices and Glossary*, ed. and trans. William J. Hill (Blackfriars/McGraw-Hill Book Company, 1966), pp. 139–154.

95 ST I-II 26.4. In addition to Hill, see Gallagher, 'The Will and Its Acts'.

96 Ibid.

97 As movement is the precursor to arriving at the end, Aquinas sees *amor concupiscentiae* as a precursor rather than an inherent rival or enemy to *amor benevolentiae*. Due to sin, the relationship between these two loves often goes awry. But this is the abuse rather than proper use of their natures, and *abusis non tollit usum*. See Cessario, 'The Theological Virtue of Hope', p. 237.

98 My exposition here follows that of Hill in Aquinas, *Hope*, pp. 138–157.

99 ST I 82.3.

100 Ibid. Hill in Aquinas, *Hope*, p. 157.

101 See ST 17.7, 8, and Hill in Aquinas, *Hope*, pp. 157–158.

102 ST II-II 23.8.

103 ST I-II 40.7: 'In so far as hope regards one through whom something becomes possible to us, love is caused by hope.... Because by the very fact that we hope that good will accrue to us through someone, we are moved towards him as to our own good; and thus we begin to love him'.

104 See Doyle, *The Promise of Christian Humanism*, p. 89.
105 ST II-II 17.8.
106 ST II-II 23.1.
107 ST I-II.113.4.
108 ST II-II 17.5, 8.
109 For example, fasting or celibacy may be acts of infused temperance proximately and thus bear the 'form' of infused temperance. But they are further ordained to charity's ultimate end of union with God, and so are 'in-formed' by charity remotely. See ST II-II 63.4.
110 ST II-II.23.6, 8.
111 ST II-II.17.3.
112 Ephesians 4:24, from the Vulgate translation.
113 See Porter, *Nature as Reason*, p. 143; and more generally, Servais Pinckaers, *L'Evangile et la morale* (Saint-Paul, 1990).
114 ST II-II 20.1.
115 Pieper, *On Hope*, p. 49.
116 My account of sloth is much indebted to Rebecca Konyndyk DeYoung, 'Sloth: Some Historical Reflections on Laziness, Effort, and Resistance to the Demands of Love', in Kevin Timpe and Craig A. Boyd, *Virtues and Their Vices* (Oxford University Press, 2014), pp. 177–198.
117 For Aquinas on sloth as a cause of despair, see ST II-II 20.4. On sloth generally, see ST II-II 35 and Thomas Aquinas, *On Evil*, ed. and trans. Richard J Regan and Brian Davies (Oxford University Press, 2003), pp. 361–390. Pieper also gives an excellent contemporary discussion of sloth as a gateway to despair in *On Hope*, pp. 54–60.
118 ST II-II.35.1.
119 ST II-II 20.4. See also Pieper, *On Hope*, pp. 67–72.
120 ST II-II 21.1.
121 Ibid.
122 Ibid.
123 Ibid.
124 ST II-II 19. For a Thomistic overview of the gift of fear, see Merkt, *Sacra Doctrina and Christian Eschatology*, pp. 279–285.
125 ST II-II 19.3.
126 ST II-II 19.4.
127 ST II-II 19.5, 6.
128 ST II-II 19.6.
129 Aquinas writes: 'That some who have hope fail to obtain happiness, is due to a fault of the free will in placing the obstacle of sin, but not to any deficiency in God's power or mercy, in which hope places its trust' (ST II-II 18.4). My interpretation of certitude follows that of Walter M. Conlon, 'The Certitude of Hope', in *The Thomist* 10 (1947): 76–119, 226–252.
130 Friedrich Nietzsche, *The Anti-Christ* in *Twilight of the Iodls and the Anti-Christ*, trans. R. Hollingdale (Penguin, 1968), pp. 58, 60.
131 Jean-Jacques Rousseau, *On the Social Contract* (Courier Dover Publications, 2012), p. 95.

132 Algernon Charles Swinburne, *Selected Poems* (D. C. Heath & Company, 1905), p. 73.

133 See Ourida Mostefai and John T. Scott, *Rousseau and 'L'Infame': Religion, Toleration, and Fanaticism in the Age of Enlightenment* (Rodopi, 2009), p. 9.

134 Cited in Robert Merrihew Adams, *A Theory of Virtue: Excellence in Being for the Good* (Oxford University Press, 2008), p. 97.

135 See Darlene Fozard Weaver, *Self Love and Christian Ethics* (Cambridge University Press, 2002). Weaver clearly distinguishes self-love from self-preoccupation and conventional models of autonomy. A proper self-love will be embodied and reflexive rather than disembodied and narcissistic, and it will complement rather than compete with moral responsibility (Weaver's views on responsibility owe much to William Schweiker, *Responsibility and Christian Ethics*. New edition [Cambridge University Press, 1999]). While developing her own model of self-love, Weaver draws on Aquinas and presents his account of self-love as compatible with her own. See esp. pp. 132–134, 164. She also shows affinities for the account of Jean Porter, herself a Thomist. See pp. 89–91.

136 Richard Parish, *Catholic Particularity in Seventeenth-Century French Writing: 'Christianity Is Strange'* (Oxford University Press, 2011), p. 177.

137 Cited in Adams, *A Theory of Virtue*, p. 97.

138 Ibid. Parish, *Catholic Particularity in Seventeenth-Century French Writing*, p. 177.

139 See ibid., pp. 170–185.

140 Timothy P. Jackson, *Love Disconsoled: Meditations on Christian Charity* (Cambridge University Press, 2010), p. 30.

141 Ibid., p. 162.

142 Ibid. 'If there is a proper place for self-love, as the second love commandment implies, then utter loss of self cannot be the essence of *agape*', p. 158.

143 Stout also seems to think Jackson's critiques of hope are sound and should alter current thinking in Christian theology. See *Democracy and Tradition*, pp. 256, 336 n. 43.

144 Jackson, *Love Disconsoled*, pp. ix–xii.

145 Ibid., p. 169.

146 Ibid., p. 132.

147 Ibid., p. xii.

148 Ibid., p. 200.

149 Ibid., p. x.

150 Ibid., pp. 130–131.

151 Ibid., p. 133.

152 Ibid., p. 162.

153 Ibid., p. 167. Jackson warns us not to make 'immortality-as-endless-life' into a 'motive for charity' (p. 163) and says that 'To insist on resurrection as something owed the life of love smacks of trying to strike a lawlike bargain with God' (p. 30).

154 C. S. Lewis, *The Weight of Glory and Other Addresses* (HarperSanFrancisco, 2001), pp. 26–27.

155 Aquinas, *Summa Contra Gentiles* Bk 3, Pt 2, Q. 153. I will cover this section later.

156 Jackson rejects the idea that *agape* is essentially friendship, thereby distancing him from Aquinas' view of charity as friendship. Yet he does believe that 'a cooperative friendship with God' may be 'the ideal *consummation* of love' (p. 81). Moreover, Jackson depicts *agape* 'as participation in the life of God' (p. 163), and the broader point of both Lewis and Aquinas is that the beatific vision is precisely that 'participation' in a more perfect and consummated form rather than a separate end distinct from that participation.

157 Ibid., p. 163.

158 For the historical biblical meaning of 'face to face' as referring to a 'direct encounter with God', see Richard B. Hays, *First Corinthians: Interpretation : A Bible Commentary for Teaching and Preaching* (Westminster John Knox Press, 2011), pp. 229–231.

159 See Jackson, *Love Disconsoled*, pp. 160–166, and especially p. 167.

160 Ibid., p. 163.

161 Ibid., p. 169.

162 Ibid., pp. 162, 167.

163 Ibid., p. 159.

164 Ibid.

165 Ibid., p. 30.

166 In Aquinas' terms, this sinks hope far below the level of a virtue, perhaps sinking it below the level of action altogether into what he calls a *velleitas*: a passing, spontaneous wish which gives rise to no intentions and is not even an object of deliberation. See Gallagher, 'The Will and Its Objects', p. 81.

167 Ibid. Jackson, *Love Disconsoled*, p. 167.

168 Ibid., p. 170.

169 G. E. M. Anscombe, *Intention* (Harvard University Press, 2000). The 'idle wish' corresponds closely to what Aquinas calls a *velleitas*.

170 See William Childs Robinson, 'Eschatology of the Epistle to the Hebrews: A Study in the Christian Doctrine of Hope', *Encounter* 22.1 (1 December 1961): 37–51.

171 Ibid. Jackson, *Love Disconsoled*, p. 166.

172 Ibid., p. 152.

173 Ibid., p. 165.

174 Ibid., p. 166.

175 Jackson says that St. Paul was simply mistaken in his claim that: 'If Christ has not been raised, then our preaching is in vain and your faith is vain.... If for this life only we have hoped in Christ, we are of all men most to be pitied' (1 Cor 15:14, 19). See *Love Disconsoled*, p. 165.

176 Ibid., p. 174.

177 Stout, *Ethics after Babel*, p. 186.

178 Jackson states: 'we can be supremely confident that an agapic God grants perdurability to the righteous *if* their ever being loving itself requires this' (p. 170). It is the need to do this rather than the power of God to do this that Jackson doubts, which makes an important difference.

179 Ibid.

180 Ibid., p. 15.

181 See ST II-II 17.3.

182 For an excellent treatment of this verse in context, see Richard B. Hays, *The Moral Vision of the New Testament: Community, Cross, New Creation, a Contemporary Introduction to New Testament Ethics*. First edition (HarperOne, 1996), pp. 179–181.

183 Jackson, *Love Disconsoled*, p. 169.

184 Ibid., p. 129.

185 Ibid., pp. 132, 164, 174, 177–230.

186 Ibid., p. 197.

187 Ibid., p. 174.

188 E. R. Dodds quoted in Bernard Williams, *Shame and Necessity* (University of California Press, 2008), p. 126.

189 Ibid., p. 176.

190 Ibid., p. 159. Compared to the ardent love and desire for communion with God found in Scripture and the writings of the saints, Jackson's concession is faint and muted. As Aquinas writes: 'In every lover there is caused a desire to be united with his beloved, in so far as that is possible; as a result, it is most enjoyable to live with friends. So, if by grace man is made a lover of God, there must be produced in him a desire for union with God, according as that is possible.... Therefore, the desire for this fruition results in man from the love of God. But the desire for anything bothers the soul of the desirer, unless there be present some hope of attainment'. See Aquinas, *Summa Contra Gentiles* Bk 3, Pt 2, Q. 153.

191 Jackson, *Love Disconsoled*, p. 173.

192 Nothing in Jackson's account suggests that this annihilation, were it to occur, would discriminate between the righteous and the wicked. The problem I am discussing therefore differs from the problem of whether an all-loving, all-powerful God would engage in damnation.

193 Ibid., pp. 169–174.

194 Matthew Levering drew my attention to this passage. See his *The Betrayal of Charity: The Sins that Sabotage Divine Love* (Baylor University Press, 2011), p. 48. Though my overall critique of Jackson differs in important ways from that of Levering, I owe the use of Job and the point about annihilation to him. See pp. 49–50.

3 Rejoicing in Hope

1 William C Mattison, *Introducing Moral Theology: True Happiness and the Virtues* (Brazos Press, 2008), p. 253.

2 Ibid.

3 Ibid., p. 254.

4 ST I-II 2.8.

5 Matthew Arnold, cited in McGrath, *A Brief History of Heaven*, p. 128.

6 Ibid., p. 129.

7 William Wordsworth, *Lines Composed a Few Miles above Tintern Abbey*, lines 73–83.

8 See Dorothy L. Sayers, *Further Papers on Dante: His Heirs and His Ancestors* (Wipf & Stock Publishers, 2006), p. 189.

9 See Mattison, *Introducing Moral Theology*, pp. 254–256.

10 See the excellent treatment in George Orwell and John Carey, *Essays* (Alfred A. Knopf, 2002), pp. 504–506.

11 See Stout, *Democracy and Tradition*, pp. 105, 133–135, 165, 219.

12 *The Complete Poetical Works of William Wordsworth*, 1904, p. 340.

13 In Book Seven of the 1850 *Prelude* he asks his readership to 'forgive the pen seduced/ By specious wonders' and against mere abstract theory recommends some reasonable 'form of acquiescence in an essentially traditional way of life attached to a particular place':

> Thus, duties rising out of good possessed,
> And prudent caution needful to avert
> Impending evil, equally require
> That the whole people should be taught and trained.
> So shall licentiousness and black resolve
> Be rooted out, and virtuous habits take
> Their place; and genuine piety descend,
> Like an inheritance, from age to age.
> (Quoted in Stout, *Democracy and Tradition*, pp. 35-36.)

14 Orwell and Carey, *Essays*, pp. 503–510.

15 See David Suzuki, Adrienne Mason, and Amanda McConnell, *The Sacred Balance: Rediscovering Our Place in Nature*. Illustrated edition (Greystone Books, 1999).

16 William Shakespeare, *Romeo and Juliet*, Act 2, Scene 6.

17 For an excellent discussion, see Gabriele Taylor, *Deadly Vices* (Oxford University Press, 2008), pp. 27–30, 64–66.

18 ST I-II 40.6.

19 On magnanimity and pusillanimity, see ST II-II 129, 133. For an instructive discussion, see Herdt, *Putting On Virtue*, pp. 77–80.

20 Lewis, *The Weight of Glory*, p. 31.

21 Aristotle, *Nicomachean Ethics*, p. 265.

22 Ibid., p. 22.

23 Saint Augustine, *Confessions*. Second edition, trans. Frank J. Sheed (Hackett Publishing, 2007), p. 65.

24 Rousseau, *On the Social Contract*, p. 95.

25 ST I-II 69.4.

26 For excellent treatments of the subject, see Hays, *The Moral Vision of the New Testament*, pp. 169–187, and Wright, *Surprised by Hope*, particularly pp. 31–79.

27 ST I 13.2.

28 Ibid.

29 Aquinas believes that our language of God is neither univocal nor equivocal, but analogous. For it to be univocal, God would have to be a finite being

like ourselves. If it were equivocal, we as finite beings could not know or say anything about God. For an extensive treatment of divine predication and analogy, see David B. Burrell, *Knowing The Unknowable God: Ibn Sina, Maimonides, Aquinas* (University of Notre Dame Press, 1992).

30 ST II-II 17.2.

31 Regarding imperfect and perfect happiness, see Porter, *Nature as Reason*, pp. 158–162.

32 ST II-II 17.2, 4. This does not require us to crudely instrumentalise all created goods – as though I were merely 'using' my wife or the community as a ladder to hope's end and nothing more. The love and commitment expressed by virtuous activities and enjoyments I partake of through and with them may be sought for their own sakes, while also further and ultimately for the sake of the ultimate end.

33 In a different but related way, Aquinas says that the resurrected saints will have both an *aurea* or crown indicating their deserved perfect beatitude and an *aureole* or wreath indicating the particular quality of their earthly merits. For example, a distinctive *aureole* will belong to doctors, martyrs, and virgins. He is making a different point from the one I am making now, but what I want to emphasise is that there is a certain continuity to imperfect and perfect happiness. See ST III *Supplementum* 96.1.

34 See Walter M. Abbott and Lawrence Shehan, *The Documents of Vatican II with Notes and Comments by Catholic, Protestant, and Orthodox Authorities*, trans. Joseph Gallagher (America Press, Inc., 2012), p. 237. For similar interpretations of how the eschaton as it will fully be has begun to break into this world, see Robert A. Guelich, *The Sermon on the Mount: A Foundation for Understanding* (W Publishing Group, 1982), esp. pp. 78–79; and William D. Davies and Dale C. Allison, *Matthew 1–7: Volume 1* (Bloomsbury, 2004), p. 440.

35 ST II-II 69.4.

36 See Sayers, *Further Papers on Dante*; Charles Williams, *The Figure of Beatrice* (Apocryphile Press, 2005).

37 Dante, *Purgatorio*, canto XXXI.

38 Orwell and Carey, *Essays*, p. 557.

39 Ibid.

40 If the dead are not raised, hedonism is not the only reasonable option. By Aristotelian lights, it is a very foolish and vicious option. But I take St. Paul to be speaking descriptively, not normatively. Disbelief in the afterlife would not make hedonism wise, just easier to fall into.

41 The wicked pictured by the biblical author are not Epicureans or Sadducees, but those who 'espouse a practical atheism and attribute man's origin to chance'. They 'resolve to persecute the just man because his life and words are a reproach to them'. See Patrick W. Skehan, *The Literary Relationship between the Book of Wisdom and the Protocanonical Wisdom Books of the Old Testament* (The Catholic University of America Press, 1938), pp. 40–65.

42 Ibid.

43 Orwell and Carey, *Essays*, p. 557.

44 Ibid., p. 989.

45 Ibid.

46 See 'Breaking News via Seeking Alpha', http://seekingalpha.com/news/70810.

47 W. H. Auden, *Collected Poems* (First Vintage Reprint Edition, 1991), p. 276.

48 Ibid., p. 556.

49 See Neil Postman, *Amusing Ourselves to Death: Public Discourse in the Age of Show Business*. Revised edition (Penguin Books, 2005).

50 Nicholas Boyle, *Who Are We Now?: Christian Humanism and the Global Market from Hegel to Heaney* (University of Notre Dame Press, 1999), p. 86.

51 Plato quoted in Williams, *Shame and Necessity*, p. 156.

52 See William Mattison, 'Hope', in Michael W Austin and R. Douglas Geivett, *Being Good: Christian Virtues for Everyday Life* (W. B. Eerdmans, 2012), pp. 116–119.

53 ST I-II 69.1.

54 Jane Austen, *Mansfield Park* (Everyman's Library Classics, [1702] 1992), p. 36.

55 Hope may also give rise not just to joy, but to a pining and disconsolation we do not enjoy. As Aquinas says: 'Nothing prevents the same thing, in different ways, being the cause of contraries. And so hope, inasmuch as it implies a present appraising of a future good, causes pleasure; whereas, inasmuch as it implies absence of that good, it causes affliction'. See ST I-II 32.3. Yet the two may be distinguished. I discuss the first in this chapter, and the second in the fifth chapter.

56 ST II-II 20.4.

57 *The Liturgy of the Hours Volume II – Lent and Easter*. Lea edition (Catholic Book Publishing Company, 1976), p. 893.

58 Pieper, *On Hope*, p. 41.

59 ST I-II 31.3. See also Kevin White, 'The Passions of the Soul', in Pope, *The Ethics of Aquinas*, pp. 110–112.

60 ST II-II 20.4.

61 T. S. Eliot, *Four Quartets* (Houghton Mifflin Harcourt, 2014), p. 59.

62 ST III 75.1.

63 ST III 53.1.

64 A late poem by Gerard Manley Hopkins captures the sense of 'new wonder' this *consideratio* is meant to rouse. Struggling with 'grief's gasping, joyless days, dejection', he cries, 'Enough! The Resurrection/ A heart's-clarion!' He takes heart, recalling 'In a flash, at a trumpet crash' that 'I am all at once what Christ is, since he was what I am, and/ This Jack, joke, poor potsherd, patch, matchwood, immortal diamond/ Is immortal diamond' (Gerard Manley Hopkins, *Selected Poetry*, ed. Catherine Phillips (Oxford University Press, 2008), p. 163.) Being 'immortal' matters less in a sense here than being to God a 'diamond' – that is, a precious object so beloved that it cannot be let go, even by the seemingly unanswerable fact of death.

65 ST III 57.1.

66 *King Lear*, Act 3, Scene 4.

67 The citation appears in C. S. Lewis, *A Preface to Paradise Lost* (Atlantic Publishers & Dist., 2005), p. 52.

68 According to Craig Evans, Paul contrasts and opposes Christian religious joy with the pagan bacchanalia and the religiously tinged sensual attempts at ecstasy found in the Greek mystery cults. See Craig A. Evans, 'Ephesians 5:18–19 and Religious Intoxication in the World of Paul', in *Paul's World* (Brill, 2008), pp. 181–200.

69 The literature on praise in the psalms is understandably vast. For a good treatment that complements my use of the psalms here, see Walter Brueggemann, 'Praise and the Psalms: A Politics of Glad Abandonment', *Hymn* 43 (1 October 1992): 14–18.

70 Volitional hope may overflow into and stimulate the passions, often giving rise to passions of hope. In addition, the mental reflections which volitional hope gives rise to may also cause passions of hope through mediation of the imagination. So hope in the will is often concurrent with and routinely causes passions of hope. See II-II.25.5.2, and Merkt, *Sacra Doctrina and Christian Eschatology*, p. 250.

4 Presumption and Moral Reform

1 Cited in William Hazlitt, *Table-Talk: Essays on Men and Manners* (Grant Richards, 1903), p. 197.

2 ST II-II 21.1. Pieper is almost alone among Thomistic commentators for treating presumption at any length. See his *On Hope*, pp. 65–72.

3 Stanley Hauerwas, 'Pragmatism and Democracy: Assessing Jeffrey Stout's Democracy and Tradition', *Journal of the American Academy of Religion* 78.2 (1 June 2010): 429. Hauerwas' point is not to offer a feudal anthropology. The only begging he endorses is petitionary prayer before God, not abject dependence on fellow human beings.

4 Stout, *Democracy and Tradition*, p. 116.

5 Ibid., pp. 37, 38.

6 Ibid., pp. 19–21.

7 Ibid., p. 19.

8 Ibid. p. 34.

9 ST II-II 101.

10 Stout borrows the phrase 'fossil and unhealthy air' from Whitman, ibid., p. 29. For a poet with a very different assessment of Christianity's air, consider Shakespeare's speech about Christ's nativity, uttered by Marcellus in *Hamlet*, Act 1, scene 1, when the ghost fades at 'the crowing of the cock':

> Some say that ever 'gainst that season comes
> Wherein our Saviour's birth is celebrated,
> The bird of dawning singeth all night long.
> And then, they say, no spirit dare stir abroad.
> The nights are wholesome. Then no planets strike,
> No fairy takes, nor witch hath power to charm,
> So hallowed and so gracious is the time.

11 Jeffrey Stout, *Democracy and Tradition*, p. 15. As a recent major conference by the British Academy on 'Pragmatism in Britain in the Long Twentieth Century' aims to show, the transatlantic influence has been mutual and long-standing, and is on the rise. See www.britac.ac.uk/events/2014/The_Practical_Turn.cfm.

It is also significant that of the three major targets of Stout's criticisms, only one is American (Stanley Hauerwas), the other two being British (Alasdair MacIntyre and John Milbank).

12 Stout, *Democracy and Tradition*, p. 30.

13 Ibid., p. 39.

14 Ibid., p. 25.

15 Ibid., p. 37.

16 Ibid., p. 38.

17 Ibid., p. 31.

18 Ibid., p. 26.

19 The Emersonian/Augustinian dichotomy runs throughout chapter 1 of *Democracy and Tradition*. Stout does not explain clearly what he means by 'Augustinian', but certainly he does not just mean strict Augustinians. The label appears to be convenient tag for any and all Christians who believe in Christ's mediation, the need for the Church, the reality of original sin, and the need for grace. It is in this broad sense that I will use the term in this section.

20 The point is made throughout chapter 1 of *Democracy and Tradition*, where Stout concedes that major differences exist between Augustinian and Emersonian piety, but says we may 'discern a bit more common ground' than we 'tend to notice'. Charitably interpreted, each side may be seen as 'people doing their best to offer appropriate acknowledgment of their dependence. Insofar as they do acknowledge that dependence appropriately, given their own conceptions of the sources of our existence and progress through life, they may be said to exhibit an attitude that is worthy of our respect.... *We can praise this aspect of character as a virtue for the same reason* we can praise the courage, temperance, or wisdom of someone we oppose in battle or debate' (emphasis mine). The reason is that they are exhibiting the same virtue, though they may disagree as to how it is best or most fully expressed. The implication is that Augustinians and Emersonians possess a shared virtue of piety which they bend in different directions. See especially pp. 33–34.

21 Ibid., p. 31.

22 Gilbert Keith Chesterton, *Orthodoxy* (John Lane Company, 1909), p. 240.

23 See Stout, *Ethics after Babel*, p. 188.

24 Ibid., p. 20.

25 Ibid., pp. 25, 37–38.

26 Ibid., p. 39.

27 Ibid.

28 See his comments about the need sharply to distinguish '*just* or *fitting* acknowledgment' from deferential and undemocratic forms of piety, which as the contrary of the former are implicitly characterised as *unjust* and *unfitting*. Making

the case that Emerson, Whitman, and his preferred sources do commend piety, Stout says: 'When they denounce piety as a vice, they mean piety as defined in the traditionalist way' (p. 30) – that is, the Augustinian way.

29 Stout, p. 41.
30 Ibid., p. 19.
31 Ibid., p. 116.
32 Ibid., pp. 140–161.
33 Ibid., p. 33.
34 Arthur Miller, *Death of a Salesman: Certain Private Conversations in Two Acts and a Requiem* (Penguin, 1976).
35 Cited in David A. Yamane, *The Catholic Church in State Politics: Negotiating Prophetic Demands and Political Realities* (Sheed & Ward, 2005), p. 15.
36 Pieper, *On Hope*, p. 68.
37 Mattison, *Introducing Moral Theology*, pp. 311–318.
38 ST II-II 21.1.
39 See Aquinas, *Compendium of Theology*, chapters 1 and 2.
40 Ibid., and ST II-II 17.2.
41 As the man going down from Jerusalem to Jericho is beaten, rescued by the Good Samaritan, and then put in the inn to recuperate, Aquinas follows Augustine and the Venerable Bede in seeing the human race as *homo infirmus* saved by Christ as the allegorical Good Samaritan. This allegory was made into a cautionary tale against Pelagian rigorism and spiritual elitism. Its message is that the Christian is still *homo infirmus*: that he or she is 'still in the inn, recuperating … through the healing medicine of grace'. See ST I-II. 85 1, and John Mahoney, *The Making of Moral Theology: A Study of the Roman Catholic Tradition* (Clarendon Press, 1989), p. 49.
42 ST II-II 21.4.
43 Jackson, *Love Disconsoled*, pp. 130–132.
44 Ibid., pp. 162, 169.
45 Cited in Tullian Tchividjian, *Glorious Ruin: How Suffering Sets You Free* (David C. Cook, 2012), p. 187.
46 Brown, *The Jerome Biblical Commentary*, p. 317.
47 ST II-II.17.2.3.
48 Aquinas says the error consists in the belief that God 'gives glory to those who quit from good works' (SI II-II 21.2).
49 On 'storing treasure in heaven', see the groundbreaking recent treatment by biblical scholar Gary Anderson, *Charity: The Place of the Poor in the Biblical Tradition* (Yale University Press, 2014), especially pp. 111–135.
50 ST II-II 28.1.3.
51 ST *Supp.* 93.3.
52 Ibid.
53 Throughout the second chapter.
54 See Thomas Aquinas, *Summa Contra Gentiles* Bk 3, Pt 2, Q. 153.
55 Charles Dickens, *A Christmas Carol and Other Christmas Books* (Oxford University Press, 2006), p. 1879.

56 Scrooge sees one spirit who 'who cried piteously at being unable to assist a wretched woman with an infant, whom it saw below, upon a door-step', his chief torment being that he wanted to help her, but 'had lost that power forever'. Ibid., p. 1880.

57 Pope Gregory the Great described innocent recreation as the comforting 'inn' (*stabulum*) at which the wayfarer (*homo viator*) occasionally stays to refresh himself 'on the way' (*in via*), so that he may then carry on with renewed vigour. See Gregory the Great, *Moralia* VIII, pp. 54, 92, and *Registrum Epistolarum* IX, p. 217. In this motif, ordinate recreation and enjoyments play the role of 'refreshment' (*refrigerium*). Refreshment differs from pleasure or enjoyment simply in that it restores strength and vigour to those who have exerted themselves commendably. This gives a place to this-worldly enjoyments while simultaneously cautioning against complacency, laziness, and luxuriating. The inn is somewhere you rest and then *leave* with a sense of continuing 'on the way' (*in via*).

58 ST II-II 17.3.

59 Charles Williams' novel *Descent into Hell* gives a bracing account of how injustice and lack of charity tempt to despair. The life of a miserable common labourer culminates in his being fired from his job. His existence has been one of continual abandonment by his fellow humans, and this abandonment successfully tempts him to a quiet despair in which he hangs himself. Referring to humanity as a city or republic, Williams comments:

> The Republic, of which he knew nothing, had betrayed him; all the nourishment that comes from friendship and common pain was as much forbidden to him as the poor nourishment of his body. The Republic had decided that it was better one man, or many men, should perish, than the people in the dangerous chance of helping those many. It had, as always, denied supernatural justice. He went on, in that public but unspectacular abandonment, and the sun went down on him.

Without theatrics, even without passion, the man concludes that he is ultimately worthless, alone, and unloved: that he can 'never rise to any good' to use Aquinas' bleak phrase about how dejection incubates despair (ST II-II 20.4). Even apart from the independent demands of justice and charity, hope incites one to works of justice and charity on behalf of the neighbour for whom one hopes lest he or she plunge into that 'unspectacular abandonment'. See Charles Williams, *Descent into Hell: A Novel* (W. B. Eerdmans, n.d.), pp. 27–28.

60 ST II-II 21.4.

61 Norman Vincent Peale, *The Power of Positive Thinking*. Reprint edition (Touchstone, 2003).

62 Christian Smith and Melina Lundquist Denton, *Soul Searching: The Religious and Spiritual Lives of American Teenagers*. Reprint edition (Oxford University Press, 2009), p. 171.

63 Cited by Ross Douthat in www.theatlantic.com/personal/archive/2009/04/theology-has-consequences/56091/.

64 Ibid.

65 Smith and Denton, *Soul Searching*, pp. 163–164.

66 God becomes 'something like a combination Divine Butler and Cosmic Therapist: he's always on call, takes care of any problems that arise, professionally helps his people to feel better about themselves, and does not become too personally involved in the process'. Ibid., p. 165.

67 Ibid. Douthat.

68 Council of Trent (1551): DS 1676.

69 William Tyndale and John Frith, *The Works of the English Reformers: William Tyndale and John Frith* (Ebenezer Palmer, 1831), p. 524.

70 Friedrich Nietzsche, *Thus Spoke Zarathustra*, trans. Walter Kaufmann, in *The Portable Nietzsche* (Penguin, 1977), p. 332.

71 For two impressive efforts to read the eternal recurrence as existential and parabolic, see Alexander Nehamas, *Nietzsche: Life as Literature* (Harvard University Press, 1990), pp. 141–169; Christopher Janaway, 'Nietzsche on Morality, Drives, and Human Greatness', in Christopher Janaway and Simon Robertson, *Nietzsche, Naturalism, and Normativity* (Oxford University Press, 2012), pp. 183–201.

72 Nietzsche, *The Will to Power* (New York: Vintage, 1968), p. 373; *Thus Spoke Zarathustra*, p. 264. For a full treatment in the secondary literature, see Nehamas, *Nietzsche: Life as Literature*, pp. 6–7, 141–169.

73 Friedrich Nietzsche, Bernard Williams, and Josefine Nauckhoff, *Nietzsche: The Gay Science: With a Prelude in German Rhymes and an Appendix of Songs* (Cambridge University Press, 2001), p. 341.

74 Friedrich Nietzsche, Rolf-Peter Horstmann, and Judith Norman, *Nietzsche: Beyond Good and Evil: Prelude to a Philosophy of the Future* (Cambridge University Press, 2002), p. 56.

75 Walter Kaufmann, *Beyond Good and Evil*. First Thus edition (Vintage, 1966), p. 259.

76 Nietzsche, *The Will to Power*, p. 545.

77 In Nietzsche's account, whatever another person says or does to me, so long as it psychologically registers on me at all, will become a feature in my identity (ibid.; Nehamas, *Nietzsche: Life as Literature*, pp. 6–7, 141–169). But embracing this seems to require embracing a certain will to powerlessness. Since every feature of me is as defining as every other feature, any change which another person works on me is defining. The changes which their casual words or grand gestures effect will therefore *construct* me as the person I am (so do other things, including my own willing, but the point remains). Nietzsche advises us not just to accept the eternal recurrence, but to embrace it ('to crave nothing more fervently than this ultimate eternal confirmation and seal', *The Gay Science*, p. 341). Given the view of identity presupposed, this seems to require embracing and indeed 'craving' a certain will to powerlessness before other people, who may make, unmake, define, and redefine me whether I consent to it or not.

78 Williams, *The Sense of the Past*, p. 317.

79 I have borrowed and altered here Stanley Hauerwas' phrase 'the gift of time enough for love'. See Stanley Hauerwas, John Berkman, and Michael Cartwright, *The Hauerwas Reader* (Duke University Press, 2001), p. 587.

80 Dante, *Paradiso*, Canto IX, l. 103–105.

81 The topic of the third chapter in this book.

82 ST II-II 19.3.

83 ST II-II 19.4.

84 See Daniel Castelo, 'The Fear of the Lord as Theological Method', *Journal of Theological Interpretation* 2.1 (1 March 2008): 147–160.

85 ST II-II 19.1.

86 It is possible to act unjustly from motives of false mercy, for example, by indulging kindness to the point where one harms other people by not telling them difficult but important truths (e.g., the doctor who hides a distressing or terminal diagnosis) or by giving people harmful things when not doing so would cause them pain or distress (e.g., the friend who enables a drug addiction, or the overindulgent parent who badly spoils a child). Presumption imputes this kind of false mercy to the divine nature.

87 By 'the soul' here I mean the respect in which the self does not simply cease with death, however we go on to explain this. The soul with its need to be saved was once an overriding concern in moral theology and Christian thought. Worries about dualism and the marginal place of eschatology even in Christian ethics have changed this. The topic requires separate treatment, but all that needs to be said here is that hope requires *some role* for the soul, and that the Resurrection prevents this role from being dualistic. For a fascinating discussion of these issues from a philosophical perspective, see Bernard Williams, 'The Theological Appearance of the Church of England: An External View', in Wood and Williams, *Essays and Reviews*, pp. 17–23.

88 Jim Crace, *Harvest* (Vintage, 2013), p. 64.

89 For primary sources, see Edmund Burke and Adam Phillips, *A Philosophical Enquiry into the Origin of Our Ideas of the Sublime and Beautiful*. Reissue edition (Oxford University Press, n.d.); Patrick Frierson, *Kant: Observations on the Feeling of the Beautiful and Sublime and Other Writings*, trans. Professor Paul Guyer. First edition (Cambridge University Press, 2011); Walter John Hipple Jr., *The Beautiful, the Sublime, & the Picturesque: In Eighteenth-Century British Aesthetic Theory*. First edition (Southern Illinois University Press, 1957); Marjorie Hope Nicolson and William Cronon, *Mountain Gloom and Mountain Glory: The Development of the Aesthetics of the Infinite*. Reprint edition (University of Washington Press, 1997).

90 Ibid. Burke and Phillips, *A Philosophical Enquiry*, pp. 53–57.

91 Joseph Addison, *Spectator* 412, vol. vi, p. 59.

92 Ibid. Burke and Phillips, *A Philosophical Enquiry*, p. 54.

93 Nicolson and Cronon, *Mountain Gloom and Mountain Glory*, pp. 271–324.

94 Obviously not all sources or instances of fear are good. My claim is only that *some* are.

95 The discussion is found in R. Otto, *The Idea of the Holy*. Second edition, trans. John W. Harvey (Oxford University Press, 1958).

96 For a forceful and updated restatement of Otto's thesis with respect to the Bible, see Samuel Terrien, 'The Numinous, the Sacred and the Holy in Scripture', *Biblical Theology Bulletin: A Journal of Bible and Theology* 12.4 (1 November 1982): 99–108.

97 Otto, *The Idea of the Holy*, pp. 60–65.

98 Ibid., pp. 31–35, 71–80.

99 Ibid., p. 52.

100 ST II-II 19.11.

101 ST II-II 19.2.

102 According to Aquinas, wonder is a cause of pleasure (I-II 32.8), and wonder or amazement of a certain type exhibits religious fear (I-II 41.4).

103 Dante, *Paradiso*, canto 25.

104 In contrast to what he takes traditional Christian piety to be, Jeffrey Stout calls for a 'piety cleansed of sadomasochistic tendencies by democratic self-respect' (*Democracy and Tradition*, p. 39). But the humbled awe I have connected in different ways with the sublime, the numinous, and the gift of fear is neither 'sadomasochistic' nor self-disrespecting. (Spiritual fear may be pegged to perceived bad moral and spiritual performance, but where this sense is accurate it implies that we have not respected our dignity *enough*.) Such awe, frequently accompanied by a sudden awareness of one's smallness before something vast and admirable, does not require a lower overall estimation of our self-worth.

Consider by analogy that the astronaut who views the earth from space, the traveller who feels dwarfed by a mountain range or an endless expanse of sea, may rightly experience that thrill of admiration and sense of their own smallness which I am here calling humbled awe. This perception would not entail that they themselves were insignificant, unimportant, or devalued. The same relation may obtain in spiritual experience. The Psalmist's meditation provides a good example:

> O Lord, our Lord
> How majestic is your name in all the earth ...
> When I look at your heavens, the work of your fingers,
> the moon and the stars that you have established;
> what are human beings that you are mindful of them,
> mortals that you care for them? (Ps 8: 1, 3–4)

Importantly, this reflection transitions to a *heightened* sense of human worth and self-respect: 'Yet you have made them a little lower than God, and crowned them with glory and honor' (Ps 8: 5). In this respect, belief in the *imago dei* leverages the very sense of our smallness to be struck anew by the incalculable greatness of human dignity (further ratified, for Christians, by the Incarnation).

105 Cited in Legh Richmond, *The Fathers of the English Church: Or, A Selection from the Writings of the Reformers and Early Protestant Divines of the Church of England* (John Hatchard, 1807), p. 17.

5 Despair and Consolation

1 Julian of Norwich, *Revelations of Divine Love* (Cosimo, Inc., 2007), p. 48.
2 Charles Schmidt, *The Social Results of Early Christianity* (Wm. Isbister, 1889), p. 328.
3 See Robert Louis Wilken, *The Christians as the Romans Saw Them*. Second edition (Yale University Press, 2003), pp. 164–180.
4 Foot, *Natural Goodness*, p. 85.
5 Ibid., pp. 95–96.
6 John Henry Newman, *The Idea of a University* (Library of Alexandria, 1925), p. 4. However, the tension should not be overstated. Aquinas is in my view correct to say that the mean of infused virtue, while it transcends that of acquired virtue, does not abolish the end which acquired virtue is proportioned to. Hence his insistence that while fasting may be an instance of infused rather than acquired temperance, it is wrong to fast to the point of damaging one's health. In addition, finitude entails that any given happy life involves choices and commitments which exclude other possibilities for a happy life. For instance, the choices to marry rather than stay a leisured bachelor, or to become an artist rather than a politician. Such choices embark one on a way of life which will be happy in a different way from other alternatives, seeking different characteristic activities and virtuous pursuits. This is true also of the infused/acquired virtues in the choices they often lead to. See the helpful discussion of the issue in Bonnie Kent, 'Habits and Virtues (Ia IIae, qq. 49–70)', in Pope, *The Ethics of Aquinas*, pp. 123–126.
7 See ST I-II 69, 70.
8 ST I-II 5.3, 69.4.
9 Current representative treatments include William D. Davies and Dale C. Allison, *The Gospel According to Matthew, Volume I* (T. & T. Clark, 1988); Guelich, *The Sermon on the Mount* (W Publishing Group, 1982); and Hans Dieter Betz, *The Sermon on the Mount* (Fortress Press, 1995), William Mattison III, 'The Beatitudes and Moral Theology: A Virtue Ethics Approach', *Nova et Vetera* 11.3 (2013): 819–848; and Servais Pinckaers, *The Pursuit of Happiness – God's Way: Living the Beatitudes*. Reprint edition (Wipf & Stock Publishers, 2011).
10 Concerning the gifts of the Holy Spirit in Aquinas, see M. J. Nicholas, 'Les Dons du Saint-Esprit', in *Revue Thomiste* 92 (1992): 141–153.
11 Aquinas is not unusual in following the order of Matthew's beatitudes and making Luke's supplementary. For an excellent discussion of the biblical and patristic sense of 'beatitude' (*makarios, beatitudo*) as happiness, as well as questions about their ordering, see Mattison, 'The Beatitudes and Moral Theology', 819–830.

12 ST I-II 70.2.

13 ST I-II 108.3.

14 ST I-II 18.7.

15 ST I-II 69.4.

16 The suggestion, however, is that they are nonetheless happy-making. To give but one example: St. Francis ministered to lepers and performed other feats which most of us would lack the imagination to conceive of, let alone the nerve to follow through with. But while his day job of radical charity involved serious sacrifices, like many of the saints he gives the curious impression of enjoying a kind of happy life that is genuine, contagious, and awe-inspiring.

17 The case of Tolstoy is discussed along these lines in Orwell and Carey, *Essays*, p. 1194.

18 See Bernard McGinn, *The Foundations of Mysticism: Origins to the Fifth Century* (Crossroad, n.d.), pp. 12–55.

19 Ibid. McGinn; Boethius and Victor Watts, eds., *The Consolation of Philosophy* (Penguin Classics, 2000); Thomas a Kempis, *The Imitation of Christ*. Revised Sub edition (Vintage, 1998).

20 ST I-II 69.2.

21 ST I-II 69.4.

22 Ibid.

23 Dante, *The Portable Dante*. Reissue edition (New Penguin USA, 2003), p. 10.

24 John R. Bowlin, *Contingency and Fortune in Aquinas's Ethics* (Cambridge University Press, 2010), pp. 12–18.

25 Ibid., p. 14.

26 Ibid., p. 216.

27 Ibid., p. 218.

28 Cited in Jackson, *Love Disconsoled*, p. 145.

29 Bowlin, *Contingency and Fortune in Aquinas's Ethics*, p. 220.

30 ST I-II 35.1.

31 Pope Gregory the Great, *Morals on the Book of Job*, trans. and ed. John Henry Parker (Oxford University Press, 1850), Bk. 13.45.88.

32 ST I-II 20.4.

33 See Aquinas' points about how a virtuous habit may be lost or diminished in ST I-II 52.1-3.

34 Bowlin, *Contingency and Fortune in Aquinas's Ethics*, p. 220.

35 Graham Greene, *The Heart of the Matter*. Great Books edition (Penguin, 1999).

36 Orwell, *Essays*, pp. 1338, 1340.

37 St. Francis de Sales, *A Serious Call to a Devout and Holy Life* (Westminster John Knox Press, 1968), pp. 111–113.

38 ST II-II 17.4.

39 ST II-II 109.6.

40 Taking prayer in a very broad sense: not just as the discrete recitation of a formula, but as an activity of mind and will, directed to God, and expressed in various ways.

41 ST I-II 20.4.

42 The point is not to effect a gimmick, as though hope were a religious analgesic obtained by mental gymnastics. It is a matter of attending to and waiting for divine help – what Aquinas calls *auxilium* grace – help which one expects with complete trust.

43 Luke's Gospel states that in his terrible agony 'there appeared to him an angel from heaven, strengthening him (ἐνισχύων αὐτὸν)' (Lk 22:43). The Greek ἐνισχύων is sometimes translated as 'comforting', with religious art depicting a consolatory angel providing Christ much-needed solace. But 'strengthening' is a much more accurate translation than 'comforting', with its connotations of encouraging and bracing the will to persevere in doing something possible but arduous.

44 The foiled retirement of the prophet Elijah provides a suggestive analogue. After the contest on Mount Carmel, Elijah fled into the wilderness to die. He had been persecuted by the powerful for years, acquitted himself admirably, but decided his story was finished. The Bible says that 'he went a day's journey into the wilderness, and came and sat down under a broom tree; and he asked that he might die, saying, 'It is enough; now, O Lord, take away my life; for I am no better than my fathers' (1 Kings 19:4). Elijah prematurely declares his journey at an end. He falls asleep and an angel wakens him, saying, 'Arise and eat' (19:5). He eats but then lies down again to die. The angel then reappears saying: 'Arise and eat, else the journey will be too great for you'. So the journey is as yet unfinished. At this point Elijah recommits to carrying on. He 'arose', ate his meal, 'and went in the strength of that food forty days and forty nights to Horeb the mount of God' (21:8). Amid the temptation to quit Elijah receives divine help and encouragement and makes a renewed commitment to persevere. As Elijah 'went on the strength of that food', the wayfarer tempted to sluggishness or despair need not give up the wilderness. Instead, he or she may consider the divine favours which console hope with the prospect of success, and renew the commitment to persevere 'on the strength' of the divine *auxilium* provided by the sacraments and other sources of grace.

45 See John M. Cooper, 'Aristotle on Friendship', in Rorty, *Essays on Aristotle's Ethics*, pp. 315–339.

46 Our daily bread, among other ends of the Lord's Prayer, is not itself a motion of grace. The idea is that hope ordains even natural goods to our supernatural end by seeking them *as* parts of our overall journey to hope's end. See ST II-II 17 2.2.

47 See Aquinas, *Compendium of Theology*, pp. 213–232.

48 Given that this account presupposes 'cooperative grace', I take it that *auxilium* is present throughout every aspect of the process, and doing the main work. Since it would be silly to describe matters from God's point of view, I have merely sketched the human side so as to give some content to the idea that our agency is engaged.

49 John Henry Newman, *Dream of Gerontius* (Schwartz, Kirwin & Fauss, 1916), p. 8.

50 William F. May as quoted in Jeffrey Stout's *Ethics after Babel*, p. 275.

51 Aquinas notes that despair often arises from forms of *acedia* to which misery tempts us. See ST II-II.20.4.

52 The *ars moriendi* literature begins in earnest in the early fifteenth century. This was the century of 'the Black Death', when 30–60 per cent of the European population was killed and a whole culture was thrown into post-traumatic shock. Death was not just on the mind; it dominated the aesthetics of the age. The decaying corpse, mere food for worms, the ornately carved cadaver tomb, the *danse macabre*, and woodcuts of death personified all predominate in poetry, music, and art. Alongside this emphasis on the *macabre* emerges the *ars moriendi*, whose tone is quite different. The pioneering work is Jean Gerson's 1408 *De arte moriendi*. This was a true handbook for the dying process, one written *ad populum* and not just *ad clerum*. The book was divided into six sections on 1) what the patristic and later authorities said about death; 2) how the dying person or *Moriens* should resist the five sins of faithlessness, impatience, pride, worldliness, and despair; 3) a brief catechism; 4) prayers and principles for imitating Christ's dying; and 5) prayers to be said around the bed of the dying. For a century, Gerson's *De arte* was the standard *ars moriendi* manual. It was widely copied and made into woodcuts displaying the death-struggle over the five sins, with vivid images of angels and demons competing to influence the dying. See Johan Huizinga, *The Waning of the Middle Ages* (Dover Publications, 2013), pp. 124–135.

53 See Christopher Vogt, *Patience, Compassion, Hope, and the Christian Art of Dying Well* (Rowman & Littlefield Publishers, 2004), pp. 17–25, 36–39.

54 See Jennifer Herdt, 'Frailty, Fragmentation, and Social Dependency in the Cultivation of Christian Virtue', in Snow, *Cultivating Virtue*, p. 231.

55 For an excellent and pioneering treatment of this problem, see Michael Banner, *The Ethics of Everyday Life: Moral Theology, Social Anthropology, and the Imagination of the Human* (Oxford University Press, 2014), pp. 107–134.

56 Ibid., p. 118.

57 See Athena McLean, *The Person in Dementia: A Study of Nursing Home Care in the US*. Second revised edition (Broadview Press Ltd, 2006); P. Kontos, 'Embodied Selfhood: An Ethnographic Exploration of Alzheimer's Disease', in Annette Leibing and Lawrence Cohen, *Thinking about Dementia: Culture, Loss, and the Anthropology of Senility* (Rutgers University Press, 2006), pp. 195–217.

58 Allen Verhey, *The Christian Art of Dying: Learning from Jesus* (W. B. Eerdmans, 2011), pp. 11–23.

59 ICEL, *Pastoral Care of the Sick* (Catholic Book Publishing Corp., 1991).

60 For example, St. Francis of Assisi spoke words of welcome to 'our Sister Bodily Death'. It bears mentioning that he also stressed the need for repentance given the possibility of damnation so as to prevent hope from lapsing into complacent presumption (*Letter to All the Faithful*, v. 82).

61 Parts of this section have been adapted from my 'The Theological Virtue of Hope and the Art of Dying', *Studies in Christian Ethics* 29.3 (Summer 2016).

I am grateful to Susan Parsons and to SAGE Publications for permission to rework this material.

62 ST II-II 17.6. This ordering should not be thought of as discrete steps which sequentially follow each other. They will typically overlap and may occur simultaneously, making the order psychological, not chronological.

63 Kenneth Burke, *The Philosophy of Literary Form* (University of California Press, 1974), p. 160.

6 The Problem of Worldliness

1 Mathetes, *Epistle to Diognetus* 5.

2 Tomasi, 'Homo Viator: From Pilgrimage to Religious Tourism via the Journey', pp. 1–9.

3 Brown, *The Cult of the Saints*, pp. 69–70.

4 See Gerhart B. Ladner, 'Homo Viator: Mediaeval Ideas on Alienation and Order', *Speculum* 42.2 (1 April 1967): 233–242.

5 Ibid., p. 235.

6 For excellent overviews of the topic and its history, see Ladner, 'Homo Viator', and also C. S. Lewis, *Studies in Words* (Cambridge University Press, 2013), pp. 214–269.

7 Ladner, 'Homo Viator', pp. 250–251.

8 See Stanley B. Marrow, 'Kosmos in John', *The Catholic Biblical Quarterly* 64 (2002): 90–102; Richard B. Hays, *The Moral Vision of the New Testament: Community, Cross, New Creation: A Contemporary Introduction to New Testament Ethics*. First edition (HarperOne, 1996), pp. 169–181; and Raymond Brown, 'The Pater Noster as Eschatological Prayer', in *New Testament Essays* (Bruce Publishing Co., 1965), pp. 217–253.

9 Marrow, 'Kosmos in John', pp. 95–100.

10 Brown, 'The Paternoster as Eschatological Prayer', pp. 217–225.

11 Tomasi, 'Homo Viator: From Pilgrimage to Religious Tourism via the Journey', pp. 1–9.

12 Mathetes, *Epistle to Diognetus* 5.

13 Augustine, *De Civitate Dei* Bk. XIV, Ch. 28.

14 See Ladner, 'Homo Viator', pp. 233–242.

15 This interpretation has garnered the support of much biblical scholarship. In addition to Marrow, see Raymond E. Brown, *The Epistles of John* (Yale University Press, 1995), pp. 293–328. For a shorter treatment, see Bruce Vawter, 'The Johannine Epistles', in Brown, *The Jerome Biblical Commentary*, pp. 407–409.

16 Aquinas, ST I-II.108.3.4.

17 See ST I 114.2, III 41.1; and Episcopal Church, *Book of Common Prayer* (Oxford University Press, 2007), pp. 54–60.

18 Dante Alighieri, *The Divine Comedy Part II: Purgatory*, trans. Mark Musa (Penguin Books, 1984), canto 19, p. 133. My interpretation of Dante on worldliness is indebted to Anthony Esolen in *Purgatory* (Modern Library, 2004), p. 458.

19 Geoffrey Chaucer, *The Canterbury Tales*, General Prologue, pp. 292–298.

20 Ibid., The Parson's Tale, pp. 390–480, 740–800.

21 Edmund Spenser, *The Faerie Queen*, II, vii, pp. 7–19.

22 William Shakespeare, *As You Like It*, Act 2, Scene 1; Act 5, Scene 4.

23 William Law, *A Serious Call to a Devout and Holy Life*, ed. John Meister et al. (Westminster John Knox Press, 1968), p. 110.

24 See the 'divisions of fear' and 'worldly fear' in the question on fear (II-II.19, 2, 3). There Aquinas depicts (inordinate) 'worldly love' as the enemy of hope's love, and consequently 'worldly fear' as the opposite of hope's fear. Elsewhere he describes 'the world' qua tempting as: 'excessive attachment to the goods of this life' (versus the future life), 'worldly riches and fame' (III.41.1), the 'ambition for renown and honors', and 'honors, riches, and pleasures' (ST I-II.108.3.4). Undue attachment to such external goods is a nursery of despair: 'for the love of those pleasures leads man to have a distaste for spiritual things, and not to hope for them as arduous goods. In this way despair is caused' (II-II.20.4). Worldliness breaks down the habit of hope by disposing us overmuch to present, this-worldly ends.

25 ST II-II 19.3.

26 ST II-II 21.1.

27 John Henry Newman, 'Temporal Advantages', in *Parochial and Plain Sermons* (Ignatius Press, 1987), pp. 1445–1446.

28 Ibid., pp. 1449.

29 Aquinas, *Compendium of Theology*, pp. 314–315.

30 ST II-II 20.1.

31 ST II-II 17.1.

32 ST II-II 20.4.

33 Ibid.

34 Ibid.

35 In Thomistic terms, such consummate idolatry consists in putting one's ultimate end in something other than God. In addition to constituting theological despair, Aquinas would also regard it as a grave sin against charity (see ST II-II 24.12).

36 Aquinas was therefore quite right to see sloth or *acedia* as a characteristic cause of despair. He calls it the 'sorrow of the world' (II-II 35.3) and foresees in it the precursor to full abandonment of hope (II-II 20.4).

37 Homer, *The Odyssey*, trans. Robert Fitzgerald, *The Odyssey* (Farrar, Straus, and Giroux, 1998), Bk IX 94–97, p. 148.

38 William Shakespeare, *Twelfth Night*, Act 2, Scene 3.

39 See Pope Gregory the Great, *Moralia* VIII, pp. 54, 92, and *Registrum Epistolarum* IX, p. 217; and Augustine *Sermo* xiv, pp. 4, 6, *Sermo*, Lxxx, p. 7 and *Tractatus in Johannem* XL, p. 10.

40 What I am calling 'worldliness' generally corresponds to what Thomas calls '*amor mundanus*': the inordinate 'worldly love ... whereby a man trusts in the world as his end, so that worldly love is always evil' (ST II-II 19.3). Such love is for 'worldly goods' (*bona mundi*): that is, 'external goods' (*bona exteriora*

[ST II-II.19.2]) which consist of four things: i) wealth; ii) honour; iii) fame and glory; and by extension iv) power (I-II.2.4.).

41 ST 118.2, and *Disputed Questions on Evil* XIII.1. and ad 6, XXXI.2.

42 See, for instance, Dante, *The Inferno*, Canto VII.

43 On the seductive pursuit of power as its own end leading to unbridled *libido dominandi*, see Augustine, *De Civitate Dei*, Bk II.

44 ST II-II 162.2., II-II 162.4.

45 See ST II-II 130–132, II-II 132.4.

46 See Rebecca Konyndyk DeYoung, *Glittering Vices: A New Look at the Seven Deadly Sins and Their Remedies* (Brazos Press, 2009), pp. 61–68.

47 Obviously these worldly ends are mutually reinforcing and typically overlap. The distinction sought in fame and honours routinely pairs with avarice and its pricy, high-end, name-brand lifestyle. Likewise, the avaricious typically do not just want money and possessions, but the atmosphere of success, prestige, and glamour that go with them. So while we may analytically dissect different temptations of 'the world', concretely they tend to overlap.

48 My account of consumerism is indebted to Benjamin R. Barber, *Consumed: How Markets Corrupt Children, Infantilize Adults, and Swallow Citizens Whole* (W. W. Norton, 2007), especially pp. 3–37, 81–212; Lizabeth Cohen, *A Consumer's Republic: The Politics of Mass Consumption in Post-war America* (Knopf, 2003); and David Cloutier, 'The Problem of Luxury in the Christian Life', *Journal of the Society of Christian Ethics* 32.1 (2012): 3–20.

49 Since multinational corporations owe allegiance to no country, citizenry, or people, it is very difficult for citizens of any particular country to hold them directly accountable, and citizens have little or no influence on the international bureaucracies which exercise corporate oversight. Widespread boycotting, petitions with signatories in the hundreds of thousands, and media shaming have some clout, but have been too seldom used to effect much change. See Mathias Koenig-Archibugi, 'Transnational Corporations and Public Accountability', *Government and Opposition* 39.2 (1 April 2004): 234–259.

50 On the need both to appeal to and increase greed and vainglory in consumers, see Cohen, *A Consumer's Republic*, pp. 112–165. On 'costly emblems of lifestyle', see Stout, *Democracy and Tradition*, pp. 225, 291–294; and David Hollinger, *Postethnic America: Beyond Multiculturalism* (Basic Books, 1995), pp. 15–21.

51 Ronald D. Michman and Edward M. Magee, *The Affluent Consumer: Marketing and Selling the Luxury Lifestyle* (Praeger, 2006), pp. 105, 148.

52 Quoted in Cloutier, 'The Problem of Luxury', p. 13.

53 As Pope Gregory the Great says: 'when the disturbed heart has lost the satisfaction of joy within, it seeks for sources of consolation without, and is more anxious to possess external goods, the more it has no joy on which to fall back within'. See *Morals on the Book of Job*, Bk. 13.45.89.

54 See *The Book of Common Prayer* (The Episcopal Church, 1971), p. 577.

55 Newman, *Parochial and Plain Sermons*, p. 1429. More generally, see Ladner, 'Homo Viator', pp. 239–240.

56 William Mattison interprets spiritual poverty as a compound of (1) 'humility' and (2) a 'refusal to seek ultimate comfort in material possessions'. See his excellent 'The Beatitudes and Moral Theology: A Virtue Ethics Approach', p. 829. Spiritual poverty as (1) resists pride and arrogance, and as (2) it resists avarice. Hence, spiritual poverty is a remedy to worldliness; possibly the chief remedy. Aquinas notes that it disengages us from 'honors and riches', voiding both a 'proud and puffed up spirit' and the search for 'greatness . . . in external goods' (II-II.19.12).

57 Aquinas, ST I-II 108.3.

58 ST II-II 19.12.

59 Guelich, *The Sermon on the Mount*, p. 69.

60 Ibid., p. 68.

61 Davies and Allison, *Matthew 1–7*, p. 445. The sense in which it can be said of the poor that 'theirs is' (present tense) the kingdom of heaven is in part as a 'futuristic or proleptic present' which promises future reversal (p. 446.) At the same time, the blessing is due not just to what is promised in the future, but to the consolation that takes place now. There is a 'vividness and confidence' conveyed by the beatitude. 'The world will be turned upside down' (p. 445), and there are 'hints' of this beginning even now: 'God's promise for the future is now being fulfilled in Jesus' person and ministry. . . . On the one hand, God's sovereign rule has arrived in this age in the person of his Son and is recognised by the community of "understanding believers". . . . On the other hand, it has not yet arrived in all its visible power and glory' (Guelich, *The Sermon on the Mount*, pp. 78–79). Allison says that Matthew pictures the hearers of the beatitudes as consoled, so that the blessing is not just about future reversal but begins even now: 'When Jesus speaks, the drudgery and difficulties of day-to-day life fade away and the bliss of life to come proleptically appears. Time is, however briefly, overcome, and the saints are refreshed' (Davies and Allison, *Matthew 1–7*, p. 440).

62 Guelich, *The Sermon on the Mount*, p. 75.

63 Pope Benedict XVI, *Jesus of Nazareth: From the Baptism in the Jordan to the Transfiguration* (Bloomsbury Publishing PLC, 2008), p. 75.

64 Matthew is generally seen to accent the 'spiritualised' or 'ethicised' dimension of poverty more than Luke, but there is agreement that both sets of beatitudes emerge from Isaiah 61, and that Matthew's 'poor in spirit' are ultimately 'no different from Luke's poor' (Guelich, *The Sermon on the Mount*, pp. 70, 75). Both evangelists appear to have the same people in mind even though they draw them up somewhat differently.

65 Davies and Allison, *Matthew 1–7*, p. 444.

66 Hans Dieter Betz and Adela Yarbro Collins, *The Sermon on the Mount: A Commentary on the Sermon on the Mount, Including the Sermon on the Plain* (Augsburg Fortress, 1995), pp. 115–116.

67 If the two were incompatible, Christians would have to think they were 'harming' the degraded poor by giving them material help, since this would expel them from the beatitude. But this is absurd, and certainly the evangelists do not think this way. See Guelich, *The Sermon on the Mount*, p. 87.

68 Betz and Collins, *The Sermon on the Mount*, p. 116.

69 ST II-II.19.12. The neediness and vulnerability of the human condition is also emphasised by Aquinas, who cites for spiritual poverty the Psalm verse: 'Some hope in chariots and some in horses; but we will call upon the name of ... our God' (II-II. 19.12).

70 The difference is not total, however. Some if not most of Matthew's 'poor' began well-off. The apostle Matthew himself had been a tax collector (Matt 9:9) and likely well-to-do. Many of the apostles came from professions which would likely enough provide for basic needs as construed at the time. But when they follow Jesus they renounce their security. 'In doing so, they showed themselves to be *the poor*, namely, those who stood empty-handed, without a power base and pretense, before God' (Guelich, *The Sermon on the Mount*, p. 71).

71 Betz and Collins, *The Sermon on the Mount*, p. 108.

72 ST II-II 19.12.

73 Aquinas regards literal voluntary poverty as the ideal of spiritual poverty while allowing that it may take other forms as well. See I-II 69.3 and II-II 19.12.

74 Gregory of Nyssa particularly recommends this practice as an expression of poverty of spirit. See *The Lord's Prayer, The Beatitudes,* trans. Hilda C. Graef (Paulist Press, 1990), p. 93.

75 See, for example, Alphonsus Maria de'Liguori, *The 12 Steps to Holiness and Salvation*, trans. Cornelius J. Warren (Tan Books, 1986), pp. 73–91.

76 This is his interpretation of Matthew 24. See Richard Hays, 'Scripture-Shaped Community: The Problem of Method in New Testament Ethics', *Interpretation* 44 (1990): 53.

77 Augustine, *Teaching Christianity: De Doctrina Christiana*, trans. Edmund Hill, O.P. (New York City Press, 1996), pp. 101–168.

78 Law, *A Serious Call*, XVIII, p. 118.

79 What would a lifestyle of simplicity look like today among the middle and upper classes with the means to live luxuriously? Unfortunately, this topic is underdeveloped. For excellent and pioneering exceptions, see Cloutier, 'The Problem of Luxury', pp. 3–20; and Shannon Hayes, *Radical Homemakers: Reclaiming Domesticity from a Consumer Culture*, (Left to Write Press, 2010). The biblical scholar Raymond Brown asked whether the beatitude of poverty is 'impossible in a world where worth is measured by salary, home, car, and TV'. He suggests as a contemporary instance of the beatitude 'those Christian parents who bring into the world large families, despite knowing that each child means more privation of clothing, amusements, leisure. The Sermon finds its hearers even in the twentieth century' (p. 340).

80 Francis de Sales, *Introduction to the Devout Life*, trans. John Ryan (Image Books, 1986), p. 160.

81 Ibid.

82 To take a contemporary example, Pope Francis has repeatedly sought the poor out personally in unscripted ways and deeply moved people by spending time with them in unaffected fellowship. See John Allen Jr., 'Thoughts on Francis as 'Person of the Year',' accessed 10 January 2014, http://ncronline.org/blogs/ncr-today/thoughts-francis-person-year.

83 For Augustine's correlation of poverty of spirit with the gift of fear, see *The Preaching of St. Augustine, 'Our Lord's Sermon on the Mount'*, ed. Jaroslav (Fortress Press, 1973), pp. 112–116.

84 Besides Ladner, see Thomas à Kempis *Imitatio Christi* 1.1, 1.17; Ernst Troeltsch and James Luther Adams, *The Social Teaching of the Christian Churches: 2 Volume Set Vols. I and II*, trans. Olive Wyon (Westminster John Knox Press, 1992), vol. II, pp. 691–729; Justo L. Gonzalez, *Story of Christianity: Vol. 1.: The Early Church to the Dawn of the Reformation* (HarperCollins, 2010), pp. 73–78, pp. 136–143; *The Story of Christianity, Vol. 2: The Reformation to the Present Day*, pp. 53–60. For Tertullian and Tolstoy, see Richard Niebuhr, *Christ and Culture* (Harper Torchbooks, n.d.), pp. 49–56.

85 See Ladner, 'Homo Viator', pp. 234–238.

86 Ibid., p. 252.

87 See Gonzalez, *The Story of Christianity, Vol. 1*, pp. 53–58, and Rousseau, *The Social Contract*, pp. 142–155.

88 Much of this chapter is adapted from my article 'The Christian as Homo Viator: A Resource in Thomas Aquinas for Overcoming "Worldly Sin and Sorrow"', in *The Journal of the Society of Christian Ethics* 34.2 (Fall/Winter 2015): 101–121. I am grateful for permission from the *JSCE* and Georgetown University Press to re-work some of this material.

7 Hope and the Earthly City

1 ST I-II 63.4.

2 For representative discussions in the literature, see Saul Kripke, 'Identity and Necessity', in Michael J. Loux, *Metaphysics: Contemporary Readings* (Routledge, 2008), pp. 218–250; Sydney Shoemaker, 'Personal Identity: A Materialist Account', in Peter van Inwagen and Dean W. Zimmerman, *Metaphysics: The Big Questions* (Oxford: Blackwell Publishing, 2008), pp. 296–309; Peter van Inwagen, *Ontology, Identity, and Modality: Essays in Metaphysics* (Cambridge University Press, 2001), pp. 144–158; and Michael J. Loux, *Nature, Norm, and Psyche: Explorations in Aristotle's Philosophical Psychology* (Scuola Normale Superiore, 2004), pp. 22–40.

3 ST I 75.4.

4 Alasdair C MacIntyre, *After Virtue: A Study in Moral Theory* (University of Notre Dame Press, 2007), p. 172.

5 Orwell and Carey, *Essays*, p. 150.

6 ST II-II 101.1.

7 Obviously, family and country are not the only sources of individual and social birth and nourishment. But they are representative and serve as convenient bookends between which we may place other social groups, from one's town and neighbourhood to one's *alma mater* and home parish.

8 Despite the verbal echoes, I am using the motif of 'two cities' differently to Augustine in his *City of God*, as I later discuss. For a full contemporary treatment of the latter, see Bruce W. Speck, 'Augustine's Tale of Two Cities: Teleology/

Eschatology in The City of God', *Journal of Interdisciplinary Studies* 8.1–2 (1 January 1996): 104–130.

9   See ST II-II 26.6.

10 See, for example, Stout, *Democracy and Tradition*, pp. 140–161. For Hauerwas' denial of the sectarian charges made against him, see Stanley Hauerwas, *Christian Existence Today: Essays on Church, World, and Living in Between*. Reissue edition (Wipf & Stock Publishers, 2010), pp. 3–21.

11 John Milton, *The Poetical Works of John Milton: With Notes of Various Authors, Principally from the Edition of Thomas Newton, Charles Dunster, and Thomas Warton, to Which Is Prefixed, Newton's Life of Milton* (W. Baxter, 1824), p. 117.

12 This is not to deny the existence of real martyrs, but to distinguish them from pseudo-martyrs.

13 The Matthew scholars W. D. Davies and Dale Allison argue that the critics of Jesus saw his entry into 'joyous fellowship with others' as too lax and wanting in asceticism. Hence the charge that he and his disciples should fast, and the accusations that he was a 'glutton' and a 'drunkard'. See W. D. Davies and Dale C. Allison, *Matthew: Volume 2: 8–18* (Bloomsbury Publishing, 1999), pp. 261–264.

14 ST III 40.2.

15 Orwell, *Essays*, pp. 292, 294. Orwell notes the obvious point that while the items of cultural attachment vary over the decades and centuries, so that some become 'dated', the general attachment is to a persisting identification: 'What can the England of 1940', he writes, 'have in common with the England of 1840? But then, what have you in common with the child of five whose photograph your mother keeps on the mantelpiece? Nothing, except that you happen to be the same person' (p. 292).

16 Samuel Johnson and James Boswell, *A Journey to the Western Islands of Scotland AND The Journal of a Tour to the Hebrides*, ed. Peter Levi. Reprint edition (Penguin Classics, 1984), p. 141.

17 Wilken, *The Christians as the Romans Saw Them*, pp. 164–183.

18 Charles Wells Moulton, *The Library of Literary Criticism of English and American Authors: V. 3 1730–1784* (University of Michigan Library, 2009), p. 199.

19 See ST II-II 33.1.

20 I am indebted here to Jeffrey Stout's discussion of principled alienation in *Democracy and Tradition*, pp. 298–300.

21 C. S. Lewis, *The Four Loves*. Second Printing edition (Mariner Books, 1971), pp. 27–28.

22 G. K. Chesterton, *A Short History of England* (The Floating Press, 2011), p. 110.

23 MacIntyre, *After Virtue*, p. 263.

24 Stanley Hauerwas and William H. Willimon, *Resident Aliens: Life in the Christian Colony*. First edition (Abingdon Press, 2008), p. 35.

25 Nicholas Wolterstorff, *Until Justice and Peace Embrace: The Kuyper Lectures for 1981 Delivered at the Free University of Amsterdam* (W. B. Eerdmans, 1983), chapter 5; Stout, *Democracy and Tradition*, pp. 296–300.

26 In his magisterial work, *The English and Their History*, the Cambridge historian Robert Tombs tracks the subtle differences and continuities between 'Britishness' and the UK sovereign state, on one hand, and 'Englishness' and England, on the other. The former compared to the latter, he suggests:

> is more redolent of ... Westminster than Hackney, 'Rule Brittania' than 'The Roast Beef of Old England', swaggering John Bull than egalitarian Robin Hood'. The feeling for 'England' was and is more emotive, human and earthy: 'old England', 'England expects', 'speak for England', even 'traditional English Christmas' and 'full English breakfast'. 'Oh to be in Britain/ Now that April's there', or 'in UK's green and pleasant land' would be utterly incongruous'. (Robert Tombs, *The English and Their History*. Allen Lane, 2014, p. 877)

It bears mentioning that Tombs sees 'Englishness' not as opposed to 'Britishness', but as a partly distinct, partly continuous quality that is fully compatible with it.

27 Dante, *The Portable Dante*, p. 256.

28 Dante, *Paradiso*, canto xxv, 295–297.

29 Doyle, *The Promise of Christian Humanism*, p. 38.

30 See ibid., pp. 12–16.

31 See ibid., pp. 18–22.

32 Boyle, *Who Are We Now?*, p. 86.

33 Doyle, *The Promise of Christian Humanism*, p. 5.

34 Ibid., pp. 124–125.

35 Ibid., p. 113.

36 Ibid., p. 115.

37 Ibid., p. 115.

38 Dominic Doyle, 'The Dialectic Unfolding of the Theological Virtues: "Tayloring" Christian Identity to a Secular Age', *Gregorianum* 92 [2011]: 687–707.

39 Doyle, *The Promise of Christian Humanism*, p. 132.

40 Ibid., pp. 126–127.

41 Ibid., p. 96.

42 Ibid., p. 98.

43 Ibid., p. 99.

44 Ibid.

45 When describing legitimate humanism, Doyle repeatedly falls back on phrases such as 'the human good', 'justice and human flourishing in the present life', 'the present human good', etc. See, for example, pages 2, 5, and 38. The opposite of humanism is anything that detracts from the human good and flourishing, in particular what 'harms the human' (p. 5). Structurally, Doyle's humanism appears to overlap with what ethicists tend to call eudaimonism, though his humanism takes on many further particulars (e.g., particular views about social justice, a narrative of modern identity, and so forth).

46 Ibid., p. 102.

47 In addition to my treatment in Chapter 1, see ST I-II 3.2, 5.3, 5.4.

48 See Porter, *Nature as Reason*, pp. 158–162.
49 Ibid., p. 160.
50 Doyle, *The Promise of Christian Humanism*, p. 112.
51 Ibid., p. 126.
52 ST I-II 17.3.
53 ST I-II 17.4.
54 See Cessario, 'The Theological Virtue of Hope', p. 236.
55 Merkt, *Sacra Doctrina and Christian Eschatology*, p. 354.
56 One reason it cannot be taken as a 'legitimate development' of Aquinas is as follows. Aquinas believes each virtue is a *habitus* in potency to acts of that same virtue, and that those acts reduce the potency of that virtue into act (ST I-II 52.1–3). The consequence is that no virtue, whether faith or anything else, just operates at the level of 'potency'. In addition, the potency of a given virtue is actualised by the acts of *that* virtue (ST I-II 54.2). Each virtue also involves prudence (ST I-II 57), and the supernatural virtues all involve charity (ST II-II 23.8). But the act of one virtue is never simply collapsed into the habit of another. Likewise, nothing in Aquinas supports the view that the habit of faith is itself actualised by acts of hope. Granted the mediation of charity, faith insofar as it is in potency is actualised by acts of faith, hope by acts of hope, charity by acts of charity, and so on with each virtue (see the discussion on how 'like acts cause like habits' at ST I-II 52.3). Each of the theological virtues is itself in 'motion' (Dante's portrayal of them 'circling in a dance' in the earthly paradise above Purgatory captures this magnificently; see *Purgatorio*, canto XXIX). If it were otherwise, then either some virtues could not be actualised at all, or the acts of many virtues would actually be the acts of other virtues. But this is a needless tangle entirely alien to Aquinas' thought.
57 Besides the above, see the discussion of hope's final cause in the second chapter, as well as the discussion of proximate ends and of Bowlin's Stoic hope in the fifth chapter.
58 I take it that the point of such imagery is not to speculate about the physics or geography of the *eschaton*, but to suggest an immensity of glory, healing, grandeur, and reconciliation which transcend anything we have ever experienced to be possible. Without *that* sense of transcendence – which the mythological colouring evokes – our concept of the *eschaton* might still be wholly circumscribed by the conditions of the eudaimonia gap, and dreadfully incapable of suggesting what hope seeks.
59 I am not using the term 'earthly city' here in the Augustinian (normative) sense of the city of man opposed to the city of God, but in an everyday (descriptive) sense of all of the neighbours with whom we share bonds. The former has in view a city it defines in advance as lacking grace, and therefore unsusceptible to the agency of hope. The latter does not address this question, since it is describing our neighbours generally, whom we certainly *hope* are in a state of grace (or, at the very least, that as many as possible are or will come to be). Yet such hope is not to be confused with wrongheaded *beliefs* about who, factually, is or is not in grace: a topic spectacularly beyond our qualifications.
60 *Gaudium et Spes*, 39.

61 See Mattison, 'Hope', in Austin and Geivett, *Being Good*, p. 122.

62 ST I-II 91.1.

63 Thomas Merton and Sue Monk Kidd, *New Seeds of Contemplation*. Reprint edition (New Directions, 2007), p. 90.

64 Indeed, the joint validation of natural happiness and natural virtue (including justice) would likely be a far more promising and mutually validating starting point for Christian and secular citizens to engage in cooperative moral and civic projects than Stout's blatantly Emersonian *pietas*. Serious proposals along those lines would of course require separate and extensive work.

65 ST I-II 69.4.

66 Hare, *The Moral Gap*, p. 253.

67 Since I am trying to undermine the appearance of Church/world dualism in this chapter, I have focused more on the good ways in which the hopeful may be related to their homeland. This is not because citizenship is a more important social membership to Christians than the Church, but only because it is the one I am emphasising so as to counter old stereotypes about hope.

68 See John Pollock, *Wilberforce* (Chariot Victor Publishing, 1986), pp. 51–90.

69 Cited in Great Britain Parliament, *The Parliamentary History of England from the Earliest Period to the Year 1803* (Printed by T. C. Hansard, 1817), p. 278.

70 Pollock, *Wilberforce*, p. 211.

71 Stout, *Democracy and Tradition*, p. 59.

72 *Gaudium et Spes*, 39.

73 For a treatment of this verse and theme, see Richard Hays, 'Here We Have No Lasting City', in Richard Bauckham, *The Epistle to the Hebrews and Christian Theology* (W. B. Eerdmans, 2009), especially pp. 183–186.

74 ST II-II 26.13. Elsewhere he explains that the order of charity presupposes and perfects the order of natural loves according to which our bond with neighbours is greater or lesser depending on our degree of fellowship (*societatis*) with them in terms of kinship, citizenship, and so forth. 'For the affection of charity, which is the inclination of grace, is no less orderly than the natural appetite, which is the inclination of nature. For each inclination proceeds from the divine wisdom' (ST II-II 26.6).

75 C. S. Lewis, *The Four Loves* (Harcourt Brace, 1960), p. 187.

76 The biblical scholar Robert Mounce interprets this as developing Isaiah's claim that the 'wealth of the nations shall come' to Jerusalem (Is 60:5) with the difference that whereas the Isaiah reference is to 'the choicest of earthly treasures', the author of Revelation makes the wealth 'symbolic' of spiritual riches related to 'human culture'. See Robert H. Mounce, *The Book of Revelation* (W. B. Eerdmans, 1998), pp. 396–397.

77 ST I-II 4.8.

78 John Milton, *Paradise Lost*, Book III, verses 61–63.

79 ST I-II 63.4.

80 ST I-II 4.5.

81 Porter, *Nature as Reason*, p. 160.

82 *Torrens voluptatis* is the Vulgate phrase in Ps 36:8. Aquinas states that the disembodied *beatus* enjoys the full intensity of perfect happiness at once, but that he or she does not yet enjoy it in every way appropriate to a rational animal. In other words, one will not become *happier* after the resurrection, but there will in effect be a more completed version of oneself to enjoy the happiness. In ST I-II 4.5, Aquinas writes: 'separation from the body is said to hold the soul back from tending with all its might to the vision of the Divine Essence. For the soul desires to enjoy God in such a way that the enjoyment also may overflow into the body, as far as possible. And therefore, as long as it enjoys God, without the fellowship of the body, its appetite is at rest in that which it has, in such a way, that it would still wish the body to attain to its share'. See also ST I-II 4.1–8.

83 In his 2 Corinthians commentary, Paul Barnett interprets being 'further clothed' as referring to the receipt of 'the resurrection body' which 'will occur at the Parousia'. See Paul Barnett, *The Second Epistle to the Corinthians* (W. B. Eerdmans, 1997), p. 261.

84 ST I-II 69.4.

85 Ibid.

86 C. S. Lewis, *Letter to Malcolm: Chiefly on Prayer* (Houghton Mifflin Harcourt), p. 90.

87 No created good is too little to reflect something of the creator and furnish the opportunity for adoration ('Nothing is too little for so little a creature as man', Samuel Johnson said). The destination of the wayfarer is the heavenly *patria* or 'homeland'. As Scripture puts it, we are bound for 'The Father's house' (John 14:2). But such terms and appeals would be uninteresting, perhaps even meaningless, unless the word 'home' served to suggest something important with respect to heaven. The secret of a good home is that it is a commodious extension of personality into three-dimensional space, so that it both signifies and effects a sense of belonging, security, and comfort. The notion of a homeland regards the people as a kind of group personality analogously extended onto the country itself. Scripture and the tradition characterise heaven desirably as our true *patria* or homeland: the place where we ultimately and eternally belong. This presupposes and builds on a relish for the familiar, the homely, and the sense of belonging. Everyday and ordinary pleasures, far from being irrelevant, faintly signify the perfect sense of being at home and of belonging which are proper to the *patria*. This helps preclude the view of eternal life as simply an immersion into the alien – a view of heaven fit to cause a trauma of dislocation. Julian of Norwich went so far as to apply the quality of 'homeliness' directly to God. Since the creator is the innermost reality in any creature, to be in right relationship with the creator is to be 'at home' in God. See Julian of Norwich, Edmund Colledge, and James Walsh, *Showings* (Paulist Press, 1978), pp. 60, 129, 181.

88 *Gaudium et Spes* makes the related point that "when man gives himself to the various disciplines of philosophy, history and of mathematical and natural science, and when he cultivates the arts" we may come through material things

to "a more sublime understanding of truth, goodness, and beauty." This perception better disposes "the human spirit" to regard invisible things, so that we are "more easily drawn to the worship and contemplation" of the heavenly and uncreated. See *Gaudium et Spes*, 57.

89 ST I-II 3.2. See also Carlos Leget, 'Eschatology', in Van Nieuwenhove and Wawrykow, *The Theology of Thomas Aquinas*, pp. 365–385.

Select Bibliography

Abbott, Walter M. and Lawrence Shehan. *The Documents of Vatican II with Notes and Comments by Catholic, Protestant, and Orthodox Authorities*. Translated by Joseph Gallagher. America Press, Inc., 2012.

Adams, Robert Merrihew. *A Theory of Virtue: Excellence in Being for the Good.* Oxford University Press, 2008.

Alighieri, Dante and Mark Musa. *The Divine Comedy, Vol. 3: Paradise*. Reprint edition. Penguin Classics, 1986.

Annas, Julia. *The Morality of Happiness*. Oxford University Press, 1995.

Anscombe, Gertrude E. M. *Intention*. Harvard University Press, 2000.

Aquinas, Thomas. *Compendium of Theology*, trans. Cyril Vollert and Richard A. Munkelt. Angelico Press, 2012.

Quaestiones disputatae de malo. Vol. 23 in *Opera Omnia iussa edita Leonis XIII P.M.* Rome/Paris: Commissio Leonina/J. Vrin, 1982.

Quaestiones disputatae De virtutibus, quaestio 4. Rome: Marietti, 1965.

Lectura super Evangelium S. Matthaei. Rome: Marietti, 1951.

In Epistolam I ad Corinthios. In *Opera omnia*, Parma edition, vol. 13. New York: Musurgia, 1949.

In Epistolam ad Hebraeos. In *Opera omnia*, Parma edition, vol. 13. New York: Musurgia, 1949.

In Epistolam ad Romanos. In *Opera Omnia*, Parma edition, vol. 13. New York: Musurgia, 1949.

Sententia Libri Ethicorum. In *Opera omnia*, Leonine edition, vol. 47/1. Rome: Ad Sanctae Sabinae, 1969.

Summa contra gentiles. In *Opera Omnia*, Leonine edition, vols. 13-15. Rome: 1982.

Summa theologiae. In *Opera Omnia*, Leonine edition, vols. 4-12. Rome: 1982. Except where otherwise indicated, quotations in English have been taken from *Summa theologica*, trans. Fathers of the English Dominican Province, 5 vols. Allen, TX: Christian Classics, 1981.

Aristotle. *The Nicomachean Ethics*. Translated by W. D. Ross. Revised by J. L. Ackrill and J. O. Urmson. Oxford University Press, 1998.

Augustine. *The Preaching of St. Augustine, 'Our Lord's Sermon on the Mount.'* Edited by Jaroslav. Fortress Press, 1973.

Teaching Christianity: De Doctrina Christiana. Translated by Edmund Hill, O.P. New York City Press, 1996.

Augustine and Frank J. Sheed. *Confessions.* Second edition. Hackett Publishing, 2007.

Austen, Jane. *Mansfield Park.* Everyman's Library Classics, 1992.
Persuasion, 1992.

Austin, Michael W. and R. Douglas Geivett. *Being Good: Christian Virtues for Everyday Life.* W. B. Eerdmans, 2012.

Banner, Michael. *The Ethics of Everyday Life: Moral Theology, Social Anthropology, and the Imagination of the Human.* Oxford University Press, 2016.

Barber, Benjamin R. *Consumed: How Markets Corrupt Children, Infantilize Adults, and Swallow Citizens Whole.* W. W. Norton, 2007.

Barnett, Paul. *The Second Epistle to the Corinthians.* W. B. Eerdmans, 1997.

Bauckham, Richard. *The Epistle to the Hebrews and Christian Theology.* W. B. Eerdmans, 2009.
Theology of Jürgen Moltmann. Continnuum-3PL, 1995.

Benhabib, Seyla. *Situating the Self: Gender, Community, and Postmodernism in Contemporary Ethics.* First edition. Routledge, 1992.

Betz, Hans Dieter and Adela Yarbro Collins. *The Sermon on the Mount: A Commentary on the Sermon on the Mount, Including the Sermon on the Plain.* Augsburg Fortress, 1995.

Bloch, Ernst. *The Principle of Hope.* Basel Blackwell, three volumes, 1986.

Boethius, Ancius and Victor Watts. *The Consolation of Philosophy.* Penguin Classics, 2000.

Bowlin, John R. *Contingency and Fortune in Aquinas's Ethics.* Cambridge University Press, 2010.

Boyle, Nicholas. *Who Are We Now?: Christian Humanism and the Global Market from Hegel to Heaney.* University of Notre Dame Press, 1999.

'Breaking News via Seeking Alpha'. Accessed 7 June 2014. http://seekingalpha .com/news/70810.

Brown, Peter. *The Cult of the Saints: Its Rise and Function in Latin Christianity.* University of Chicago Press, 1981.

Brown, Raymond. *The Epistles of John.* Yale University Press, 1995.
The Jerome Biblical Commentary. Two volumes in one. Prentice Hall, 1968.

Brueggemann, Walter. 'Praise and the Psalms: A Politics of Glad Abandonment'. *Hymn* 43 (1 October 1992): 14–18.

Bunston, Terry, Deborah Mings, Andrea Mackie, and Diane Jones. 'Facilitating Hopefulness'. *Journal of Psychosocial Oncology* 13.4 (16 May 1996): 79–103.

Burge, Gary M. 'A Specific Problem in the New Testament Text and Canon: The Woman Caught in Adultery'. *Journal of the Evangelical Theological Society* 27.2 (June 1984): 141–148.

Burke, Edmund and Adam Phillips. *A Philosophical Enquiry into the Origin of Our Ideas of the Sublime and Beautiful.* Reissue edition. Oxford University Press, n.d.

Burke, Kenneth. *The Philosophy of Literary Form.* University of California Press, 1974.

Burrell, David B. *Knowing the Unknowable God: Ibn Sina, Maimonides, Aquinas.* University of Notre Dame Press, 1992.

Cahill, Lisa Sowle. *Global Justice, Christology and Christian Ethics.* Cambridge University Press, 2015.

Castelo, Daniel. 'The Fear of the Lord as Theological Method'. *Journal of Theological Interpretation* 2.1 (1 March 2008): 147–160.

Chesterton, Gilbert Keith. *Orthodoxy*. John Lane Company, 1909.

A Short History of England. The Floating Press, 2011.

Clarke, David. 'Faith and Hope'. *Australasian Psychiatry* 11.2 (1 June 2003): 164–168.

Cloutier, David. 'The Problem of Luxury in the Christian Life'. *Journal of the Society of Christian Ethics* 32.1 (2012): 3–20.

Cohen, Lizabeth. *A Consumer's Republic: The Politics of Mass Consumption in Post-war America*. Knopf, 2003.

The Complete Poetical Works of William Wordsworth, 1904.

Conlon, Walter M. 'The Certitude of Hope'. *The Thomist* 10 (1947): 76–119, 226–252.

Crace, Jim. *Harvest*. Vintage, 2013.

Dante Alighieri. *The Divine Comedy Part II: Purgatory*. Translated by Mark Musa. Penguin Books, 1984.

The Portable Dante. Reissue edition. Penguin USA, 2003.

Purgatory. Modern Library, 2004.

Davies, William D. and Dale C. Allison. *The Gospel According to Matthew, Volume I*. T. & T. Clark, 1988.

Matthew: Volume 2: 8–18. Bloomsbury Publishing, 1999.

Matthew 1–7: Volume 1. Bloomsbury 3PL, 2004.

Delaney, C. F., ed. *Rationality and Religious Belief*. University of Notre Dame Press, 1980.

de'Liguori, Alphonsus Maria. *The 12 Steps to Holiness and Salvation*. Translated by Cornelius J Warren. Tan Books, 1986.

DeYoung, Rebecca Konyndyk. *Glittering Vices: A New Look at the Seven Deadly Sins and Their Remedies*. Brazos Press, 2009.

Dickens, Charles. *A Christmas Carol and Other Christmas Books*. Oxford University Press, 2006.

Dorrien, Gary. *Reconstructing the Common Good: Theology and the Social Order*. Wipf & Stock Publishers, 2008.

Doyle, Dominic. 'The Dialectic Unfolding of the Theological Virtues: "Tayloring" Christian Identity to a Secular Age', *Gregorianum* 92 [2011]: 687–707.

The Promise of Christian Humanism: Thomas Aquinas on Hope. Crossroad Publishing Company, 2012.

Edge, Deckle. *The Weight of Glory*. New edition. HarperOne, 2009.

Elliot, David. 'The Christian as Homo Viator: A Resource in Thomas Aquinas for Overcoming "Worldly Sin and Sorrow"'. *The Journal of the Society of Christian Ethics* 34.2 (Fall/Winter 2015): 101–121.

'Defining the Relationship Between Health and Well-Being in Bioethics'. *The New Bioethics* 22.1 (Spring 2016): 4–17.

'The Theological Virtue of Hope and the Art of Dying'. *Studies in Christian Ethics* 29.3 (Summer 2016): 301–307.

'The Turn to Classification in Virtue Ethics: A Review Essay'. *Studies in Christian Ethics* 29.4 (November 2016): 477–488.

Eubank, Nathan. 'Storing up Treasure with God in the Heavens: Celestial Investments in Matthew 6:1–21'. *Catholic Biblical Quarterly* 76.1 (1 January 2014): 77–92.

Fitzmyer, Joseph A. *Romans*. Yale University Press, 1993.

Foot, Philippa. *Natural Goodness*. Oxford University Press, 2001.

Frierson, Patrick. *Kant: Observations on the Feeling of the Beautiful and Sublime and Other Writings*. Translated by Professor Paul Guyer. First edition. Cambridge University Press, 2011.

Geuss, Raymond. 'The Future of Theological Ethics'. *Studies in Christian Ethics* 25.2 (2012).

Gollwitzer, Helmut, Käthe Kuhn, and Reinhold Schneider. *Dying We Live: The Final Messages and Records of the Resistance*. Wipf & Stock Publishers, 2009.

Gonzalez, Justo L. *Story of Christianity Vol. 1. The Early Church to the Dawn of the Reformation*. HarperCollins, 2010.

The Story of Christianity Vol. 2. The Reformation to the Present Day. Second edition. HarperOne, 2010.

Graham, Gordon. *Evil and Christian Ethics*. Cambridge University Press, 2000.

Greene, Graham. *The Heart of the Matter*. Great Books edition. Penguin, 1999.

Gregory of Nyssa. *The Lord's Prayer, The Beatitudes*. Translated by Hilda C. Graef. Paulist Press, 1990.

Guelich, Robert A. *The Sermon on the Mount: A Foundation for Understanding*. W Publishing Group, 1982.

Hammond, Paul. *The Poems of John Dryden*. Pearson Education, 1995.

Hare, John E. *The Moral Gap: Kantian Ethics, Human Limits, and God's Assistance*. New edition. Oxford University Press, 1997.

Harvey, John, 'The Nature of the Infused Moral Virtues'. *Proceedings of the Tenth Annual Convention of the Catholic Theological Society of America* 10: 172–221.

Hauerwas, Stanley. *Christian Existence Today: Essays on Church, World, and Living in Between*. Reissue edition. Wipf & Stock Publishers, 2010.

'Pragmatism and Democracy: Assessing Jeffrey Stout's Democracy and Tradition'. *Journal of the American Academy of Religion* 78.2 (1 June 2010): 429.

Hauerwas, Stanley, John Berkman, and Michael Cartwright. *The Hauerwas Reader*. Duke University Press, 2001.

Hauerwas, Stanley and William H. Willimon. *Resident Aliens: Life in the Christian Colony*. First edition. Abingdon Press, 2008.

Hayes, Shannon. *Radical Homemakers: Reclaiming Domesticity from a Consumer Culture*. Left to Write Press, 2010.

Hays, Richard B. *First Corinthians: Interpretation: A Bible Commentary for Teaching and Preaching*. Westminster John Knox Press, 2011.

The Moral Vision of the New Testament: Community, Cross, New Creation, A Contemporary Introduction to New Testament Ethics. First edition. HarperOne, 1996.

'Scripture-Shaped Community: The Problem of Method in New Testament Ethics'. *Interpretation* 44 (1990): 53.

Hazlitt, William. *Table-Talk: Essays on Men and Manners*. Grant Richards, 1903.

Herdt, Jennifer. *Putting on Virtue: The Legacy of the Splendid Vices*. Reprint edition. University of Chicago Press, 2012.

Herzog, Frederick, ed., *The Future of Hope: Theology as Eschatology*. Herder & Herder, 1970.

Hipple, John Walter, Jr. *The Beautiful, the Sublime, & the Picturesque: In Eighteenth-Century British Aesthetic Theory*. First edition. Southern Illinois University Press, 1957.

Hollinger, David. *Postethnic America: Beyond Multiculturalism*. Basic Books, 1995.

Homer. *The Odyssey*. Translated by Robert Fitzgerald. Farrar, Straus, and Giroux, 1998.

Hooft, Stan van. *Hope*. Routledge, 2014.

Hopkins, Gerard Manley. *Selected Poetry*. Edited by Catherine Phillips. Oxford University Press, 2008.

Huizinga, Johan. *The Waning of the Middle Ages*. Dover Publications, 2013.

Hursthouse, Rosalind. *On Virtue Ethics*. Oxford University Press, 1999. http://site.ebrary.com/id/10273328.

ICEL. *Pastoral Care of the Sick*. Catholic Book Publishing Corp., 1991.

Inglis, John. 'Aquinas' Replication of the Acquired Moral Virtues: Rethinking the Standard Philosophical Interpretation of Moral Virtue in Aquinas'. *Journal of Religious Ethics* 27.1 (1999): 3–27.

Jackson, Timothy P. *Love Disconsoled: Meditations on Christian Charity*. Cambridge University Press, 2010.

   The Priority of Love: Christian Charity and Social Justice. Princeton University Press, 2009.

Janaway, Christopher and Simon Robertson, eds. *Nietzsche, Naturalism, and Normativity*. Oxford University Press, 2012.

Johnson, Samuel and James Boswell. *A Journey to the Western Islands of Scotland and the Journal of a Tour to the Hebrides*. Edited by Peter Levi. Reprint edition. Penguin Classics, 1984.

Julian of Norwich. *Revelations of Divine Love*. Cosimo, Inc., 2007.

Julian (of Norwich), Edmund Colledge, and James Walsh. *Showings*. Paulist Press, 1978.

Kant, Immanuel. *Critique of Judgment*. Translated by Werner S. Pluhar. Hackett Publishing Company, Inc., 1987.

   Critique of Practical Reason. Translated, with an introduction by L. W. Beck. Library of Liberal Arts / Bobbs-Merrill. 1956.

   Critique of Practical Reason. Translated by Mary Gregor. Cambridge University Press, 1997.

   Critique of Pure Reason. Translated by Paul Guyer. Cambridge University Press, 1998.

   Groundwork of the Metaphysic of Morals. Translated by H. J. Paton. HarpPeren, 1964.

Kaufmann, Walter. *Beyond Good and Evil*. First Thus edition. Vintage, 1966.

Kempis, Thomas a. *The Imitation of Christ*. Rev sub edition. Vintage, 1998.

Koenig-Archibugi, Mathias. 'Transnational Corporations and Public Accountability'. *Government and Opposition* 39.2 (1 April 2004): 234–259.

La, Gottschalk. 'Hope and Other Deterrents to Illness'. *American Journal of Psychotherapy* 39.4 (October 1985): 515–524.

Ladner, Gerhart B. 'Homo Viator: Mediaeval Ideas on Alienation and Order'. *Speculum* 42.2 (1 April 1967): 233–259.

Law, William. *A Serious Call to a Devout and Holy Life*. Edited by John Meister et al. Westminster John Knox Press, 1968.

Leibing, Annette and Lawrence Cohen, eds. *Thinking about Dementia: Culture, Loss, and the Anthropology of Senility*. Rutgers University Press, 2006.

Levering, Matthew. *The Betrayal of Charity: The Sins that Sabotage Divine Love*. Baylor University Press, 2011.

Lewis, Clive Staples. *Letter to Malcolm: Chiefly on Prayer*. Houghton Mifflin Harcourt.
  The Four Loves. Harcourt Brace Jovanovich, 1960.
  The Four Loves. Second Printing edition. Mariner Books, 1971.
  A Preface to Paradise Lost. Atlantic Publishers & Dist, 2005.
  Studies in Words. Cambridge University Press, 2013.
  The Weight of Glory and Other Addresses. HarperSanFrancisco, 2001.

Lonergan, Bernard. *Grace and Freedom: Operative Grace in the Thought of St. Thomas Aquinas*. Edited by J. Patout Burns, S.J. Darton, Longman & Todd, 1971.

Long, Steven. 'On the Possibility of a Purely Natural End for Man'. *The Thomist* 64 (2006): 211–237.

Loux, Michael J., ed. *Metaphysics: Contemporary Readings*. Routledge, 2008.
  Nature, Norm, and Psyche: Explorations in Aristotle's Philosophical Psychology. Scuola Normale Superiore, 2004.

MacIntyre, Alasdair C. *After Virtue: A Study in Moral Theory*. University of Notre Dame Press, 2007.

Mahoney, John. *The Making of Moral Theology: A Study of the Roman Catholic Tradition*. Clarendon Press, 1989.

Mansini, Guy. '*Duplex Amor* and the Structure of Love in Aquinas'. *Thomistica* (1995): 127–196.

Marrow, Stanley B. 'Kosmos in John'. *The Catholic Biblical Quarterly* 64 (2002): 90–102.

Mattison, William C. 'The Beatitudes and Moral Theology: A Virtue Ethics Approach'. *Nova et Vetera* 11.3 (2013): 819–848.
  Introducing Moral Theology: True Happiness and the Virtues. Brazos Press, 2008.
  'Movements of Love: A Thomistic Perspective on Eros and Agape'. *Journal of Moral Theology* 1.2 (2012): 31–60.

McGinn, Bernard. *The Foundations of Mysticism: Origins to the Fifth Century*. Crossroad, n.d.

McGrath, Alister E. *A Brief History of Heaven*. Blackwell Publishers, 2003.

McInerny, Ralph, Saint Thomas Aquinas, and Aristotle. *Commentary on Aristotle's 'Nicomachean Ethics'*. Translated by C. I. Litzinger. New edition of revised edition. Dumb Ox Books, 1993.

McKay, Angela. 'Prudence and Acquired Moral Virtue'. *The Thomist* 69 (2005): 535–556.

McLean, Athena. *The Person in Dementia: A Study of Nursing Home Care in the US*. Second revised edition. Broadview Press Ltd, 2006.

Merkt, Joseph T. *Sacra Doctrina and Christian Eschatology: A Test Case for a Study of Method and Content in the Writings of Thomas Aquinas*. The Catholic University of America Press, 1982.

Merton, Thomas and Sue Monk Kidd. *New Seeds of Contemplation*. Reprint edition. New Directions, 2007.

Michman, Ronald D. and Magee, Edward M. *The Affluent Consumer: Marketing and Selling the Luxury Lifestyle*. Praeger, 2006.

Miller, Arthur. *Death of a Salesman: Certain Private Conversations in Two Acts and a Requiem*. Penguin, 1976.

Milton, John. *The Poetical Works of John Milton: With Notes of Various Authors, Principally from the Edition of Thomas Newton, Charles Dunster, and Thomas Warton, to Which Is Prefixed, Newton's Life of Milton*. W. Baxter, 1824.

Moltmann, Jürgen. 'Christian Hope: Messianic or Transcendent? A Theological Discussion with Joachim of Fiore and Thomas Aquinas'. *Horizons* 12.2 (September 1985): 328–348.

The Crucified God: The Cross of Christ as the Foundation and Criticism of Christian Theology. New edition. SCM Press, 2001.

The Future of Creation. Annotated edition. Augsburg Fortress Publishers, 2000.

God in Creation. First edition. SCM Press, 2000.

On Human Dignity: Political Theology and Ethics. First edition. Fortress Press, 2007.

Religion, Revolution, and the Future. Scribner, 1969.

Theology of Hope. New edition. SCM Press, 2010.

The Trinity and the Kingdom: The Doctrine of God. Fortress Press edition. Fortress Press, 1993.

Morris, William. *The Earthly Paradise*, Prologue, l. 12, 978.

Mostefai, Ourida and John T. Scott. *Rousseau and 'L'Infame': Religion, Toleration, and Fanaticism in the Age of Enlightenment*. Rodopi, 2009.

Moulton, Charles Wells. *The Library of Literary Criticism of English and American Authors: V. 3 1730–1784*. University of Michigan Library, 2009.

Mounce, Robert H. *The Book of Revelation*. W. B. Eerdmans, 1998.

Nagel, Thomas. *The View from Nowhere*. New edition. Oxford University Press, 1989.

Nehamas, Alexander. *Nietzsche: Life as Literature*. Harvard University Press, 1990.

Newman, John Henry. *Dream of Gerontius*. Schwartz, Kirwin & Fauss, 1916.

The Idea of a University. Library of Alexandria, 1925.

Parochial and Plain Sermons. Ignatius Press, 1987.

Nicholas, M. J. 'Les Dons du Saint-Esprit', in *Revue Thomiste* 92 (1992): 141–153.

Nicolson, Marjorie Hope and William Cronon. *Mountain Gloom and Mountain Glory: The Development of the Aesthetics of the Infinite*. Reprint edition. University of Washington Press, 1997.

Niebuhr, Richard. *Christ and Culture*. Some Underlining edition. Harper Torchbooks, n.d.

Nietzsche, Friedrich. *The Anti-Christ* in *Twilight of the Iodls and the Anti-Christ*. Translated by R. Hollingdale. Penguin, 1968.

The Portable Nietzsche. Penguin, 1977.

The Will to Power. Vintage, 1968.

Nietzsche, Friedrich, Rolf-Peter Horstmann, and Judith Norman. *Nietzsche: Beyond Good and Evil: Prelude to a Philosophy of the Future*. Cambridge University Press, 2002.

Nietzsche, Friedrich, Bernard Williams, and Josefine Nauckhoff. *Nietzsche: The Gay Science: With a Prelude in German Rhymes and an Appendix of Songs*. Cambridge University Press, 2001.

None. *The Liturgy of the Hours Volume II – Lent and Easter*. Lea edition. Catholic Book Publishing Company, 1976.

Nussbaum, Martha C. *The Fragility of Goodness*. Cambridge University Press, 2001. *Women and Human Development: The Capabilities Approach*. New edition. Cambridge University Press, 2001.

Orwell, George. *Essays*. Everyman, 2002.

Orwell, George and John Carey. *Essays*. Alfred A. Knopf, 2002.

Otto, R. *The Idea of the Holy*. Second edition, trans. John W. Harvey. Oxford University Press, 1958.

Parish, Richard. *Catholic Particularity in Seventeenth-Century French Writing: 'Christianity Is Strange.'* Oxford University Press, 2011.

Parliament, Great Britain. *The Parliamentary History of England from the Earliest Period to the Year 1803*. Printed by T. C. Hansard, 1817.

Peale, Norman Vincent. *The Power of Positive Thinking*. Reprint edition. Touchstone, 2003.

Pearson, Keith Ansell. *A Companion to Nietzsche*. John Wiley & Sons, 2008.

Perry, John, ed. *God, the Good, and Utilitarianism: Perspectives on Peter Singer*. Cambridge University Press, 2014.

Pieper, Josef. *On Hope*. Ignatius Press, 1986.

Pinckaers, Servais, Op. *The Pursuit of Happiness – God's Way: Living the Beatitudes*. Reprint edition. Wipf & Stock Publishers, 2011.

L'Evangile et la morale. Saint-Paul, 1990.

The Pinckaers Reader: Renewing Thomistic Moral Theology. Edited by John Berkman and Craig Steven Titus. The Catholic University of America Press, 2005.

The Sources of Christian Ethics. The Catholic University of America Press, 1995.

Pollock, John. *Wilberforce*. Chariot Victor Publishing, 1986.

Pope Benedict XVI. *Jesus of Nazareth: From the Baptism in the Jordan to the Transfiguration*. Bloomsbury Publishing PLC, 2008.

Pope Gregory the Great, *Morals on the Book of Job*. Translated and edited by John Henry Parker. Oxford University Press, 1850.

Pope, Stephen J., ed. *The Ethics of Aquinas*. Georgetown University Press, 2002.

Porter, Jean. *Moral Action and Christian Ethics*. New edition. Cambridge University Press, 1999.

Nature as Reason: A Thomistic Theory of the Natural Law. W. B. Eerdmans, 2005.

Postman, Neil. *Amusing Ourselves to Death: Public Discourse in the Age of Show Business*. Revised edition. Penguin Books, 2005.

Richmond, Legh. *The Fathers of the English Church: Or, A Selection from the Writings of the Reformers and Early Protestant Divines of the Church of England*. John Hatchard, 1807.

Robinson, William Childs. 'Eschatology of the Epistle to the Hebrews: A Study in the Christian Doctrine of Hope'. *Encounter* 22.1 (1 December 1961): 37–51.

Rorty, Amélie. *Essays on Aristotle's Ethics*. University of California Press, 1980.

Rousseau, Jean-Jacques. *On the Social Contract*. Courier Dover Publications, 2012.

The Social Contract. Translated by Frederick Watkins. University of Wisconsin Press, 1986.

Sales, St. Francis de. *Introduction to the Devout Life*. Translated by John Ryan. Image Books, 1986.

A Serious Call to a Devout and Holy Life. Westminster John Knox Press, 1968.

Sayers, Dorothy L. *Further Papers on Dante: His Heirs and His Ancestors*. Wipf & Stock Publishers, 2006.

Scaer, David P. 'Jürgen Moltmann and His "Theology of Hope"'. *Journal of the Evangelical Theological Society* 13.2 (1 March 1970): 69–79.

Schmidt, Charles. *The Social Results of Early Christianity*. Wm. Isbister, 1889.

Schweiker, William. *Responsibility and Christian Ethics*. New edition. Cambridge University Press, 1999.

Sethi, Sheena and Martin E. P. Seligman. 'Optimism and Fundamentalism'. *Psychological Science* 4.4 (1 July 1993): 256–259.

Sidgwick, Henry. *Methods of Ethics*. Seventh revised edition. Hackett Publishing Co, Inc., 1981.

Skehan, Patrick W. *The Literary Relationship between the Book of Wisdom and the Protocanonical Wisdom Books of the Old Testament*. The Catholic University of America Press, 1938.

Smith, Christian and Melina Lundquist Denton. *Soul Searching: The Religious and Spiritual Lives of American Teenagers*. Reprint edition. Oxford University Press, 2009.

Snow, Nancy E., ed. *Cultivating Virtue: Perspectives from Philosophy, Theology, and Psychology*. Oxford University Press, 2014.

'Virtue and Flourishing'. *Journal of Social Philosophy* 39.2: p. 229.

Speck, Bruce W. 'Augustine's Tale of Two Cities: Teleology/Eschatology in The City of God'. *Journal of Interdisciplinary Studies* 8.1–2 (1 January 1996): 104–130.

Springs, Jason, Cornel West, Richard Rorty, Stanley Hauerwas, and Jeffrey Stout. 'Pragmatism and Democracy: Assessing Jeffrey Stout's Democracy and Tradition'. *Journal of the American Academy of Religion* 78.2 (1 June 2010): 413–448.

Staley, Kevin. 'Happiness: The Natural End of Man?' *The Thomist* 53.2 (1989): 215–234.

Stout, Jeffrey. *Democracy and Tradition*. Princeton University Press; Hebrew Union College Press, 2004.

Democracy and Tradition. New edition. Princeton University Press, 2009.

Ethics after Babel: The Languages of Morals and Their Discontents. Princeton University Press, 2001.

Suzuki, David, Adrienne Mason, and Amanda McConnell. *The Sacred Balance: Rediscovering Our Place in Nature*. Illustrated edition. Greystone Books, 1999.

Swinburne, Algernon Charles. *Selected Poems*. D. C. Heath & Company, 1905.

Taylor, Gabriele. *Deadly Vices*. Oxford University Press, 2008.

Tchividjian, Tullian. *Glorious Ruin: How Suffering Sets You Free*. David C. Cook, 2012.

Terrien, Samuel. 'The Numinous, the Sacred and the Holy in Scripture'. *Biblical Theology Bulletin: A Journal of Bible and Theology* 12.4 (1 November 1982): 99–108.

Thomas, Richard J. Regan and Brian Davies. *On Evil*. Oxford University Press, 2003.

Timpe, Kevin and Craig A. Boyd, eds. *Virtues and Their Vices*. Oxford University Press, 2014.

Tombs, Robert. *The English and Their History*. Allen Lane, 2014.

Torrell, Jean-Pierre. *Saint Thomas Aquinas: Spiritual Master v. 2*. The Catholic University of America Press, 2003.

　Surnaturel: A Controversy at the Heart of Twentieth-Century Thomistic Thought. Edited by Serge-Thomas Bonino. Translated by Robert Williams. Revised by Matthew Levering. Sapientia Press, 2009.

Troeltsch, Ernst and James Luther Adams, *The Social Teaching of the Christian Churches: 2 Volume Set Vols. I and II*. Translated by Olive Wyon. Westminster John Knox Press, 1992.

Tyndale, William and John Frith. *The Works of the English Reformers: William Tyndale and John Frith*. Ebenezer Palmer, 1831.

Van Inwagen, Peter. *Ontology, Identity, and Modality: Essays in Metaphysics*. Cambridge University Press, 2001.

Van Inwagen and Dean W. Zimmerman. *Metaphysics: The Big Questions*. Oxford: Blackwell Publishing, 2008.

Van Nieuwenhove, Rik and Joseph Peter Wawrykow. *The Theology of Thomas Aquinas*. University of Notre Dame Press, 2005.

Verhey, Allen. *The Christian Art of Dying: Learning from Jesus*. W. B. Eerdmans, 2011.

Vogt, Christopher. *Patience, Compassion, Hope, and the Christian Art of Dying Well*. Rowman & Littlefield Publishers, 2004.

Wawrykow, Joseph Peter. *God's Grace and Human Action: 'Merit' in the Theology of Thomas Aquinas*. University of Notre Dame Press, 1995.

　The Westminster Handbook to Thomas Aquinas. Westminster John Knox Press, 2005.

Weaver, Darlene Fozard. *Self Love and Christian Ethics*. Cambridge University Press, 2002.

Wilken, Robert Louis. *The Christians as the Romans Saw Them*. Second edition. Yale University Press, 2003.

　The Will to Power. Vintage, 1968.

Willard, Dallas. *A Place for Truth*. InterVarsity Press, 2010.

Williams, Bernard. *The Sense of the Past: Essays in the History of Philosophy*. Edited by Myles Burnyeat. Princeton University Press, 2007.

　Shame and Necessity. University of California Press, 2008.

Williams, Charles. *Descent into Hell: A Novel*. W. B. Eerdmans, n.d.

　The Figure of Beatrice. Apocryphile Press, 2005.

Wolterstorff, Nicholas. *Until Justice and Peace Embrace: The Kuyper Lectures for 1981 Delivered at the Free University of Amsterdam*. W. B. Eerdmans, 1983.

Wood, Michael and Bernard Williams. *Essays and Reviews: 1959–2002*. Princeton University Press, 2014.

Wright, N. T. *Surprised by Hope: Rethinking Heaven, the Resurrection, and the Mission of the Church*. First edition. HarperOne, 2008.

Yamane, David A. *The Catholic Church in State Politics: Negotiating Prophetic Demands and Political Realities*. Sheed & Ward, 2005.

Index